Qualitative Reasoning

Qualitative Reasoning
Modeling and Simulation with Incomplete Knowledge

Benjamin Kuipers

The MIT Press
Cambridge, Massachusetts
London, England

© 1994 Massachusetts Institute of Technology

This book was set in Computer Modern by Patrick A. O'Donnell and was printed and bound in the United States of America.

Library of Congress Cataloging-in-Publication Data

Kuipers, Benjamin.
    Qualitative reasoning: modeling and simulation with incomplete
knowledge / Benjamin Kuipers.
       p.   cm. — (Artificial intelligence)
    Includes bibliographical references and index.
    ISBN 0–262–11190–X
    1. Artificial intelligence. 2. Simulation methods. 3. Reasoning.
I. Title. II. Series: Artificial intelligence (Cambridge, Mass.)
Q335.K78 1994
006.3'3—dc20   94–7954
                                                                            CIP

To my father and mother,
who taught me about
mathematics and the mind.

Contents

List of Figures

List of Tables

Series Foreword

Artificial intelligence is the study of intelligence using the ideas and methods of computation. Unfortunately, a definition of intelligence seems impossible at the moment because intelligence appears to be an amalgam of so many information-processing and information-representation abilities.

Of course psychology, philosophy, linguistics, and related disciplines offer various perspectives and methodologies for studying intelligence. For the most part, however, the theories proposed in these fields are too incomplete and too vaguely stated to be realized in computational terms. Something more is needed, even though valuable ideas, relationships, and constraints can be gleaned from traditional studies of what are, after all, impressive existence proofs that intelligence is in fact possible.

Artificial intelligence offers a new perspective and a new methodology. Its central goal is to make computers intelligent, both to make them more useful and to understand the principles that make intelligence possible. That intelligent computers will be extremely useful is obvious. The more profound point is that artificial intelligence aims to understand intelligence using the ideas and methods of computation, thus offering a radically new and different basis for theory formation. Most of the people doing work in artificial intelligence believe that these theories will apply to any intelligent information processor, whether biological or solid state.

There are side effects that deserve attention, too. Any program that will successfully model even a small part of intelligence will be inherently massive and complex. Consequently, artificial intelligence continually confronts the limits of computer-science technology. The problems encountered have been hard enough and interesting enough to seduce artificial intelligence people into working on them with enthusiasm. It is natural, then, that there has been a steady flow of ideas from artificial intelligence to computer science, and the flow shows no sign of abating.

The purpose of this series in artificial intelligence is to provide people in many areas, both professionals and students, with timely, detailed information about what is happening on the frontiers in research centers all over the world.

J. Michael Brady
Daniel G. Bobrow
Randall Davis

Preface

This book describes a body of work that I have been involved with for about fifteen years. It represents a particular point of view on one of the most stimulating areas in artificial intelligence research. I originally entered this area in order to understand human commonsense and expert reasoning. What I found was a body of mathematics and potentially useful technology that has kept me enthralled since then, even though it has led, in some ways, quite a distance from human commonsense knowledge. (However, by chapter 14, we will have returned to many of the commonsense knowledge themes introduced in chapter 1.) The area has lost none of its excitement in fifteen years, though the "hot topics" have shifted as the research community solves each problem and moves on to the next.

Because I love teaching, the book is written as a textbook, with practice and research problems at the ends of the chapters, even though there are few courses devoted to qualitative reasoning. Some of the problems and comments in the text are intended to suggest research directions that I believe will be fruitful, as the field continues its rapid progress.

The primary intended readers are advanced students and researchers in AI or its applications. Prerequisites are a substantial introduction to artificial intelligence, plus calculus and preferably differential equations. I would like scientists and engineers who are not AI researchers (but who have had a solid introduction to AI) to be able to use this book as a self-contained education in qualitative modeling and simulation methods.

In order to support detailed exploration and experimentation with these ideas, the Lisp source code for the QSIM program is available to interested readers. The program is not advertised or warranted as a software product, and is distributed via `ftp` for research purposes only.

host: `cs.utexas.edu` (`128.83.139.9`)
file: `/ftp/pub/qsim/README`
or email to: `kuipers@cs.utexas.edu`.

Over fifteen years, I have accumulated an enormous intellectual and personal debt to the large number of people who have contributed to the completion of this book. Inevitably, I will have forgotten to include the name of someone I should thank here. If you are that person, please accept my apology and thanks at the head of the list.

I would particularly like to thank Peter Szolovits and Jerome Kassirer, who invited me into the area of AI in medicine, and who helped me find the problem of how people, expert physicians in this case, understand mechanisms. Both have continued to be good friends and helpful colleagues.

I have been privileged to collaborate with a number of very fine students and more senior scientists, all of whom have contributed to my education and to the substance and quality of the body of work presented here: Karl Åström, Andrew Bailey, Ray Barriess, Dan Berleant, Giorgio Brajnik, David Bridgeland, Catherine Catino, Charles Chiu, Daniel Clancy, James Crawford, David Dalle Molle, Daniel Dvorak, Thomas Edgar, Christopher Eliot, Adam Farquhar, Pierre Fouché, Evangelina Gazi, Akira Hayashi, Herbert Kay, Yihwa Kiang, Ina Kraan, Wood Wai Lee, Richard Mallory, Raman Rajagopalan, Sowmya Ramachandran, Bradley L. Richards, Jeff Rickel, Bob Schrag, Benjamin Shults, David Throop, Lyle Ungar, Jack Vinson, Tom Vinson, Takashi Watanabe, Andrew Whinston, and Larry Widman.

A long list of people have contributed to this work over the last fifteen years, with help that ranged from thorough examination of the manuscript, to scorching criticism that demanded a careful answer, to a stimulating discussion or insightful suggestion at just the right moment. My thanks to Hal Abelson, Gautam Biswas, Danny Bobrow, Johan deKleer, Jon Doyle, Richard Doyle, Brian Falkenhainer, Boi Faltings, Ken Forbus, Tony Gorry, Walter Hamscher, Jim Hunter, Liliana Ironi, Roy Leitch, Jane MacFarlane, Ray Mooney, Bruce Porter, Todd Quinto, Elisha Sacks, Vijay Saraswat, Mario Stefanelli, Sara Strandtman, Peter Struss, Gerry Sussman, Dan Weld, and Mike Wellman.

I am very grateful for assistance with preparation of the manuscript from my secretaries Bess Sullivan, Linh Pham, and Phuong Pham, and my students Herbert Kay, Raman Rajagopalan, Sowmya Ramachandran, and Robert Schrag. My editors at MIT Press, Bob Prior and Jenya Weinreb, have been exceedingly helpful.

Most of this work has taken place in the Qualitative Reasoning Group at the Artificial Intelligence Laboratory, Computer Science Department, The University of Texas at Austin. However, early portions took place at the Laboratory for Computer Science, Massachusetts Institute of Technology, and the Mathematics Department, Tufts University.

I am very grateful to the funding agencies who have supported the research on qualitative reasoning that made this book possible: National Science Foundation (MCS-8303640, DCR-8417934, DCR-8512779, IRI-8602665, IRI-8905494, IRI-9017047); National Aeronautics and Space Administration (NAG 2-507, NAG 9-512, NCC 2-760, NAG 9-665); National Library of Medicine (R23 LM03603, R01 LM04125, R01 LM04374, R01 LM04515); and the Jet Propulsion Laboratory at California Institute of Technology. Naturally, no endorsement of the ideas expressed here is implied.

This book has been in draft since the mid-1980s, and manuscript copies have been used in courses for a number of years. Some of the material presented in this book appeared in earlier form in other publications: chapter 1 (Kuipers, 1993b; Kuipers, 1993a), chapter 2 (Kuipers, 1989), chapters 3, 4, and 5 (Kuipers, 1984; Kuipers, 1986; Kuipers, 1988a; Dalle Molle *et al.*, 1988), chapter 6 (Kuipers and Kassirer, 1985), chapter 9 (Kuipers and Berleant, 1988; Kuipers and Berleant, 1990), chapter 10 (Kuipers and Chiu, 1987; Kuipers *et al.*, 1991), chapter 11 (Fouché and Kuipers, 1992; Lee and Kuipers, 1988; Lee and Kuipers, 1993), chapter 12 (Kuipers, 1987; Kuipers, 1988b), and chapter 14 (Crawford *et al.*, 1990; Farquhar, 1993).

And finally, I am especially grateful to my wife, Laura Lein, and our children, Anna, Rebecca, and David, who prevented when possible, and tolerated when not, the single-mindedness required by a project of this size. Their love and support has been the foundation.

Qualitative Reasoning

1 Introduction to Qualitative Reasoning

1.1 Incomplete Knowledge

The world is infinitely complex. Our knowledge of the world is finite, and therefore always incomplete. The marvel is that we function quite well in the world in spite of never fully understanding it.

This book examines methods for representing and reasoning with incomplete knowledge about physical mechanisms: bathtubs, tea kettles, automobiles, furnaces, refrigerators, electrical circuits, chemical processing plants, the physiology of the body, and so on, *ad infinitum*.

Bathtubs and tea kettles are mechanisms that "everybody" understands — most people would say that knowledge about how bathtubs and tea kettles work is part of *common sense*. Chemical processing plants and medical physiology are domains for experts with knowledge gained through years of experience and specialized training. Nonetheless, important parts of these two kinds of knowledge seem to be represented and used in much the same way. The expert is characterized as much by his or her "trained intuition," "educated guesses," and "expert common sense" as by the ability to use specialized instruments or advanced computational methods.

Both commonsense and expert knowledge are always incomplete. No one understands down to the last detail how any mechanism actually works. Even if it were possible to construct a model of, say, the oil furnace in my basement, down to the level of quantum electrodynamics, the model would be absurdly, uselessly large. More realistically, even if I have a "good enough" model of my oil furnace, I probably don't recall the actual number of BTUs produced by burning a gallon of oil, or the flow rate of the oil spray nozzle in gallons per hour. Worse, once something has gone wrong and I am trying to diagnose a fault in the mechanism, my knowledge is by definition incomplete. I don't yet realize that the problem is a dirty and partially clogged oil spray nozzle, and I will probably never know exactly what the reduced flow rate was, even after I am satisfied that I have found and corrected the problem. How is it possible for people to cope with the demands of the physical world, usually quite successfully, with such incomplete knowledge?

Part of the answer seems to be that people can build and use *qualitative* descriptions of mechanisms in the physical world. A qualitative description is one that captures distinctions that make an important, qualitative difference, and ignores others. The level at which a bathtub overflows is a qualitatively important point that a qualitative description distinguishes from levels even a little bit less. A wide range of lower levels is aggregated under the single qualitative description, "partly full."

Undoubtedly, the ability to focus on the important distinctions and ignore the unimportant ones is an excellent way to cope with incomplete knowledge. But how do we formalize this insight? A number of researchers in artificial intelligence are working to apply qualitative descriptions of the physical world to problem solving at a commonsense and expert level.[1] The goal of this book is to present a unified theoretical framework for the field of *qualitative reasoning about physical mechanisms*.

This framework is built around the QSIM algorithm for qualitative simulation, and the QSIM representation for qualitative differential equations. The viewpoint expressed in this book is based on the belief that the various representations and inference methods in this area can best be understood in terms of their relationship to differential equations and the tasks of model building and model simulation.

1.2   Building Models; Using Models

A model is a (small) finite description of an infinitely complex reality, constructed for the purpose of answering particular questions.

- If I wish to answer questions about the orbits of the moon around the earth and the earth around the sun, I may describe the earth, sun, and moon in terms of point masses, positions, velocities, and forces.

- If I am interested in the phases of the moon and the possibility of eclipses, I need to reason about the positions, shapes, and diameters of the three bodies.

- If I ask why the full moon looks like a disk rather than a sphere, I need to consider the reflective properties of the dust that covers the surface of the moon.

- The romantic and superstitious descriptions of the moon, and its relationship to the human psyche and culture, require yet other simplified models of reality, but ones that are outside of the domain of physical mechanisms we will discuss.

Sometimes we will need to use multiple models to answer a question. To explain the phenomenon of eclipses, we might first use a point-mass description to determine

---

[1] The material presented here builds on the work of an extraordinarily exciting and productive community of researchers, who have developed a vision of qualitative reasoning. No list can be adequate, especially in a rapidly expanding area, but some of the significant early contributors are Johan de Kleer, Ken Forbus, Danny Bobrow, Pat Hayes, Brian Williams, Reid Simmons, Ernie Davis, Olivier Raiman, Peter Struss, Elisha Sacks, Dan Weld, Brian Falkenhainer, Boi Faltings, Yumi Iwasaki, and Herb Simon.

the orbits of the earth around the sun, and the moon around the earth, applying a set of simplifying assumptions that is inconsistent with the phenomenon of eclipses! Once we understand the orbits, we can change models, introduce spherical shapes and conical shadows, and determine whether eclipses can occur, how frequently, whether they will be partial or total, and how long they might last.

Thus, the process of reasoning with models breaks down into two major sub-problems:

1. Out of all the possible ways of describing the world, select an appropriate model or combination of models to answer a particular question.

2. Given a model (e.g., of the structure of a mechanism), simulate it or otherwise analyze it to make explicit some facts about the world that are implicit in that description of the world (e.g., its predicted behavior).

As we shall see, research in qualitative reasoning has addressed both of these problems. The *model-building* problem is the more open-ended of the two problems. While important steps have been taken, it is clear that we have only scratched the surface of a large problem.

Once we specify the representation for models, the *model-simulation* problem is more tightly constrained, so we have seen correspondingly more technical progress. The existence of this book is motivated, in part, by an emerging consensus about the value of a model representation that captures incomplete, qualitative knowledge of continuous quantities.

The organization of this book reflects its pedagogical purpose, with each chapter providing a foundation for later ones. However, its conceptual framework is that of figure 1.1, in which the model-building task and the model-simulation task communicate through the intermediate representation of qualitative differential equations (QDEs).

• Model building requires modeling assumptions that specify which aspects of the world are negligible and which should be included in the model, and the closed-world assumption to transform a collection of fragments into a model. Although model building comes first in figure 1.1, we will postpone our treatment of it until chapters 13 and 14, after we learn how models are represented and simulated.

• The QSIM representation for QDEs and the QSIM algorithm for qualitative simulation are introduced in chapter 2. Then:

  • Chapters 3, 4, and 5 present the representation and algorithms formally and in detail.

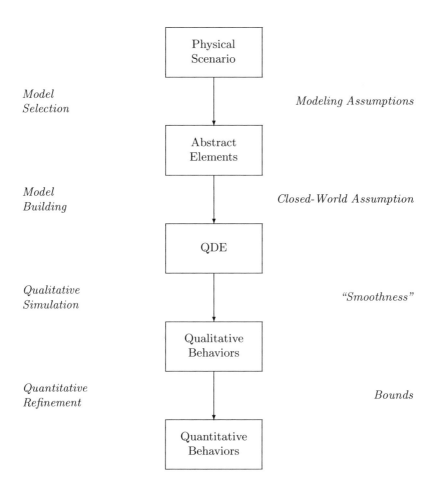

Figure 1.1
Major steps in qualitative modeling and simulation.

Each step requires particular types of assumptions. Using qualitative models makes this set of assumptions tractable. (In practice, this linear chain is augmented with loops.)

- Chapter 6 provides some larger examples.

- Chapters 7 and 8 show how to reason with the steady-state assumption and across region transitions.

- Chapters 10, 11, and 12 describe more sophisticated methods for reasoning with higher-order derivatives, energy constraints, phase portraits, and time-scale decompositions of qualitative models.

Much care is taken to preserve a guarantee that all behaviors consistent with the QDE model are covered by the qualitative prediction.

- Chapter 9 shows how quantitative and semi-quantitative information can be unified with the behaviors predicted by qualitative simulation to produce stronger, more precise predictions without losing the coverage guarantee.

The qualitative reasoning framework in figure 1.1 provides two benefits over traditional engineering approaches to modeling and simulation. First, the representations are designed to express states of incomplete knowledge that are common in human knowledge but are hard to express using traditional methods. Second, the inference methods are designed to be essentially deductive, so that assumptions are explicit and guarantees are provided that every step is sound.

As we shall see, much work remains to be done to bind all the steps into a unified framework, to make each step tractable and efficient as well as expressive and sound, and to apply these methods to complex real problems. Nonetheless, we have already seen successful uses of qualitative reasoning methods to:

- predict the possible behaviors of a heterogeneous control system and prove its stability (chapter 12 and Kuipers and Åström, 1994);

- construct qualitative phase portraits of incompletely known generalizations of the Lienard equation and other dynamical systems (chapter 11 and Lee and Kuipers, 1993);

- predict all behaviors under normal and fault conditions to perform a hazard and operability study of a nitric acid synthesis plant (chapter 14 and Catino, 1993);

- model, simulate, and explain the physiological mechanisms by which a green plant responds to water stress (chapter 14 and Rickel and Porter, 1992);

- monitor streams of observations from (simulated) vacuum chamber pump-down and propylene glycol synthesis plants, to discriminate between healthy and faulty conditions (chapter 9, Kay and Kuipers, 1993; Vinson and Ungar, 1993).

Qualitative modeling and simulation are key inference methods for problem-solvers for the major tasks of model-based reasoning: monitoring, diagnosis, design, planning, and explanation.

Monitoring Given a model of the system and a behavior predicted by that model, track an observation stream by unifying it with the qualitative behavior to get a quantitatively bounded prediction. Identify discrepancies via contradictions between observations and the prediction. When multiple models or behaviors are proposed, track them in parallel.

Diagnosis Given one or more models of a faulty device, proposed by some process such as dependency tracing from discrepancies, unify each qualitative behavior predicted from each model with the available observations, refuting inconsistent ones. Compute probabilities or other likelihood scores to order the remaining predictions. Analyze the predictions to select the best next observation to discriminate among models.

Design Given a model representing the incomplete knowledge available at the current state of the design process, predict the behaviors of the model consistent with known qualitative and quantitative constraints. Check the predictions against the specifications for the device being designed. If all behaviors satisfy the specifications, any fully specified instance of the current design will be acceptable. Select one to optimize cost or some other criterion. If some behaviors violate the specifications, search for additional qualitative or quantitative constraints that will prevent (i.e., refute) those behaviors.

Planning Planning a sequence of actions to achieve a goal is a special case of designing an artifact to meet given specifications. Given a plan, and a model of the world, simulate the evolving state of the world before, during, and after each action in the plan. Evaluate and refine as described under Design.

Explanation Given a set of observations of the world, find one or more models consistent with the observations. (See Monitoring and Diagnosis.) Extract the relevant features of the those models and communicate them to the user.

As we proceed through the book, numerous examples will be given, many simple pedagogical ones, and many less simple to illustrate the direction of applications research. To begin, however, we must start with some very basic questions about quantity, change, and incomplete knowledge.[2]

1.3 Partial Knowledge of Quantity

A quantity is a real-valued attribute of a physical object. However, a real number contains an infinite amount of information and human knowledge is finite, so our knowledge even of a single real number must be incomplete. There are many ways to represent incomplete knowledge in a description of a quantity and its value.

1.3.1 Interval Arithmetic

In interval arithmetic, incomplete knowledge of the real value of a quantity x is expressed as a closed interval $[lb, ub]$ representing the knowledge that $lb \leq x \leq ub$. The theory of interval arithmetic has become quite sophisticated (Moore, 1966; Moore, 1979; Alefeld and Herzberger, 1983), showing that many functions defined on real numbers have natural extensions to the domain of interval values.

We will use interval arithmetic to express semi-quantitative annotations on qualitative behavior predictions (chapter 9).

1.3.2 Nominal, Ordinal, Interval, Ratio

Statisticians distinguish among different types of knowledge that can be embodied in real-valued data according to the operations that can legitimately be applied to that data (Stevens, 1946).

- **Nominal** data can only be compared for equality or inequality.

- **Ordinal** data can be compared for order as well as equality.

- **Interval** data can be subtracted to determine the difference between two values. Conversely, a difference can be added to one value to get another.

- **Ratio** data can be added, subtracted, multiplied, or divided.

For example, the number on a football player's jersey is nominal data, used only to identify the individual, not to rank him. Rank in class is ordinal data: differences or ratios of rank are not meaningful. Temperature on the Fahrenheit

---

[2]Warren S. McCulloch (1965) tells about a conversation between himself as a young Haverford student and the great Quaker philosopher, Rufus Jones. "Warren," said he, "what is thee going to be?" And I said, "I don't know." "And what is thee going to do?" And again I said, "I have no idea; but there is one question I would like to answer: What is a number, that a man may know it, and a man, that he may know a number?" He smiled and said, "Friend, thee will be busy as long as thee lives."

or Celsius scale is interval data, since zero degrees is an arbitrary reference point. Mass, heat energy, and temperature on the Kelvin scale are all ratio data, since zero represents a true zero magnitude.

The import of this classification is that different descriptions and inference methods require different kinds of data. For example, the median can be computed from ordinal data, but the arithmetic mean requires interval data, and the geometric mean requires ratio data.

Qualitative reasoning methods are based primarily on *ordinal* knowledge of real-valued quantities, because human perception and memory seem to be particularly sensitive to ordinal relationships, especially with "landmark" values (Goldmeier, 1972).

1.3.3   Landmark Values

Landmark values are the "natural joints" that break a continuous set of values into qualitatively distinct regions. A landmark value is a symbolic name for a particular real number, whose numerical value may or may not be known. It serves as a precise boundary for a qualitative region. The qualitative properties of a value in the set depend primarily on its ordinal relations with the landmarks.

For example, a natural set of qualitative regions for the temperature of water is defined by the following landmarks:

$$AbsoluteZero \cdots Freezing \cdots Boiling \cdots \infty.$$

For a model with constant (though possibly unknown) pressure, the qualitatively distinct values for temperature of water are the landmark values and the open intervals between them.

Similarly, angles in a triangle can be described in the following qualitative terms, which include conventional names for open intervals as well as landmark values.

$$Zero \quad \cdots\cdots \quad Right \quad \cdots\cdots \quad Straight$$
$$(acute) \qquad (obtuse)$$

Note that there is no imprecision *at all* about the landmark *Right,* while describing an angle θ as *Acute* only asserts the ordinal relations $Zero < \theta < Right$. Any angle in the interval $(Zero, Right)$ has the same qualitative description.

1.3.4   "Fuzzy" Values

"Fuzzy" values are qualitative descriptions without precise boundaries. For example, when describing values of a continuous scalar quantity such as the amount of

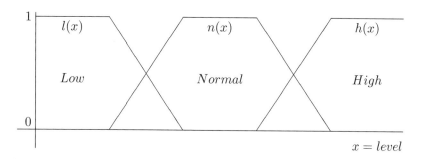

Figure 1.2
Appropriateness measures for fuzzy qualitative terms.

water in a tank, there are no meaningful landmark values representing the boundaries between *low* and *normal,* or between *normal* and *high.* Linguistic terms such as these refer to *fuzzy sets* of numbers.

Fuzzy sets were originally developed by Lotfi Zadeh (Zadeh, 1965; Yager *et al.,* 1987) to formalize qualitative concepts without precise boundaries. A fuzzy set, S, within a domain, D, is represented by a *membership function, $s : D \rightarrow [0,1]$,* generalizing the traditional representation of a set by a characteristic function $\sigma : D \rightarrow \{0,1\}$. This generalization of the set-membership function is the foundation of a great deal of mathematical, computational, and engineering research.

We interpret the value of $s(x)$, for $x \in D$, as a measure of the *appropriateness* of describing x with the descriptor S. *Appropriateness measure* is technically synonymous with the terms *membership function* and *possibility measure* as used in the fuzzy research community. However, it seems to me that a more intuitively compelling view of fuzzy representation is to interpret a fuzzy value not as a set but as a qualitative description of a scalar value, and the characteristic function not as representing partial set-membership, but as a measure of the *appropriateness* of the qualitative description.

Figure 1.2 illustrates three membership functions defining the appropriateness of applying the qualitative descriptors $\{low, medium, high\}$ to quantitatively defined levels of water in a tank.

The landmark-value and fuzzy-value qualitative representations are very distinct, and have different advantages and disadvantages, although their relationship has not yet been fully explored (though see Shen and Leitch 1992 and Kuipers and Åström 1991; 1994). Detailed reviews of fuzzy representations are available in Dubois and Prade, 1980; Dubois and Prade, 1988; and Yager *et al.,* 1987.

It is not uncommon to observe applications of qualitative reasoning that do violence to both representations by arbitrarily selecting landmark values to represent precise boundaries between inherently fuzzy descriptors.

Qualitative representation is complex: models can be built at different levels of detail and for different purposes; values can be described in terms of landmarks or fuzzy descriptors; qualitative descriptions can be augmented with quantitative information. The QSIM framework is a step toward clarifying these distinctions.

Consider, for example, the breaking-point of a string as a function of tension. For a given string, the breaking-point serves as a landmark value separating qualitatively distinct regions of behavior. Across a population of strings, the quantitative value of the breaking-point has a certain distribution. This provides a certain degree of knowledge, and leaves a certain degree of uncertainty, about the numerical value named by the landmark. Chapter 9 presents a method for representing and reasoning with this type of semi-quantitative knowledge. At a finer level of detail, the breaking-point is not a single value but is the result of a continuous process of stretching and deterioration of the fibers that make up the string. Chapter 12 shows how time-scale abstration can be used to express coupled descriptions of the same phenomenon at very slow and very fast time-scales.

1.4   Partial Knowledge of Continuous Change

In most ways, and at most times, the world changes continuously. As with scalar quantities, complete knowledge of continuous change requires an infinite amount of information. Thus, we need finite, symbolic methods for describing continuous change.

1.4.1   Discrete State Graphs

People often seem to describe the changing world in discrete terms, such as events, actions, states, and state-changes. A variety of representations have been developed for describing action and change in discrete terms, including finite-state causal graphs (Schank, 1973; Rieger and Grinberg, 1977; Patil *et al.*, 1981), situation calculus (McCarthy and Hayes, 1969; Lifschitz, 1987), and temporal logic (McDermott, 1982; Shoham, 1988).

Discrete state graphs are useful at a level of abstraction where the continuity of change and the continuous dynamics of behavior are not critical. Because they do not exploit the properties of continuity, they have difficulty reasoning about variables with values moving toward limits, dynamic phenomena involving a balance of forces, or the effect of perturbations on feedback systems.

Qualitative reasoning, as described here, provides a level of description between discrete state graphs and the continuous world: continuous change is described symbolically, but in a way that obeys the constraints of continuity. Recent work on causal reasoning builds on qualitative representations to clarify the roles and properties of causal knowledge (Horn, 1990; Borchardt, 1992; Amsterdam, 1993; Vescovi *et al.*, 1993; Iwasaki *et al.*, 1993).

1.4.2 Differential Equations

The QSIM qualitative model representation is closely related to differential equations as a language for describing aspects of the world.

To clarify and illustrate the role of qualitative descriptions of the world, let us begin with the physicist's view of the world. We observe some physical system in the world that exhibits some actual behavior over time. By a *system*, we simply mean some subset of the entire world whose behavior, and whose interaction with the rest of the world, we believe can be sensibly described. The mechanism of an individual grandfather's clock is a good example of a system. The set of all clock pendulums in New England is undeniably a subset of the world, but there is probably no interesting description of its behavior or its interaction with the rest of the world, so it is not a good example of a system.

The physicist can use the language of differential equations for describing a system and drawing inferences about it. A differential equation represents the structure of the system by selecting certain continuous variables that characterize the state of the system, and certain mathematical constraints on the values those variables can take on. One use of a differential equation description of a system is to predict the behavior of the system over time: a set of continuous functions of time that describe the way the variables of the system evolve over time starting from a given initial state. In figure 1.3, the top row represents the infinite complexity of the real-world system, while the bottom row represents descriptions of that system and its behavior in terms of differential equations and their solutions. Since the description makes fewer distinctions than are actually present in the real system, it is an *abstraction* of the real system.

If a differential equation model adequately describes the structure of a physical system, the behavior predicted by the solution to the differential equation will describe the actual behavior of the physical system. In other words, the upper and

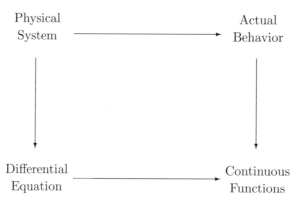

Figure 1.3
A differential equation model is an abstraction of the real world.
A model is a finite tool for predicting or explaining the behavior of an infinitely complex world.

lower paths through figure 1.3 give the same result, or *commute*. A model with this property is useful because we can use it to predict aspects of the behavior of a physical system, and we have confidence that the actual system will behave in the same way.

The *language* of differential equations can be used to state accurate models that make accurate predictions, or faulty models that make inaccurate or incoherent predictions. Its strength comes from the *expressive power* to state models that capture the dynamic character of the world, and the *inferential power* to derive predictions from those models. Differential equations are the single most powerful mathematical tool of modern science and engineering, for exactly this reason.

1.4.3   Abstraction from Numerical to Symbolic Values

I can write a differential equation model describing a ball dropped from a height of two meters, including the numerical values of constants in the differential equation:

$$\frac{d^2x}{dt^2}(t) = -9.8 \; m/sec^2, \; x(t_0) = 2 \; m, \; v(t_0) = 0 \; m/sec.$$

I can use this equation to predict the position of the ball at future times, either by simulating it numerically or by solving it analytically, to get

$$x(t) = (-4.9t^2 + 2) \; m.$$

However, I can get a better result by providing *less* information, and using a model with *more* generality,

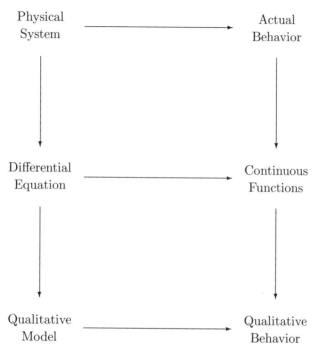

Figure 1.4
Qualitative models are abstractions of differential equations.

Since the qualitative representation corresponds to human states of incomplete knowledge, a person may have the knowledge to formulate a QDE model when an ODE model would be too precise.

Since QDEs and their behaviors are abstractions of ODEs and their solutions, we can provide a guarantee that the qualitative behaviors cover all solutions to corresponding ODEs.

$$\frac{d^2x}{dt^2}(t) = -g, \quad x(t_0) = x_0, \quad v(t_0) = v_0,$$

whose solution is

$$x(t) = -\frac{1}{2}gt^2 + v_0 t + x_0.$$

By replacing numerical constants with symbolic names, the new differential equation represents a state of relatively incomplete knowledge. As a result, I now have a more general model, applicable to a wide range of different conditions. I can apply the model and derive useful predictions even if I don't know the numerical values corresponding to the symbolic names g, v_0, and x_0.

This abstraction from numerical values to symbolic names depends on the fact that the familiar arithmetic operations that we perform on numbers have corresponding algebraic operations on symbolic names and expressions.[3]

1.4.4   Abstraction to Qualitative Values and Relations

The QSIM representation was developed, in part, to make explicit and precise the abstraction relationship between the qualitative representations and the theory of differential equations (figure 1.4). Accordingly, QSIM models can be called *qualitative differential equations* or QDEs.

There are two fundamental improvements in expressive power as we abstract from ordinary to qualitative differential equations.

1. A functional relationship between two variables may be incompletely known, specified only as being in the class of monotonically increasing (or decreasing) functions. For example, one might want to say that the rate of flow from a drain at the bottom of a tank increases with the amount of water in the tank without saying that the increase is linear, or specifying any other particular function.

2. The real number line in which variables take their values is described in terms of a finite set of qualitatively significant "landmark values" and the intervals between them. For example, a variable describing water temperature might have landmark values for the freezing and boiling points of water.

Naturally, the expressive power to state models with incomplete knowledge is useful only if we also have the inferential power to draw useful conclusions from those models!

1.5   References

This framework has evolved over the last decade or so, attempting to maximize conceptual clarity while providing a clear place (or at least a "hook") for the many research contributions in the field.

The field of qualitative reasoning is fortunate to have several excellent volumes that collect critical papers and provide "snapshots" of the state of the field. A more complete bibliography appears at the end of this book.

---

[3]Early steps toward the invention of algebra had taken place in Egypt by approximately 1700 BC, as demonstrated by the Rhind Papyrus (Newman, 1956). The identification of algebra as a useful language for expressing incomplete knowledge was a major revolution in mathematics.

- Daniel G. Bobrow (Ed.). *Qualitative Reasoning about Physical Systems*. Cambridge, MA: Bradford Books/MIT Press, 1985. Reprint of a special issue of the *Artificial Intelligence Journal* **24**, 1984.

  This volume, which represents research done between about 1980 and 1984, was very influential in the development of two productive research areas within artificial intelligence: qualitative reasoning and model-based reasoning.

- Daniel S. Weld and Johan de Kleer (Eds.). *Readings in Qualitative Reasoning About Physical Systems*. Los Altos, CA: Morgan Kaufman, 1989.

  This volume collects many of the best papers in qualitative reasoning, along with a comprehensive bibliography. It includes several of the papers from Bobrow, 1985, some earlier work providing important context, and many of the papers that have influenced the subsequent growth of the area.

- Johan de Kleer and Brian Williams (Eds.). Special volume, Qualitative Reasoning about Physical Systems II. *Artificial Intelligence Journal* **51**, 1991.

- Boi Faltings and Peter Struss (Eds.). *Recent Advances in Qualitative Physics*, MIT Press, 1992.

  These two volumes collect a number of excellent papers representing recent progress in the field.

1.5.1 Comparisons

Several of the seminal approaches to qualitative reasoning slice up the world in different ways, so it is useful to discuss briefly how they fit into the QSIM framework presented here. Although many alternative views have been presented, I will restrict my attention to positions in Bobrow, 1985.

- Confluences (de Kleer and Brown, 1984). Confluences are an alternate representation for qualitative differential equations, discussed in section 3.4.3. Confluence models are often created from component-connection descriptions of electrical circuits, as described in chapter 13. Simulation frequently takes place under the quasi-equilibrium assumption, as discussed in chapter 7. The qualitative behaviors resulting from simulation are represented by an envisionment (state-transition graph) as discussed in section 5.7.

- Qualitative Process Theory (Forbus, 1984) is viewed here primarily as a model-building method, recognizing idealized views and processes in the description of the physical situation, and accumulating a set of influences capable of supporting simulation, as discussed in chapter 14. Our framework is compatible with this model, but we introduce an explicit transformation from influences to the QDE representation to clarify the distinction between model building and model simulation. Like confluences, QP Theory uses envisionments to represent qualitative behaviors.

• Temporal Constraint Propagation (Williams, 1984a; Williams, 1986). Like confluences, a set of TCP constraints is derived from a component-connection description of a physical circuit (chapter 13). Like QSIM, the TCP simulation rules are carefully grounded in the mathematics of continuous function (chapter 3), but the representation for states, time, and qualitative values are different, supporting somewhat different strengths and weaknesses in simulation.

2 Concepts of Qualitative Simulation

In order to introduce the concepts of qualitative simulation, we will go through an elementary modeling exercise, illustrating how qualitative modeling differs from more traditional numerical methods.

We can explore these concepts by looking at the U-tube: a simple, two-tank fluid-flow system. The structure of the U-tube is simple and clear, and its behaviors are easily deduced. Nonetheless, there is enough complexity to motivate the basic features of qualitative simulation systems. Furthermore, this closed two-compartment system can serve as a model for many more complex systems such as electrolyte flow between cellular and extracellular fluid, investment flow between stocks and bonds, and electron flow between regions in a solid state device.

2.1 Qualitative Structure

The U-tube consists of two tanks (named **A** and **B**) connected by a flow channel (figure 2.1). We assume that the momentum of water flowing through the channel is not a significant factor.

Each tank holds a certain amount of water, which produces a certain pressure at the bottom. Since the state of the U-tube system may change over time, these

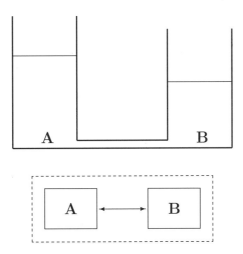

Figure 2.1
The U-tube: a closed two-compartment system.

magnitudes are represented by the *variables*, $amtA(t)$, $amtB(t)$, $pressureA(t)$, and $pressureB(t)$, which are continuous real-valued functions of time.

Reasoning qualitatively, and not knowing the exact size and shape of each tank, we know that the pressure at the bottom of a tank increases with the amount of water in it, but we don't know the exact relationship. We express this state of incomplete knowledge by saying that there is some unspecified monotonically increasing function relating $amtA$ to $pressureA$:

$$pressureA = M^+(amtA). \tag{2.1}$$

The term M^+ refers to an unspecified member of the class of monotonically increasing functions. We may also use M^+ to refer to the entire class and write

$$pressureA = f(amtA) \text{ for some } f \in M^+.$$

We can express incomplete qualitative knowledge about the values taken on by the variables $amtA$ and $pressureA$ at any given time. Instead of specifying numerical values in the real number line, the value of a variable is described qualitatively in terms of its *quantity space*. Each quantity space is defined by an ordered set of *landmark values*. The quantity spaces for $amtA$ and $pressureA$ are:

$amtA$ $0 \cdots AMAX \cdots \infty$
$pressureA$ $0 \cdots\cdots\cdots\cdots \infty$

The landmarks $-\infty$, 0, and ∞ have known mathematical properties and may be used in any quantity space. Other landmarks are symbols whose meanings are specific to the particular quantity space, and are defined only by their relations with other landmarks. Thus, the landmark $AMAX$, representing the maximum capacity of tank A, is somewhere in the interval $(0, \infty)$, but otherwise unspecified. Since $amtA$ and $pressureA$ are necessarily non-negative, the lower bounds of the quantity spaces are both 0, and negative values cannot even be described.

The U-tube is a closed system, so the total amount of water is fixed.

$$amtA + amtB = total \tag{2.2}$$

$$constant(total) \tag{2.3}$$

In the case of the U-tube, we have additional knowledge about the M^+ function relating $amtA$ and $pressureA$. We know that it passes through the origin: there is a correspondence between $amtA = 0$ and $pressureA = 0$. (Following normal mathematical usage, we will write this as the *corresponding values* pair $(0,0)$.) We also assert that the relation $pressureA = M^+(amtA)$ has corresponding values at (∞, ∞), which has the effect of excluding a horizontal or vertical asymptote.

There is a similar (but not necessarily identical) monotonically increasing function relating $amtB$ to $pressureB$, so we can write

$$pressureB = M^+(amtB). \tag{2.4}$$

Remember that M^+ is not the name of an individual function, but a description that applies to a class of functions.

The pressure difference between the two tanks is another important variable:

$$pAB = pressureA - pressureB \tag{2.5}$$

The flow between A and B is a monotonic function of the pressure difference, with corresponding values $(-\infty, -\infty)$, $(0, 0)$, and (∞, ∞):

$$flowAB = M^+(pAB) \tag{2.6}$$

Finally, we observe that $flowAB$ represents the rate of change of $amtB$ and the inverse of the rate of change of $amtA$.

$$\frac{d}{dt}amtB = flowAB \tag{2.7}$$

$$\frac{d}{dt}amtA = -flowAB \tag{2.8}$$

These *qualitative constraints* (equations 2.1–2.8), along with their corresponding values and the quantity spaces of their variables, describe the qualitative structure of the U-tube system. Figure 2.2 shows a graphical form of this set of constraints, along with the QSIM representation of the QDE. Since some of our computations later on will involve propagation of information across constraints, a graphical notation helps clarify the information flow.

The quantity spaces for the variables of this system are

total	$0 \cdots \infty$
amtA	$0 \cdots AMAX \cdots \infty$
pressureA	$0 \cdots \infty$
amtB	$0 \cdots BMAX \cdots \infty$
pressureB	$0 \cdots \infty$
pAB	$-\infty \cdots 0 \cdots \infty$
flowAB	$-\infty \cdots 0 \cdots \infty.$

The quantity spaces define a descriptive "language" representing the set of qualitative distinctions that can be expressed by this model, at least at its initial state.

The constraints and corresponding values are

constraints	corresponding values
$amtA + amtB = total$	
$pressureA = M^+(amtA)$	$(0,0), (\infty, \infty)$
$pressureB = M^+(amtB)$	$(0,0), (\infty, \infty)$
$pressureA - pressureB = pAB$	
$flowAB = M^+(pAB)$	$(-\infty, -\infty), (0,0), (\infty, \infty)$
$\frac{d}{dt}amtB = flowAB$	
$\frac{d}{dt}amtA = -flowAB$	

By combining the constraints and eliminating intermediate variables, we could rewrite this QDE in a notation that emphasizes its similarity to an ordinary differential equation.

$$\frac{d}{dt}amtB = f(g(amtA) - h(amtB)), \quad f, g, h \in M^+$$

Since f, g, and h are unknown monotonic functions, and may well be non-linear, this equation is intractable analytically.

The physical structure of the U-tube implies that this description has a limited domain of validity. We specify the boundaries of the *operating region* for this QDE in two ways. First, the landmark 0 is the lower bound of the quantity spaces of several variables. Thus, negative values for $amtA$, for example, are not even expressible within this QDE. Second, operating region *transitions* can be explicitly triggered by a variable taking on a certain qualitative value. In figure 2.2, the U-tube model specifies two such transitions. In either case, if the simulator detects that a behavior is crossing a boundary of the current operating region, simulation within that region stops, perhaps to be resumed in another operating region. Chapter 8 discusses this topic in detail. Later, in chapters 13 and 14, we will discuss how a set of constraints like this can be derived from a physical description of a mechanism.

2.2   Qualitative Knowledge of State

Like our incomplete knowledge of structure — the qualitative constraints and quantity spaces — we have incomplete knowledge of the state of the U-tube at any given moment. Its state is described by the qualitative values of the variables: $amtA$, $amtB$, $total$, $pressureA$, $pressureB$, pAB, and $flowAB$.

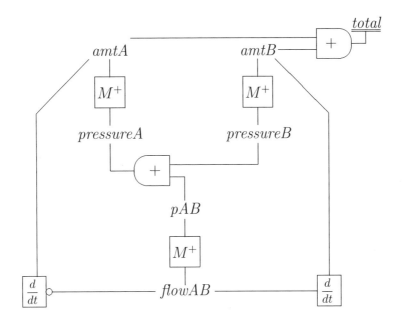

```
(define-QDE U-Tube
  (quantity-spaces
     (amtA       (0 AMAX inf))
     (pressureA  (0 inf))
     (amtB       (0 BMAX inf))
     (pressureB  (0 inf))
     (pAB        (minf 0 inf))
     (flowAB     (minf 0 inf))
     (-flowAB    (minf 0 inf))
     (total      (0 inf)))
  (constraints
     ((M+ amtA pressureA)          (0 0) (inf inf))
     ((M+ amtB pressureB)          (0 0) (inf inf))
     ((add pAB pressureB pressureA))
     ((M+ pAB flowAB)              (minf minf) (0 0) (inf inf))
     ((minus flowAB -flowAB))
     ((d/dt amtB flowAB))
     ((d/dt amtA -flowAB))
     ((add amtA amtB total))
     ((constant total)))
  (transitions
     ((amtA (AMAX inc)) -> tank-A-overflow)
     ((amtB (BMAX inc)) -> tank-B-bursts)))
```

Figure 2.2
U-tube constraint diagram and QSIM QDE.

2.2.1   Qualitative State Is Dynamic

As the system changes with time, we will need to describe the sequences of qualitative states that it may pass through. Suppose that we fill tank A until it overflows, ignoring tank B. The sequence of qualitative magnitudes of the variable $amtA$ will be

$$amtA(t): \qquad 0 \longrightarrow (0, AMAX) \longrightarrow AMAX$$

meaning that after the time that $amtA(t) = 0$ and until $amtA(t) = AMAX$ the value of $amtA(t)$ is somewhere in the open interval $(0, AMAX)$. This is not the whole story, however.

In order to predict a behavior like that of $amtA$, we will need to determine the transitions from one qualitative state to another. In addition to qualitative magnitude in the quantity space, we need to know the direction of change of each variable. Thus, for each variable, we describe its qualitative state in terms of its magnitude (in the quantity space) and its direction of change: increasing, decreasing, or steady. For example, the qualitative state of $amtA$ in the midst of filling has two components, magnitude and direction of change, and is written $\langle (0, AMAX), inc \rangle$. When tank A is filled to the top, the behavior of $amtA$ over time can be described as follows:

$$
\begin{array}{cccccc}
time: & t_0 & & (t_0, t_1) & & t_1 \\
amtA(t): & \langle 0, inc \rangle & \longrightarrow & \langle (0, AMAX), inc \rangle & \longrightarrow & \langle AMAX, std \rangle
\end{array}
$$

We can capture the same description of the behavior of an individual variable with a *qualitative plot* (cf. figure 2.3).

However, before we can predict behavior, we must define an initial state.

2.3   Predicting Behavior from Initial Conditions

A qualitative simulation problem specifies a QDE as a set of variables, their quantity spaces, and their constraints with corresponding values. Then an initial state is given, and we want to know the possible behaviors.

Suppose we start with tank A full and tank B empty. We thus begin with the following information:

$$
t = t_0 \Longrightarrow \boxed{\begin{array}{lcl} amtA & = & \langle AMAX, ? \rangle \\ amtB & = & \langle 0, ? \rangle \end{array}}
$$

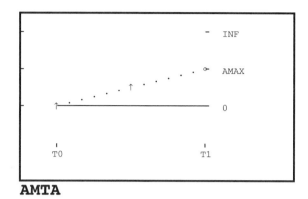

AMTA

Figure 2.3
Qualitative plot of the behavior of $amtA(t)$ as tank A of the U-tube is filled exactly to the top.

$$time: \quad t_0 \qquad\qquad (t_0, t_1) \qquad\qquad\qquad t_1$$
$$amtA(t): \quad \langle 0, inc \rangle \quad \longrightarrow \quad \langle (0, AMAX), inc \rangle \quad \longrightarrow \quad \langle AMAX, std \rangle$$

- Landmark values in a quantity space are arranged on the vertical axis, and landmark time-points are along the horizontal axis;
- qualitative values are plotted at, or midway between, landmark points;
- the symbol plotted ($\uparrow$, $\downarrow$, $\circ$) represents the direction of change;
- dots connecting symbols have no significance.

In order to simulate the system, we need a *complete* qualitative state description: a qualitative magnitude and direction of change for each variable. How much information must be provided to specify an unique initial state? This question is hard to answer in general, because qualitative constraints are weaker than the corresponding quantitative constraints. At a minimum, one should specify magnitudes for all the independent variables in the QDE (those appearing in `constant` constraints), and for integrated variables, that is, those appearing as the first argument to a `d/dt` constraint.

2.3.1 Propagating to the Complete Initial State

Given the initially specified information, we can propagate locally across constraints to determine more about the qualitative state (figure 2.4). Here we are able to propagate to determine the initial state of the U-tube completely.

1. Because of the corresponding value at $(0, 0)$,

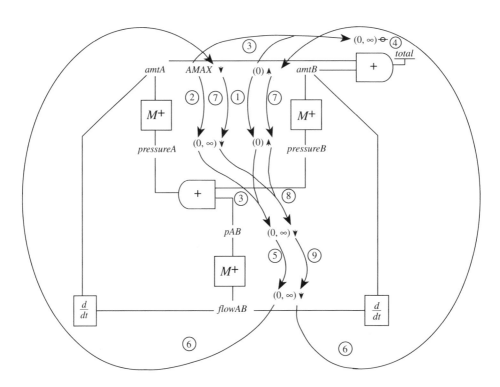

Figure 2.4
Propagation to derive U-tube(t_0).

$amtB = 0 \Longrightarrow pressureB = 0$.

2. Because of corresponding values at $(0,0)$ and (∞,∞), we can conclude that

$amtA = AMAX \Longrightarrow pressureA = (0,\infty)$.

Because of the absence of landmarks, this is the best description for the value of
$pressureA$ expressible in its quantity space.

3. An addition constraint has an implicit set of corresponding values at $(0,0,0)$, so

$amtA = AMAX \wedge amtB = 0 \Longrightarrow total = (0,\infty)$

and

$$pressure A = (0, \infty) \land pressure B = 0 \Longrightarrow pAB = (0, \infty).$$

4. Constant values have direction of change[1] *std*:

$$constant(total) \Longrightarrow [d(total)/dt] = std.$$

5. The corresponding values at $(0,0)$ and (∞, ∞) of the constraint $flow AB = M^+(pAB)$ then give us

$$pAB = (0, \infty) \Longrightarrow flow AB = (0, \infty).$$

6. The derivative constraints can now determine the directions of change of $amt A$ and $amt B$.

$$flow AB = (0, \infty) \quad \Longrightarrow \quad [d(amt A)/dt] = dec$$
$$\land [d(amt B)/dt] = inc.$$

The known directions of change for $amt A$, $amt B$, and *total* are consistent with the addition constraint.

7. The directions of change propagate through monotonic functions:

$$[d(amt A)/dt] = dec \Longrightarrow [d(pressure A)/dt] = dec$$

$$[d(amt B)/dt] = inc \Longrightarrow [d(pressure B)/dt] = inc.$$

8. Directions of change also propagate through the addition constraint:

$$[d(pressure A)/dt] = dec \quad \land \quad [d(pressure B)/dt] = inc$$
$$\Longrightarrow \quad [d(pAB)/dt] = dec.$$

9. The last propagation completes the state:

$$[d(pAB)/dt] = dec \Longrightarrow [d(flow AB)/dt] = dec.$$

The final result of this propagation is a complete qualitative description of the state of the U-tube at the initial instant, t_0.

---

[1] If x is a variable, we can describe the sign of its value as $[x]$, and its direction of change as $[dx/dt]$ or $[\dot{x}]$.

$$t = t_0 \Longrightarrow \begin{array}{lcl} amtA & = & \langle AMAX, dec \rangle \\ pressureA & = & \langle (0, \infty), dec \rangle \\ amtB & = & \langle 0, inc \rangle \\ pressureB & = & \langle 0, inc \rangle \\ pAB & = & \langle (0, \infty), dec \rangle \\ flowAB & = & \langle (0, \infty), dec \rangle \\ total & = & \langle (0, \infty), std \rangle \end{array}$$

Although this inference propagates around a network of constraints, it does not represent changes taking place over time. It derives mathematical consequences from given information about the rest of the state description at a particular instant in time.

This gives us a complete initial state for simulation. The qualitative state description shows us that several of the variables are changing. We can predict the evolution of the U-tube system over time by looking at the nature of the possible qualitative changes.

2.3.2   Predicting the Next State

Each variable changes continuously with time, so it is relatively easy to predict the successor(s) to a given state. Since at the initial instant t_0, $amtB = 0$ and increasing, then in the next qualitative state, $amtB > 0$ and still increasing. Similarly with $pressureB$. The same approach handles $amtA = \langle AMAX, dec \rangle$. However, $pressureA$ is within an open interval, so it would require a finite amount of time to reach the boundary of its interval, while $amtA$ or $amtB$ can move off a landmark value instantaneously. Thus we get the next state description, specifying the qualitative values the variables must have over some open time-interval following t_0. The subsequent simulation will show what event determines the time-point t_1 that terminates this interval.

$$t \in (t_0, t_1) \Longrightarrow \begin{array}{lcl} amtA & = & \langle (0, AMAX), dec \rangle \\ pressureA & = & \langle (0, \infty), dec \rangle \\ amtB & = & \langle (0, BMAX), inc \rangle \\ pressureB & = & \langle (0, \infty), inc \rangle \\ pAB & = & \langle (0, \infty), dec \rangle \\ flowAB & = & \langle (0, \infty), dec \rangle \\ total & = & \langle (0, \infty), std \rangle \end{array}$$

Before we continue, there are a few technicalities we need to observe.

• We are actually presuming that not only the variables but their derivatives vary continuously with time. That is, the variables of the system are *continuously differentiable* functions of time.

• Although we speak of the "next state," since the underlying process we are describing is continuous, strictly speaking a given state has no immediate successor state. However, the qualitative state description changes only at discrete points, so the "next state" of a mechanism refers to the next qualitatively distinct description in that sequence.

Time is modeled as an alternating sequence of time-points and open time-intervals. Our first state description represented the qualitative state of the U-tube at the initial instant t_0. The change from that point in time puts us into an open interval (t_0, t_1) on the time-line, during which the qualitative description remains fixed, until we reach another distinguished time-point t_1 when a qualitative change takes place. Thus, the second state description applies not to a single instant in time but to every time t in the interval (t_0, t_1). Since several variables are changing, the mechanism is changing during that interval, and the description reflects that fact. However, since it has not crossed any qualitative boundary, the *qualitative description* of the changing system remains constant during (t_0, t_1).

2.3.3   Moving to a Limit

Now we need to determine the qualitative change that defines the time t_1 that terminates the interval (t_0, t_1). There are several kinds of qualitative changes:

• A variable that is moving toward a limit may reach it.

• A variable that is equal to a landmark value may move off it.

• A variable may start or stop moving.

In this example, all six variables are moving toward various limits, for a theoretical maximum of $4^6 - 1 = 4095$ possible combinations of qualitative changes. The constraints and corresponding values, however, greatly reduce this set. In the end, we are left with only a single unresolved ambiguity: the race between $amtB \to BMAX$ and $flowAB \to 0$. There are no constraints to resolve this ambiguity, so our prediction will branch on all possibilities. (Physical intuition confirms that both possibilities are reasonable, since we don't know the relative sizes of tanks A and B.)

A branching prediction simply means that the qualitative description of the system does not contain enough information to specify its future qualitative state description uniquely.

The three possible complete qualitative states at t_1 follow:

t	$t_{1(a)}$	$t_{1(b)}$	$t_{1(c)}$
$amtA$	$\langle(0, AMAX), std\rangle$	$\langle(0, AMAX), std\rangle$	$\langle(0, AMAX), dec\rangle$
$pressureA$	$\langle(0, \infty), std\rangle$	$\langle(0, \infty), std\rangle$	$\langle(0, \infty), dec\rangle$
$amtB$	$\langle BMAX, std\rangle$	$\langle(0, BMAX), std\rangle$	$\langle BMAX, inc\rangle$
$pressureB$	$\langle(0, \infty), std\rangle$	$\langle(0, \infty), std\rangle$	$\langle(0, \infty), inc\rangle$
pAB	$\langle 0, std\rangle$	$\langle 0, std\rangle$	$\langle(0, \infty), dec\rangle$
$flowAB$	$\langle 0, std\rangle$	$\langle 0, std\rangle$	$\langle(0, \infty), dec\rangle$
$total$	$\langle(0, \infty), std\rangle$	$\langle(0, \infty), std\rangle$	$\langle(0, \infty), std\rangle$

$t_{1(a)}$ $amtB$ and $flowAB$ reach their limits together, so the U-tube reaches equilibrium with tank B brimming full.

$t_{1(b)}$ $flowAB = 0$ while $amtB < BMAX$, so we reach an equilibrium state with tank B partially filled. (Figure 2.5 shows this behavior.)

$t_{1(c)}$ $amtB$ reaches $BMAX$ while $flowAB > 0$, so tank B overflows. (The current model of the U-tube ceases to apply, so we must make a transition to a new model. Figure 2.6 shows a transition to a model in which tank B has burst and all the water in the system drains out.)

The fourth possibility, that neither variable reaches its limit, means that no qualitative change has taken place and is already adequately described by the state representing the time-interval (t_0, t_1). The QSIM representation is designed so that every open time-interval has a terminating time-point.

This non-deterministic prediction is represented as a branching tree of qualitative states, alternating time-points and time-intervals, in which the behaviors are the paths from root to leaves:

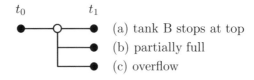

t_0 t_1

(a) tank B stops at top
(b) partially full
(c) overflow

This type of non-deterministic prediction is an important feature of qualitative simulation. A specific U-tube is a deterministic mechanism and cannot choose arbitrarily which behavior to take. However, our qualitative description is incomplete and does not contain enough information to determine which behavior will be the real one. There are different physical U-tubes that satisfy the same qualitative constraints and initial state exhibiting each of the three possible behaviors, so all three behaviors are genuine.

One might hope that qualitative simulation would give us exactly the set of possible behaviors consistent with the partial knowledge expressed by the qualitative structure description. In other words, (a) every behavior of any mechanism satisfying the constraints will be predicted, and (b) every predicted behavior will be the real behavior of some mechanism satisfying the constraints. As we have seen, this is true for the U-tube. Although the first half (a) can be guaranteed in general, the second half (b) cannot. After establishing the necessary preliminaries, these results will be proved in section 5.6.

Figures 2.5 and 2.6 show corresponding qualitative and numerical simulations illustrating two branches of the behavior tree for this U-tube scenario. The numerical models, of course, contain numerical assumptions not required by the qualitative models. In the models we have constructed, when tank B passes its maximum capacity, it bursts, losing its own contents immediately and allowing the contents of tank A to drain away as well, eventually emptying the entire system. Figure 2.5 shows the behavior where equilibrium is achieved before tank B becomes full. Figure 2.6 shows the behavior where tank B overflows and bursts.

2.3.4   Creating New Landmark Values

In the second case $(t_{1(b)})$ described previously (figure 2.5), the U-tube system reaches equilibrium while $amtB$ is still in the open interval $(0, BMAX)$, so its qualitative state is described as

$$amtB(t_{1(b)}) = \langle (0, BMAX), std \rangle.$$

The value of $amtB$ when $t = t_{1(b)}$ is a critical value of the function $amtB(t)$: its value when its derivative becomes zero. The critical value may be sufficiently important that it should be given a name so it can be referred to later. It may represent an important qualitative distinction that will be useful in other contexts. This is exactly what we mean by a "landmark value."

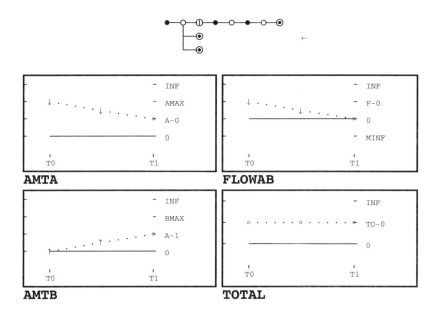

U-Tube

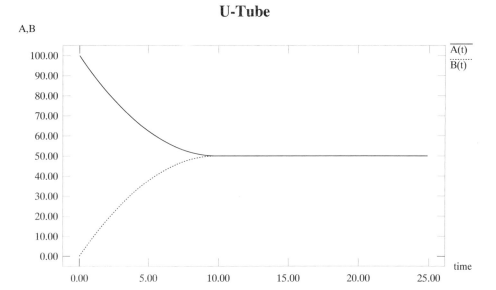

Figure 2.5
Qualitative and numerical simulations of the U-tube reaching equilibrium.

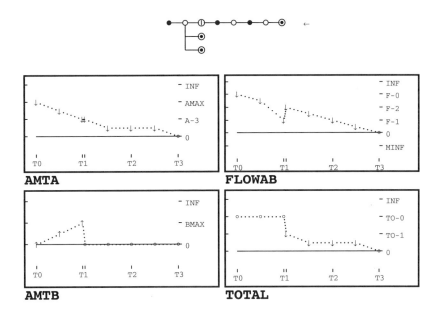

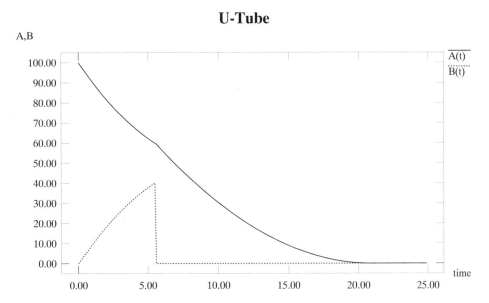

Figure 2.6
Qualitative and numerical simulations of the U-tube overflowing and bursting.

Since $amtB(t_{1(b)})$ lies strictly between two existing landmarks, we can give it a name, e.g., a_1, and insert it as a new landmark into the quantity space for $amtB$.[2]

$amtB \qquad 0 \cdots a_1 \cdots BMAX \cdots \infty.$

Following this strategy for the other variables that reach critical values between landmarks, we augment the quantity spaces for the U-tube system.

$amtA \qquad\qquad 0 \cdots a_0 \cdots AMAX \cdots \infty$
$pressureA \qquad 0 \cdots p_0 \cdots \infty$
$amtB \qquad\qquad 0 \cdots a_1 \cdots BMAX \cdots \infty$
$pressureB \qquad 0 \cdots p_1 \cdots \infty$
$pAB \qquad\qquad -\infty \cdots 0 \cdots \infty$
$flowAB \qquad\quad -\infty \cdots 0 \cdots \infty$
$total \qquad\qquad 0 \cdots to_0 \cdots \infty.$

Several constraints can now define new corresponding values from the new equilibrium state, representing the meaning of these new landmarks through their relationships with the constraints.

constraints	new corresponding values
$pressureA = M^+(amtA)$	(a_0, p_0)
$pressureB = M^+(amtB)$	(a_1, p_1)
$pressureA - pressureB = pAB$	$(p_0, p_1, 0)$
$flowAB = M^+(pAB)$	
$flowAB = \frac{d}{dt} amtB$	
$flowAB = -\frac{d}{dt} amtA$	
$amtA + amtB = total$	$(AMAX, 0, to_0), (a_0, a_1, to_0)$

Actually, the landmark to_0 and the corresponding value tuple $(AMAX, 0, to_0)$ were created at time-point t_0.

The final equilibrium state of the system along this branch of the tree can now be described more precisely in terms of the new landmarks.

---

[2]QSIM constructs new landmarks from a root made up of the first one or two letters of the variable name.

$$t = t_{1(b)} \Longrightarrow \begin{array}{lcl} amtA & = & \langle a_0, std \rangle \\ pressureA & = & \langle p_0, std \rangle \\ amtB & = & \langle a_1, std \rangle \\ pressureB & = & \langle p_1, std \rangle \\ pAB & = & \langle 0, std \rangle \\ flowAB & = & \langle 0, std \rangle \\ total & = & \langle to_1, std \rangle \end{array}$$

New landmarks and corresponding values are meaningful only on their own branch of the state tree. For example, the landmark a_0, representing the amount of water in tank A when the U-tube reaches equilibrium, has no significance along the branch in which tank B overflows. Along that branch, there is a different new landmark, a_3, representing the value of $amtA$ when the overflow occurred.

The three paths through the tree of qualitative states represent the three possible behaviors of the system. Each qualitative graph represents a single behavior, so we need three qualitative graphs to capture these possibilities.

2.4   Example: Ballistic Trajectory in Two Dimensions

To provide another elementary example, consider a qualitative model of the trajectory of a ball, described in two dimensions, assuming gravity but no friction.

2.5   Problems

1. Hand simulate the behaviors of a simple one-tank "bathtub" model from t_0 to t_1, starting with $amount(t_0) = 0$, $inflow(t_0) = if^*$.

```
(define-QDE Minimal-Bathtub
  (quantity-spaces
    (amount    (   0 full inf))
    (outflow   (   0      inf))
    (inflow    (   0 if*  inf))
    (netflow   (minf 0    inf)))
  (constraints
    ((M+ amount outflow)          (0 0) (inf inf))
    ((add netflow outflow inflow))
    ((d/dt amount netflow))
    ((constant inflow)))
  (transitions
    ((amount (full inc)) -> overflow)))
```

```
(define-QDE Simple-Trajectory
  (text   "2-D Trajectory, no friction.")
  (quantity-spaces
    (x    (0 inf))                       ; position
    (y    (0 inf))                       ; position
    (vx   (minf 0 inf))                  ; velocity
    (vy   (minf 0 inf))                  ; velocity
    (g    (minf G* 0)))                  ; gravity (constant)
  (constraints
    ((d/dt x vx))
    ((d/dt y vy))
    ((d/dt vy g))
    ((constant vx))
    ((constant g))))

(defun fire-simple-projectile ()
  (let ((init (make-new-state :from-qde Simple-Trajectory
                              :assert-values '((x (0 nil))
                                               (y (0 nil))
                                               (vx ((0 inf) nil))
                                               (vy ((0 inf) nil))
                                               (g (g* std)))
                              :text "Fire projectile")))
    (qsim init)
    (qsim-display init)))
```

Figure 2.7
The 2D-Trajectory QDE.

2. Hand simulate the behaviors of the "gravity" model from t_0 to t_2, starting with $y(t_0) = 0$, $v(t_0) = v^*$, $a(t_0) = g$. (What happens if you continue to t_3?)

```
(define-QDE Gravity
   (quantity-spaces
       (y (     0    inf))
       (v (minf  0 v0 inf))
       (a (minf g 0    inf)))
   (constraints
       ((d/dt y v))
       ((d/dt v a))
       ((constant a))))
```

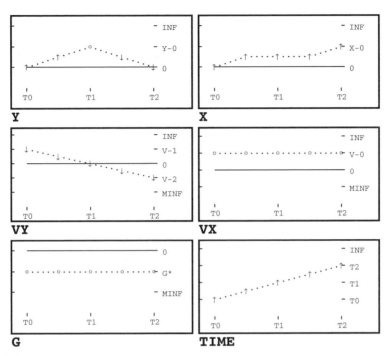

Figure 2.8
Unique behavior of the trajectory in 2-D.

3. Hand simulate the behaviors of the "simple spring" model from t_0 to t_4, starting with $x(t_0) = x^*$, $v(t_0) = 0$. (What happens if you continue beyond t_4?)

```
(define-QDE Simple-Spring
  (quantity-spaces
    (x  (minf 0 x0 inf))
    (v  (minf 0    inf))
    (a  (minf 0    inf)))
  (constraints
    ((d/dt x v))
    ((d/dt v a))
    ((M- a x)      (0 0) (minf inf) (inf minf))))
```

3 The QSIM Representation

3.1 Introduction

We have now been introduced to the basic concepts of qualitative modeling and simulation in QSIM: variables, quantity spaces, qualitative values, constraints, corresponding values, limit analysis, and region transitions. In this chapter, we define the elements of the qualitative representation formally, by showing how they correspond with the familiar elements — the real number line, continuous functions, algebraic and differential relationships — of the elementary theory of differential equations. Adequate background in calculus and differential equations can be found in many textbooks; my favorites are Spivak, 1967, and Boyce and DiPrima, 1969.

This correspondence justifies the vertical (abstraction) arrows in figure 3.1, and therefore justifies our use of the term *qualitative differential equation* for qualitative descriptions of physical mechanisms. Because we can justify this abstraction relation, the qualitative representation is not merely metaphorically *like* a differential equation; it actually *is* a differential equation, albeit describing the world at a coarser granularity than is usual with ordinary differential equations.

We will often say that an ordinary differential equation "abstracts to", "is an instance of", or "satisfies" the corresponding qualitative differential equation. Similarly with descriptions of initial values and behaviors.

Later, in chapter 5, after we have developed the machinery that underlies qualitative simulation, we will consider the bottom horizontal arrow in figure 3.1, representing the inference from qualitative structure to qualitative behavior.

3.1.1 Qualitative Differential Equations

DEFINITION 1 A *qualitative differential equation* (QDE) is a tuple of four elements, $\langle V, Q, C, T \rangle$, each of which will be defined below.

- V is a set of *variables*, each of which is a "reasonable" function of time.

- Q is a set of *quantity spaces*, one for each variable in V.

- C is a set of *constraints* applying to the variables in V. Each variable in V must appear in some constraint.

- T is a set of *transitions*, which are rules defining the boundary of the domain of applicability of the QDE.

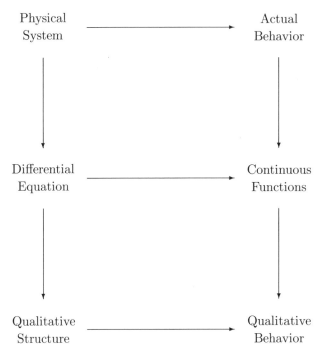

Figure 3.1
Abstraction from the world, to differential equations and their solutions, to qualitative models.

In this discussion, I will attempt to describe not only *how* the qualitative representation is defined but *why* it was defined that way, and not some other plausible way.

3.2   Symbolic Descriptions of Continuous Change

Differential equations model the world of continuous change. Qualitative reasoning is based on discrete symbol structures. How can the two be compatible?

The key intuition is that, although the world changes continuously, it changes *qualitatively* only at isolated points. In order to formalize this intuition, we focus our attention on a subset of the things that can happen in a continuous world, for which useful qualitative reasoning is possible. We will also need to craft the qualitative representation with care, to capture no more and no less than what we need from differential equations and continuous functions.

In this section, we will formalize the qualitative description of the behavior of a continuous function

$$f(t) : \Re^* \to \Re^*$$

in terms of the qualitative variables representing f and t, the quantity spaces representing the domain and range of the function $f(t)$, and the qualitative values that represent the value of $f(t_i)$ for any specific t_i.

3.2.1   Qualitative Variables

The variables in a QDE represent time-varying quantities. In order for qualitative reasoning to be possible, we must restrict variables to correspond to functions of time whose behavior is *reasonable*.

First, a reasonable function must be *continuously differentiable*: if v is a variable, then both $v(t)$ and its derivative $v'(t)$ are continuous. Transitions between domains will make it possible to represent isolated discontinuities between regions of continuous behavior.

Second, it is convenient to consider each variable, including time, to range over the *extended* real number line, $\Re^*$, which includes the endpoints $-\infty$ and $+\infty$. The function $v : [0, \infty] \to \Re^*$ is defined to be continuous at ∞ exactly if $\lim_{t \to \infty} v(t)$ exists. Using the extended real number line allows us to use the invariant that the value of a variable always lies in a closed interval defined by landmark values. It also allows us to describe asymptotic approach to a limit, as reaching the limit at $t = \infty$. For example, both e^{-t} and e^t are reasonable functions on $[0, \infty]$, but $\sin t$ is not.

Third, we will need to avoid functions of time whose qualitative properties change infinitely often in a finite interval. For example, the function $f(t) = t^2 \sin 1/t$ is continuously differentiable, but its behavior changes infinitely quickly around $t = 0$. An additional restriction is required to prevent $f'(t)$ from behaving unreasonably around the endpoints of its domain, even without crossing zero.

We can summarize these properties in the definition of a reasonable function. Unless otherwise mentioned, all variables will be considered to be reasonable functions of time.

DEFINITION 2   Where $[a, b] \subseteq \Re^*$, the function $f : [a, b] \to \Re^*$ is a *reasonable function over* $[a, b]$ if

1. f is continuous on $[a, b]$,

2. f is continuously differentiable on (a, b),

3. f has only finitely many critical points in any bounded interval, and

4. the one-sided limits $\lim_{t \to a+} f'(t)$ and $\lim_{t \to b-} f'(t)$ exist in $\Re^*$. Define $f'(a)$ and $f'(b)$ to be equal to these limits.

3.2.2   Quantity Spaces

A *quantity space* captures the intuition that, for reasonable functions at least, there are only a few qualitatively important *landmark values*.[1]

DEFINITION 3   A *quantity space* is a finite, totally ordered set of symbols, the *landmark values*

$$l_1 < l_2 < \cdots < l_k.$$

Each landmark is a symbolic name, representing a particular value in $\Re^*$ whose actual value is often unknown. A quantity space normally contains the landmarks $-\infty$, 0, and $+\infty$, though the QSIM program allows these to be omitted where their explicit presence is not necessary (e.g., section 8.6).

Under the usual QSIM semantics, the quantity space representing the range for a reasonable function $f(t)$ must include a landmark value corresponding to each *critical value* of $f(t)$: the value of $f(t)$ when $f'(t) = 0$. This requires us to introduce new landmarks if critical points are discovered during simulation. Under the alternative envisionment semantics (section 5.7) new landmarks are not created, so some critical values may fall in the intervals between landmarks.

Time, represented by the qualitative variable *time*, has the quantity space

$$t_0 < t_1 < \cdots < t_n < \infty.$$

DEFINITION 4   A time-point $t \in [a, b]$ is a *distinguished* or *landmark time-point* of the reasonable function f if t is a boundary element of the set $\{t \in [a, b] \mid f(t) = x$, where $x \in \Re^*$ is represented by a landmark value of $f\}$.

---

[1]Consistency in terminology suggests that quantity spaces should be called "qualitative value spaces." However, the current usage, from the Naive Physics Manifesto (Hayes, 1979; 1985b), is firmly established.

The restriction to *boundary* values of t handles the possibility that $f(t)$ remains constant at some landmark value over a time-interval. Only the endpoints of that interval are landmark time-points.

PROPOSITION 1   Any reasonable function $f : [a, b] \rightarrow \Re^*$ defined over a bounded interval $[a, b]$ has a finite set of landmark time-points,

$a = t_0 < t_1 < \cdots < t_n = b,$

in its domain, and a finite set of landmark values,

$l_1 < l_2 < \cdots < l_k,$

in its range.

3.2.3   Qualitative Values

A qualitative variable v, and its quantity space $l_1 < \cdots < l_k$, define a symbolic language — a finite set of meaningful distinctions — for describing the values of a reasonable function $f(t) : [a, b] \rightarrow \Re^*$. At any time t, we can describe the qualitative value of $f(t)$ in terms of its ordinal relationships with the landmarks in its quantity space, and its direction of change.

That is, the qualitatively expressible values for a variable v are the landmark values and the open intervals bounded by landmark values. For most purposes, we will only consider open intervals bounded by *adjacent* landmark values.

DEFINITION 5   The *qualitative value* of $f(t)$, $QV(f, t)$, with respect to the quantity space $l_1 < l_2 < \cdots < l_k$, is the pair $\langle qmag, qdir \rangle$, where

$$qmag = \begin{cases} l_j & \text{if } f(t) = l_j, \text{a landmark value} \\ (l_j, l_{j+1}) & \text{if } f(t) \in (l_j, l_{j+1}) \end{cases}$$

$$qdir = \begin{cases} inc & \text{if } f'(t) > 0 \\ std & \text{if } f'(t) = 0 \\ dec & \text{if } f'(t) < 0. \end{cases}$$

For example, suppose $x(t)$ takes its values in the quantity space

$x: \qquad -\infty \cdots 0 \cdots A \cdots B \cdots \infty.$

If x starts at equilibrium at A and moves to a new equilibrium at B, then its sequence of qualitative values could be described as

$$x(t) : \langle A, std \rangle \to \langle (A, B), inc \rangle \to \langle B, std \rangle. \tag{3.1}$$

Notice that although the function $x(t)$ changes continuously, so there is no immediate successor time to a given time t, the *qualitative description* of the value of $x(t)$ changes only at discrete points. Thus, the concept of a "next state" of x is meaningful when referring to the qualitative descriptions, even though it is not when referring to the continuous function.

PROPOSITION 2   Where $a = t_0 < \cdots < t_n = b$ are the distinguished time-points of f, consider $s, t \in (a, b)$ such that $t_i < s < t < t_{i+1}$ for some i. Then $QV(f, s) = QV(f, t)$.

Proof   By the Intermediate Value Theorem and the definition of distinguished time-point, since f is continuously differentiable, $f(t)$ cannot pass a landmark value, and $f'(t)$ cannot change signs between adjacent distinguished time-points. ∎

This justifies our basic intuition that the qualitative value of the function is constant over intervals between landmarks. Hence, we may make the following definitions.

DEFINITION 6   For adjacent distinguished time-points t_i and t_{i+1}, define $QV(f, t_i, t_{i+1})$, the *qualitative value of f on (t_i, t_{i+1})*, to be $QV(f, t)$ for any $t \in (t_i, t_{i+1})$.

DEFINITION 7   The *qualitative behavior* of f on $[a, b]$ is the sequence of qualitative values of f,

$$QV(f, t_0), QV(f, t_0, t_1), QV(f, t_1) \ldots QV(f, t_{n-1}, t_n), QV(f, t_n),$$

alternating between qualitative values at distinguished time-points, and qualitative values on intervals between distinguished time-points.

DEFINITION 8   A *system* is a set $F = \{f_1 \ldots f_m\}$ of reasonable functions $f_j : [a, b] \to \Re^*$ over the same domain, each with its own set of landmarks and distinguished time-points. The *distinguished time-points of a system* F are the union of the distinguished time-points of the individual functions $f_j \in F$. The *qualitative state* of a system F of m functions is the m-tuple of individual qualitative states:

$$\begin{aligned} QS(F, t_i) &= \langle QV(f_1, t_i), \ldots QV(f_m, t_i) \rangle \\ QS(F, t_i, t_{i+1}) &= \langle QV(f_1, t_i, t_{i+1}), \ldots QV(f_m, t_i, t_{i+1}) \rangle \end{aligned}$$

If t_i and/or t_{i+1} are not distinguished time-points of a particular f_j, then t_i and the interval (t_i, t_{i+1}) must be between two distinguished time-points of f_j, say t_k and t_{k+1}. Then $QV(f_j, t_i)$ and $QV(f_j, t_i, t_{i+1})$ are defined to be the same as the containing $QV(f_j, t_k, t_{k+1})$.

THEOREM 1 (BEHAVIOR ABSTRACTION) If $F = \{f_1 \dots f_m\}$ is a set of reasonable functions $f_j : [a, b] \to \Re^*$ defined over a bounded interval $[a, b]$, then the qualitative behavior of F is described by the sequence of qualitative states of F,

$$QS(F, t_0), QS(F, t_0, t_1), QS(F, t_1), \dots, QS(F, t_n),$$

where $a = t_0$ and $t_n = b$. That is,

- for any qualitative state $QS(F, t_i, t_{i+1})$ over a time-interval, and any $f_j \in F$, $QV(f_j, t)$ has the same value for all t in (t_i, t_{i+1});
- for any pair of adjacent qualitative states $QS(F, t_i), QS(F, t_i, t_{i+1})$, or $QS(F, t_i, t_{i+1}), QS(F, t_{i+1})$, there is some $f_j \in F$ such that $QV(f_j, t_i) \neq QV(f_j, t_i, t_{i+1})$ or $QV(f_j, t_i, t_{i+1}) \neq QV(f_j, t_{i+1})$, respectively.

Proof Follows directly from proposition 2 and definitions 6, 7, and 8. ∎

This discussion clarifies the concept of the "next state." Every state has a qualitative description $QS(F, t)$, but that description changes only at discrete landmark time-points, and remains constant on the open intervals between them. The "next state" of a system is more properly called the "next distinct qualitative state description" of the system. Time is thus represented as an alternating sequence of time-points and time-intervals.

3.3 Defining the Qualitative Constraints

The state of a system at a time t is described in terms of the values of some set of variables $\{x, y, \dots\}$, each of which is a reasonable function of time.

The relationships among these variables are expressed by qualitative constraints that hold for each t. The first few — *add*, *mult*, *minus*, *d/dt*, and *constant* — are familiar mathematical relations.

`(add x y z)`	$\equiv$	$x(t) + y(t) = z(t)$
`(mult x y z)`	$\equiv$	$x(t) \cdot y(t) = z(t)$
`(minus x y)`	$\equiv$	$y(t) = -x(t)$
`(d/dt x y)`	$\equiv$	$\frac{d}{dt}x(t) = y(t)$
`(constant x)`	$\equiv$	$\frac{d}{dt}x(t) = 0$

The functional constraints — M^+ and M^- — express incomplete, qualitative knowledge about a functional relationship. The function relating the variables is known only to lie in the class M^+ of monotonically increasing functions.

(M+ x y) $\equiv$ $y(t) = f(x(t)), f \in M^+$
(M- x y) $\equiv$ $y(t) = -f(x(t)), f \in M^+$

DEFINITION 9 M^+ is the set of reasonable functions $f : [a, b] \to \Re^*$ such that $f' > 0$ over (a, b).

Allowing $f'(a)$ or $f'(b)$ to be zero or infinite permits more plausible behavior at region boundaries.

DEFINITION 10 M_0^+ is the set of $f \in M^+$ such that $f(0) = 0$.

Actually, the set M^+ is somewhat more restrictive than the set of monotonic functions. For example, $f(x) = x^3$ does not belong to M^+ over the domain $\Re^*$ because $f'(0) = 0$. This restriction is necessary to enable the propagation rule

if $y = f(x)$, where $f \in M^+$, then $[\dot{y}] = [\dot{x}]$.

3.3.1   Abstracting Structure from ODE to QDE

Using the constraint definitions, we can define precisely the abstraction relation between qualitative differential equations (QDEs) and ordinary differential equations (ODEs). If a mechanism can be described by an ODE meeting certain restrictions, there is a corresponding but weaker QDE describing the same mechanism. "Weaker" means that any behavior that satisfies the ODE must satisfy the QDE, but not necessarily vice versa.

Given a suitable ODE, we can decompose it into an equivalent set of simultaneous equations by introducing terms for each subexpression. When this process is complete, each equation can be mapped to a qualitative constraint. For example, consider the ODE

$$\frac{d^2u}{dt^2} - \frac{du}{dt} + \arctan ku = 0. \tag{3.2}$$

The simultaneous equations (a) and the qualitative constraints (b) are derived as follows:

(a)	(b)
$v_1 = du/dt$	`(d/dt u v1)`
$v_2 = dv_1/dt$	`(d/dt v1 v2)`
$v_3 = ku$	`(mult k u v3)`
$v_4 = \arctan v_3$	`(M+ v3 v4)`
$v_2 - v_1 + v_4 = 0$	`(add v2 v4 v1)`

Quantity spaces for the variables $\{u, v_1, \ldots, v_4, k\}$ are constructed by adding to the base quantity space $\{-\infty, 0, +\infty\}$ landmarks representing the values of constants and domain and range boundary values for monotonic functions. Constraints are augmented with corresponding values where they are known to take on values uniquely representable within the quantity spaces. In the previous example, the variable v3 receives the quantity space (`minf l1 0 l2 inf`), while the monotonic function constraint (`M+ v3 v4`) receives the corresponding values (`l1 minf`), (`0 0`), and (`l2 inf`).

Any solution $u(t)$ to equation (3.2) uniquely determines the auxiliary functions $v_1 \ldots v_4$, and so defines a solution to the simultaneous equations (a). Each constraint in (b) is mathematically equivalent to the corresponding equation, with the exception of the M^+, which is less restrictive. Therefore, the function $u(t)$ must also satisfy the constraints (b). The introduction of the monotonic function constraint, of course, requires that the corresponding function from the ODE (in this case, arctan) have non-zero derivative on the interior of its domain.

We may summarize this discussion as the following theorem.

THEOREM 2 (STRUCTURAL ABSTRACTION)   Let

$$F[u(t), u'(t), \ldots, u^{(n)}] = 0 \tag{3.3}$$

be an ordinary differential equation of order n, to be satisfied by a function $u : [a, b] \to \Re^*$, where F is defined only in terms of the arithmetic operations addition, multiplication, and negation, along with functions of continuous and strictly non-zero derivative. Then a qualitative differential equation $QDE = \langle V, Q, C, T \rangle$ can be defined, corresponding with equation (3.3), such that any reasonable function $u : [a, b] \to \Re^*$ that satisfies equation (3.3) also satisfies QDE.

In such a case we say that QDE is a *structural abstraction* of the ODE represented by equation (3.3).

This syntactic procedure for decomposing an ODE into simultaneous equations generates a unique set of constraints from a given QDE. However, different monotonic functions may be mapped to the same M^+ constraint, so a given qualitative differential equation can be the abstraction of multiple ODEs.

3.3.2   Corresponding Values

Corresponding values are tuples (pairs or triples, usually) of landmark values that
the variables in some constraint can take on at the same time. They provide a
mutual constraint between the meaning of a QSIM constraint and the meaning of
landmark values in the quantity spaces of the variables.

In the case of an *add* constraint, whose meaning is already precisely specified, a
corresponding value triple (p, q, r) where p, q, and r are landmarks in the appropriate quantity spaces, provides a constraint $p + q = r$ on the real numbers that
p, q, and r can stand for. In the case of incompletely specified monotonic function
constraints such as M^+ or M^-, a corresponding value pair (p, q) provides a mutual
constraint on the possible values of p and q, and on the shape of the functional
relation $f \in M^+$.

For example, the constraint $level = M^+(amount)$ in a model of a bathtub encapsulates the incompletely known geometry of the container:

```
((M+ amount level) (0 0) (full top) (inf inf))
```

The corresponding value pairs of the constraint encode the following information:

- $(0, 0)$ means that $amount = 0$ iff $level = 0$. That is, the implied monotonic
function $f \in M^+$ must pass through $(0, 0)$.

- $(full, top)$ constrains the meanings of the landmarks in their respective quantity
spaces to refer to different aspects of the same event.

- (∞, ∞) constrains the function $f \in M^+$ to eliminate the possibility of horizontal
or vertical asymptote.

Horizontal and vertical asymptotes in the shape of monotonic function constraints
are expressed as corresponding value tuples with one infinite and one finite landmark.

Similarly, the constraint (`add netflow outflow inflow`) represents the relationship $netflow(t) = inflow(t) - outflow(t)$. This *add* constraint might have the
corresponding value triple $(0, of_{27}, if_{27})$, which encodes the information that the
landmarks of_{27} and if_{27} refer to the same value. Section 3.8.6 discusses equality
of landmarks in different quantity spaces. Section 3.8.2 discusses an extension of
corresponding values to non-landmark values.

3.4 The Domain of Signs

Zero (0) is the prototypical landmark, dividing the positive numbers $(+)$ from the negative numbers $(-)$ on the real line. This set of qualitative values is called the *Domain of Signs:*

$$\mathcal{S} = \{+, 0, -\}.$$

For some purposes we need to express ignorance of the sign of a quantity, so we add a qualitative value to get the *extended signs:*

$$\mathcal{S}' = \{+, 0, -, ?\}.$$

Using these simple domains, we can provide simple criteria for checking the qualitative constraints against qualitative values, and prove some useful algebraic properties of the qualitative representation.

In the following chart, we summarize the fundamental definitions of the sign values in terms of intervals, the compact bracket notation used to avoid confusion with other symbols, the single-character abbreviated notation used where no confusion is possible, and two notations when signs are used for directions of change. The notations are mathematically equivalent "syntactic sugar" used for clarity in different contexts.

Fundamental	*Signs (Compact)*	*Signs (Abbreviated)*	*QSIM qdirs*	*Plot symbols*
$(0, \infty)$	$[+]$	$+$	*inc*	↑
0	$[0]$	0	*std*	⊖
$(-\infty, 0)$	$[-]$	$-$	*dec*	↓
$(-\infty, +\infty)$	$[?]$	$?$	*ign*	*

3.4.1 Sign-Valued Operators

Certain qualitative operators are applied to values in $\Re^*$ and return signs as values:

- $[x]_0 = sign(x) = \begin{cases} [+] & \text{if } x > 0 \\ [0] & \text{if } x = 0 \\ [-] & \text{if } x < 0. \end{cases}$

  $[x]$ as an abbreviation for $[x]_0$ is acceptable where no ambiguity is possible.

- $[x]_{x_0} = sign(x - x_0)$, where x_0 serves as a reference value for the variable x.

- $[\dot{x}] = [dx/dt] = sign(dx/dt)$.

- $[x]_\infty = \begin{cases} [+] & \text{if } x = +\infty \\ [0] & \text{if } x \text{ is finite} \\ [-] & \text{if } x = -\infty \end{cases}$

The $[\dot{x}]$ notation is motivated by the standard engineering notation in which $\dot{x}$ represents dx/dt. Note that the use of ∂x for $[dx/dt]_0$ is obsolete because of the potential for confusion with notations for partial derivatives. An additional operator is defined later: $[x]_{(a,b)}$ on page 63.

For example, these operators provide several different ways to describe the behavior of $x(t)$ in equation (3.1) above, increasing from equilibrium at A to B, as follows:

	$QSIM$		$[x]_0$	$[x]_A$	$[x]_B$	$[\dot{x}]$
$x(t_0)$	$=$	$\langle A, std \rangle$	$+$	0	$-$	0
$x(t_0, t_1)$	$=$	$\langle (A, B), inc \rangle$	$+$	$+$	$-$	$+$
$x(t_1)$	$=$	$\langle B, std \rangle$	$+$	$+$	0	0

In perturbation analysis problems, it is common for a set of variables $\{x, y, z\}$ to have a set of related reference values $\{x^*, y^*, z^*\}$. In such a case, we may write $[x]_*$, $[y]_*$, and $[z]_*$, to mean the sign of each variable with respect to *its own* reference value.

3.4.2 Qualitative Addition: Function or Relation?

Addition over the real numbers is a *function* that takes two real values and returns a third: $+ : \Re \times \Re \to \Re$. It may seem plausible to define addition over the signs in the same way:

$+ : \mathcal{S} \times \mathcal{S} \to \mathcal{S}.$

This is not possible, however, since the sum of the qualitative values $[+]$ and $[-]$ is ambiguous, so the addition function cannot be single-valued. To represent addition as a function, it must be defined over the *extended* signs:

$+ : \mathcal{S}' \times \mathcal{S}' \to \mathcal{S}'.$

This, in turn, means that other qualitative constraints, such as multiplication, must be defined over $\mathcal{S}'$ as well. Table 3.1(a) gives the definitions of the qualitative addition and multiplication functions.

In general, we cope with the problem of ambiguity by representing qualitative addition and multiplication not as functions, but as *relations*, taking three qualitative

(a) Arithmetic operations defined as functions:

+	[+]	[0]	[−]	[?]
[+]	[+]	[+]	[?]	[?]
[0]	[+]	[0]	[−]	[?]
[−]	[?]	[−]	[−]	[?]
[?]	[?]	[?]	[?]	[?]

$$+ : \mathcal{S}' \times \mathcal{S}' \to \mathcal{S}'$$

×	[+]	[0]	[−]	[?]
[+]	[+]	[0]	[−]	[?]
[0]	[0]	[0]	[0]	[0]
[−]	[−]	[0]	[+]	[?]
[?]	[?]	[0]	[?]	[?]

$$\times : \mathcal{S}' \times \mathcal{S}' \to \mathcal{S}'$$

(b) Arithmetic operations defined as relations:

add	[+]	[0]	[−]
[+]	[+]	[+]	[+]/[0]/[−]
[0]	[+]	[0]	[−]
[−]	[+]/[0]/[−]	[−]	[−]

$$add : \mathcal{S} \times \mathcal{S} \times \mathcal{S} \to \{T, F\}$$

mult	[+]	[0]	[−]
[+]	[+]	[0]	[−]
[0]	[0]	[0]	[0]
[−]	[−]	[0]	[+]

$$mult : \mathcal{S} \times \mathcal{S} \times \mathcal{S} \to \{T, F\}$$

Table 3.1
Qualitative addition and multiplication tables.

values and returning a truth value:

$$add \quad : \quad \mathcal{S} \times \mathcal{S} \times \mathcal{S} \to \{T, F\}$$
$$mult \quad : \quad \mathcal{S} \times \mathcal{S} \times \mathcal{S} \to \{T, F\}$$

Table 3.1(b) gives the sets of triples for which the *add* and *mult* relations hold over the signs (not extended signs). When qualitative addition and multiplication are viewed as functions, uncertainty can propagate throughout a complex expression, resulting in more uncertainty than if they are viewed as relations. (See problem 11.) The *minus* relation is handled similarly.

For simplicity and clarity, we will continue to use infix-equation notation for the *add* and *mult* relations:

$$[x] + [y] = [z] \quad \equiv \quad add([x], [y], [z])$$
$$[x] \cdot [y] = [z] \quad \equiv \quad mult([x], [y], [z])$$

Furthermore, since *mult* is a function over $\mathcal{S}$, we may occasionally use embedded product terms.

3.4.3   Confluences

Confluences are equations in signs, $\mathcal{S}' = \{+, 0, -, ?\}$, or qualitative expressions evaluating to signs, such as combinations of the qualitative operators $[x]_0$, $[x]_*$, and $[\dot{x}]$. Confluences are the form of qualitative constraints developed by de Kleer and Brown (1984) and used in their qualitative physics.

For example, consider the familiar law $F = ma$, where we know that the mass m is positive and constant: $[m]_0 = [+]$ and $[\dot{m}] = 0$. We can transform this equation into a confluence to draw several useful qualitative conclusions:

- Force and acceleration are in the same direction:

$$[F]_0 = [ma]_0 = [m]_0[a]_0 = [a]_0$$

- A change to either force or acceleration results in a change to the other in the same direction:

$$[\dot{F}] = [d(ma)/dt] = [m]_0[\dot{a}] + [a]_0[\dot{m}] = [\dot{a}]$$

- Perturbations to force and acceleration (with no perturbation to mass: $[m]_* = [0]$) are in the same direction:

$$[F]_* = [ma]_* = [a]_0[m]_* + [m]_0[a]_* = [a]_*$$

Although confluences are similar in many ways to the qualitative constraints as we have defined them, they are not strictly identical. In particular, a monotonic function constraint such as

```
((M+ amount level) (0 0))
```

means that some monotonic function f exists, such that $level = f(amount)$ and $f(0) = 0$. We know very little about f, but we do know that it represents a functional relationship.

The corresponding confluences are

$$[level]_0 = [amount]_0 \text{ and } [d(level)/dt] = [d(amount)/dt],$$

which say that the sign of the magnitude and the sign of the derivative of $level(t)$ and $amount(t)$ must always be identical. They do not, however, say that the two values are related by a function. Thus, observations of the relationship between $amount(t)$ and $level(t)$ at one time do not necessarily support conclusions about their relationship later.

3.4.4 Hybrid Sign-Real Algebra

The axioms that define the legal manipulations of confluences have been formalized by Williams (1988; 1991), Dormoy and Raiman (1988), and Bylander (1991). This section closely follows the development in Williams (1991) of a hybrid, sign-real algebra called SR1.

The basic intuition behind SR1 is that many constraints are algebraic relations among real-valued variables. These constraints can be manipulated as algebraic equations in familiar ways. Other constraints, representing incomplete qualitative knowledge, can be expressed as similar algebraic relations among sign-valued terms. The hybrid sign-real algebra SR1= $\langle \Re \cup \mathcal{S}', +, \times, [\cdot] \rangle$ is essentially the union of the familiar real algebra $\langle \Re, +, \times \rangle$ with the sign algebra $\langle \mathcal{S}', +, \times \rangle$, along with the sign-valued operator $[\cdot]$ for mapping from $\Re$ to $\mathcal{S}'$. SR1 explains how it is possible to do certain algebraic manipulations on constraints in the real algebra, then map the constraints into the sign domain for other inferences.

In this discussion, we will use the letters a, b, c, $\ldots$, to denote elements of $\Re$; the letters s, t, u, $\ldots$, for elements of $\mathcal{S}'$; and x, y, z for elements of $\Re \cup \mathcal{S}'$ of unspecified type. Note that 0 is an element of both $\Re$ and $\mathcal{S}'$, but it will sometimes be notationally convenient to view 0 as equivalent to $\{0\}$ so that each element of $\mathcal{S}'$ can be treated as a subset of $\Re$.

The operators of SR1 are defined as follows. If $x \in \Re$, then $[x] = sign(x)$; if $x \in \mathcal{S}'$, then $[x] = x$. If $x, y \in \Re$, then $x + y$ and $x \times y$ are defined as in the familiar real algebra. If either $x \notin \Re$ or $y \notin \Re$, then $x + y = [x] + [y]$ and $x \times y = [x] \times [y]$, where the results of operations on $\mathcal{S}'$ are given in table 3.1(a).

Except for the lack of an additive inverse in $\langle \mathcal{S}', +, \times \rangle$, the two halves of this hybrid algebra have quite similar properties, as shown by the following table of axioms.

Axioms	$\langle \Re, +, \times \rangle$	$\langle \mathcal{S}', +, \times \rangle$
Identity	$a + 0 = a$	$s + 0 = s$
	$a \times 1 = a$	$s \times [+] = s$
Zero	$a \times 0 = 0$	$s \times 0 = 0$
Inverse	$a + (-a) = 0$	**none**
	$a \times (a^{-1}) = 1$ if $a \neq 0$	$s \times (s^{-1}) = [+]$ if $0 \notin s$
Commutative law	$a + b = b + a$	$s + t = t + s$
	$a \times b = b \times a$	$s \times t = t \times s$
Associative law	$(a + b) + c = a + (b + c)$	$(s + t) + u = s + (t + u)$
	$(a \times b) \times c = a \times (b \times c)$	$(s \times t) \times u = s \times (t \times u)$
Distributive law	$a \times (b + c) = a \times b + a \times c$	$s \times (t + u) = s \times t + s \times u$

The main implication of a lack of additive inverse is that there is no cancellation law for $\langle \mathcal{S}', + \rangle$:

$$s + u = t + u \not\Leftrightarrow s = t \tag{3.4}$$

Similarly,

$$s + t = u \not\Leftrightarrow s = u - t \tag{3.5}$$

and

$$s = t \not\Leftrightarrow s - t = 0. \tag{3.6}$$

Therefore, it is not possible to apply equation-solving methods such as Gaussian elimination to sign equations.

There is, however, a unique multiplicative inverse, so $\langle \mathcal{S}', \times \rangle$ does have a cancellation law:

$$s \times u = t \times u \Leftrightarrow s = t \text{ for } 0 \notin u \tag{3.7}$$

and

$$s \times t = u \Leftrightarrow s = u \times t^{-1}. \tag{3.8}$$

Even without an additive inverse, we can define unary negation and binary subtraction operators:

$$-s = [-] \times s \tag{3.9}$$

$$s - t = s + (-t) \tag{3.10}$$

that have the following desirable properties:

$$-(-s) = s \tag{3.11}$$

$$-(s + t) = -s - t. \tag{3.12}$$

Similarly,

$$(s^{-1})^{-1} = s \text{ for } 0 \notin s \tag{3.13}$$

$$(s \times t)^{-1} = s^{-1} \times t^{-1} \text{ for } 0 \notin s, t. \tag{3.14}$$

The major benefit of mapping an expression from $\langle \Re, +, \times \rangle$ to $\langle \mathcal{S}', +, \times \rangle$ is that it can often be dramatically simplified, primarily because a qualitative value not containing zero is its own multiplicative inverse.

$$s \times s = [+] \text{ for } 0 \notin s \tag{3.15}$$

$$s^{-1} = s \text{ for } 0 \notin s. \tag{3.16}$$

This gives us a simpler version of the multiplicative cancellation law (3.8):

$$s \times t = u \iff s = t \times u. \tag{3.17}$$

With the natural definition of exponentiation as repeated multiplication, we get, for any integer i and any $s \in \mathcal{S}'$,

$$s^{2i} = s^2 \tag{3.18}$$

and

$$s^{2i} \times s = s, \tag{3.19}$$

which allow us to collapse any polynomial expression to quadratic.

Addition can be simplified and ignorance propagated:

$$s + s = s, \tag{3.20}$$

$$s + [?] = [?], \tag{3.21}$$

$$s \times [?] = [?]. \tag{3.22}$$

When we move from $\langle \Re, +, \times \rangle$ to $\langle \mathcal{S}', +, \times \rangle$, $[\cdot]$ is a homomorphism for multiplication,

$$[a \times b] = [a] \times [b] \tag{3.23}$$

$$[-a] = -[a] \tag{3.24}$$

$$[a^n] = [a]^n, \tag{3.25}$$

but not for addition,

$$[a + b] \neq [a] + [b] \tag{3.26}$$

$$[a - b] \neq [a] - [b]. \tag{3.27}$$

Together, these properties allow complex sign expressions to be simplified and canonicalized. Williams (1991) provides proofs for these and other properties of SR1 and demonstrates their application to the analysis of simple control systems via a program called MINIMA.

3.5 Evaluating the Qualitative Constraints

We have defined what the qualitative constraints *mean* as algebraic relations. Now we translate the definitions into efficient criteria for checking whether a proposed tuple of qualitative values for its variables might satisfy a given constraint. While SR1 is close to what we need to define satisfaction criteria for QSIM constraints, it is not exactly right (problem 12). Accordingly, our constraint-checking conditions are expressed as relations over sign-valued terms, much in the spirit of SR1 but not strictly within it.

Qualitative constraint satisfaction is efficiently checked because the representation of quantity spaces as linear lists such as

```
(x (minf 0 a b inf))
```

makes it easy to evaluate sign-valued terms such as $[x]_a = [x - a]_0$. (Problem 9.)

For each constraint, we define a set of easily checked conditions that are used to test proposed tuples of qualitative values. The assertion of correctness for these conditions follows a simple schema, whose proofs are left for problem 13 at the end of the chapter.

THEOREM 3 (CONSTRAINT SCHEMA)   Each QSIM constraint C is associated with a set $\{P_1, \dots P_n\}$ of conditions that are easily evaluated given a tuple of qualitative values for the variables appearing in C, such that

$$C \to P_1 \wedge \cdots \wedge P_n. \tag{3.28}$$

Proposed tuples of qualitative values for variables in C can be refuted using the contrapositive of (3.28),

$$\neg P_1 \vee \cdots \vee \neg P_n \to \neg C. \tag{3.29}$$

Each condition P_i can then be used as a *conservative filter*: if a proposed tuple of qualitative values for the variables in C violates any condition P_i associated with C, it violates C, and hence can be validly discarded.

3.5.1 Monotonic Function Constraints

The QSIM constraint ((M+ x y) ... (xi yi) ...) represents the assertion that $y = f(x)$ for some $f \in M^+$, and that $f(x_i) = y_i$ for each corresponding value pair (x_i, y_i). This constraint implies the following conditions, which are easily evaluated on qualitative descriptions of the values of x and y.

1. $[\dot{x}] = [\dot{y}]$, unless x or y is at the endpoint of its range.

That is, the directions of change of x and y must be the same in the *interior* of the range $[a, b]$ of the monotonic function f, since the definition of $f \in M^+$ requires only that $f' > 0$ on the open interval (a, b).

2. If (x_i, y_i) is a pair of corresponding values, then $[x]_{x_i} = [y]_{y_i}$.

That is, the two values must be on the same side of the landmarks in each pair of corresponding values.

Similarly, the QSIM constraint ((M- x y) ... (xi yi) ...) implies that $[\dot{x}] = -[\dot{y}]$ and $[x]_{x_i} = -[y]_{y_i}$ for every pair of corresponding values (x_i, y_i).

3.5.2 Qualitative Addition

The QSIM constraint ((ADD x y z) (x1 y1 z1) ...) represents the relation $x + y = z$ with corresponding values $\{(x_1, y_1, z_1), \ldots\}$. This constraint implies the following conditions, which are easily evaluated on qualitative descriptions of the values of x, y, and z.

1. $([\dot{x}], [\dot{y}], [\dot{z}])$ must satisfy the qualitative addition relation $[\dot{x}] + [\dot{y}] = [\dot{z}]$:

add	$[+]$	$[0]$	$[-]$
$[+]$	$[+]$	$[+]$	$[+]/[0]/[-]$
$[0]$	$[+]$	$[0]$	$[-]$
$[-]$	$[+]/[0]/[-]$	$[-]$	$[-]$

2. If (x_i, y_i, z_i) is a triple of corresponding landmark values for $x + y = z$, then

$$[x]_{x_i} + [y]_{y_i} = [z]_{z_i}$$

according to the preceding qualitative addition relation table.

This can be easily demonstrated by subtracting the two equations:

$$
\begin{array}{ccccc}
x & + & y & = & z \\
x_i & + & y_i & = & z_i \\
\hline
(x - x_i) & + & (y - y_i) & = & (z - z_i)
\end{array}
$$

The *add* constraint always has the implicit corresponding value tuple $(0, 0, 0)$.

3. Since variables take their values over the *extended* reals, the landmark values $+\infty$ and $-\infty$ can appear in proposed value and corresponding value tuples. To evaluate the consistency of tuples including infinite values, we use the sign-valued operator

$$[x]_\infty \quad = \quad \begin{cases} [+] & \text{if } x = +\infty \\ [0] & \text{if } x \text{ is finite} \\ [-] & \text{if } x = -\infty. \end{cases}$$

The constraint $x + y = z$ then implies the relation

$$[x]_\infty + [y]_\infty = [z]_\infty.$$

3.5.3   Qualitative Multiplication

The QSIM constraint `((MULT x y z) (x1 y1 z1) ... )` represents the relation $x \cdot y = z$ with corresponding values $\{(x_1, y_1, z_1), \ldots\}$. This constraint implies the following conditions, which are easily evaluated on qualitative descriptions of the values of x, y, and z.

1. The signs of the variables must be consistent — $[x]_0 [y]_0 = [z]_0$ — except for the special case $[0] \cdot [\pm\infty] = [?]$.

The multiplication table for signs is, of course, the following

$mult$	$[+]$	$[0]$	$[-]$
$[+]$	$[+]$	$[0]$	$[-]$
$[0]$	$[0]$	$[0]$	$[0]$
$[-]$	$[-]$	$[0]$	$[+]$

2. Directions of change must be consistent: $[y]_0 [\dot{x}] + [x]_0 [\dot{y}] = [\dot{z}]$.

This follows directly from the product rule for the derivative of a product: $(xy)' = x'y + xy'$. Notice that if $x, y > 0$, $[x]_0 = [y]_0 = [+]$, so this criterion becomes identical to the direction-of-change test for addition: $[\dot{x}] + [\dot{y}] = [\dot{z}]$.

3. Where (x_i, y_i, z_i) is a corresponding value triple for the constraint $x \cdot y = z$, with $x_i, y_i, z_i \neq 0$, the absolute magnitudes of the values are compared with the magnitudes of the corresponding values by the criterion

$$[|x|]_{|x_i|} + [|y|]_{|y_i|} = [|z|]_{|z_i|}.$$

(Problem 5 proves this relation.) If x and x_i have the same sign, $[|x|]_{|x_i|}$ is easy to determine by ordinal comparisons. If they have opposite signs, $[|x|]_{|x_i|}$ cannot in general be determined, since there may be no correspondence between the landmarks on the positive and negative sides of the quantity space.

4. The interaction between infinite and zero values in the MULT constraint can be expressed in the condition

$$[\log |x|]_\infty + [\log |y|]_\infty = [\log |z|]_\infty.$$

Note that the sign-valued term $[\log |x|]_\infty$ is easy to evaluate for qualitative values of x.

3.5.4 Qualitative Negation

The QSIM constraint ((MINUS x y) (x1 y1) ...) represents the relation $y = -x$ with corresponding values $\{(x_1, y_1), \ldots\}$. This constraint implies the following conditions, which are easily evaluated on qualitative descriptions of the values of x and y.

1. $[\dot{x}] = -[\dot{y}]$.
2. If (x_i, y_i) is a pair of corresponding values, then $[x]_{x_i} = -[y]_{y_i}$.

   That is, the two values must be on opposite sides of the landmarks in each pair of corresponding values.

   The *minus* constraint has implicit corresponding values $(0, 0)$, $(+\infty, -\infty)$, and $(-\infty, +\infty)$.

3.5.5 Qualitative Derivatives

The QSIM constraint ((d/dt x y)) represents the relation $y = \frac{d}{dt}x$, which can have no corresponding values. This constraint implies the following condition.

1. $[\dot{x}] = [y]_0$ — the sign of the "rate" variable determines the direction of change of the "level" variable.

3.5.6 The Constant Constraint

The QSIM constraint ((CONSTANT x)), or ((constant x a)) where a is a landmark in the quantity space for x, represents the assertion that the variable x is constant. This constraint implies the following conditions:

1. $[\dot{x}] = 0$.
2. $[x]_a = 0$, if the landmark a has been specified.

3.5.7 Non-Monotonic Function Constraints

There are non-monotonic generalizations of the M^+ and M^- constraints:

- U^+ and U^- functions are concave up and concave down, respectively, and monotonic on each side of an extreme point.

- S^+ and S^- functions are monotonically increasing or decreasing, respectively, within a given interval, but become constant (i.e., saturate) outside that interval.

Problems 7 and 8 define these constraints, and they are discussed in more detail in chapter 8 on region transitions.

3.6 Multivariate Constraints

While the basic QSIM constraints have fixed numbers of arguments, usually two or three, there are a number of useful constraints that have arbitrary numbers of arguments.

3.6.1 The Multivariate Monotonic Function Constraint

The QSIM multivariate monotonic function constraint,

```
(((M s1 ...  sn) x1 ...  xn y) (a1 ...  an a0) ...  ),
```

generalizes the definition of monotonic function constraint to handle functions of several variables:

$$y = f(x_1, \ldots x_n), \text{ where } [\partial f / \partial x_i] = s_i, \text{ for } s_i \in \mathcal{S}.$$

The multivariate monotonic function constraint provides generality required in a variety of contexts, including time-scale abstraction in chapter 12 and automatic generation of qualitative models in chapter 14. A more extensive discussion of the properties of these constraints is provided by Wellman (1991).

Fortunately, the qualitative criteria for checking this constraint are easily evaluated on a tuple of qualitative values for $x_1, \ldots x_n$ and y. We use the notational convention that x_0 refers to y, that a_0 stands for a landmark of y in a corresponding value tuple, and that $s_0 = [-]$.

1. At each time t, for i, j in $0..n$, one of the following holds:

   - for all i, $[s_i][x_i] = [0]$;
   - for some i, $[s_i][x_i] = [?]$;
   - for some i and j, $[s_i][x_i] = [+]$ and $[s_j][x_j] = [-]$.

2. At each time t, for i, j in $0..n$, one of the following holds:

   - for all i, $[s_i][\dot{x}_i] = [0]$;

- for some i, $[s_i][\dot{x}_i] = [?]$;
- for some i and j, $[s_i][\dot{x}_i] = [+]$ and $[s_j][\dot{x}_j] = [-]$.

3. If $(a_1, \ldots a_n, a_0)$ is a corresponding value tuple for this constraint, then at each time t, for i, j in $0..n$, one of the following holds:

- for all i, $[s_i][x_i]_{a_i} = [0]$;
- for some i, $[s_i][x_i]_{a_i} = [?]$;
- for some i and j, $[s_i][x_i]_{a_i} = [+]$ and $[s_j][x_j]_{a_j} = [-]$.

4. Infinite values in corresponding value tuples of the M constraint raise some subtle and difficult issues. Problem 18 asks you to resolve them.

3.6.2 The Signed-Sum Constraint

The signed-sum constraint, SSUM,

```
(((SSUM s1 ...  sn) x1 ...  xn y) (a1 ...  an a0) ...  )
```

where $s_i \in \mathcal{S}$, is more specific than the M constraint, since the arguments are combined strictly additively:

$$\bar{s}_1 x_1 + \cdots + \bar{s}_n x_n = y, \text{ where } \bar{s}_i = \begin{cases} +1 & \text{if } s_i = [+] \\ 0 & \text{if } s_i = [0] \\ -1 & \text{if } s_i = [-] \end{cases}$$

The following conditions for checking the SSUM constraint are easily evaluated on qualitative descriptions of the values of the variables y, $x_1 \ldots x_n$.

1. At each time t, for i, j in $0..n$, one of the following holds:

- for all i, $[s_i][x_i] = [0]$;
- for some i, $[s_i][x_i] = [?]$;
- for some i and j, $[s_i][x_i] = [+]$ and $[s_j][x_j] = [-]$.

2. At each time t, for i, j in $0..n$, one of the following holds:

- for all i, $[s_i][\dot{x}_i] = [0]$;
- for some i, $[s_i][\dot{x}_i] = [?]$;
- for some i and j, $[s_i][\dot{x}_i] = [+]$ and $[s_j][\dot{x}_j] = [-]$.

3. If $(a_1, \ldots a_n, a_0)$ is a corresponding value tuple for this constraint (using a_0 to represent a landmark value for y), then at each time t, for i, j in $0..n$, one of the following holds:

- for all i, $[s_i][x_i]_{a_i} = [0]$;

- for some i, $[s_i][x_i]_{a_i} = [?]$;
- for some i and j, $[s_i][x_i]_{a_i} = [+]$ and $[s_j][x_j]_{a_j} = [-]$.

Multivariate addition constraints help the modeler avoid irrelevant and under-constrained intermediate variables that are required if only the basic constraints are available. For example, using only the **add** constraint, a conservation-of-mass constraint $A + B + C = Total$ on the contents of three tanks would require two constraints

```
((add A B D))
((add D C Total))
```

and a new intermediate variable D whose behavior can raise distinctions that are not significant to the modeler.

3.6.3 The Sum Constraint

The QSIM constraint

```
((SUM x1 ...  xn y) (a1 ...  an a0) ...  ),
```

which represents the relation $x_1 + \cdots + x_n = y$ with corresponding value tuples $\{(a_1, \ldots a_n, a_0), \ldots\}$, is an abbreviation for

```
(((SSUM + ...  +) x1 ...  xn y) (a1 ...  an a0) ...  ).
```

The conservation-of-mass constraint $A + B + C = Total$ is naturally expressed as `((SUM A B C Total))`.

3.6.4 The Sum-Zero Constraint

The QSIM constraint

```
((SUM-ZERO x1 ...  xn) (a1 ...  an) ...  ),
```

which represents the relation $x_1 + \cdots + x_n = 0$ with corresponding value tuples $\{(a_1, \ldots a_n), \ldots\}$, is an abbreviation for

```
(((SSUM - ...  -) x2 ...  xn x1) (a2 ...  an a1) ...  ).
```

3.7   Transitions

The transitions associated with a QDE define the limits of the region of applicability of the QDE, and optionally specify a transition to a new QDE if that limit is reached. For example, the U-tube model of chapter 2 included the transition

```
((amtB (BMAX inc)) -> tank-B-bursts).
```

DEFINITION 11   A *transition* is a rule of the form

$$condition \rightarrow transition\text{-}function$$

where

• The *condition* is a pattern of the form $(\langle variable \rangle (\langle qmag \rangle \langle qdir \rangle))$, or a boolean combination of such patterns. It succeeds at a state when the values of the specified variables match the corresponding description.

• The *transition function* is applied to the current state if the condition succeeds. It returns a new qualitative state, perhaps defined with respect to a new QDE, from which simulation can resume.

The transition function is responsible for establishing the correspondence between the pre- and post-transition states. If no transition function is provided, simulation stops along the current behavior.

Transitions are discussed in detail in chapter 8. They can be used to represent known transitions between QDEs or as an escape to a model-building process.

3.8   Discussion: Quantity Spaces

3.8.1   Low Resolution of Quantity Spaces

A quantity space defines a low-resolution language of qualitative descriptions for incompletely known quantities. The advantage of a low-resolution representation is that we represent only a few important distinctions. The disadvantages are that only some distinctions are expressible, and that inference with ordinal relations is quite weak.

Suppose we have three variables, A, B, and C, with the following quantity spaces, and the relationship $A + B = C$.

$$A: \quad 0 \quad \cdots \quad a_3 \quad \cdots \quad a_6 \quad \cdots \quad a_9 \quad \cdots \quad \infty$$
$$B: \quad 0 \quad \cdots \quad b_7 \quad \cdots \quad b_{14} \quad \cdots \quad b_{21} \quad \cdots \quad \infty$$
$$C: \quad 0 \quad \cdots \quad c_{10} \quad \cdots \quad c_{20} \quad \cdots \quad c_{30} \quad \cdots \quad \infty$$

Suppose that each landmark represents a real number whose true (but unknown) value is equal to its subscript. The qualitative reasoner's knowledge of the landmark values consists only of the ordering relations implied by the quantity spaces and the four given corresponding value tuples,

$$(0,0,0), \quad (a_3, b_7, c_{10}), \quad (a_6, b_{14}, c_{20}), \quad (a_9, b_{21}, c_{30}).$$

There are plenty of other facts *we* know about addition, but they are inexpressible in the simple language provided by these quantity spaces.

We can demonstrate certain aspects of qualitative representation with three examples of the addition of qualitative interval values. We assert information about A and B, then use the qualitative constraints to filter the set of all possible values for the remaining variable, C.

1. $A = (0, a_3)$ and $B = (0, b_7)$ implies $C = (0, c_{10})$.

This conclusion is obvious both in quantitative interval arithmetic and in qualitative arithmetic, enforced by the corresponding values $(0,0,0)$ and (a_3, b_7, c_{10}).

2. Given $A = (a_3, a_6)$ and $B = (0, b_7)$, if we use the true numerical values of the landmarks and interval arithmetic, we can deduce that $C = (3, 13)$. However, having much less information, the qualitative reasoner can only deduce that $C = (0, c_{20})$. This is appropriate, since there are assignments of numerical values to A and B consistent with any of $C = (0, c_{10})$, $C = c_{10}$, and $C = (c_{10}, c_{20})$.

3. Similarly, given $A = (a_6, a_9)$ and $B = (0, b_7)$, interval arithmetic on the true numerical values would tell us that $C = (6, 16)$. Only the qualitative interval $C = (0, c_{20})$ is consistent with the true values, but the best inference we can draw using corresponding value tuples is $C = (0, c_{30})$. This is because the only applicable corresponding landmark value tuples are $(0,0,0)$ and (a_9, b_{21}, c_{30}). (Check it yourself!)

3.8.2   Generalized Corresponding Values

We can extend the language for asserting corresponding value relationships among landmarks, to permit assertions such as $a_9 + b_7 < c_{20}$. This statement is compatible with the finite language of the quantity spaces, and allows the third example to produce the best expressible result, $C = (0, c_{20})$.

One might think that a very large number of such assertions would be necessary. However, many of these inequalities are already consequences of the corresponding value tuples. For example, the inequality $a_3 + b_{14} < c_{20}$ need not be explicitly asserted, since it is implied by the corresponding value tuple (a_6, b_{14}, c_{20}) and the inequality $a_3 < a_6$, which is represented by the quantity space of A.

In this example, the only two inequalities that are not already covered are $a_9 + b_7 < c_{20}$ and $a_3 + b_{21} > c_{20}$. We represent these inequalities by generalizing corresponding value tuples to include interval values as well as landmarks: $(a_9, b_7, (c_{10}, c_{20}))$ and $(a_3, b_{21}, (c_{20}, c_{30}))$.

Suppose (p, q, r) is a corresponding value tuple for the constraint $add(x, y, z)$, where p, q, and r may be either landmarks or open intervals. Treating a landmark as the singleton set containing its value, the meaning of the corresponding value (p, q, r) is

There is some x_1 in p, y_1 in q, z_1 in r, such that $x_1 + y_1 = z_1$.

When p, q, and r are all landmarks, this definition reduces to the previous definition that $p + q = r$. However, if some or all are intervals, it simply asserts that a tuple of values satisfying the constraint lies *somewhere* in the specified interval(s).

Recall that the addition constraint $add(x, y, z)$ implies that, for each corresponding value tuple (x_i, y_i, z_i), a proposed tuple of values (x, y, z) must satisfy the qualitative addition relation $[x]_{x_i} + [y]_{y_i} = [z]_{z_i}$ on signs. In order to use generalized corresponding values to filter possible assignments of values to variables, we must extend the definition of $[x]_p$ to handle the case where the reference value p is an interval.

- When the reference value p is a landmark,

$$[x]_p = \begin{cases} + & \text{if } x > p \\ 0 & \text{if } x = p \\ - & \text{if } x < p. \end{cases}$$

- When the reference value is an interval (a, b),

$$[x]_{(a,b)} = \begin{cases} + & \text{if } x \geq b \\ ? & \text{if } a < x < b \\ - & \text{if } x \leq a. \end{cases}$$

This method extends straightforwardly to the other constraints.

3.8.3 Associative Law Violations

The low resolution of the quantity-space representation means that the associative law, $(A + B) + C = A + (B + C)$, may not hold for qualitative constraints. One order of operations may result in more "rounding up" of the intervals than another order.

In the last section, we evaluated $C = A + B$. We can extend that set of quantity spaces:

$$
\begin{array}{llllll}
A: & 0 & \cdots & a_3 & \cdots & a_6 & \cdots & a_9 & \cdots & \infty \\
B: & 0 & \cdots & b_7 & \cdots & b_{14} & \cdots & b_{21} & \cdots & \infty \\
C: & 0 & \cdots & c_{10} & \cdots & c_{20} & \cdots & c_{30} & \cdots & \infty \\
D: & 0 & \cdots & d_8 & \cdots & d_{16} & \cdots & d_{24} & \cdots & \infty \\
E: & 0 & \cdots & e_{18} & \cdots & e_{36} & \cdots & e_{54} & \cdots & \infty
\end{array}
$$

Given interval values $A = (0, a_3)$, $B = (0, b_7)$, and $D = (0, d_8)$, we evaluate $E = (A + B) + D = A + (B + D)$, using C as an intermediate variable in each case.

One order of evaluation gives us $E = (A + B) + D = (0, e_{18})$:

$$
\underbrace{\underbrace{A + B}_{C} + D}_{E} \qquad \underbrace{\underbrace{(0, a_3) + (0, b_7)}_{(0, c_{10})} + (0, d_8)}_{(0, e_{18})}
$$

The other order gives $E = A + (B + D) = (0, e_{36})$:

$$
\underbrace{A + \underbrace{B + D}_{C}}_{E} \qquad \underbrace{(0, a_3) + \underbrace{(0, b_7) + (0, d_8)}_{(0, c_{30})}}_{(0, e_{36})}
$$

One might think that $C = (0, b_7) + (0, d_8)$ would evaluate to $(0, c_{20})$, rather than $(0, c_{30})$, but the strongest relevant corresponding value tuple that can be expressed in the quantity spaces for the variables in $B + D = C$ is (b_{14}, d_{16}, c_{30}). If we use generalized corresponding values to express the relation $b_7 + d_8 < c_{20}$, then we will be able to deduce the stronger intermediate conclusion $C = (0, c_{20})$. The final result, $E = (0, e_{36})$, is not changed, however, because of the resolution of the quantity space for E.

3.8.4 The Selection Problem

When a particular variable appears more than once in an expression (or equivalently, when two variables are connected by more than one path of constraints), qualitative inference may give an unnecessarily inclusive result. The same problem arises in interval arithmetic (Moore, 1966; Moore, 1979).

For example, suppose we know that $y = x - x$, where $x \in (0, \infty)$. Then,

$$
\begin{aligned}
y &= x - x \\
&= (0, \infty) - (0, \infty) \\
&= (-\infty, \infty).
\end{aligned}
$$

Obviously, even though it includes the correct answer $y = 0$, the broad range for y is spurious, because two occurrences of the variable x cannot select different values from the range $(0, \infty)$. (Hence the name "Selection Problem.")

In some cases, the selection problem can be avoided by algebraically rewriting an expression to have only a single occurrence of each variable. For example, in the following case, still with $x \in (0, \infty)$, the second form provides a much narrower bound than the first.

$$
\begin{aligned}
y &= \frac{x}{x+1} \quad &\rightarrow& \quad \frac{(0,\infty)}{(1,\infty)} &=& \quad (0, \infty) \\
&= 1 - \frac{1}{x+1} \quad &\rightarrow& \quad 1 - \frac{1}{(1,\infty)} &=& \quad 1 - (0, 1) = (0, 1).
\end{aligned}
$$

3.8.5 Distributive Law Violations

An important instance of the Selection Problem is the failure of the Distributive Law. Interval arithmetic has only a weaker property known as *subdistributivity*:

$$A \cdot (B + C) \subseteq A \cdot B + A \cdot C.$$

The following example demonstrates subdistributivity using numerical intervals, in order to separate this phenomenon from "rounding up" due to the low-resolution quantity-space representation for intermediate and final results. In this case, $A \cdot (B + C)$ provides a strictly better bound on the result than $A \cdot B + A \cdot C$.

$$
\begin{aligned}
[1, 2] \cdot ([-4, -3] + [5, 6]) &= [1, 2] \cdot [1, 3] &=& [1, 6] \\
[1, 2] \cdot [-4, -3] + [1, 2] \cdot [5, 6] &= [-8, -3] + [5, 12] &=& [-3, 9]
\end{aligned}
$$

Struss (1988b; 1990) showed that the only finite quantity space in which qualitative values satisfy both the associative and distributive laws is the simplest quantity space:

$$-\infty \cdots 0 \cdots \infty.$$

(If it may have infinitely many landmarks, then a quantity space with a landmark representing every integer satisfies these laws.) As soon as we add non-trivial landmarks or require variable resolution — both surely important properties in a qualitative representation — we must give up both laws.

3.8.6   Unrelated Quantity Spaces

Quantity spaces in QSIM are completely unrelated structures. Landmarks in different quantity spaces have no *a priori* relationship, even if they have the same print-names. Thus, any intended relationship among landmarks across quantity spaces must be made explicit in corresponding values of suitable constraints.

Consider a closed system of two equal-sized tanks, where the landmarks $AMAX$ and $BMAX$ represent the capacities of the tanks A and B respectively. Then the amounts in the two systems may be represented with respect to the two quantity spaces,

$$A: \quad 0 \cdots AMAX \cdots \infty$$
$$B: \quad 0 \cdots BMAX \cdots \infty.$$

In order to represent the fact that $AMAX$ and $BMAX$ refer to the same value, we need to assert that $A(t) + B(t) = Total(t)$, and assert the corresponding value tuples

$$(AMAX, 0, T^*) \text{ and } (0, BMAX, T^*)$$

of the constraint $add(A, B, Total)$, for some landmark T^* of $Total$. This encoded information represents the equality of the two landmarks for QSIM's purposes, but it is somewhat less general than a logical or algebraic assertion that $AMAX = BMAX$.

3.9   Example: Algebraic Manipulation

To illustrate how algebraic manipulation might be required for a real problem, consider an example of a tank with hot and cold water inputs and one output of mixed water (Dalle Molle *et al.*, 1988) (figure 3.2). Suppose the flow rates and temperatures of the hot, cold, and output streams are represented by the constants F_h, T_h, F_c, T_c, F_o, T_o, respectively. T_o is the same as the temperature T of the mixed tank.

We can model this system with two equations, where W is the overall mass of water in the tank and $H = WT$ is the overall heat content of the water.

- A mass balance:

$$W' = F_h + F_c - F_o = F_h + F_c - M^+(W). \tag{3.30}$$

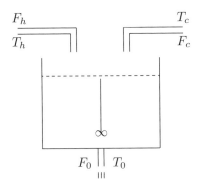

Figure 3.2
The hot-cold mixing tank.

- A heat balance:

$$H' = F_h T_h + F_c T_c - F_o T_o = F_h T_h + F_c T_c - M^+(W)T_o. \qquad (3.31)$$

If we attempt to determine the response of this tank to an increased flow of cold water (F_c), we will get unacceptable amounts of ambiguity. Mass simply increases to a new level with increased inflow and outflow, but the sign of heat balance (H') is ambiguous, because both the inflow ($F_c T_c$) and outflow ($F_o T_o$) of heat are increased.

In order to reason successfully with this system, we must change the variables of interest, focusing on mass and temperature rather than mass and heat. In order to do this, we define the overall input flow-rate F_{in} and average input temperature T_{in}, defined by

$$F_{in} \quad = \quad F_c + F_h \qquad (3.32)$$

$$T_{in} \quad = \quad \frac{F_c T_c + F_h T_h}{F_c + F_h}. \qquad (3.33)$$

Since F_h, T_h, F_c, and T_c are all constant, the new variables F_{in} and T_{in} are also constants in the model.

Unfortunately, equation (3.33) is still ambiguous, since F_c appears in both numerator and denominator. We eliminate this problem by rewriting the expression for T_{in} in two equivalent forms:

$$T_{in} = T_h - \frac{F_c}{F_{in}}(T_h - T_c) \tag{3.34}$$

$$T_{in} = T_c + \frac{F_h}{F_{in}}(T_h - T_c). \tag{3.35}$$

Although either expression can be ambiguous under some circumstances, together they always determine an unambiguous change to T_{in} when either flow rate or either temperature is changed.

With this algebraic restructuring of the model, there were no further problems with ambiguity, and qualitative simulation gave a tractable set of behaviors representing all and only the possible qualitative behaviors of the hot-cold mixing tank.

3.10   Problems

1. If x, y, and z are real numbers such that $x + y = z$, prove that $[x]_0 + [y]_0 = [z]_0$. If qualitative addition is represented as a function, how is equality defined?

2. If x, y, z, a, b, and c are real numbers such that $x + y = z$ and $a + b = c$, prove that $[x]_a + [y]_b = [z]_c$.

3. Where x and y are real numbers, prove

$$[xy]_* = [x]_0[y]_* + [y]_0[x]_*.$$

   Are additional hypotheses necessary?

4. Why does the add constraint have the corresponding values $(0, 0, 0)$ but the mult constraint does not?

5. Prove the third criterion for the consistency of a triple of qualitative values (x, y, z) with the constraint $x \cdot y = z$ and the corresponding value triple (x_1, y_1, z_1), where $x_1, y_1, z_1 \neq [0]$.
   Consider the equation

$$\left| \frac{x}{x_1} \right| \cdot \left| \frac{y}{y_1} \right| = \left| \frac{z}{z_1} \right|$$

from which we can conclude

$$(\log|x| - \log|x_1|) + (\log|y| - \log|y_1|) = (\log|z| - \log|z_1|).$$

Since log is a monotonic function, it does not affect the ordinal comparison $[\log|x| - \log|x_1|]_0 = [|x| - |x_1|]_0$, so we can conclude that

$$[|x|]_{|x_1|} + [|y|]_{|y_1|} = [|z|]_{|z_1|}.$$

6. Justify the exception $[0] \cdot [\pm\infty] = [?]$ to the multiplication constraint sign check, by considering the relation $(-1/x) \cdot x = -1$ as $x \to \infty$.

7. It is useful to define a functional constraint that is monotonic within a specified region but "saturates" and becomes constant outside its region of monotonic behavior. Define the qualitative constraint

$$y = S^+(x)_{(a,b)(c,d)},$$

represented $((\text{S+ } x\ y\ (a\ b)\ (c\ d)))$, to refer to some reasonable function f, such that $f(x) = b$ for $x \leq a$, and $f(x) = d$ for $x \geq c$, while $f'(x) > 0$ for $a < x < c$. (An S^- constraint can also be defined, in the obvious way.) Of course, $a < c$ must be landmarks in the quantity space of x, and $b < d$ must be landmarks in the quantity space of y.

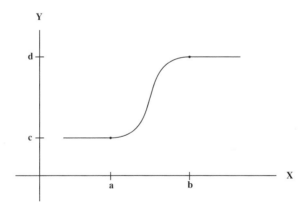

Specify how a pair of qualitative values for $x(t)$ and $y(t)$ are to be checked for consistency with the S^+ constraint and any known corresponding values.

8. It is also useful to define a U^+ constraint,

$$y = U^+(x)_{(a,b)}$$

which describes a "concave up" reasonable function f such that $f'(x) < 0$ for $x < a$, $f'(x) = 0$ for $x = a$, and $f'(x) > 0$ for $x > a$. (U^- is defined similarly.)

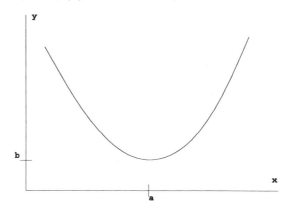

Note that the famous "Laffer curve" relating tax rate to tax revenue is a U^- curve. U^+ and U^- constraints often arise as an assertion about the relationship between two distinct monotonic influences on the same variable.

Specify how a pair of qualitative values for $x(t)$ and $y(t)$ are to be checked for consistency with a U^+ constraint and any known corresponding values.

9. Write efficient functions in Lisp to take a qualitative value x, a landmark a, and a quantity space, and return the value in S of the following:

(a) $[x]_a$

(b) $[\log |x|]_\infty$

10. With the simplest possible quantity spaces, provide the qualitative descriptions, in terms of M^+ relations and corresponding values, of the following functional relations:

(a) $y = 1/x$

(b) $y = \log x$

(c) $y = 1 - e^{-x}$

(d) $y = x^3 + x$

11. Suppose we define the qualitative arithmetic *functions*

$+ : \mathcal{S}' \times \mathcal{S}' \to \mathcal{S}'$

$\times : \mathcal{S}' \times \mathcal{S}' \to \mathcal{S}'$

as discussed in section 3.4.2.

Given the set of equations

$$
\begin{aligned}
x &= [+] \\
y &= [-] \\
z &= x + y \\
w &= z \cdot z,
\end{aligned}
$$

find all solutions to this set of equations under two circumstances:

(a) treating addition and multiplication as the qualitative functions $+$ and $\times$;

(b) treating addition and multiplication as the three-argument relations *add* and *mult*.

12. (Research Problem.) While SR1 is close to what we need to define satisfaction criteria for QSIM constraints, it is not exactly right. One issue is that QSIM is defined over the *extended* reals, so that $+\infty$ and $-\infty$ are landmark values. Another is QSIM's treatment of addition and multiplication as relations rather than functions. A careful reconciliation of QSIM and SR1 would be of considerable value.

13. Carefully state and prove an instance of equation (3.28) where C is the following constraint:

(a) (M+ x y)

(b) (minus x y)

(c) (add x y z)

(d) (mult x y z)

(e) (d/dt x y)

(f) (constant x)

14. Define a QSIM constraint ((dy/dx y x rate)) representing the relation $\frac{dy}{dx} = rate$. Because of the chain rule,

$$
\frac{dy}{dx} \cdot \frac{dx}{dt} = \frac{dy}{dt},
$$

this constraint implies the following condition:

(a) $[\dot{y}] = [\dot{x}][rate]_0$.

15. Show how a single M^+ constraint can be unsatisfiable, by having inconsistent corresponding values.

16. Is it possible for a tuple of qualitative value descriptions to satisfy all the conditions of a single constraint C, while no assignment of real values and rates of change exists that satisfies the constraint?

17. (Research Problem.) We noted on page 44 that the function $f(x) = x^3$ does not belong to M^+ over the domain $\Re^*$ because $f'(0) = 0$. However, $g_\epsilon(x) = x^3 + \epsilon x$ does belong to M^+ for any $\epsilon > 0$. Therefore, $f(x)$ is in some sense on the *boundary* of the set M^+. How can we make use of this?

18. (Research Problem.) Determine the possible behaviors of multivariate monotonic functions consistent with corresponding value tuples including infinite values. Develop an easily checkable condition for testing a proposed tuple of qualitative values for consistency with such a corresponding value tuple.

19. Demonstrate that neither side of the algebraic equivalence

$$x'(t) = -y'(t) \equiv x(t) + y(t) = \text{constant}$$

subsumes the other under qualitative reasoning.

20. (Research Problem.) How can a qualitative simulator take advantage of the linearity of a relationship like $y = kx$ when it is known, without sacrificing the ability to handle arbitrary monotonic functions when linearity is not known? Is it possible to define a qualitative category of linear relationships $L^+ \subseteq M^+$?

The qualitative constraint filtering algorithms exploit only very weak properties of the constraints: much less than the full algebraic and quantitative significance of the add, mult, and minus constraints.

Stronger properties of the arithmetic constraints are exploited by more sophisticated parts of QSIM, such as algebraic derivation of higher-order derivative constraints (chapter 10) and application of quantitative information to a qualitative behavior (chapter 9).

For example, QSIM treats the linear relationship, $y = kx$, represented as

```
((mult k x y))
((constant k)),
```

the same as the weaker monotonic relationship $y = f(x)$, for $f \in M^+$, represented as

```
((M+ x y) (0 0) (minf minf) (inf inf)).
```

The arithmetic constraints (`add x y z`) and (`minus x y`) are also very weak.

The problem this raises is that a qualitative simulator, given constraints specifying a linear relationship, could predict behaviors that are only possible for non-linear monotonic relationships, and are therefore spurious. The genuine linear solution is predicted as well, of course.

4 Solving Qualitative Constraints

4.1 Introduction

The basic computational operation in qualitative simulation is finding all solutions to a given set of qualitative constraints, consistent with other given information. There are several different problems that are solved using this operation. In all cases, we start with a qualitative differential equation, specifying a set of variables, their quantity spaces, and constraints applied to them.

- Given a set of partially specified qualitative values, find all completely specified qualitative states consistent with the constraints in the QDE.

  This transforms an initial specification into a set of complete initial states for simulation, and determines completely specified results from region transitions.

- Given a qualitative state and a set of possible successor values to the value of each variable, find all complete consistent states that can be created by assigning a successor value to each variable.

  This is used (in the next chapter) to predict all possible successors to a given state. The successor values for each variable are predicted from continuity alone.

- Given a stable equilibrium state and a perturbation from that state, determine the new equilibrium states consistent with the perturbation.

  This is used in chapter 7 to solve comparative statics problems.

In this chapter, we will discuss two methods for solving sets of constraints, and illustrate them with examples from qualitative simulation.

1. *Constraint propagation* methods are efficient, local, and psychologically plausible. Unfortunately, they don't always succeed.

2. *Constraint satisfaction* methods can be guaranteed to find all solutions to the constraints, but are computationally expensive in the worst case. Fortunately, excellent constraint satisfaction algorithms exist, and are typically quite efficient.

4.2 Constraint Propagation

Observations of humans solving problems suggest that a common reasoning step is to propagate qualitative descriptions from one variable to another across the connecting constraints. For example, when an expert physician explains a physiological mechanism, the explanation can be analyzed to reveal descriptions of continuous variables and the constraints among them (Kuipers and Kassirer, 1984).

A: When there is a very low albumin in the serum,
there are two forces which cause edema in my thinking —
the hydrostatic and oncotic forces
and we have actually opposed forces,
forces *[...break...]* formation is secondary to
the hydrostatic force of the blood going through the capillaries
and causing the transudation of fluid,
as well as the osmotic force within the blood vessels
that is secondary to the proteins in the plasma
which tend to draw fluid
from the interstitial spaces into the blood vessels.
And also there is the forces in the extracellular space:
there are certain proteins which tend to pull water
out of the blood vessels;
and there is a hydrostatic force I believe also in the interstitial spaces
which can counteract the force of the fluid
coming out from within the vessels.

Once the variables and constraints are described, the physician predicts the behavior of the mechanism by propagating the effects of a change through the constraints.

And if you have a very low albumin in the serum,
there will be a decreased osmotic pressure,
and make it easier for the fluid to go out into the interstitial spaces.

Section 6.3.1 describes this phenomenon in more detail and provides a qualitative model.

The idea behind constraint propagation is straightforward. Given the QSIM constraint that $y = M^+(x)$,

$$[x]_* = [+] \implies [y]_* = [+].$$

Given the constraint that $x + y = z$,

$$[x]_0 = [+] \text{ and } [z]_0 = [-] \implies [y]_0 = [-].$$

More generally, if a constraint has values for all but one of its arguments, and if those values along with the definition of the constraint determine the value of the remaining argument uniquely, then the constraint may assert that value to the remaining argument. This may, of course, put another constraint in the position where it has enough knowledge about all but one of its arguments, so the process continues.

In Chapter 2, we traced through an example of constraint propagation whereby a small amount of initial information about the U-tube

$$t = t_0 \Longrightarrow \boxed{\begin{array}{rcl} amtA & = & \langle AMAX, ? \rangle \\ amtB & = & \langle 0, ? \rangle \end{array}}$$

is propagated through the constraints of the QDE to produce a complete qualitative description of its state at t_0.

$$t = t_0 \Longrightarrow \boxed{\begin{array}{rcl} amtA & = & \langle AMAX, dec \rangle \\ pressureA & = & \langle (0, \infty), dec \rangle \\ amtB & = & \langle 0, inc \rangle \\ pressureB & = & \langle 0, inc \rangle \\ pAB & = & \langle (0, \infty), dec \rangle \\ flowAB & = & \langle (0, \infty), dec \rangle \\ total & = & \langle (0, \infty), std \rangle \end{array}}$$

Because constraint propagation is a local operation, it is convenient to draw the set of constraints as graphically linking the variables of the QDE (figure 2.4). Each constraint can be thought of as a small local processor that has access to the values of the variables it is directly attached to. Whenever one of its associated variables receives some new information, the constraint "wakes up" and decides whether it knows enough to draw any new conclusions. If so, it passes the news on to the affected variables, and the process continues.

A clear exposition of constraint propagation, including the complete Lisp code for a simple constraint propagator for numerical values, can be found in Abelson and Sussman, 1985, (section 3.3.5). A clear discussion of constraint propagation with interval values can be found in Davis, 1987.

The computational sequence of the propagation process does not represent the passage of time in the system being modeled, but it does reflect certain logical dependencies among the values of the variables. This ordering can be interpreted as specifying the causal order of changes in the system. A fascinating exchange of views on this topic occurs in Iwasaki and Simon, 1986a; de Kleer and Brown, 1986; and Iwasaki and Simon, 1986b, which are reprinted in Weld and de Kleer, 1990.

4.2.1 Propagation Is Efficient

Propagation of constraints can be very efficient when solving constraint-satisfaction problems of a suitable form. Consider the ideal case of a linear chain of variables and constraints, one variable for each letter of the alphabet.

$a = M^+(b),\ b = M^+(c),\ \ldots\ x = M^+(y),\ y = M^+(z).$

Given the initial fact that $[\dot{a}] = [+]$, it clearly takes 25 steps for constraint propagation to determine the unique solution for the derivatives of the variables in the system:

$[\dot{a}] = [\dot{b}] = [\dot{c}] = \ldots = [\dot{x}] = [\dot{y}] = [\dot{z}] = [+].$

An algorithm that generates possible solutions and tests them against the constraints must explore a space of 3^{26} possible solutions to find consistent values for $[\dot{a}], [\dot{b}], \ldots [\dot{z}]$. Of course, as we shall see, a good constraint-satisfaction algorithm does not explicitly generate the entire space of 3^{26} assignments.

4.2.2 Propagation Can Be Blocked

Since some constraint must have values for all but one of its variables before propagation can take place, it is possible for a collection of constraints to be blocked, so that no individual constraint is in a position to propagate any value, even though only one global solution is possible. The voltage divider (Sussman and Steele, 1980) provides a simple example where constraint propagation is blocked (figure 4.1).

A number of methods have been proposed by various researchers to unblock the propagation process while preserving its efficiency and cognitive realism.

• Sussman and Stallman (1975) propagate a symbolic value (e.g., $v_2 = a$) through the constraints, giving symbolic expressions for the values, then solve for a. The cost of this approach is that the values propagated are drawn from the domain of algebraic expressions rather than the domain of numerical values, qualitative values, or signs. Solving the resulting expression for a (or $[a]$) can be costly.

• de Kleer and Brown (1984) impose a causal order on the variables linked by the constraints associated with particular types of components. When solving for the effect of a perturbation, if propagation is blocked, assume that any unknown variable x that is "upstream" in the causal order is unaffected by the perturbation, i.e., $[x]_* = 0$. This allows a value to be propagated "downstream." In a case where a feedback loop produces a causal order that loops back on itself, revise the

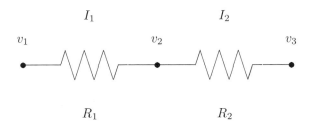

$$[R_1] = [+]$$
$$[R_2] = [+]$$
$$I_1 = I_2$$
$$I_1 \cdot R_1 = v_1 - v_2$$
$$I_2 \cdot R_2 = v_2 - v_3$$

Figure 4.1
The voltage divider and its constraints.

Given $[v_1] = [+]$ and $[v_3] = 0$, it is easy to see that the only consistent solution in the domain $\{+, 0, -\}$ is $[v_2] = [+]$, $[I_1] = [I_2] = [+]$, but no constraint has exactly one unknown variable, so no propagation can take place.

assumption about the "unaffected" variable once it appears in a downstream role.

In the voltage divider in figure 4.1, given a perturbation $([v_1]_* = [+]$, $[v_3]_* = 0$, $[R_1]_* = [R_2]_* = 0)$, we would assume that $[I_1]_* = 0$ in order to propagate $[v_1]_* = [+] \Rightarrow [v_2]_* = [+]$. Then we propagate $[v_2]_* = [+]$, $[v_3]_* = [0] \Rightarrow [I_2]_* = [+]$, and finally revise $[I_1]_*$ to be $[+]$.

• Sussman and Steele (1980) create an abstract view of the voltage divider as a single resistor described by

$$R_{total} = R_1 + R_2$$
$$I_{total} = I_1 = I_2$$
$$I_{total} \cdot R_{total} = v_1 - v_3$$

to allow the propagation $[v_1] = [+]$, $[v_3] = [0] \Rightarrow [I_{total}] = [+]$. Then propagate back to the more detailed view to get $[v_2] = [+]$.

In general, local propagation is possible when the constraints of the system can be viewed as equations in the following form:

$$x_1 = c$$
$$x_2 = f_1(x_1)$$
$$x_3 = f_2(x_1, x_2)$$
$$\ldots$$

where $f_1, f_2 \ldots$ represent explicit expressions that can be evaluated.

Where there are simultaneous equations such as

$$x_1 = g_1(x_1, x_2)$$
$$x_2 = g_2(x_1, x_2),$$

more powerful constraint-satisfaction methods are required.

4.3   Constraint Satisfaction

We can find all solutions to a set of constraints by viewing the problem in more general terms as a *constraint-satisfaction problem* (CSP). For more on constraint satisfaction, see Mackworth, 1977; Mackworth, 1992; Freuder, 1978; and Dechter, 1992.

DEFINITION 12   A *constraint-satisfaction problem* is a triple $\langle V, D, P \rangle$ consisting of

• a set $V = \{v_1, \ldots, v_n\}$ of variables;

• a set of sets $D = \{D_1, \ldots, D_n\}$, such that each D_i is the domain of possible values for the corresponding variable v_i; and

• a set $P = \{P_1, \ldots, P_m\}$ of constraint relations, where each P_j refers to some subset of the variables in V, and every v_i in V appears in some P_j in P.

DEFINITION 13   An *assignment* for a constraint-satisfaction problem $\langle V, D, P \rangle$ is an n-tuple, $\langle x_1, \ldots x_n \rangle$ with $x_i \in D_i$. An assignment $\langle x_1, \ldots x_n \rangle$ is *valid* for $\langle V, D, P \rangle$ if every $P_j \in P$ is true under the substitution $\{v_1/x_1, \ldots, v_n/x_n\}$.

DEFINITION 14   The *solution* to a constraint-satisfaction problem $\langle V, D, P \rangle$ is the set of valid assignments for $\langle V, D, P \rangle$.

In qualitative simulation, appropriate constraint-satisfaction problems $\langle V, D, P \rangle$ can be formulated easily and automatically from the information in the QDE.[1]

• The variables $v_i \in V$ are just the variables in the QDE.

• The domain D_i for a variable v_i is constructed in different ways for different purposes. The domain of all possible qualitative values for v_i is easily constructed from the quantity space for v_i in the QDE. (Problem 3.) Initial value information or continuity constraints may be used to select a subset of this initial domain. For qualitative simulation problems, the domains D_i are always finite.

• The set P of constraints is the union of the conditions P_j associated with the QSIM constraints in the QDE. These conditions are the consequents of theorem 3 in chapter 3,

$$C \to P_1 \wedge \cdots \wedge P_n,$$

instantiated for each QSIM constraint in the QDE.

Much of the inference in QSIM can be viewed as generating and solving appropriate constraint-satisfaction problems. For purely qualitative simulation, the variables are QSIM variables, and have finite domains of qualitative value descriptions. Later, when we treat semi-quantitative simulation in chapter 9, the variables in the CSP will be landmarks and other qualitative elements of the behavior description, and they will have infinite domains consisting of intervals with endpoints in $\Re^*$.

4.3.1 Constraint Filtering

There is a straightforward algorithm for finding a complete, exact solution to a CSP with finite domains (table 4.1).

PROPOSITION 3   Given a constraint-satisfaction problem $\langle V, D, P \rangle$, the set of assignments returned by the algorithm `CSP-Solver` is all and only the valid assignments of $\langle V, D, P \rangle$.

Proof The initial set of all possible assignments generated in step 1 contains all valid assignments. No valid assignment could be discarded in step 2. Every invalid assignment must violate some constraint in P, so it would be discarded in step 2. Therefore, the remaining set must contain exactly the valid assignments. ∎

---

[1] For this discussion of constraint-satisfaction problems, "constraints" refers to the easily checkable conditions P_i defined in theorem 3 on page 54, while "QSIM constraints" refers to the qualitative algebraic, differential, and monotonic function constraints C appearing in the QDE.

Algorithm **CSP-Solver**:

Given a constraint satisfaction problem $\langle V, D, P \rangle$

1. Generate every possible assignment $\langle x_1, \ldots, x_n \rangle$ of values to variables in V.

2. Test each assignment against each constraint, discarding ("filtering out") those that violate any constraint.

3. Return the remaining set of assignments.

Table 4.1
The CSP-Solver algorithm.

Unfortunately, `CSP-Solver` is intractable in all but the simplest cases, since the set of assignments is the product space of the domains. If there are n variables and each domain has size d, the number of assignments is d^n.

Fortunately, we can be considerably more clever about the representation of the product space of assignments, so that individual constraint violations can eliminate entire subspaces of the product space, rather than just a single assignment. The worst-case performance is still exponential, but typical performance is vastly improved. At the same time, we preserve the guarantee that the algorithm produces all and only the solutions that satisfy the constraints.

Rather than filtering complete assignments, we consider progressively larger sets of variables, from individual variables, to tuples of variables associated with individual constraints, to pairs of tuples associated with adjacent constraints, to the entire set V. At each step, inconsistencies can be detected that filter out corresponding portions of the product space of all assignments.

We exploit the framework of node, arc, and path consistency developed by Mackworth (1977), formalizing methods such as the Waltz algorithm (Waltz, 1972).[2] Currently in QSIM we use node and arc consistency, but not path consistency. In part to deal with the fact that QSIM constraints are not restricted to arity ≤ 2 as are constraints in Mackworth's formulation, we use the dual to his constraint graph; in our graph, constraints are nodes, and variables are edges, as in the formulation of Freuder (1978). Node consistency considers p-tuples of variables associated with individual constraints of arity p, removing those that violate the constraint. Arc consistency ensures that tuples assigned to adjacent nodes assign the same values

---

[2]The Waltz filtering algorithm is illustrated by a visually compelling animation in the memorable 1972 MIT AI Lab film, "The Eye of the Robot."

Algorithm **Cfilter**:

Given a QDE and partial state information $\bar{D}$, generate a constraint satisfaction problem $\langle V, D, P \rangle$ and solve it.

1. (Domain restriction.) For each variable v_i in the QDE, obtain its domain of values D_i by intersecting $\bar{D}_i \in \bar{D}$ with the full set of possible qualitative values defined by the quantity space for v_i. V is the set of variables v_i, and D is the set of D_i

2. (Node consistency.) P is the set of conditions P_j from all the QSIM constraints C_i in the QDE. For each QSIM constraint C_i with arity k, applying to a tuple $\langle v_{i_1}, \ldots, v_{i_k} \rangle$ of variables, form all tuples $\langle x_{i_1}, \ldots, x_{i_k} \rangle$ of values, where $x_{i_j} \in D_{i_j}$.

   - Filter each tuple of values against each condition associated with C_i, according to the theorem schema

   $$\neg P_1 \vee \cdots \vee \neg P_n \rightarrow \neg C_i,$$

   discarding those tuples that violate any P_j.

3. (Arc consistency.) For each QSIM constraint C_i in the QDE, and each adjacent QSIM constraint C_j sharing the common variable v,

   - for each tuple associated with C_i (which assigns a value, say x, to v), discard it unless some tuple associated with C_j also assigns x to v.

4. (Exhaustive search.) Generate all possible assignments of the remaining tuples to QSIM constraints that imply consistent sets of assignments of values to variables. (See problem 5.) This gives the set of all valid assignments of $\langle V, D, P \rangle$.

Table 4.2
The Cfilter algorithm.

to shared variables. Finally, we use an exhaustive backtracking search algorithm to generate all complete assignments $\langle x_1, \ldots, x_n \rangle$ from the remaining tuples.

The `Cfilter` algorithm (table 4.2) applies this method to the problem of generating and solving the constraint-satisfaction problem $\langle V, D, P \rangle$ defined by a given QDE and partial state information. We will represent partial state information as a set $\bar{D}$ of sets $\bar{D}_i$ restricting the domain of possible qualitative values for each $v_i \in V$. $\bar{D}$ can represent user-supplied information, or be specified by state-successor rules.

The constraints P in the constraint-satisfaction problem are the easily checked conditions implied by the QSIM constraints (theorem 3). However, `Cfilter` also uses the QSIM constraints C to organize and index the variables, values, and tuples as they are built up into valid assignments.

THEOREM 4 (CFILTER COMPLETENESS)   Given a QDE and initial state information $\bar{D}$, the algorithm Cfilter returns a set of assignments including all and only the valid assignments of $\langle V, D, P \rangle$, where V is the set of variables in the QDE, D is the set of domains for variables in V consistent with the quantity spaces in the QDE and partial state information in $\bar{D}$, and P is the set of easily checked conditions associated with the QSIM constraints in the QDE.

Proof   Essentially the same as proposition 3: all assignments are considered; all and only the invalid ones are discarded.

All assignments are considered, albeit implicitly, because in step 1, all legal variable values are explicitly created; in step 2, all legal tuples of values for each QSIM constraint are formed; and in step 4, all consistent assignments of tuples to QSIM constraints are exhaustively formed from the remaining tuples. Since every variable must appear in at least one constraint, an assignment of tuples to QSIM constraints is consistent if and only if the corresponding assignment of values to variables is consistent.

Only invalid assignments are discarded. In step 2, a tuple is discarded only if it explicitly violates some condition P_j. In that case, no assignment containing that tuple could be valid. In step 3, a tuple is discarded only if it assigns a value to a variable that is inconsistent with every tuple associated with some other constraint that also assigns a value to that variable. Thus, no valid complete assignment can contain the discarded tuple.

Every invalid assignment is discarded. In step 4, every assignment $\langle x_1, \ldots, x_n \rangle$ consistent with the remaining tuples is explicitly generated. Suppose one of these is invalid. Then, by definition 13, it must violate some condition $P_j \in P$. But each P_j is associated with some QSIM constraint C_i, and the restriction of the invalid assignment to the variables in C_i is a tuple $\langle x_{i_1}, \ldots, x_{i_k} \rangle$ associated with C_i. This tuple violates the condition P_j and must have been filtered out in step 2. This contradicts the assumption of the existence of the invalid assignment.   ∎

The Cfilter algorithm, as presented in table 4.2, is neatly separated into steps to simplify its presentation and proof. In the QSIM program, the steps are interleaved for increased efficiency. Domain values are generated, and constraints are checked, in an order heuristically selected to increase the likelihood of early detection of inconsistencies, and to increase the effect of early pruning. These algorithmic permutations, however, do not affect the validity of theorem 4.

It is worth noting that theorem 4 means that the `Cfilter` algorithm is sound and complete as a solution algorithm for a given constraint-satisfaction problem $\langle V, D, P \rangle$. On the other hand, the set P of easily checked conditions may not capture all implications of the QSIM constraints C in a given QDE. This gap is partially responsible for the phenomenon of spurious behaviors in qualitative simulation (section 5.6.2).

4.4   Constraint-Filtering Examples

We will illustrate the `Cfilter` algorithm in operation with two examples of successor generation in qualitative simulation: the bathtub (one-compartment equilibrium system), and the spring (energy-conserving harmonic oscillator).[3] Dynamic qualitative simulation, which is discussed in detail in the next chapter, exploits continuity constraints to allow us to propose a small set of candidate values for the successor state of each changing variable.

4.4.1   Successor Generation for the Bathtub Model

The minimal bathtub model has four variables and four constraints (figure 4.2). If we start filling the empty bathtub at a constant rate

$$t = t_0 \Longrightarrow \boxed{\begin{aligned} amount &= \langle 0, ? \rangle \\ inflow &= \langle if^*, std \rangle \end{aligned}},$$

we can easily complete the qualitative state at t_0 and predict its successor state describing the open interval (t_0, t_1).

	t_0	(t_0, t_1)	t_1
$amount$	$\langle 0, \uparrow \rangle$	$\langle (0, full), \uparrow \rangle$	?
$outflow$	$\langle 0, \uparrow \rangle$	$\langle (0, \infty), \uparrow \rangle$	?
$inflow$	$\langle if^*, \ominus \rangle$	$\langle if^*, \ominus \rangle$	?
$netflow$	$\langle (0, \infty), \downarrow \rangle$	$\langle (0, \infty), \downarrow \rangle$	?

We will demonstrate the constraint-filtering algorithm on the process of determining the possible states at t_1.

[3]To watch the progress of the constraint-filtering algorithm when running the QSIM program, set the switch `*trace-count*` to `t`.

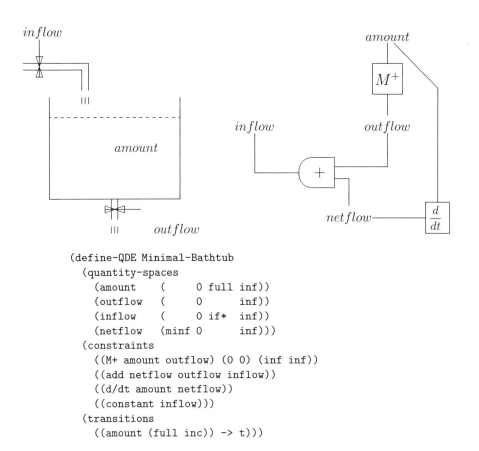

```
(define-QDE Minimal-Bathtub
  (quantity-spaces
    (amount    (     0 full inf))
    (outflow   (     0      inf))
    (inflow    (     0 if*  inf))
    (netflow   (minf 0      inf)))
  (constraints
    ((M+ amount outflow) (0 0) (inf inf))
    ((add netflow outflow inflow))
    ((d/dt amount netflow))
    ((constant inflow)))
  (transitions
    ((amount (full inc)) -> t)))
```

Figure 4.2
Minimal bathtub model.

Domain Restriction   For the state at t_1, the set of possible values is constrained
by continuity, by the bounding landmark values, and by the current direction of
change. The next chapter formalizes this as a table of successor rules for qualitative
values. For now, however, we simply propose a set of possible values for each
variable independently. These are the sets $\bar{D}_i$ used in Step 1 of `Cfilter`.

	t_1
amount	$\{\langle full, \uparrow\rangle, \langle full, \ominus\rangle, \langle (0, full), \uparrow\rangle, \langle (0, full), \ominus\rangle\}$
outflow	$\{\langle \infty, \uparrow\rangle, \langle \infty, \ominus\rangle, \langle (0, \infty), \uparrow\rangle, \langle (0, \infty), \ominus\rangle\}$
inflow	$\{\langle if^*, \ominus\rangle\}$
netflow	$\{\langle 0, \downarrow\rangle, \langle 0, \ominus\rangle, \langle (0, \infty), \downarrow\rangle, \langle (0, \infty), \ominus\rangle\}$

Node Consistency For each constraint, we form all tuples (pairs or triples) of possible values for its variables, and test them against the definition of the constraint. This allows us to eliminate many of the possible combinations.

The $\times$ entries in the tables show which tuples are inconsistent, and according to which criterion. Blank entries survive to the next stages of filtering.

- `((M+ amount outflow) (0 0) (inf inf))`

outflow			amount	
	$\langle full, \uparrow\rangle$	$\langle full, \ominus\rangle$	$\langle (0, full), \uparrow\rangle$	$\langle (0, full), \ominus\rangle$
$\langle \infty, \uparrow\rangle$	$\times^2$	$\times^1$	$\times^2$	$\times^1$
$\langle \infty, \ominus\rangle$	$\times^1$	$\times^2$	$\times^1$	$\times^2$
$\langle (0, \infty), \uparrow\rangle$		$\times^1$		$\times^1$
$\langle (0, \infty), \ominus\rangle$	$\times^1$		$\times^1$	

The $\times$ entries are eliminated because

1. they violate the requirement that $[d(amount)/dt] = [d(outflow)/dt]$; and

2. they violate the corresponding value at (∞, ∞).

Constraint filter: $(16) \rightarrow (4)$ tuples.

- `((add netflow outflow inflow))`

  This table represents a set of 16 triples for $\langle netflow, outflow, inflow\rangle$, each of which includes the value $inflow = \langle if^*, \ominus\rangle$.

outflow			netflow	
	$\langle 0, \downarrow\rangle$	$\langle 0, \ominus\rangle$	$\langle (0, \infty), \downarrow\rangle$	$\langle (0, \infty), \ominus\rangle$
$\langle \infty, \uparrow\rangle$	$\times^4$	$\times^3$	$\times^4$	$\times^3$
$\langle \infty, \ominus\rangle$	$\times^3$	$\times^4$	$\times^3$	$\times^4$
$\langle (0, \infty), \uparrow\rangle$		$\times^3$		$\times^3$
$\langle (0, \infty), \ominus\rangle$	$\times^3$		$\times^3$	

The $\times$ entries are eliminated because

3. they violate the requirement that

$$[d(netflow)/dt] + [d(outflow)/dt] = [d(inflow)/dt]; and$$

4. it is impossible for $\infty + finite = finite$.

Constraint filter: $(16) \rightarrow (4)$ tuples.

- `((d/dt amount netflow))`

$netflow$	amount			
	$\langle full, \uparrow \rangle$	$\langle full, \ominus \rangle$	$\langle (0, full), \uparrow \rangle$	$\langle (0, full), \ominus \rangle$
$\langle 0, \downarrow \rangle$	$\times^5$		$\times^5$	
$\langle 0, \ominus \rangle$	$\times^5$		$\times^5$	
$\langle (0, \infty), \downarrow \rangle$		$\times^5$		$\times^5$
$\langle (0, \infty), \ominus \rangle$		$\times^5$		$\times^5$

The $\times$ entries are eliminated because

5. they violate the requirement that $[d(amount)/dt] = [netflow]_0$.

Constraint filter: $(16) \rightarrow (8)$ tuples.

Arc Consistency All surviving tuples satisfy the arc consistency test, so no possibilities are eliminated in this example.

Exhaustive Search Driven by the remaining viable tuples of values, exhaustive backtracking search creates all sets of consistent global assignments of values to the variables. (Problem 5.)

	1	2	3	4
$amount$	$\langle full, \uparrow \rangle$	$\langle full, \ominus \rangle$	$\langle (0, full), \uparrow \rangle$	$\langle (0, full), \ominus \rangle$
$outflow$	$\langle (0, \infty), \uparrow \rangle$	$\langle (0, \infty), \ominus \rangle$	$\langle (0, \infty), \uparrow \rangle$	$\langle (0, \infty), \ominus \rangle$
$inflow$	$\langle if^*, \ominus \rangle$	$\langle if^*, \ominus \rangle$	$\langle if^*, \ominus \rangle$	$\langle if^*, \ominus \rangle$
$netflow$	$\langle (0, \infty), \downarrow \rangle$	$\langle 0, \ominus \rangle$	$\langle (0, \infty), \downarrow \rangle$	$\langle 0, \ominus \rangle$

Global Filtering We have now identified all four possible assignments of qualitative values to variables consistent with the given set of QSIM constraints. However, one of them (number 3) is not useful in the context of qualitative *simulation*. Although solution number 3 is a valid assignment, consistent with the constraints, it is identical to the description of the qualitative state over (t_0, t_1). Thus, it is deleted by the *No Change* filter (discussed in section 5.4.1). The remaining three solutions are possible successor states at t_1.

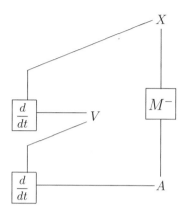

```
(define-QDE Simple-Spring
  (quantity-spaces
    (A  (minf 0      inf))
    (V  (minf 0 v-0 inf))
    (X  (minf 0      inf)))
  (constraints
    ((d/dt X V))
    ((d/dt V A))
    ((M- A X) (0 0) (minf inf) (inf minf)))))
```

Figure 4.3
The QDE for the simple spring model.

4.4.2 Successor Generation for the Spring Model

We can illustrate other properties of the Cfilter algorithm by considering the model of an oscillating spring (figure 4.3).

Domain Restriction Prior to the point we will look at, the values for the variables at t_0 and (t_0, t_1) are the following:

	t_0	(t_0, t_1)	t_1
X	$\langle 0, \uparrow \rangle$	$\langle (0, \infty), \uparrow \rangle$	?
V	$\langle v_0, \ominus \rangle$	$\langle (0, v_0), \downarrow \rangle$	?
A	$\langle 0, \downarrow \rangle$	$\langle (-\infty, 0), \downarrow \rangle$	?

For the state at t_1, the sets of possible values, $\bar{D}_i$, for each variable considered individually, are the following:

	t_1
X	$\{\langle\infty,\uparrow\rangle, \langle\infty,\ominus\rangle, \langle(0,\infty),\uparrow\rangle, \langle(0,\infty),\ominus\rangle\}$
V	$\{\langle 0,\downarrow\rangle, \langle 0,\ominus\rangle, \langle(0,v_0),\downarrow\rangle, \langle(0,v_0),\ominus\rangle\}$
A	$\{\langle-\infty,\downarrow\rangle, \langle-\infty,\ominus\rangle, \langle(-\infty,0),\downarrow\rangle, \langle(-\infty,0),\ominus\rangle\}$

Node Consistency   For each constraint, form all tuples of possible variable values, and test them against the definition of the constraint.

- `((d/dt X V))`

V	X			
	$\langle\infty,\uparrow\rangle$	$\langle\infty,\ominus\rangle$	$\langle(0,\infty),\uparrow\rangle$	$\langle(0,\infty),\ominus\rangle$
$\langle 0,\downarrow\rangle$	$\times^1$		$\times^1$	
$\langle 0,\ominus\rangle$	$\times^1$		$\times^1$	
$\langle(0,v_0),\downarrow\rangle$		$\times^1$		$\times^1$
$\langle(0,v_0),\ominus\rangle$		$\times^1$		$\times^1$

The $\times$ entries are eliminated because

1. they violate the requirement that $[\dot{X}] = [V]_0$.

Constraint filter: $(16) \rightarrow (8)$ tuples.

- `((d/dt V A))`

V	A			
	$\langle-\infty,\downarrow\rangle$	$\langle-\infty,\ominus\rangle$	$\langle(-\infty,0),\downarrow\rangle$	$\langle(-\infty,0),\ominus\rangle$
$\langle 0,\downarrow\rangle$				
$\langle 0,\ominus\rangle$	$\times^2$	$\times^2$	$\times^2$	$\times^2$
$\langle(0,V_0),\downarrow\rangle$				
$\langle(0,V_0),\ominus\rangle$	$\times^2$	$\times^2$	$\times^2$	$\times^2$

The $\times$ entries are eliminated because

2. they violate the requirement that $[\dot{V}] = [A]_0$.

Constraint filter: $(16) \rightarrow (8)$ tuples.

- ((M- A X) (0 0) (minf inf) (inf minf))

A	X			
	$\langle\infty,\uparrow\rangle$	$\langle\infty,\ominus\rangle$	$\langle(0,\infty),\uparrow\rangle$	$\langle(0,\infty),\ominus\rangle$
$\langle-\infty,\downarrow\rangle$		$\times^3$	$\times^4$	$\times^3$
$\langle-\infty,\ominus\rangle$	$\times^3$		$\times^3$	$\times^4$
$\langle(-\infty,0),\downarrow\rangle$	$\times^4$	$\times^3$		$\times^3$
$\langle(-\infty,0),\ominus\rangle$	$\times^3$	$\times^4$	$\times^3$	

The $\times$ entries are eliminated because

3. they violate the requirement that $[\dot{X}] = -[\dot{A}]$; and

4. they violate the corresponding value $(-\infty,\infty)$.

Constraint filter: $(16) \to (4)$ tuples.

Arc Consistency   At this point, each constraint has associated with it a list of tuples of values. Step 3 in `Cfilter` deletes tuples that cannot match any tuple of an adjacent QSIM constraint. Deleting tuples from one constraint may eliminate possible shared values with other adjacent constraints as well, so the arc consistency test propagates through the network of constraints.

In the model of the spring, we can apply it to the sets of tuples as follows:

- ((d/dt X V))

X	V	
$\langle\infty,\uparrow\rangle$	$\langle(0,v_0),\downarrow\rangle$	
$\langle\infty,\uparrow\rangle$	$\langle(0,v_0),\ominus\rangle$	$\times^1$
$\langle\infty,\ominus\rangle$	$\langle0,\downarrow\rangle$	
$\langle\infty,\ominus\rangle$	$\langle0,\ominus\rangle$	$\times^2$
$\langle(0,\infty),\uparrow\rangle$	$\langle(0,v_0),\downarrow\rangle$	
$\langle(0,\infty),\uparrow\rangle$	$\langle(0,v_0),\ominus\rangle$	$\times^1$
$\langle(0,\infty),\ominus\rangle$	$\langle0,\downarrow\rangle$	
$\langle(0,\infty),\ominus\rangle$	$\langle0,\ominus\rangle$	$\times^2$

- `((d/dt V A))`

V	A
$\langle 0, \downarrow \rangle$	$\langle -\infty, \downarrow \rangle$
$\langle 0, \downarrow \rangle$	$\langle -\infty, \ominus \rangle$
$\langle 0, \downarrow \rangle$	$\langle (-\infty, 0), \downarrow \rangle$
$\langle 0, \downarrow \rangle$	$\langle (-\infty, 0), \ominus \rangle$
$\langle (0, v_0), \downarrow \rangle$	$\langle -\infty, \downarrow \rangle$
$\langle (0, v_0), \downarrow \rangle$	$\langle -\infty, \ominus \rangle$
$\langle (0, v_0), \downarrow \rangle$	$\langle (-\infty, 0), \downarrow \rangle$
$\langle (0, v_0), \downarrow \rangle$	$\langle (-\infty, 0), \ominus \rangle$

- `((M- X A) (0 0) (minf inf) (inf minf))`

X	A
$\langle \infty, \uparrow \rangle$	$\langle -\infty, \downarrow \rangle$
$\langle \infty, \ominus \rangle$	$\langle -\infty, \ominus \rangle$
$\langle (0, \infty), \uparrow \rangle$	$\langle (-\infty, 0), \downarrow \rangle$
$\langle (0, \infty), \ominus \rangle$	$\langle (-\infty, 0), \ominus \rangle$

The $\times$ entries are eliminated because

1. no tuple associated with `((d/dt V A))` includes the value $V = \langle (0, v_0), \ominus \rangle$; and

2. no tuple associated with `((d/dt V A))` includes the value $V = \langle 0, \ominus \rangle$.

This reduces the number of tuples to be considered by the more expensive exhaustive search step.

Exhaustive Search Driven by the remaining viable tuples of values, we assign values to the variables, producing sets of consistent global assignments. Four complete assignments are valid.

	1	2	3	4
X	$\langle \infty, \uparrow \rangle$	$\langle \infty, \ominus \rangle$	$\langle (0, \infty), \uparrow \rangle$	$\langle (0, \infty), \ominus \rangle$
V	$\langle (0, v_0), \downarrow \rangle$	$\langle 0, \downarrow \rangle$	$\langle (0, v_0), \downarrow \rangle$	$\langle 0, \downarrow \rangle$
A	$\langle -\infty, \downarrow \rangle$	$\langle -\infty, \ominus \rangle$	$\langle (-\infty, 0), \downarrow \rangle$	$\langle (-\infty, 0), \ominus \rangle$

Global Filtering The complete state descriptions may now be considered by the global filters, which are discussed in more detail in the next chapter.

- Solutions 1 and 2 are eliminated by a filter that considers the implications of infinite values for variables (section 5.4.2).

Algorithm **State-Completion**:

1. Given a description of a state, S.

   - If S is complete, stop. Assert $complete(S)$.

2. Apply propagation to obtain a more complete description of S.

   - If S is complete, stop. Assert $complete(S)$.

3. Apply `Cfilter` to derive all possible completions $\{S_1, \ldots S_n\}$ of S. Assert $completion(S, S_i)$ and $complete(S_i)$ for each S_i.

Table 4.3
The State-Completion algorithm.

- Solution 3 is discarded by the *No Change* filter because it is identical to the predecessor state (t_0, t_1) and hence does not describe a qualitative change to the system.

Solution 4 is left as the only globally consistent solution for the state of the system at t_1.

$$t = t_1 \Longrightarrow \begin{array}{|rcl|} \hline X & = & \langle (0, \infty), \ominus \rangle \\ V & = & \langle 0, \downarrow \rangle \\ A & = & \langle (-\infty, 0), \ominus \rangle \\ \hline \end{array}$$

4.5 Completing the Initial State Description

Qualitative simulation typically begins by finding all complete qualitative state descriptions consistent with the information given about the initial state.

A qualitative state description is *complete* if every variable has a qualitative magnitude, described as a landmark or an open interval between adjacent landmarks in its quantity space, and a qualitative direction of change.

Given a QDE and a (possibly incomplete) description of $State(t_0)$, we can use the constraint-propagation and constraint-satisfaction algorithms to derive all possible qualitative descriptions for $State(t_0)$ consistent with the given information.

The propagation algorithm does not branch to provide more than one completion. However, it is possible for propagation to be blocked, even though the available information determines the state uniquely.

Consider several examples of incompletely specified initial states.

• Suppose we create an initial state for the simple bathtub example of figure 4.2 in which we assert

$$t = t_0 \Longrightarrow \boxed{\begin{array}{rcl} amount & = & \langle (0, full), ? \rangle \\ inflow & = & \langle if^*, std \rangle \end{array}}$$

This will be consistent with three complete state descriptions (problem 1), with significantly different resulting behaviors.

• Suppose we provide no initial state information at all about the simple spring model in figure 4.3, except that all of the variables have finite values.

$$t = t_0 \Longrightarrow \boxed{\begin{array}{rcl} X & = & \langle (-\infty, \infty), ? \rangle \\ V & = & \langle (-\infty, \infty), ? \rangle \\ A & = & \langle (-\infty, \infty), ? \rangle \end{array}}$$

This is consistent with nine complete state descriptions (problem 2), which represent all the possible states of the spring system. As we shall see later (section 5.7), these descriptions can be linked into a "total envisionment" transition graph representing all possible behaviors of the system.

4.6 Problems

1. Given the simple bathtub QDE from figure 4.2, and the initial assertions that $amount(t_0) = (0, full)$; $inflow(t_0) = if^*$, apply Cfilter by hand to determine the consistent completions at t_0.

2. Given the simple spring QDE from figure 4.3, and the initial assertions that all values are in $(-\infty, \infty)$, apply Cfilter by hand to determine the consistent completions at t_0

3. Write a Lisp program that generates all possible qualitative values $\langle qmag, qdir \rangle$ for a variable v, given its quantity space, $l_1 < \cdots < l_k$.

4. Hand simulate an exhaustive backtracking search algorithm forming complete qualitative states at t_1 for the bathtub and spring models in section 4.4. Notice that states are created with qualitative values for all QSIM variables, but are later refuted. Why?

5. Implement a function that does an exhaustive backtracking search through the space of assignments of tuples to constraints, and returns the set of all possible assignments of values to variables. Remember that all constraints must be considered, even after all variables have been assigned values.

6. Pure constraint satisfaction can be quite expensive, especially if there are more than a few landmarks in the quantity spaces of the variables. Determine the number of qualitative values for each variable, and the number of tuples for each constraint:

   (a) for the U-tube system in chapter 2;

   (b) for a general system of k variables where variable v_i has n_i landmarks in its quantity space.

7. Design a method for interleaving constraint satisfaction with propagation to get an improved algorithm for solving for initial qualitative states. When does the added complexity pay off?

8. Determine the worst-case complexity of the `Cfilter` algorithm.

9. Create an example of a QDE with n variables, unique states at t_0 and (t_0, t_1), but 2^n consistent states at t_1.

10. (Research Problem.) In terms of the Mackworth (1977) framework, when `Cfilter` solves for assignments of tuples to QSIM constraints, it checks only for node and arc consistency before exhaustively generating all assignments. Extend the algorithm to check path consistency as well. Under what circumstances does this pay off? What if we restrict our attention to closed-loop paths?

11. (Research Problem.) Design, implement, and evaluate a parallel version of the `Cfilter` algorithm.

5 Dynamic Qualitative Simulation

5.1 Introduction

Simulation predicts the behavior of a system, given its structure. A behavior is a sequence of states that represents the temporal evolution of the system. Under a qualitative description, the sequence alternates between states representing time-points, and states representing time-intervals:

$$Behavior = [QState(t_0), QState(t_0, t_1), \ldots, QState(t_n)].$$

Qualitative simulation typically starts with a QDE and a description of the initial state, and predicts one or more possible behaviors, essentially proving a theorem of the form

$$QDE \wedge QState(t_0) \rightarrow or(Behavior_1, \ldots, Behavior_m).$$

In the last two chapters, we have developed the machinery we need to do qualitative simulation: first, the definitions of qualitative constraints, so that we can write meaningful qualitative differential equations; and second, algorithms for efficiently solving sets of constraints.

Dynamic qualitative simulation, which we will discuss in this chapter, determines the possible sequences of qualitative states that a system moves through, including both non-equilibrium and equilibrium states. This contrasts with *comparative statics* (chapter 7), which focuses on stable equilibrium states of a system, and how the equilibrium state is affected by a perturbation. There are important roles for both types of qualitative reasoning.

Qualitative simulation of possible behaviors depends on the solution to two different constraint-satisfaction problems.

1. Given a QDE and partial information about the initial state, determine all complete, consistent qualitative states $QState(t_0)$.

2. Given a QDE and a qualitative state, determine its possible immediate successors.

$$QState(t_i) \quad \rightarrow \quad or(QState_1(t_i, t_{i+1}), \ldots QState_{n_i}(t_i, t_{i+1}))$$
$$QState(t_i, t_{i+1}) \quad \rightarrow \quad or(QState_1(t_{i+1}), \ldots QState_{m_i}(t_{i+1}))$$

Qualitative behaviors are then predicted from the set of states and successor relations. Global filters are applied to test the consistency of individual successor states or entire behaviors during this process.

Given the immediate-successor relation on pairs of states, there are two principal representations for the possible behaviors of the system and corresponding algorithms for qualitative simulation.

- *Behavior tree.* Starting from one or more initial states $QState(t_0)$, grow a tree of states linked by the immediate-successor relation, so that the paths from root to leaves explicitly describe the possible behaviors.

- *Total envisionment.* Generate all possible states of the system and use the immediate-successor relation to link them into a transition graph, in which the possible behaviors are implicitly described by the paths through the graph.

5.2   The Immediate Successors of a State

There is a simple intuition behind prediction of the next qualitative state. Since a qualitative variable and its derivative are continuous functions of time, there are only a few possible transitions from one qualitative value to the next (figure 5.1). The constraints in the QDE restrict the combinations of values that can appear in a consistent assignment of values to variables.

The process of determining the successors to a given qualitative state is sometimes known as *limit analysis*. It attempts to identify the qualitative transition (typically a changing variable reaching a limit) that defines the time-point terminating a qualitatively uniform time-interval. Figure 5.1 graphically illustrates the possible qualitative value transitions.

In table 5.1, we formalize this intuition as a set of successor rules that associate with each possible qualitative value description the descriptions of its possible successors. Under a qualitative description, the successor to a given value is not uniquely determined. However, the ambiguity is tightly bounded: no variable ever has more than four possible successor values, and in many cases the successor value is unique.

The fact that table 5.1 contains all and only the possible successors follows from the Intermediate Value and Mean Value Theorems from the differential calculus. Once a set of possible successor values has been proposed for each individual variable, the set of possible successors to the current state is determined by constraint satisfaction.

Moving toward a limit point (over a time-interval)

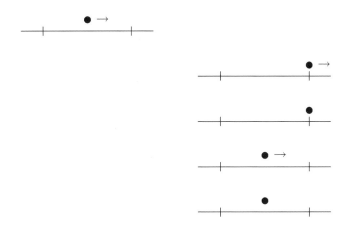

Moving from a landmark (at a time-point)

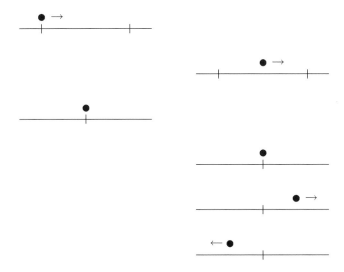

Figure 5.1
The basic qualitative value transitions.

There are only a few distinct possible behaviors for a changing value, described qualitatively with
respect to a discrete set of landmarks.

There are only a few possible successor relations from one qualitative value to the next for a continuously differentiable function $v : [a, b] \to \Re^*$. There are two sets of successor rules, depending on whether the antecedent state is a time-point or a time-interval. Let $l_{j-1} < l_j < l_{j+1}$ be three adjacent landmarks in the quantity space for v.

- **P-Successors**: point to interval.

$QV(v, t_i)$	$\Rightarrow$	$QV(v, t_i, t_{i+1})$
$\langle l_j, std \rangle$		$\langle l_j, std \rangle$
$\langle l_j, std \rangle$		$\langle (l_j, l_{j+1}), inc \rangle$
$\langle l_j, std \rangle$		$\langle (l_{j-1}, l_j), dec \rangle$
$\langle l_j, inc \rangle$		$\langle (l_j, l_{j+1}), inc \rangle$
$\langle l_j, dec \rangle$		$\langle (l_{j-1}, l_j), dec \rangle$
$\langle (l_j, l_{j+1}), inc \rangle$		$\langle (l_j, l_{j+1}), inc \rangle$
$\langle (l_j, l_{j+1}), dec \rangle$		$\langle (l_j, l_{j+1}), dec \rangle$
$\langle (l_j, l_{j+1}), std \rangle$		$\langle (l_j, l_{j+1}), std \rangle$
$\langle (l_j, l_{j+1}), std \rangle$		$\langle (l_j, l_{j+1}), inc \rangle$
$\langle (l_j, l_{j+1}), std \rangle$		$\langle (l_j, l_{j+1}), dec \rangle$

- **I-Successors**: interval to point.

$QV(v, t_i, t_{i+1})$	$\Rightarrow$	$QV(v, t_{i+1})$
$\langle l_j, std \rangle$		$\langle l_j, std \rangle$
$\langle (l_j, l_{j+1}), inc \rangle$		$\langle l_{j+1}, std \rangle$
$\langle (l_j, l_{j+1}), inc \rangle$		$\langle l_{j+1}, inc \rangle$
$\langle (l_j, l_{j+1}), inc \rangle$		$\langle (l_j, l_{j+1}), inc \rangle$
$\langle (l_j, l_{j+1}), inc \rangle$		$\langle (l_j, l_{j+1}), std \rangle$
$\langle (l_j, l_{j+1}), dec \rangle$		$\langle l_j, std \rangle$
$\langle (l_j, l_{j+1}), dec \rangle$		$\langle l_j, dec \rangle$
$\langle (l_j, l_{j+1}), dec \rangle$		$\langle (l_j, l_{j+1}), dec \rangle$
$\langle (l_j, l_{j+1}), dec \rangle$		$\langle (l_j, l_{j+1}), std \rangle$
$\langle (l_j, l_{j+1}), std \rangle$		$\langle (l_j, l_{j+1}), std \rangle$

Table 5.1
The qualitative successor rules.

5.2.1 Validity of the Qualitative Successor Table

THEOREM 5 (QUALITATIVE SUCCESSORS)   Let $v : [a, b] \to \Re^*$ be a reasonable function. Then table 5.1 contains all and only the possible qualitative descriptions for the value of v at a qualitative state and its immediate successor, where $l_{j-1} < l_j < l_{j+1}$ are adjacent landmarks in the quantity space for v.

Proof The antecedents of the successor rules cover all possible cases: a qualitative value can be equal to a landmark or between two adjacent landmarks, and the direction of change can be *inc*, *std*, or *dec*. The only excluded cases are the qualitative values $\langle l_j, inc \rangle$ and $\langle l_j, dec \rangle$ over a time-interval, which are obviously not possible.

Consider the P-successors of a qualitative value of the form $QV(v, t_i) = \langle l_j, std \rangle$. Any direction of change $[\dot{v}]$ is possible over the following time-interval. However, direction of change and displacement from l_j must have the same sign. For example, if $[\dot{v}] = inc$ over the following qualitatively uniform time-interval (t_i, t_{i+1}), then $v(t)$ must be in (l_j, l_{j+1}) as well. Otherwise, if there is some $t_a \in (t_i, t_{i+1})$ such that $v(t_a) = l_j$, then the Mean Value Theorem requires that there is some $t_b \in (t_i, t_a)$ such that $v'(t_b) = 0$, contradicting the assumption that $[\dot{v}] = inc$. Similarly, it is not possible for $v(t) < l_j$ during (t_i, t_{i+1}).

Consider the P-successors of a qualitative value $QV(v, t_i) = \langle l_j, inc \rangle$. This means that $v'(t_i)$ has some positive value $m > 0$. By the Intermediate Value Theorem, $v'(t)$ cannot reach zero without passing through all the values in the interval $(0, m)$. Therefore $[\dot{v}] = inc$ over the following interval (t_i, t_{i+1}). Just as in the previous case, the Mean Value Theorem guarantees that displacement from l_j has the same sign as direction of change.

The remaining P-successor rules follow from the same arguments, appealing to the Intermediate Value Theorem to guarantee that the endpoint of the interval (l_j, l_{j+1}) cannot be reached without using the following time-interval to pass through the points between $v(t_i)$ and the endpoint.

Consider the I-successors of a qualitative value of the form $QV(v, t_i, t_{i+1}) = \langle (l_j, l_{j+1}), inc \rangle$. By continuity, the direction of change $[\dot{v}(t_{i+1})]$ can only be *inc* or *std*. It is impossible for $v(t_{i+1}) = l_j$ by the Mean Value Theorem, so by continuity the only possible qualitative values for $v(t_{i+1})$ are the interval (l_j, l_{j+1}) and the landmark l_{j+1}. It is easy to find instances of all four combinations of values and directions of change so these rules, and the corresponding rules for $QV(v, t_i, t_{i+1}) = \langle (l_j, l_{j+1}), dec \rangle$, are valid.

Finally, if $QV(v, t_i, t_{i+1}) = \langle l_j, std \rangle$, then $v(t_{i+1})$ must have the same value, for if $v'(t_{i+1}) = m > 0$, then $v'(t)$ must have passed through the values in $(0, m)$ during the preceding interval. Likewise, if the magnitude of $v(t)$ has reached a new value at $v(t_{i+1})$, then the Mean Value Theorem requires that $v'(t)$ be non-zero during the preceding interval. The case where $QV(v, t_i, t_{i+1}) = \langle (l_j, l_{j+1}), std \rangle$ is similar.

This argument extends naturally to handle the case where the limiting landmark is $+\infty$ or $-\infty$.

Thus, we have shown that the successor rules in table 5.1 represent exactly the possible immediate successor relations for qualitative values of reasonable functions.

∎

5.3 Behavior Generation

QSIM constructs a tree of states representing the possible behaviors of the system by first finding all consistent initial states, then repeatedly linking each state with its possible successors. The behaviors are the paths from the root(s) of the tree to the leaves. Table 5.2 gives the QSIM algorithm for constructing the behavior tree.[1]

In most cases, our goal is to predict all possible behaviors, so the behavior tree is created in breadth-first order. For certain applications, such as establishing whether a particular type of behavior is possible, or incrementally growing the predicted behavior tree while monitoring an ongoing process (Dvorak and Kuipers, 1989; 1991; Dvorak, 1992), it could be appropriate to search the behavior tree in some other order.

There is no guarantee that the agenda will ever empty. Indeed, there are known sources of intractable branching that can generate infinitely many infinitely long behaviors. Intractable branching is not unique to qualitative simulation. Rather, it is the failure mode of any breadth-first problem solver. The corresponding failure mode of a depth-first problem solver is to run forever, pursuing infinitely long paths or thrashing indefinitely among alternatives. However, Leitch and Shen (1993) describe methods for guiding depth-first control of a qualitative simulator to explore the most productive behaviors first.

Intractable branching results when too many successor states survive the filtering process. Sections 3.8 and 3.9 show how to improve the filtering ability of a given set of qualitative constraints. Chapters 10 and 11 discuss additional methods for filtering out spurious qualitative behaviors. Chapter 9 discusses the use of quantitative information to filter out qualitatively consistent behaviors.

---

[1] In this book, the term "QSIM algorithm" refers to the simulation loop that builds behavior descriptions, calling Cfilter to solve constraint-satisfaction problems. In Kuipers, 1986, the same term covered much of what is now in Cfilter.

Algorithm **QSIM**:

Given $QDE = \langle V, Q, C, T \rangle$ and initial state information, predict the set of possible qualitative behaviors $\{Beh_1, \ldots, Beh_n\}$.

1. Initialize the agenda with the set of complete initial states $QState(t_0)$ consistent with the QDE and given initial state information using the State-Completion algorithm (section 4.5). `Cfilter` treats initial state information as domain restrictions $\bar{D}_i$ on the variables v_i in the QDE.

2. If the agenda is empty, or a resource limit has been exceeded, stop. The paths from roots to leaves in the behavior tree are the behaviors $\{Beh_1, \ldots, Beh_n\}$.

- Otherwise, pop a state S from the agenda.

3. For each variable v_i in the QDE, use the qualitative successor table to determine the possible successors to $QV(v_i, S)$. These are interpreted as domain restrictions $\bar{D}_i$ by `cfilter`.

4. Determine all successor states $\{S_1, \ldots, S_k\}$ consistent with the domain restrictions $\bar{D}_i$ and the constraints in the QDE.

- If S represents a time-interval, delete the successor S_i whose values are identical with those in S. (The *No Change* filter; section 5.4.1.)

5. For each S_i, assert the relations $successor(S, S_i)$ and $predecessor(S_i, S)$, thereby adding the new states to the behavior tree.

6. Apply the global filters to each successor state S_i.

7. Add each eligible successor state to the agenda.

- A newly created state S_i is eligible for successors unless a global filter has asserted $inconsistent(S_i)$, $quiescent(S_i)$, $cycle(S_i)$, $transition(S_i)$, or $t = \infty$ at S_i.

8. Continue from step 2.

Table 5.2
The QSIM algorithm.

5.4   Global Filters

In step 6 of the QSIM algorithm, after the successors $\{S_1, \ldots S_n\}$ of S have been
determined by constraint satisfaction, each successor state S_i passes through a sequence of *global filters*, which infer new information about that state. The global filter mechanism provides an open-ended interface to arbitrarily deep inference about
qualitative states and behaviors.

One particularly important case is when a global filter can infer *inconsistent*(S_i),
detecting an inconsistency that was not visible to the explicit constraints, and
ruling out an apparently possible behavior. Another important case arises when
the qualitative description can be transformed and made more specific without loss
of validity or generality, for example by creating new landmarks or identifying new
corresponding value tuples.

Some global filters are described in more detail in this chapter; others are treated
in chapters of their own. Each of the filters described in this chapter is sound,
preserving the validity of the behavior description.

State filters have a local focus, considering only information in the current state
description and perhaps its immediate predecessor.

• *The "No Change" filter* deletes a time-point state description at which no variable
changes qualitative value. (Section 5.4.1.)

• *Infinite values* must satisfy certain additional constraints that can be checked by
considering whether the time-point represented by the current state must represent
$t = \infty$ or $t < \infty$. (Section 5.4.2.)

• A *quiescent state* is recognized if all directions of change are *std*. This analysis can be extended to determine whether the quiescent state represents a stable
equilibrium. (Section 5.4.3.)

• *New landmarks* are created to represent critical values and other significant,
uniquely determined, values in quantity spaces. (Section 5.4.4.)

• *New corresponding value tuples* are identified at time-points. (Section 5.4.5.)

• *Matching states* and *cyclic behavior* can be detected by comparing the current
state with its predecessors in the behavior tree. (Section 5.4.6.)

• *Inconsistency can be propagated* backward in the behavior tree. (Section 5.4.7.)

• *Operating region transitions* are identified by comparing current qualitative values with the antecedents of transition rules. (Chapter 8.)

- *Higher-order derivative constraints* derive expressions for higher-order derivatives to eliminate spurious branches ("chatter") from critical points. (Chapter 10.)

Behavior filters consider global information about the entire behavior terminating in the current state.

- The *analytic function constraint* allows the user to focus attention on analytic solutions to the QDE by requiring that any variable that is constant over an interval must be constant everywhere. (Section 10.5.)

- *The non-intersection constraint* applies to trajectories in a phase-plane representation of behaviors, and eliminates behaviors that intersect themselves and thereby violate the uniqueness theorem for solutions of differential equations. (Chapter 11.)

- *Global energy constraints* can detect an important class of globally inconsistent behaviors. (Chapter 11.)

- *Quantitative information* can be asserted about the landmark values and other terms in the behavior description. This can be propagated to derive inconsistencies, and thus eliminate behaviors. (Chapter 9.)

5.4.1   The "No Change" Filter

For a qualitative transition to take place from a time-interval to its concluding time-point, *some* variable must change its qualitative value. If no variable changes its value, the "successor" state is already adequately described by the preceding interval, and can therefore be filtered out without reducing the coverage of the set of predicted behaviors.

Such a "no change" state will always be generated by the constraint-satisfaction algorithm. The proposed successors for each variable necessarily include the possibility that it retains its current qualitative value while some *other* variable changes. Naturally, since the current state is consistent, the state where no variable changes qualitative value will also be found consistent.

5.4.2   Infinite Values and Infinite Time

Qualitative variables are defined over the *extended* real number line, so infinite values may be explicitly included in the quantity spaces for variables, and infinite times are allowed as interpretations for time-points.

There are constraints on the possible combinations of finite and infinite values. We extend the representation for a time-point to be able to assert a temporal attribute: $t = \infty$ or $t < \infty$.

If $t = \infty$ for a state S, then S is ineligible for further simulation and will not be added to the simulation agenda.

The following rules allow us to examine the derivative of a variable v when it takes on an infinite value, and conclude a temporal attribute.

$$v(t) < \infty \text{ and } v'(t) \neq 0 \quad \rightarrow \quad t < \infty$$
$$v(t) = \infty \text{ and } v'(t) < \infty \quad \rightarrow \quad t = \infty$$

Once a temporal attribute has been deduced for a time-point, the qualitative value and direction of change of every variable in the state must satisfy the following constraints.

$$t = \infty \quad \rightarrow \quad [v(t) < \infty \rightarrow v'(t) = 0]$$
$$t < \infty \quad \rightarrow \quad [v(t) = \infty \rightarrow v'(t) = \infty]$$

If a state S_i violates any of these rules, the filter asserts $inconsistent(S_i)$. Problem 8 asks you to prove the correctness of these rules.

5.4.3   Recognizing a Quiescent State

A state S is *quiescent* if all directions of change are *std*. We include a transformation that recognizes this situation, and asserts $quiescent(S)$. A quiescent state is normally not eligible for successors.

A quiescent state is a fixed point in the phase portrait of the dynamical system described by the QDE. A fixed point is *stable* if all flows in its immediate neighborhood point inward. It is *unstable* if any flow points outward. We can build on this intuition to analyze and label quiescent states.

Suppose we attempt to simulate forward from a quiescent state. If all behaviors are ruled out except the one remaining at the fixed point, then the fixed point is stable. If some behaviors leaving the fixed point are predicted, then the state is unstable. (See problems 2 and 3.) For example, if the fixed point is a saddle point, then the behaviors departing from the fixed point represent the unstable separatrix trajectories from the saddle point. This type of embedded call to QSIM, to determine a qualitative property of a point, can be expanded into a qualitative approach to building phase portrait descriptions of dynamical systems given a QDE (Lee and Kuipers, 1993; Lee, 1993; section 11.7).

Because coverage of all behaviors is guaranteed but it is possible for predicted behaviors to be spurious, a label of *stable(S)* is guaranteed correct, but a label of *unstable(S)* could be wrong.

5.4.4 Creating New Landmarks

Consider the last two I-successor rules in table 5.1 applied to a variable $v(t)$:

$$v(t_i, t_{i+1}) \quad\Rightarrow\quad v(t_{i+1})$$

$$\langle(l_j, l_{j+1}), inc\rangle \qquad \langle(l_j, l_{j+1}), std\rangle$$
$$\langle(l_j, l_{j+1}), dec\rangle \qquad \langle(l_j, l_{j+1}), std\rangle$$

The resulting qualitative value $v(t_{i+1}) = \langle(l_j, l_{j+1}), std\rangle$ represents a specific value $l^* \in (l_j, l_{j+1})$. It also represents a critical value of $v(t)$, because $v'(t_{i+1}) = 0$. This suggests that l^* is an important value and should be represented in the quantity space by a landmark value. Since l^* is strictly between two adjacent landmarks, it can be inserted unambiguously into the quantity space.

$$\cdots l_j \cdots \cdots l_{j+1} \cdots$$
$$\Downarrow$$
$$\cdots l_j \cdots l^* \cdots l_{j+1} \cdots$$

QSIM currently creates new landmarks under three circumstances:

1. to represent a critical value of a variable;

2. to represent the initial value of a variable;

3. to represent the value of a variable when a region transition occurs.

Since each of these cases occurs at a time-point, when the variable in question takes on a definite value, even if it is described by an interval, the introduction of the new landmark does not affect the validity of the behavior description. It may affect subsequent simulation, either by allowing knowledge to be encoded in corresponding values to allow additional pruning, or by defining a new distinction that requires additional branching.

A good example of the value of creating new landmarks arises in the spring example in section 5.5.2.

```
(define-QDE Spring
 (quantity-spaces
   (A (minf 0 inf))
   (V (minf 0 inf))
   (X (minf 0 inf)))
 (constraints
   ((d/dt X V))
   ((d/dt V A))
   ((M- A X) (0 0) (minf inf) (inf minf))))
```

The initial value is only known to be $v(t_0) = \langle(0,\infty), dec\rangle$, but since it must correspond to a specific value, we can create a landmark, v_0, in the interval $(0,\infty)$, to serve as a name for that value.

$$t = t_0 \Longrightarrow \begin{array}{rcl} X & = & \langle 0, inc\rangle \\ V & = & \langle(0,\infty), dec\rangle \\ A & = & \langle 0, dec\rangle \end{array} \Longrightarrow \begin{array}{rcl} X & = & \langle 0, inc\rangle \\ V & = & \langle v_0, dec\rangle \\ A & = & \langle 0, dec\rangle \end{array}$$

With v_0 in the quantity space of $v(t)$, the description of the following time-interval is slightly strengthened.

$$t = (t_0, t_1) \Longrightarrow \begin{array}{rcl} X & = & \langle(0,\infty), inc\rangle \\ V & = & \langle(0, v_0), dec\rangle \\ A & = & \langle(-\infty, 0), dec\rangle \end{array}$$

Simulation determines that $X'(t_1) = A'(t_1) = 0$ and allows us to create new landmarks to represent the critical values, $X(t_1) = x_1$ and $A(t_1) = a_1$.

$$t = t_1 \Longrightarrow \begin{array}{rcl} X & = & \langle(0,\infty), std\rangle \\ V & = & \langle 0, dec\rangle \\ A & = & \langle(-\infty, 0), std\rangle \end{array} \Longrightarrow \begin{array}{rcl} X & = & \langle x_1, std\rangle \\ V & = & \langle 0, dec\rangle \\ A & = & \langle a_1, std\rangle \end{array}$$

After simulating around the entire cycle (and applying the energy constraint described later in chapter 11), we obtain the following state.

$$t = t_4 \Longrightarrow \begin{array}{rcl} X & = & \langle 0, inc\rangle \\ V & = & \langle v_0, dec\rangle \\ A & = & \langle 0, dec\rangle \end{array}$$

Under this state description, we can conclude that the behavior is genuinely periodic. (See section 5.4.6.) If we were not to create new landmarks, the repeated state description at $t = t_0$ and $t = t_4$ would be

$$t = t_4 \Longrightarrow \begin{array}{rcl} X & = & \langle 0, inc\rangle \\ V & = & \langle(0,\infty), dec\rangle \\ A & = & \langle 0, dec\rangle \end{array},$$

which does not distinguish between increasing, decreasing, and periodic cycles. Thus, new landmarks make it possible to express information that could not be expressed in the qualitative behavior language without them.

The creation of new landmarks gives us a revised QDE, in that the quantity spaces have additional landmarks and hence make additional qualitative distinctions. New landmarks are specific to the qualitative behavior, so they are inherited by successors to the current state but are not shared by states in alternative behaviors.

Qualitative simulation does not require the creation of new landmarks during simulation. Landmark creation is essential for capturing certain qualitative distinctions, such as between increasing, decreasing, and stable oscillations, and to provide names for qualitatively significant values for subsequent algebraic and quantitative reasoning. However, creation of new landmarks makes matching of similar states more difficult (section 5.4.6), and can make it difficult to provide a finite qualitative description for infinite behaviors.

5.4.5 Creating New Corresponding Values

After a complete state has been constructed, if all variables connected to a given constraint currently have landmark values, a corresponding value tuple is constructed and stored with the constraint. This is particularly useful when new landmarks have been created, since the corresponding value tuples that a landmark participates in help to define its meaning. Like created landmarks, corresponding value tuples are specific to the state in which they are identified, and are inherited by successor states but not across behaviors.

New landmarks and corresponding value tuples represent information about the structure and behaviors of a system that can be exploited both during subsequent qualitative simulation based on this behavior and during semi-quantitative reasoning that refines the qualitative description with quantitative assertions about the landmark values (chapter 9).

5.4.6 Identifying Cycles

Suppose, in the course of simulating a system — say, the frictionless oscillating spring — we identify a state $S(t_4)$ that is identical with a previous state $S(t_0)$ in the same behavior. In that case, $S(t_4)$ will have the same successors as those already determined for $S(t_0)$. We can assert $cycle\_identity(S(t_4), S(t_0))$ to express the fact that the two states match, and that a cyclic behavior has been recognized.[2]

The key question is, when do two states match? There are two tests that must be passed.

---

[2]The behavior tree is tree-structured under the union of the *completion, successor*, and *transition* relations. The *cycle-identity* link allows a behavior to loop back within its own branch of the tree.

1. Both states must represent time-points rather than time-intervals.

2. The qualitative values of each variable must be "the same" in the two states.

When are two values for a variable "the same?" Both strong and weak matching criteria are used, for different purposes.

• **Strong match**. Two qualitative values match if they are equal to the same *landmark value* in the quantity space of the variable.

• **Weak match**. Two qualitative values match if they are equal to the same landmark value *or interval* in the quantity space of the variable.

A landmark is the name for a specific value, but two identical qualitative interval descriptions can refer to different values within the interval. This may, under some circumstances, collapse distinctions that are qualitatively important. For example, in the domain of signs, $[+]$ and $[-]$ are the names for the qualitative intervals $(0, \infty)$ and $(-\infty, 0)$, respectively. Allowing $[+]$ to match $[+]$ collapses the distinction between different positive values. Cycles may then be identified in an oscillating process without distinguishing increasing from decreasing, steady, or chaotic oscillation.

Strong and weak cycles are cycles that have been identified according to the strong or weak state-matching criterion, respectively. The different types of cycles support different valid implications.

• **Strong cycle**. If a qualitative behavior is a strong cycle, then every trajectory that is an instance of the cyclic behavior is periodic. This is useful when identifying qualitative properties such as periodicity or features such as limit cycles.

• **Weak cycle**. If two qualitative states weakly match, then they will have the same qualitative successor states. This makes it possible to derive the *envisionment* as a finite transition-graph representation of the set of all possible behaviors, and therefore have finite descriptions of infinite behaviors.

During behavior generation, QSIM applies the strong matching criterion for purposes of cycle detection. When a strong cycle is detected, then the system has actually returned to the same state. In particular, not only the values but also the directions of change must be the same because, in an autonomous QDE, the derivatives are determined by the magnitudes. When creating an envisionment (section 5.7), the weak state-matching criterion is used.

5.4.7   Propagating Inconsistency

Unless a state is quiescent, or represents a transition out of the current QDE and into a region for which no QDE is given, it must have a successor. Therefore, if a time-interval state has no consistent successor to represent its concluding time-point, it is inconsistent. Remember that reasonable functions are defined over the *extended* reals $\Re^* = [-\infty, +\infty]$, so asymptotic approach to a limit is treated as reaching the limit at $t = +\infty$.

If all successors of a (non-quiescent, non-transition) time-point state are found to be inconsistent, the state itself is inconsistent. Inconsistency can therefore propagate backward from the leaves of the behavior tree to the root, possibly showing that the given model and initial state description are inconsistent.

5.5   Examples

5.5.1   The Bathtub

In the last chapter, we started with a set of proposed values for the variables in the bathtub model at the qualitative time-point t_1, and traced the constraint-satisfaction algorithm as it formed all possible global states at t_1. Here, we see where the proposed values came from, starting from the QDE (figure 5.2).

1. Starting at t_0 with the empty bathtub ($amount(t_0) = 0$) and filling at a constant rate ($inflow(t_0) = \langle(0, \infty), std\rangle$), State-Completion propagates the initial information to obtain a complete qualitative state description. Since t_0 is an initial state, new landmarks if_1 and nf_1 are created to represent specific values within open intervals, and a new corresponding value tuple $(nf_1, 0, if_1)$ is created for the *add* constraint.

$$t = t_0 \Longrightarrow \boxed{\begin{array}{lcl} amount & = & \langle 0, ?\rangle \\ inflow & = & \langle(0, \infty), std\rangle \end{array}} \Longrightarrow \boxed{\begin{array}{lcl} amount & = & \langle 0, inc\rangle \\ outflow & = & \langle 0, inc\rangle \\ inflow & = & \langle if_1, std\rangle \\ netflow & = & \langle nf_1, dec\rangle \end{array}}$$

2. The next qualitatively distinct state, over the interval (t_0, t_1), is non-empty and filling. We will examine the process of determining the state at t_1 that terminates this interval.

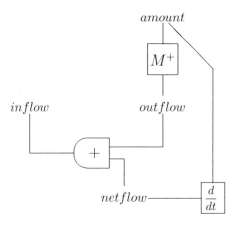

```
(define-QDE Minimal-Bathtub
  (quantity-spaces
    (amount    (    0 full inf))
    (outflow   (    0      inf))
    (inflow    (    0      inf))
    (netflow   (minf 0     inf)))
  (constraints
    ((M+ amount outflow) (0 0) (inf inf))
    ((add netflow outflow inflow))
    ((d/dt amount netflow))
    ((constant inflow))))
  (transitions
    ((amount (full inc)) -> t)))
```

Figure 5.2
Minimal bathtub model.

	t_0	(t_0, t_1)	t_1
amount	$\langle 0, \uparrow \rangle$	$\langle (0, \mathit{full}), \uparrow \rangle$	?
outflow	$\langle 0, \uparrow \rangle$	$\langle (0, \infty), \uparrow \rangle$	?
inflow	$\langle \mathit{if}_1, \ominus \rangle$	$\langle \mathit{if}_1, \ominus \rangle$	?
netflow	$\langle \mathit{nf}_1, \downarrow \rangle$	$\langle (0, \mathit{nf}_1), \downarrow \rangle$	?

3. Matching the value of each variable at (t_0, t_1) to the successor rules in table 5.1, we obtain the following sets of possible values.

	t_1
$amount$	$\{\langle full, \uparrow\rangle, \langle full, \ominus\rangle, \langle(0, full), \uparrow\rangle, \langle(0, full), \ominus\rangle\}$
$outflow$	$\{\langle\infty, \uparrow\rangle, \langle\infty, \ominus\rangle, \langle(0, \infty), \uparrow\rangle, \langle(0, \infty), \ominus\rangle\}$
$inflow$	$\{\langle if_1, \ominus\rangle\}$
$netflow$	$\{\langle 0, \downarrow\rangle, \langle 0, \ominus\rangle, \langle(0, nf_1), \downarrow\rangle, \langle(0, nf_1), \ominus\rangle\}$

4. Constraint filtering (described in detail in section 4.4.1) gives us the following four possible successor states at t_1. Successor state 3 is filtered out by the *No Change* filter (section 5.4.1) because it matches its predecessor state over the interval (t_0, t_1).

	1	2	3	4
$amount$	$\langle full, \uparrow\rangle$	$\langle full, \ominus\rangle$	$\langle(0, full), \uparrow\rangle$	$\langle(0, full), \ominus\rangle$
$outflow$	$\langle(0, \infty), \uparrow\rangle$	$\langle(0, \infty), \ominus\rangle$	$\langle(0, \infty), \uparrow\rangle$	$\langle(0, \infty), \ominus\rangle$
$inflow$	$\langle if_1, \ominus\rangle$	$\langle if_1, \ominus\rangle$	$\langle if_1, \ominus\rangle$	$\langle if_1, \ominus\rangle$
$netflow$	$\langle(0, nf_1), \downarrow\rangle$	$\langle 0, \ominus\rangle$	$\langle(0, nf_1), \downarrow\rangle$	$\langle 0, \ominus\rangle$

5. The global filters will create new landmarks to represent critical values within open intervals, and new corresponding value tuples to represent the relations among new and old landmarks. For example, consider successor state 4, where *inflow* and *outflow* reach equilibrium before *amount* reaches *full*, so the bathtub does not overflow. New landmarks are created to represent the values of *amount* and *outflow* at t_1.

$$t = t_1 \Longrightarrow \begin{array}{rcl} amount & = & \langle(0, full), std\rangle \\ outflow & = & \langle(0, \infty), std\rangle \\ inflow & = & \langle if_1, std\rangle \\ netflow & = & \langle 0, std\rangle \end{array} \Longrightarrow \begin{array}{rcl} amount & = & \langle a_1, std\rangle \\ outflow & = & \langle of_1, std\rangle \\ inflow & = & \langle if_1, std\rangle \\ netflow & = & \langle 0, std\rangle \end{array}$$

The effect of the new landmarks and corresponding values is that, after time-point t_1 and along this branch of the behavior tree, the system behaves as if it had been described as follows:

```
(define-QDE Minimal-Bathtub-at-T1-along-equilibrium-branch
  (quantity-spaces
    (amount   (      0 a-1  full inf))
    (outflow  (      0 of-1      inf))
    (inflow   (      0 if-1   *  inf))
    (netflow  (minf 0 nf-1      inf)))
  (constraints
    ((M+ amount outflow) (0 0) (a-1 of-1) (inf inf))
```

```
    ((add netflow outflow inflow)) (nf-1 0 if-1) (0 of-1 if-1))
    ((constant inflow))
    ((d/dt amount netflow)))
 (transitions
    ((amount (full inc)) -> t)))
```

6. Simulation terminates at t_1 because successor state 1 is a region transition (see chapter 8) and states 2 and 4 are quiescent. The resulting three qualitative behaviors are shown in figure 5.3.

5.5.2   The Spring

In the same way, we propose successor values for the variables in the spring model.

1. We initialize the spring model at the origin ($X(t_0) = 0$) with an initial positive velocity ($V(t_0) = (0, \infty)$). These assertions are propagated through the constraints, and a new landmark is created to represent the initial velocity, $V(t_0) = v_0$.

$$t = t_0 \implies \boxed{\begin{aligned} X &= \langle 0, ? \rangle \\ V &= \langle (0, \infty), ? \rangle \end{aligned}} \implies \boxed{\begin{aligned} X &= \langle 0, inc \rangle \\ V &= \langle v_0, std \rangle \\ A &= \langle 0, dec \rangle \end{aligned}}$$

2. The transition from t_0 to the interval (t_0, t_1) is straightforward, so we focus on the state at t_1.

	t_0	(t_0, t_1)	t_1
X	$\langle 0, \uparrow \rangle$	$\langle (0, \infty), \uparrow \rangle$	?
V	$\langle v_0, \ominus \rangle$	$\langle (0, v_0), \downarrow \rangle$	?
A	$\langle 0, \downarrow \rangle$	$\langle (-\infty, 0), \downarrow \rangle$	?

3. Matching the value of each variable at (t_0, t_1) to the successor rules in table 5.1, we obtain the following sets of possible values.

	t_1
X	$\{\langle \infty, \uparrow \rangle, \langle \infty, \ominus \rangle, \langle (0, \infty), \uparrow \rangle, \langle (0, \infty), \ominus \rangle\}$
V	$\{\langle 0, \downarrow \rangle, \langle 0, \ominus \rangle, \langle (0, v_0), \downarrow \rangle, \langle (0, v_0), \ominus \rangle\}$
A	$\{\langle -\infty, \downarrow \rangle, \langle -\infty, \ominus \rangle, \langle (-\infty, 0), \downarrow \rangle, \langle (-\infty, 0), \ominus \rangle\}$

4. Constraint filtering (described in detail in section 4.4.2) gives us the following four global states for time t_1.

	1	2	3	4
X	$\langle \infty, \uparrow \rangle$	$\langle \infty, \ominus \rangle$	$\langle (0, \infty), \uparrow \rangle$	$\langle (0, \infty), \ominus \rangle$
V	$\langle (0, v_0), \downarrow \rangle$	$\langle 0, \downarrow \rangle$	$\langle (0, v_0), \downarrow \rangle$	$\langle 0, \downarrow \rangle$
A	$\langle -\infty, \downarrow \rangle$	$\langle -\infty, \ominus \rangle$	$\langle (-\infty, 0), \downarrow \rangle$	$\langle (-\infty, 0), \ominus \rangle$

- Successor states 1 and 2 are ruled out by the global filter on infinite values (section 5.4.2).

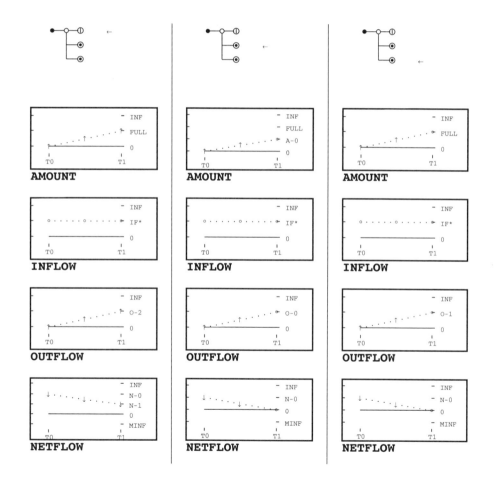

Figure 5.3
Behaviors of the bathtub model: $t_0 \rightarrow (t_0, t_1) \rightarrow t_1$.

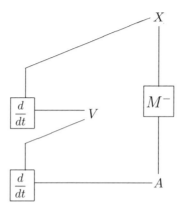

```
(define-QDE Simple-Spring
 (quantity-spaces
  (A (minf 0 inf))
  (V (minf 0 inf))
  (X (minf 0 inf)))
 (constraints
  ((d/dt X V))
  ((d/dt V A))
  ((M- X A) (minf inf) (0 0) (inf minf))))
```

Figure 5.4
The QDE for the simple spring model.

- In state 1, the values of X and V imply that $t_1 = \infty$, while the values of V and A imply that $t_1 < \infty$.

- In state 2, the values of V and A imply that $t_1 < \infty$, after which $X(t_1) = \infty$ implies that $V(t_1)$ must be infinite, but it is not.

- Successor state 3 is ruled out by the *No Change* filter (section 5.4.1) because it is identical to its predecessor, and hence does not represent a qualitative change.

5. Successor state 4 represents the only globally consistent state of the system at t_1.

$$t = t_1 \Longrightarrow \begin{array}{|ccl|} \hline X & = & \langle (0, \infty), \ominus \rangle \\ V & = & \langle 0, \downarrow \rangle \\ A & = & \langle (-\infty, 0), \ominus \rangle \\ \hline \end{array} \Longrightarrow \begin{array}{|ccl|} \hline X & = & \langle x_0, \ominus \rangle \\ V & = & \langle 0, \downarrow \rangle \\ A & = & \langle a_0, \ominus \rangle \\ \hline \end{array}$$

The values of $X(t_1)$ and $A(t_1)$ are then represented by newly created landmark values.

6. The behavior of the spring model thus far is shown in figure 5.5. Simulation will continue from t_1, with quantity spaces and corresponding values augmented as if the QDE had been defined as follows:

```
(define-QDE Simple-Spring-at-T1
  (quantity-spaces
    (A (minf a-0 0     inf))
    (V (minf     0 v-0 inf))
    (X (minf     0 x-0 inf)))
  (constraints
    ((d/dt X V))
    ((d/dt V A))
    ((M- X A) (minf inf) (0 0) (x-0 a-0) (inf minf))))
```

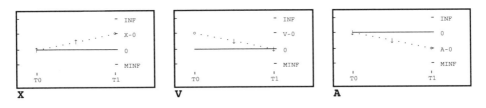

Figure 5.5
Behavior of the spring model: $t_0 \to (t_0, t_1) \to t_1$.

5.6   Guarantees

At this point, we can assemble the individual results we have proved over the past three chapters, to establish useful properties of the QSIM algorithm within the following abstraction framework.

$$\begin{array}{ccc} ODE \wedge State(t_0) & \longrightarrow & v_i : [a, b] \to \Re^* \\ \downarrow & & \downarrow \\ QDE \wedge QState(t_0) & \longrightarrow & or(Beh_1, \ldots, Beh_n) \end{array}$$

5.6.1   Guaranteed Coverage

The following theorem guarantees that the QSIM algorithm predicts every reasonable solution to every ODE described by the given QDE.

THEOREM 6 (GUARANTEED COVERAGE)   Suppose $ODE \wedge State(t_0)$ is an ordinary differential equation and initial state description, and $QDE \wedge QState(t_0)$ is a structural abstraction of $ODE \wedge State(t_0)$.

Let $u(t)$ be a solution to $ODE \wedge State(t_0)$ that determines a set Beh of reasonable functions over some domain $[a, b]$, one for each variable in QDE, via the structural abstraction relation between ODE and QDE.

If the QSIM algorithm, using only sound global filters, predicts

$$QDE \wedge QState(t_0) \rightarrow QBeh_1 \vee \cdots \vee QBeh_n \qquad (5.1)$$

then there is some i $(1 \leq i \leq n)$ such that $QBeh_i$ is an abstraction of Beh over $[a, b]$.

Viewing QSIM as a theorem prover specialized for theorems of the form (5.1) about the domain of reasonable solutions to differential equations, this means that QSIM is *sound*. That is, whenever the differential equation describing a dynamical system satisfies the antecedent of (5.1), its behavior will satisfy the consequent of (5.1).

Proof   The basic idea behind the proof is that every consistent behavior description is generated, and only inconsistent ones are filtered out.

Let QDE be the tuple $\langle V, Q, C, T \rangle$. Since Beh is a set of reasonable functions over a domain $[a, b]$, one for each variable in V, by theorem 1 it can be described by a finite qualitative behavior description

$$QS(V, t_0), QS(V, t_0, t_1), \ldots, QS(V, t_n). \qquad (5.2)$$

(Note that $QS(V, t_0)$ is equivalent to $QState(t_0)$.)

In step 1 of the QSIM algorithm (page 103) the Cfilter algorithm is guaranteed to generate all assignments of values to variables consistent with the constraints in QDE and the domain restrictions implied by $QState(t_0)$ (by theorem 4 on page 84). Since $QS(V, t_0)$ is consistent with those constraints and domain restrictions, it must be among the assignments generated.

Given a qualitative state at t_j or (t_j, t_{j+1}), the qualitative successor table is guaranteed to propose all possible successor values for each variable v_i in V (by theorem 5 on page 101). Using these values as domain restrictions, the Cfilter algorithm is guaranteed to generate all (and only) assignments for immediate successor states consistent with the constraints in QDE (again by theorem 4).

Since the initial state of behavior (5.2) is generated, and each successor state in behavior (5.2) is among the successors generated from its immediate predecessor, and since behavior (5.2) has a finite number of states, then by growing the behavior tree in breadth-first order the QSIM algorithm will generate behavior (5.2) in a finite number of steps.

Since behavior (5.2) is a description of an actual set of reasonable functions, it cannot be filtered out by any sound global filter. Therefore, behavior (5.2) must remain among the behaviors generated, and thus must be equal to $QBeh_i$ for some i ($1 \leq i \leq n$). ∎

The soundness of QSIM's prediction depends on the soundness of each filtering step, including the global filters. As we shall see in section 5.4 and later chapters, most of the global filters are carefully designed with soundness guarantees of their own. However, two important methods rely on approximations rather than validity-preserving abstraction, so they are not sound.

Derivation of higher-order derivative constraints (chapter 10) may require additional assumptions about the properties of monotonic functions. (An alternate approach that retains soundness abstracts the behavior description by collapsing certain distinctions, addressing the same concerns using a conservative filter but possibly giving weaker results.) Time-scale abstraction (chapter 12) approximates widely separated time-scales with *infinitely* separated time-scales, making it possible to decompose a complex system into several simpler systems but, like any other order-of-magnitude reasoning method, sacrificing soundness.

These and other approximation-based inference methods provide valuable qualitative insight into the behavior of a continuous system even without logical soundness. Guarantees characterizing their value to qualitative reasoning will depend on methods outside the scope of this book. However, see sections 10.4 and 12.5.

5.6.2   Incompleteness

The good news is that the predicted behaviors include all the possible ones. The bad news is that they may also include genuinely impossible ones. That is, the set of constraints and global filters is not sufficiently powerful to detect every inconsistent behavior.

DEFINITION 15   A *spurious behavior* $QBeh_i$ in a QSIM prediction

$$QDE \wedge QState(t_0) \rightarrow QBeh_1 \vee \cdots \vee QBeh_n$$

is a behavior that describes no solution to any ordinary differential equation $ODE \wedge State(t_0)$ consistent with $QDE \wedge QState(t_0)$.

Notice that the existence of spurious behaviors does not conflict with the soundness of QSIM's conclusion. One can soundly conclude $A \vee B \vee C$ even if C is false. The problem is the missed opportunity to draw the stronger conclusion $A \vee B$.

The undamped oscillator

$$\dot{x} = v$$
$$\dot{v} = -f(x), \text{ where } f \in M_0^+$$

provides a useful illustration of incomplete filtering and spurious behaviors, even though the energy filter (chapter 11) can now eliminate all spurious behaviors for this example.

Given an initial state where $x(t_0) = 0$ and $v(t_0) = v_0 > 0$, QSIM predicts a single sequence of qualitative states until reaching a three-way branch at t_4, branching on the ordering between $v(t)$ and v_0 at the time when $x(t) = 0$ after one cycle. (Because of the representation of qualitative behaviors, this event takes place at t_4 along two behaviors, but at t_5 along the third.) Figure 5.6 shows these three behaviors and their trajectories superimposed in a single qualitative x-v phase-space diagram. All three behaviors are consistent with the constraints and global filters described through this chapter. However, even with incomplete qualitative knowledge, only the strictly periodic behavior ($v(t_4) = v_0$) is a real possibility.

Consider the total energy of the oscillating system. At position $(x(t), v(t))$, the total energy is

$$E(t) = KE(t) + PE(t) = \frac{1}{2}mv^2 + m \int_0^x f(\bar{x}) \, d\bar{x}.$$

One can prove without great difficulty that the QDE for the spring implies that $dE/dt = 0$, so $E(t)$ is constant (problem 1). This means that when the spring returns to a state where $x(t) = \langle 0, inc \rangle$, $v(t)$ must have its previous value.

Why should the spurious increasing and decreasing oscillations be predicted? After all, a numerical simulation of the same equation produces a single correct prediction.

In a numerically simulated model, the value of $E(t)$ is implied by the numerical values of $x(t)$ and $v(t)$. When the values of x and v are updated at the next time-tick, the implied value of $E(t)$ remains the same.

Behaviors

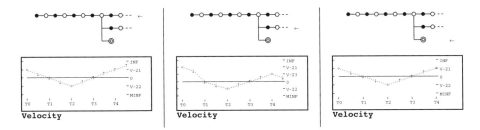

Phase Space

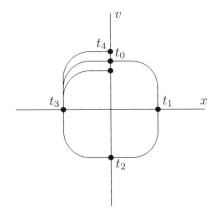

Figure 5.6
Three-way branch due to loss of implicit "energy" invariant.

In the qualitatively described system, the descriptions of the state of the system at time-point t_0 and time-interval (t_0, t_1) are the following (showing values for only x and v):

	t_0	(t_0, t_1)
x	$\langle 0, inc \rangle$	$\langle (0, \infty), inc \rangle$
v	$\langle v_0, std \rangle$	$\langle (0, v_0), dec \rangle$

At t_0, the landmark values $x = 0$ and $v = v_0$ implicitly represent the energy of the system. However, over the time-interval (t_0, t_1), the state of the system is only described as lying within open intervals for x and v. This weak description is consistent with a range of levels of total energy, not only the one implied by

$(x = 0, v = v_0)$. Since simulation takes place from each state to its immediate successor(s), information about total energy is lost by the time t_1 is reached, and is certainly not available when needed to constrain the branch at t_4 (figure 5.6). Therefore, the qualitative description does not preserve implicit information about the total system energy.

5.6.3   Discussion: Using Qualitative Predictions

Incompleteness notwithstanding, a guaranteed prediction of the form (5.1) is exactly what we need when applying qualitative simulation in the major problem-solving contexts of diagnosis and design.

Spurious behaviors can cause difficulties in both diagnosis and design, requiring additional effort to improve the model and the conclusions that can be drawn. However, since the conclusion (5.1) is guaranteed sound, the problems raised by spurious behaviors do not reduce a reasoner to incoherence. Rather, these are the usual problems of reasoning with incomplete knowledge: the inability to draw desired conclusions with available information and inference resources.

In Diagnosis   In diagnosis, we want to associate each hypothesis with a model, and to predict the consequences of that model. If all predictions from a model are false, the model is refuted, and the hypothesis is false. This is expressed by the contrapositive of (5.1):

$$\neg QBeh_1 \wedge \cdots \wedge \neg QBeh_n \quad \rightarrow \quad \neg QDE \vee \neg QState(t_0). \tag{5.3}$$

or

$$QState(t_0) \wedge \neg QBeh_1 \wedge \cdots \wedge \neg QBeh_n \quad \rightarrow \quad \neg QDE. \tag{5.4}$$

In diagnosis, the potential impact of a spurious behavior is that a model could be incorrectly retained after all of its genuine predictions had been refuted.

This approach has been explored in the MIMIC approach to model-based monitoring and diagnosis by Dvorak and Kuipers (1989; 1991); Dvorak (1992); Vinson and Ungar (1993); and in quantitative simulation and diagnosis of heat-exchanger networks by Throop (1991).

In Design   In design, we want to simulate the behavior of an incompletely specified model. If all behaviors satisfy the specifications, then any instance of the model will satisfy the specifications.

$$\frac{\begin{aligned} QDE \wedge S(t_0) \quad &\rightarrow \quad or(B_1, \dots B_n) \\ B_i \quad &\rightarrow \quad Specifications, \text{ for } i = 1, \cdots n \end{aligned}}{QDE \wedge S(t_0) \quad \rightarrow \quad Specifications} \tag{5.5}$$

If some behavior violates the specifications, it may be possible to transform the model, adding constraints to QDE, to eliminate that behavior.

In design, the potential impact of a spurious behavior is that it may falsely suggest that a design flaw must be corrected. However, it cannot lead to an incorrect guarantee of success.

This approach has been explored in the use of teleological knowledge in computer-aided design by Franke (1991; 1992); Iwasaki *et al.* (1993); and in the design and validation of fuzzy control laws by Kuipers and Åström (1991; 1994).

5.7   Total Envisionment

We have discussed qualitative simulation of a QDE as an initial-value problem, to be solved by repeatedly determining the possible successors of each state. An alternate approach is to determine all possible states, then determine which state-to-state transitions are possible. This transition graph, whose paths implicitly represent the possible qualitative behaviors, is called the *total envisionment of the QDE*.[3]

For the total envisionment to be useful, the system must have only finitely many qualitative states. The set of qualitative states is a subset of the product space of the quantity spaces and the directions of change for each variable. In order to ensure that the quantity spaces are finite, or even that they have a definite size so that the product space can be formed, we cannot allow new landmarks to be created and inserted into the quantity spaces during simulation.

Just as with prediction of successors to a given state, we can use constraint satisfaction to filter the product space down to the set of global states consistent with the constraints. State-to-state transitions are then asserted between pairs of states consistent with the qualitative successor relations in table 5.1. Figure 5.7 shows the total envisionment of the simple spring model.

5.7.1   Attainable Envisionment

The *total envisionment of a QDE* consists of the set of all possible states of the given QDE, and all possible transitions among them. The *attainable envisionment of a QDE* is the subset of states in the total envisionment reachable from a given initial state (or set of states).

---

[3]Forbus (1984) uses the term "total envisionment" in a broader sense, first generating all possible models (i.e., QDEs) consistent with a given set of facts about the world, then generating all possible states of each model, and finally linking them with all consistent state-to-state transitions. We treat model building separately from model simulation (see chapter 14).

```
(define-QDE Simple-Spring
  (quantity-spaces
   (A  (minf 0 inf))
   (V  (minf 0 inf))
   (X  (minf 0 inf)))
  (constraints
   ((d/dt X V))
   ((d/dt V A))
   ((M- A X)      (0 0) (minf inf) (inf minf))))
```

$$
\begin{array}{ccccc}
\boxed{\begin{array}{l} Y = \langle(0,\infty),\uparrow\rangle \\ V = \langle(0,\infty),\downarrow\rangle \\ A = \langle(-\infty,0),\downarrow\rangle \end{array}} & \Rightarrow & \boxed{\begin{array}{l} Y = \langle(0,\infty),\ominus\rangle \\ V = \langle 0,\downarrow\rangle \\ A = \langle(-\infty,0),\ominus\rangle \end{array}} & \Rightarrow & \boxed{\begin{array}{l} Y = \langle(0,\infty),\downarrow\rangle \\ V = \langle(-\infty,0),\downarrow\rangle \\ A = \langle(-\infty,0),\uparrow\rangle \end{array}} \\[2em]
\Uparrow & & & & \Downarrow \\[1em]
\boxed{\begin{array}{l} Y = \langle 0,\uparrow\rangle \\ V = \langle(0,\infty),\ominus\rangle \\ A = \langle 0,\downarrow\rangle \end{array}} & & \boxed{\begin{array}{l} Y = \langle 0,\ominus\rangle \\ V = \langle 0,\ominus\rangle \\ A = \langle 0,\ominus\rangle \end{array}} & & \boxed{\begin{array}{l} Y = \langle 0,\downarrow\rangle \\ V = \langle(-\infty,0),\ominus\rangle \\ A = \langle 0,\uparrow\rangle \end{array}} \\[2em]
\Uparrow & & & & \Downarrow \\[1em]
\boxed{\begin{array}{l} Y = \langle(-\infty,0),\uparrow\rangle \\ V = \langle(0,\infty),\uparrow\rangle \\ A = \langle(0,\infty),\downarrow\rangle \end{array}} & \Leftarrow & \boxed{\begin{array}{l} Y = \langle(-\infty,0),\ominus\rangle \\ V = \langle 0,\uparrow\rangle \\ A = \langle(0,\infty),\ominus\rangle \end{array}} & \Leftarrow & \boxed{\begin{array}{l} Y = \langle(-\infty,0),\downarrow\rangle \\ V = \langle(-\infty,0),\uparrow\rangle \\ A = \langle(0,\infty),\uparrow\rangle \end{array}}
\end{array}
$$

Figure 5.7
Total envisionment of the simple spring.

Initially, the product of the possible qualitative values has $(5 \cdot 3)^3 = 3375$ qualitative states, but after constraint filtering (including the filter on infinite times and infinite values), there are only nine consistent states, and eight consistent state-to-state transitions.

The QSIM algorithm (table 5.2) can compute the attainable envisionment from a given QDE and initial state description, with a few simple differences from the normal dynamic simulation mode.

- New landmarks are not created.

- The weak match criterion is used for cycle detection.

- Matching states may be found anywhere in the tree of existing states, not just among the predecessors of a state.

The resulting *cross-edges* that identify matching states make the behavior tree into a transition graph.

The size of the attainable envisionment increases with decreasing information in the initial state description, eventually becoming equal to the total envisionment when no initial state information is provided.

This simulation-based strategy for envisionment also has the advantage of enforcing the alternation between time-point and time-interval qualitative states. (See problem 12.)

5.7.2   Transition Graph or Behavior Tree?

There are relative advantages and disadvantages of these two representations for qualitative behavior.

• The envisionment provides a finite representation for infinite behaviors. There may still be an infinite number of behaviors, each infinitely long, corresponding to infinitely many possible paths through a transition graph, but the graph can be analyzed for sources, sinks, and tightly coupled, loosely coupled, and unreachable components.

   The behavior tree, by contrast, attempts to represent an infinite behavior as a path in an infinitely deep tree of states.

• The envisionment depends on enumerating all possible states before doing a simulation. This means that, in general, new landmarks cannot be created, for example to represent extremal points of an oscillatory process. This is a significant decrease in expressive power. Without the ability to create new landmarks, the distinction between increasing, steady, or decreasing oscillations cannot even be *expressed*!

• The enumeration of all possible states is an up-front cost of total envisionment (at least in current algorithms) so the complexity of qualitative simulation grows very rapidly with the size of the QDE model.

• The transition-graph representation requires the weak matching criterion for cycle detection, if any state with interval values is reachable twice in the same behavior. For example, consider the cycle in figure 5.7 showing the total envisionment of the oscillating spring. The strong matching criterion would prevent any cycle from being detected, so it would require infinitely many copies of each qualitative state.

• Both the transition-graph and the behavior-tree representations are subject to the problem of spurious behaviors — predicted behaviors that cannot occur, but

do not violate any of the explicit qualitative constraints. Spurious behaviors were
discussed in section 5.6.2.

Recently, researchers have been viewing the total envisionment as a Markov
model, annotating the transitions with probability information and drawing conclusions about the long-term behavior of the system (Doyle and Sacks, 1991; Lunze,
1992; Grossman and Werthner, 1993). Since qualitative models lack the Markov
property (section 11.8), conclusions from this description could be biased by the
impact of spurious paths.

5.8 Non-Standard Models of Time

Certain approaches to qualitative simulation have proposed the concept of "mythical time." If one uses a propagation algorithm to predict the changes that take
place in a system, there is a temptation to identify the sequence of computational
steps in the propagation algorithm with temporal or causal order in the system
being modeled. However, with plausible rules for propagation, it can take more
than one complete propagation cycle to reach the next physically meaningful state
of the system. De Kleer and Brown (1984) call the resulting intermediate states
"mythical time points."

Consider the following model in which a ball is dropped from an initial height y_0
under constant gravity.

```
(define-QDE Gravity
  (quantity-spaces
    (Y  (minf   0 y-0 inf))
    (V  (minf   0     inf))
    (A  (minf g 0     inf)))
  (constraints
    ((d/dt Y V))
    ((d/dt V A))
    ((constant A))))
  (transitions
    ((y (0 dec)) -> stop)))
```

The sequence of states predicted by the QSIM algorithm is the following.

t	t_0	(t_0, t_1)	t_1
Y	$\langle y_0, std \rangle$	$\langle (0, y_0), dec \rangle$	$\langle 0, dec \rangle$
V	$\langle 0, dec \rangle$	$\langle (-\infty, 0), dec \rangle$	$\langle (-\infty, 0), dec \rangle$
A	$\langle g, std \rangle$	$\langle g, std \rangle$	$\langle g, std \rangle$

Let us consider closely the transition from t_0 to (t_0, t_1). The set of possible successors of values at t_0 follows:

	t_0		(t_0, t_1)
	$\langle y_0, std \rangle$	$\Rightarrow$	$\langle (y_0, \infty), inc \rangle$
Y		$\Rightarrow$	$\langle (0, y_0), dec \rangle$
		$\Rightarrow$	$\langle (y_0, std \rangle$
V	$\langle 0, dec \rangle$	$\Rightarrow$	$\langle (-\infty, 0), dec \rangle$
A	$\langle g, std \rangle$	$\Rightarrow$	$\langle g, std \rangle$

Clearly, the only consistent possibility for Y is $\langle (0, y_0), dec \rangle$, since $V < 0$ over (t_0, t_1). Nonetheless, it can seem counterintuitive and non-causal for Y to decrease in value from y_0 to $(0, y_0)$ when $\dot{Y}(t_0) = 0$.

An alternate approach to simulation attempts to preserve the local inference patterns of a propagation algorithm. This approach applies a "persistence-based" successor rule like the following.

t_i		$succ(t_i)$
$\langle l, std \rangle$	$\Rightarrow$	$\langle l, nil \rangle$

To obtain a complete state, we then use a propagation rule to fill in the missing direction of change.

$$(\texttt{d/dt x y}) \quad \Rightarrow \quad [\dot{x}(t)] = [y(t)]_0$$

This propagation sequence eventually reaches the correct descriptions for (t_0, t_1) and t_1, but with an additional time-point, t_{myth}, required to propagate a change down a chain of derivative constraints. This additional time-point has been called "mythical time."

t	t_0	t_{myth}	(t_0, t_1)	t_1
Y	$\langle y_0, std \rangle$	$\langle y_0, dec \rangle$	$\langle (0, y_0), dec \rangle$	$\langle 0, dec \rangle$
V	$\langle 0, dec \rangle$	$\langle (-\infty, 0), dec \rangle$	$\langle (-\infty, 0), dec \rangle$	$\langle (-\infty, 0), dec \rangle$
A	$\langle g, std \rangle$	$\langle g, std \rangle$	$\langle g, std \rangle$	$\langle g, std \rangle$

An important consequence of using "mythical time" is that it is possible for two points in time, here t_0 and t_{myth}, to be adjacent, without a time-interval between them. The primary motivation for this step is to identify computational time during propagation with physical time in the mechanism. Thus, one must abandon the real number line as an underlying semantics for time. This is a major sacrifice, since it greatly complicates the formal relationship between qualitative reasoning and the theory of differential equations.

You might notice that the "mythical time" description resembles the "Roadrunner cartoon" scenario, in which an animated character runs off a cliff, begins to fall without losing altitude, and finally drops below its original altitude.

This type of "bug" in the inference system is an intriguing source of hypotheses about the types of inference people are actually doing. It may be that human commonsense knowledge in some cases includes inference rules that lead to "mythical time." McCloskey, Carramazza, and Green (1980) and McCloskey (1983) showed that a wide variety of non-Newtonian beliefs about physics are commonly held even by university physics majors. Clement (1983) makes additional parallels between contemporary naive physics and historical physics theories. We return to the relation between Newtonian and Aristotelean physics in section 12.4.

5.9 Problems

1. Carry out the proof discussed in section 5.6.2, that the QDE for the simple spring implies that $dE/dt = 0$, so $E(t)$ is constant.

2. Build a model of a valley — $y = U^+(x)$ — in which a mass starts at rest partway up one wall and slides frictionlessly down into the valley under the influence of gravity. Hand simulate the QSIM algorithm on this problem to determine all of its possible behaviors.

3. Build a model of a frictionless hill — $y = U^-(x)$ — in which a mass starts at rest at the very peak of the hill. Hand simulate the QSIM algorithm on this problem to determine all of its possible behaviors. Do *not* treat a quiescent state as ineligible for successor states.

4. For the bathtub and spring examples in section 5.5, apply the P-transitions in table 5.1 to the variable values at time t_0 to propose possible qualitative values for time (t_0, t_1).

5. Variables are formally defined as continuously differentiable functions whose range is a closed interval on the *extended* real number line, $[-\infty, \infty]$. Thus, the points at infinity — the landmarks $-\infty$ and $+\infty$ — are included in the quantity space. This enforces the invariant that a qualitative value is either equal to a landmark, or in an open interval bounded by two landmarks. What revisions would be

required to the transition table in table 5.1 if infinite values were excluded from the domains of the variables?

6. Create an instance of the transition table in table 5.1 that specifies the possible transitions in the $\{+, 0, -\}$ quantity space.

7. Along the other two branches of the predicted behavior of the bathtub system in section 5.5.1, determine the landmarks, the corresponding value tuples, and the states of the quantity spaces and constraints.

8. Prove the correctness of the rules in section 5.4.2, "Infinite Values and Infinite Time."

9. Formalize the temporal ordering on states in the behavior tree by observing that $completion(S_1, S_2)$ implies that $S_1 = S_2$ in the temporal order, while $successor(S_1, S_2)$ implies that $S_1 < S_2$. Show that the states in the behavior tree are partially ordered, while the behaviors are exactly the longest totally ordered subsets of the partial order.

10. Implement a stability-labeling algorithm based on the discussion in section 5.4.3, and test it on a variety of types of fixed points. Does it give the right answer on stable and unstable spiral fixed points? Why? How about vortexes?

11. By hand, construct the total envisionment of the monotonic damped spring: $x'' + f(x') + g(x) = 0$, where $f, g \in M_0^+$.

12. Can you find an example in which a total envisionment generated by the create-all-states-and-link strategy includes a path that violates the alternation between time-points and time-intervals? Or can you show that no such path can exist?

13. (Research Problem.) Are there conditions under which a differential equation $ODE \wedge State(t_0)$ would have a reasonable solution $u(t)$, but the set of functions Beh determined by the structural abstraction between ODE and QDE would not all be reasonable functions? What are those conditions?

14. (Research Problem.) Design and implement a parallel simulation algorithm that exploits the independence of the different branches of the behavior tree.

15. (Research Problem.) Can we define a useful set of QDEs, and an effective set of qualitative reasoning techniques, that will support a *completeness* theorem: all predicted behaviors are real possibilities?

16. (Research Problem.) What conclusions can be drawn by combining results from both an envisionment and a behavior simulation, that could not be drawn from one style or the other individually? How should such joint inference methods be coordinated?

6 Case Studies: Elementary Qualitative Models

There are a number of interesting and important mechanisms that can be modeled and simulated successfully using the elementary qualitative reasoning methods we have seen already. This chapter presents several examples.

- Open-ended one-tank "bathtub" system.
- Thermostat: Proportional control.
- Equilibrium mechanisms in the kidney.
  - The Starling Equilibrium.
  - Water balance.
  - Sodium balance.

6.1 One-Compartment Balance System

The world is full of "bathtubs": systems that can be viewed as a single accumulation which reflects a balance between inflow and outflow (figure 6.1). The feedback between the amount accumulated and the rate of outflow gives the system interesting dynamics.

These "bathtubs" include the water in one's bloodstream (likewise glucose, sodium, oxygen, etc.), the kinetic energy in one's automobile, the heat content of one's home, the CO_2 in one's atmosphere, the PCBs in one's water supply, the money in one's bank account, the deficit in one's economy, the population of one's country, and many others.

In this model of the bathtub, we make explicit constraints that represent different sorts of knowledge about the physical system (figure 6.2).

- $level = M^+(amount)$ represents the geometry of the container.
- $pressure = M^+(level)$ is linear in the usual open tank, but depends on the density of the fluid in the tank, and would certainly be non-linear for a balloon.
- $fp = M^+(pressure)$ represents the contribution of pressure to outflow, which is proportional to the square root of pressure, at least in the ideal case.
- $outflow = fp \cdot area$ is also proportional to the area of the orifice.

Figure 6.3 gives the QSIM QDE implementing this model, and figure 6.4 shows the typical three behaviors resulting from filling the tank from empty at a constant rate: equilibrium between inflow and outflow with the tank partly full, overflow, and equilibrium exactly at the brim.

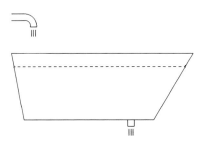

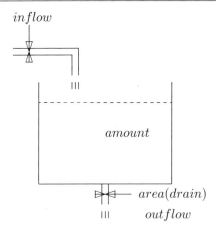

Figure 6.1
The one-tank system.

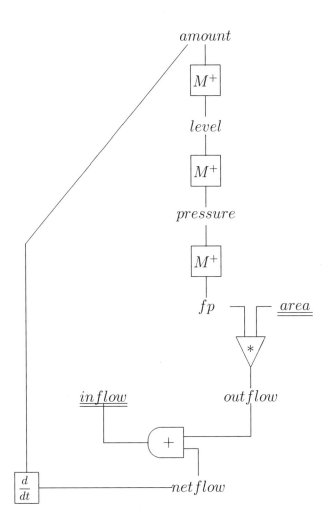

Figure 6.2
Graphical constraint model for the bathtub with drain.

```
(define-QDE Bathtub-with-drain
  (quantity-spaces
    (amount    (0 full inf))
    (level     (0 top inf))
    (pressure  (0 inf))
    (fp        (0 inf))
    (area      (0 open inf))
    (outflow   (0 inf))
    (inflow    (0 if* inf))
    (netflow   (minf 0 inf)))
  (constraints
    ((M+ amount level)      (0 0) (full top) (inf inf))
    ((M+ level pressure)    (0 0) (inf inf))
    ((M+ pressure fp)       (0 0) (inf inf))
    ((mult fp area outflow))
    ((add netflow outflow inflow))
    ((d/dt amount netflow))
    ((constant inflow))
    ((constant area)))
  (transitions
    ((level (top inc)) -> tub-overflows)))

(defun fill-bathtub-open-drain ()
  (let ((init (make-new-state :from-qde Bathtub-with-drain
                              :assert-values '((inflow (if* std))
                                               (drain   (open std))
                                               (amount (0 nil)))
                              :text "Filling at constant rate")))
    (qsim init)
    (qsim-display init)))
```

Figure 6.3
QSIM code for the bathtub model.

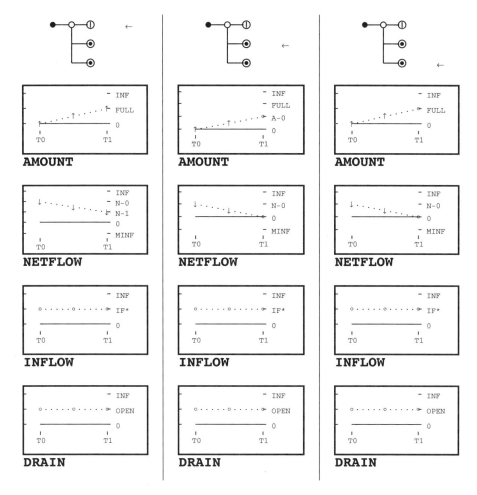

Figure 6.4
The three behaviors predicted by the bathtub model.

6.2   Thermostat: Proportional Control

The familiar home thermostat controls temperature by turning the furnace on or off when certain thresholds are crossed. Our thermostat model has two aspects:

1. The general structure of the home, as a container for heat, with heat flows to the environment and from a furnace, affected by exogenous variables such as the outside temperature, the insulation factor, the thermal mass of the house, the heating capacity of the furnace, and the desired setpoint temperature.[1]

2. The controller model, which determines the rate of heatflow from the furnace as a function of the error between setpoint and inside temperature.

Qualitative simulation predicts three possible behaviors in response to a sudden decrease in outside temperature. The behavior shown in figure 6.7 is the typical case: an increase in heatflow until it balances the heat loss to the environment. The other two behaviors represent the cases where the heater reaches its maximum capacity.

Notice that when steady state is reached, the inside temperature has not been restored to the setpoint. This type of steady-state offset is an important qualitative property of proportional control. Since the system's response increases with the magnitude of the error term, if there is a steady-state deviation in the environment, then there must be a steady-state error to provide a continuing response. On-off control (section 8.5) and Proportional-Integral control (section 11.6) take different approaches to eliminating this problem.

6.3   Equilibrium Mechanisms in the Kidney

These models were constructed as part of a cognitive study of causal and qualitative reasoning in expert physicians (Kuipers and Kassirer, 1984), which presented subjects with a problem involving a slightly atypical case of a kidney disorder called the *nephrotic syndrome*.[2]

In the nephrotic syndrome, a patient retains salt and water and suffers swelling (*edema*) of the face and legs; the swelling is an important diagnostic finding. Because of a self-induced low-salt diet, this particular patient experienced no swelling,

---

[1] In later cases, this structural model is shared by several different thermal control models. In other models, we replace the proportional controller with an on-off controller (section 8.5), or a proportional-integral (PI) controller (section 11.6).

[2] The technical content of this and other medical examples is neither complete nor up-to-date, and should be treated as purely illustrative.

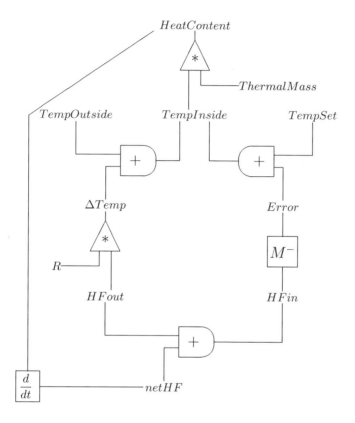

Figure 6.5
Heater structure.

though other signs and laboratory results allowed an unambiguous diagnosis to be made. The atypical case lets us compare three different models of the same subject: the model of salt and water handling by the healthy kidney, the pathophysiology of nephrotic syndrome, and the idiosyncracies of this particular patient.

The nephrotic syndrome case illustrates qualitative reasoning about equilibrium processes, which are central to many physiological mechanisms. Two important equilibrium processes are disturbed in the nephrotic syndrome: the transfer of salt

```
(define-QDE Thermostat-Proportional
  (quantity-spaces
    (heat     (0 inf)                        "Heat content")
    (mass     (0 inf)                        "Thermal mass")
    (TempIn   (0 RoomTemp inf)               "Temp(inside)")
    (TempOut  (0 Cold RoomTemp Hot inf)      "Temp(outside)")
    (TempSet  (0 RoomTemp inf)               "Temp(set)")
    (dTemp    (minf 0 inf)                    "dTemp(in,out)")
    (error    (minf 0 inf)                    "error=in-set")
    (R        (0 inf)                         "Heat flow resistance")
    (HFout    (minf 0 inf)                    "Heat flow (to environment)")
    (HFin     (minf 0 inf)                    "Heat flow (from heater/cooler)")
    (netHF    (minf 0 inf)                    "net Heat Flow"))
  (constraints
    ((mult TempIn Mass Heat))
    ((add TempOut dTemp TempIn)     (RoomTemp 0 RoomTemp) )
    ((add TempSet error TempIn)     (RoomTemp 0 RoomTemp) )
    ((mult R HFout dTemp))
    ((add HFout netHF HFin))
    ((m- error HFin)               (0 0) (minf inf) (inf minf))
    ((d/dt Heat netHF))
    ((constant Mass))
    ((constant TempOut))
    ((constant TempSet))
    ((constant R))))

(defun low-temp ()
  (let* ((normal (make-new-state :from-qde        Thermostat-Proportional
                                 :assert-values '((HFin     (0 std))
                                                  (Heat     ((0 inf) std))
                                                  (TempIn   (RoomTemp nil))
                                                  (Mass     ((0 inf) std))
                                                  (TempOut  (RoomTemp std))
                                                  (TempSet  (RoomTemp std))
                                                  (R        ((0 inf) std)))
                                 :text "Normal state; room temperature."))
         (start (make-new-state :from-state   normal
                                :inherit      '(Mass TempSet R TempIn)
                                :assert-values '((HFin     (0 nil))
                                                 (TempOut (Cold std)))
                                :text "Suddenly cold outdoors; furnace off.")))
    (qsim start)
    (qsim-display start)))
```

Figure 6.6
QDE for the proportional-control thermostat model.

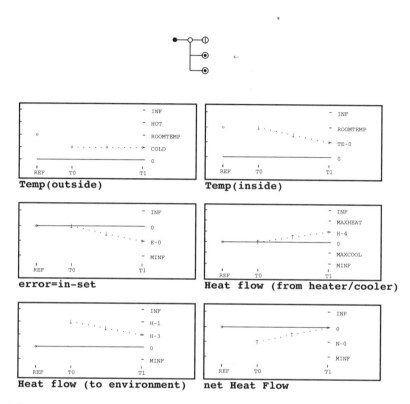

Figure 6.7
Unique behavior predicted for the proportional thermostat model.

and water across capillary walls (the *Starling equilibrium*), and the transfer of salt and water from the plasma into the urine. The Starling equilibrium determines the flow of water between the plasma and the tissues (the spaces between the cells), according to the balance of competing *hydrostatic pressure* and *oncotic pressure* in the plasma and in the tissues. The second important equilibrium, also controlled by the kidney, determines the total amount of salt and water in the body. Under normal circumstances, if the body contains too much salt and water, the kidney excretes more of each into the urine; if there is too little, it cuts back on excretion.

In the nephrotic syndrome, both of these equilibria are shifted to new stable points, changing the quantity of salt and water in the body and causing problems for the patient. The basic cause of nephrotic syndrome is that the diseased kidney excretes protein that it was supposed to retain, and consequently plasma proteins (particularly albumin) are depleted. The amount of protein in the plasma determines its oncotic pressure, and hence is an important factor in the Starling equilibrium. With less protein in the blood, the Starling equilibrium shifts, moving some water from the plasma into the tissues. This movement of extra water into the tissues in itself usually causes no clinical manifestations. However, the shift of water to the tissues leaves the plasma volume low, so the kidney starts to retain water rather than allowing it to be excreted in the urine. The Starling equilibrium, of course, continues to shift much of this additional fluid into the tissues, and substantial edema develops. From the patient's point of view, this accumulation can produce as much as fifty pounds of extra water in the legs and abdomen. To understand the mechanism of edema in nephrotic syndrome requires an understanding of both equilibria and their interaction.

Retention of salt by the kidney is central to the mechanism whereby the kidney retains water. In response to a contraction of plasma volume, the kidney's primary response is to retain salt. Salt retention, in turn, is what causes water retention. The particular patient whose history formed the basis of the experiment had selected a low-salt diet, so the kidney was unable to retain much salt or water, and the edema was consequently much less than a physician would expect, based on the severe decrease in blood proteins.

6.3.1   The Starling Equilibrium Mechanism

The Starling equilibrium is essentially a complex U-tube. The plasma (P) and interstitial (I) compartments are the two tanks of the U-tube, and the balance between them is controlled by four forces: the hydrostatic and oncotic pressures in the two tanks.

The QDE model of the Starling equilibrium is shown in figures 6.8 and 6.9. Responding to a sudden decrease in $amt(protein, P)$, the model predicts a single qualitative behavior as shown in figure 6.10.

6.3.2   Water Balance

Water balance is controlled by a system based around anti-diuretic hormone (ADH), which responds primarily to changes in the concentration of sodium in the plasma, and affects the net excretion of water through two pathways.

• The *amount* of water in the plasma, $amt(water, P)$, influences the glomerular filtration rate, which is the water taken out of the blood into the nephron.

• The *concentration* of sodium in the plasma, $c(Na, P)$, controls the secretion of ADH, which in turn influences reabsorption of water from the nephron back into the blood.

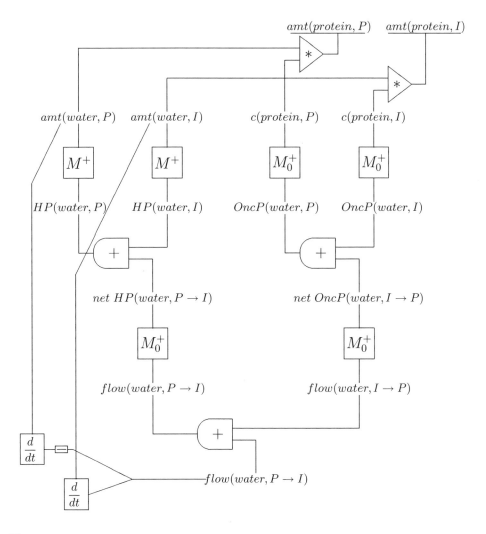

Figure 6.8
Starling equilibrium structure.

```
(Define-QDE Starling
  (quantity-spaces
    (PP      (0 inf)        "amt(protein,P)")
    (PI      (0 inf)        "amt(protein,I)")
    (AFP     (0 inf)        "amt(water,P)")
    (WI      (0 inf)        "amt(water,I)")
    (ECW     (0 inf)        "extra-cellular water")
    (CPP     (0 inf)        "c(protein,P)")
    (CPI     (0 inf)        "c(protein,I)")
    (HPP     (0 inf)        "HP(water,P->I)")
    (HPI     (0 inf)        "HP(water,I->P)")
    (OPI     (0 inf)        "OncP(water,I->P)")
    (OPP     (0 inf)        "OncP(water,P->I)")
    (HPPI    (0 inf)        "net HP(water,P->I)")
    (OPIP    (0 inf)        "net OncP(water,I->P)")
    (FWPI    (minf 0 inf)   "flow(water,P->I)")
    (FWIP    (minf 0 inf)   "flow(water,I->P)")
    (NFPI    (minf 0 inf)   "net flow(water,P->I)")
    (MNFPI   (minf 0 inf)   "-NFPI"))
  (constraints
    ((mult WI CPI PI))
    ((mult AFP CPP PP))
    ((add AFP WI ECW))
    ((M+ AFP HPP)                  (0 0) (inf inf))
    ((M+ WI HPI)                   (0 0) (inf inf))
    ((M+ CPP OPI)                  (0 0) (inf inf))
    ((M+ CPI OPP)                  (0 0) (inf inf))
    ((M+ HPPI FWPI)                (0 0) (inf inf))
    ((M+ OPIP FWIP)                (0 0) (inf inf))
    ((add HPI HPPI HPP))
    ((add OPP OPIP OPI))
    ((add FWIP NFPI FWPI))
    ((d/dt AFP MNFPI))
    ((d/dt WI NFPI))
    ((minus NFPI MNFPI)            (0 0) (inf minf) (minf inf))
    ((constant pp))
    ((constant pi))
    ((constant ecw)))
  (unreachable-values (opip 0))))
```

Figure 6.9
The Starling equilibrium QDE.

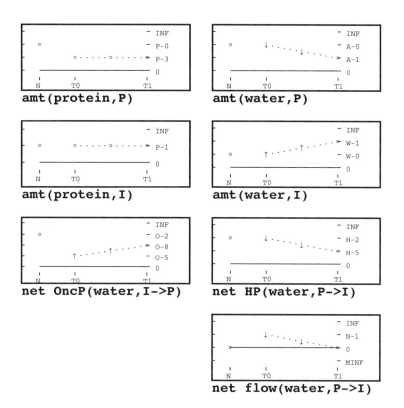

Figure 6.10
Unique behavior of the Starling equilibrium.

Low plasma protein causes a decrease in plasma oncotic pressure, which causes a net flow of water from the plasma to the interstitial compartment, until increasing hydrostatic pressure in that compartment restores the system to balance.

This model assumes that two variables are essentially constant, at least when considered on the time-scale of this equilibrium (i.e., minutes):

- the amount of sodium in the plasma, $amt(Na, P)$; and
- the rate of water intake, $net\ flow(water, ingest \rightarrow P)$.

In the example shown, starting the normal steady state, a sudden increase in water intake rate (from a transfusion, for example) causes volume to increase, and hence water excretion, until the balance between inflow and outflow is restored (figure 6.13).

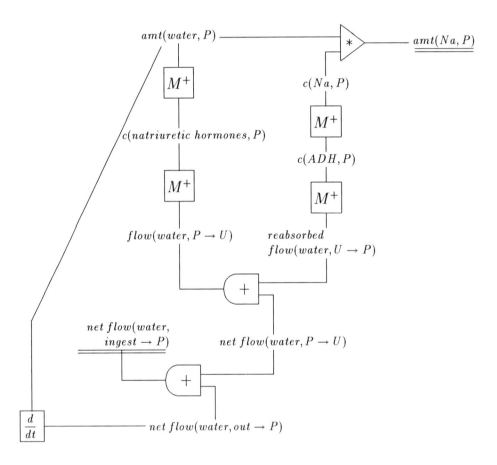

Figure 6.11
Constraint model for the water balance system.

```
(define-QDE Water-Balance
  (text "Water balance via ADH")
  (quantity-spaces
    (afp   (0 inf)        "amt(water,P)")
    (ecw   (0 inf)        "extra-cellular water")
    (wi    (0 inf)        "amt(water,I)")
    (anp   (0 inf)        "amt(Na,P)")
    (nfwip (0 inf)        "net flow(water,in->P)")
    (cnh   (0 inf)        "c(natriuretic-hormones,P)")
    (cnp   (0 inf)        "c(Na,P)")
    (cadh  (0 inf)        "c(ADH,P)")
    (rfup  (0 inf)        "reabs.flow(water,U->P)")
    (nfpu  (0 inf)        "net flow(water,P->U)")
    (ffwpu (minf 0 inf)   "flow(water,P->U)")
    (nfwop (minf 0 inf)   "net flow(water,out->P)"))
  (constraints
    ((M+ afp wi)          (0 0)  (inf inf))
    ((M+ afp cnh)         (0 0)  (inf inf))
    ((M+ cnh ffwpu)       (0 0)  (inf inf))
    ((mult afp cnp anp))
    ((add afp wi ecw))
    ((add rfup nfpu ffwpu))
    ((M+ cnp cadh)        (0 0)  (inf inf))
    ((M+ cadh rfup)       (0 0)  (inf inf))
    ((d/dt afp nfwop))
    ((add nfpu nfwop nfwip))
    ((constant anp))
    ((constant nfwip)))
  (unreachable-values (nfpu 0))))

(defun high-water-intake ()
  (let* ((normal (make-new-state :from-qde    Water-Balance
                                 :assert-values '((afp   ((0 inf) std))
                                                  (anp   ((0 inf) std))
                                                  (nfwip ((0 inf) std)))))
         (init (make-new-state :from-state normal
                               :inherit '(afp anp)
                               :perturb '((nfwip +))
                               :text "Increased water intake")))
    (qsim init)
    (qsim-display init :reference-states '((N ,normal)))))
```

Figure 6.12
The water balance QDE.

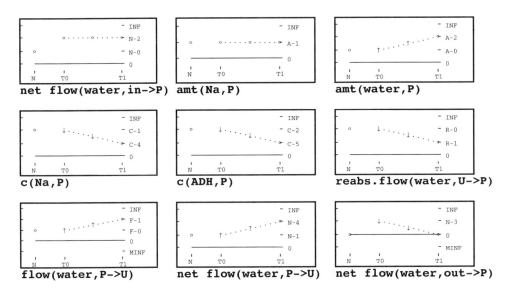

Figure 6.13
Unique behavior of water balance mechanism.

An increased rate of water intake causes an increased plasma water volume, which causes decreased plasma sodium concentration and decreased ADH concentration. This decreases water reabsorption in the tubules of the kidney, which causes increased water excretion until the system reaches balance.

6.3.3   Sodium Balance

Sodium balance is maintained by a system based around aldosterone, which responds primarily to changes in the *volume* of the plasma; i.e., to the amount of *water* in the plasma. Aldosterone controls the reabsorption of filtered sodium from the nephron back into the blood. This mechanism is based around the assumption that changes in plasma volume reflect changes in plasma sodium. Thus, its assumptions are as follows:

- The rate of sodium intake, $flow(Na, ingest \rightarrow P)$, is constant.

- The monotonic function relation

$$amt(water, P) = M^+(amt(Na, P))$$

can be treated as instantaneous.

The functional relation between $amt(Na, P)$ and $amt(water, P)$ represents one view of the behavior of the water balance system. The abstraction of the dynamic

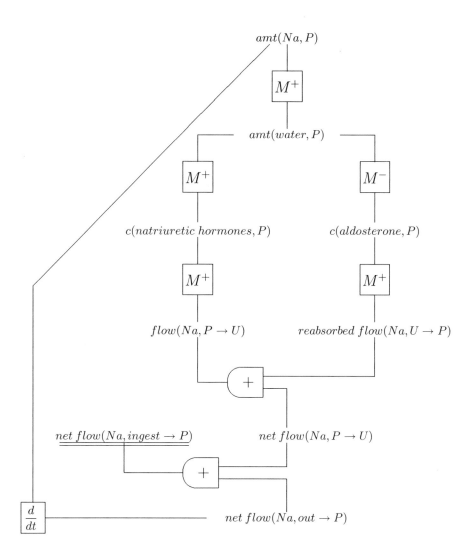

Figure 6.14
Constraint model for the sodium balance system.

```
(define-QDE SODIUM-BALANCE
  (text "Sodium balance via aldosterone")
  (quantity-spaces
    (anp   (0 inf)       "amt(Na,P)")
    (afp   (0 inf)       "amt(water,P)")
    (cnh   (0 inf)       "c(natriuretic-hormones,P)")
    (ffnpu (0 inf)       "flow(Na,P->U)")
    (caldo (0 inf)       "c(aldosterone,P)")
    (rfnup (0 inf)       "reabs.flow(Na,U->P)")
    (nfnpu (0 inf)       "net flow(Na,P->U)")
    (nfnip (0 inf)       "net flow(Na,in->P)")
    (nfnp  (minf 0 inf)  "net change(Na,P)"))
  (constraints
    ((M+ anp afp)            (0 0) (inf inf))
    ((M+ afp cnh)            (0 0) (inf inf))
    ((M+ cnh ffnpu)          (0 0) (inf inf))
    ((M- afp caldo)          (0 inf) (inf 0) )
    ((M+ caldo rfnup)        (0 0) (inf inf))
    ((add rfnup nfnpu ffnpu))
    ((add nfnpu nfnp nfnip))
    ((d/dt anp nfnp))
    ((constant nfnip)))
  (unreachable-values (nfnpu 0) (anp 0 inf))))

(defun high-salt-intake ()
  (let* ((normal (make-new-state :from-qde      Sodium-Balance
                                 :assert-values '((anp   ((0 inf) std))
                                                  (nfnip ((0 inf) std)))))
         (init   (make-new-state :from-state normal
                                 :inherit    '(anp)
                                 :perturb    '((nfnip +))
                                 :text "High salt intake")))
    (qsim init)
    (qsim-display init :reference-states '((N ,normal)))))
```

Figure 6.15
The sodium balance QDE.

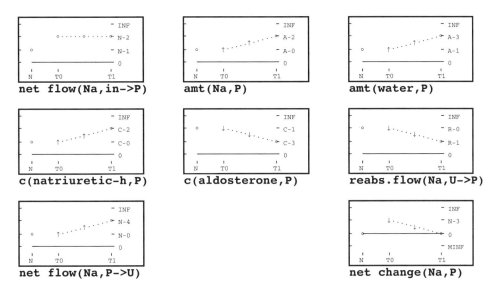

Figure 6.16
Unique behavior of sodium balance mechanism.

An increased rate of sodium intake causes the plasma sodium level to rise, which causes the plasma water volume to rise (via the water balance mechanism). This causes increased water outflow via natriuretic hormones, and decreased reabsorption via aldosterone. Sodium excretion thus increases until it balances the increased intake rate.

behavior of one system into an instantaneous relationship from the point of view of another system is justified by the fact that the water balance system (which equilibrates in minutes) is much faster than the sodium balance system (equilibrates in hours to days). (See chapter 12.)

In the example shown (figure 6.16), starting from a normal steady state, a sudden increase in sodium intake rate (from a high-sodium diet, for example) simultaneously causes the amounts of sodium and water in the plasma to increase. In response to the increased water volume, more sodium is excreted (i.e., less is reabsorbed) until increased excretion balances the increased intake. Notice, however, that in the new steady state, water volume remains increased.

6.4 Problems

1. Extend the `Simple-Trajectory` model (section 2.4) to include air resistance monotonically increasing with velocity:

(a) in still air;

(b) in a constant-velocity wind.

2. A major advantage of qualitative modeling is that pathophysiology is naturally derived from knowledge of the normal physiological mechanisms. Build qualitative models of various disorders by simple modifications of the normal water and sodium balance mechanism descriptions.

- Too much ADH. The Syndrome of Inappropriate Secretion of Anti-Diuretic hormone (SIADH) can be modeled by eliminating one of the M^+ constraints in the water balance structure and declaring $c(ADH, P)$ to be high and constant.

- Not enough ADH. Diabetes Insipidus can be modeled by breaking either of two constraints in the structure, leaving water reabsorption abnormally low.

- Too much aldosterone. Primary hyperaldosteronism can be modeled by breaking the constraint between $amt(water, P)$ and $c(aldosterone, P)$, and declaring $c(aldosterone, P)$ to be high and constant.

- Not enough aldosterone. Hypoaldosteronism can be modeled similarly.

7 Comparative Statics

7.1 The Quasi-Equilibrium Assumption

In this chapter, we consider an important special case of qualitative model: one where we can assume that the system is always at, or very near, a point of stable equilibrium. We say that such a model satisfies the *quasi-equilibrium assumption*. In such a situation, we are interested in the relationship between an initial equilibrium state and the state resulting from a small perturbation to the system; this is the problem of *comparative statics*.

In previous chapters, our concern has been with *dynamic* behavior: some sudden event places a system in a non-equilibrium state, from which the system moves according to the constraints in its QDE, perhaps eventually reaching an equilibrium state, perhaps not. Comparative statics is concerned with the initial and final equilibrium states, but not with the dynamic behavior between them. This focus lets us deal with fewer distinctions among behaviors, since we can ignore the transient states. It is also a bit easier to solve comparative statics problems, since we need only solve the constraints in the QDE, rather than doing dynamic simulation.

However, these benefits depend on three aspects of the quasi-equilibrium assumption. First, the behaviors must start from, and lead to, *equilibrium* states. Second, the equilibrium states must be *stable*. Third, the perturbations must be *small*.

We view the quasi-equilibrium assumption as a kind of *time-scale abstraction*, in which we treat the dynamic behavior leading from one equilibrium to another as taking place "instantaneously," leaving us with only static constraints describing the locus of equilibrium states.

Comparative statics has been extensively developed and widely applied in economics. Samuelson (1983) presents comparative statics and a variety of related qualitative mathematical methods, along with extensive examples of their application in economics. This classic volume provided the mathematical foundations for economics in the last half of the twentieth century. Iwasaki and Simon (1986a) and Kalagnanam, Simon, and Iwasaki (1991) include summaries of this work addressed to the artificial intelligence community.

Loop analysis is a type of comparative statics applied to qualitative models of stable equilibrium systems expressed in the form of signed directed graphs. Puccia and Levins (1985) describe loop analysis in great detail, providing a large number of examples from ecology and other areas, along with stability criteria for complex systems.

7.2 Solving Comparative Statics Problems

With the machinery we have already developed, it is relatively simple to define a procedure **QSEA** (for "Quasi-Static Equilibrium Analysis") that solves comparative statics problems. By convention, we will refer to the initial reference state for a comparative statics problem as r, and to the final state or states resulting from the perturbation as s.

Algorithm **QSEA**:

1. Start with a QDE.

2. Define an initial stable reference state r in one of the basic qualitative states of the QDE.

3. Specify a direction of perturbation $[x(s)]_* \in \{+, 0, -\}$ for each exogenous variable x in the QDE, with respect to its value in the reference state.

4. Use `Cfilter` to form all complete qualitative states s consistent with the perturbed values and the constraints of the QDE.

5. Filter out any state s for which the perturbation $r \to s$ is not small.

DEFINITION 16 The *basic qualitative states* of a QDE are the qualitative states definable in terms of the initial quantity spaces in the QDE. The *basic qualitative value* of a variable is its value described in terms of the initial quantity spaces in the QDE.

Since QSIM can create new landmarks representing new qualitative distinctions, several qualitative states after simulation may fall within a single basic qualitative state.

DEFINITION 17 A perturbation $r \to s$ is *small* if for every variable x in the QDE, either

- the basic qualitative value of $x(r)$ is an open interval and the basic qualitative value of $x(s)$ is the same interval; or

- the basic qualitative value of $x(r)$ is a landmark and the basic qualitative value of $x(s)$ is either the same landmark or one of the immediately adjacent open intervals.

Normally, comparative statics problems are defined by specifying a reference state r whose basic qualitative state includes interval values. Since perturbations are small, the resulting final states s must lie within the same basic qualitative state as

r. Occasionally, we will consider cases where the basic qualitative state of r has only landmark values, so the final states s may lie in adjacent basic qualitative states.

When specifying the initial perturbation, if the variable x has the quantity space $\cdots x_1 \cdots x_2 \cdots x_3 \cdots$, and $x(r) = \langle x_2, std \rangle$ in the reference state, then $[x(s)]_* = [+]$ means that $x(s) = \langle (x_2, x_3), std \rangle$. That is, $x(s)$ must be within the immediate adjacent interval.

When solving for the states s consistent with a given perturbation from r, we add a constraint to enforce the quasi-equilibrium assumption:

For all variables x in the QDE, $[\dot{x}] = 0$.

Recall that the derivative constraint, ((d/dt x y)), implies that $[\dot{x}] = [y]_0$, so we can also conclude that $[y]_0 = 0$ in this case. In section 7.3.3, we generalize this assumption to allow comparative reasoning statics about slowly moving equilibrium states.

Comparative statics is only valid when the states r and s represent stable equilibrium states. For now, we will simply assume stability, returning to examine the question carefully in section 7.4.

7.3 Example: The Water Tank

The water tank — a one-compartment equilibrium system — serves well to illustrate this situation. The system and its QDE are shown in figure 7.1. For comparative statics problems, it is important to know the exogenous variables of the QDE. They are specified in the **independent** clause of the QDE. It may be possible to identify the exogenous variables of a QDE automatically from the structure of the constraints in the QDE, using the dependency-tracing algorithms in Simon, 1952; Iwasaki and Simon, 1986a; and Iwasaki, 1988. (Problem 3.)

Since comparative statics is concerned with the effects of small perturbations from an initial reference state, we will be able to do most of our reasoning in the domain of signs, $\mathcal{S} = \{+, 0, -\}$, using the confluence representation (section 3.4). Recall that the term $[x]_0$ represents the sign of x; $[x]_a = [x - a]_0$ represents the deviation from some reference value a of the variable x; and $[x]_*$ represents the deviation of x from its value in some reference state. The unsubscripted form $[x]$ is used as an abbreviation for $[x]_0$.

7.3.1 Solve for Basic Qualitative States

Reasoning about perturbations using $[x]_*$ terms frequently depends on knowledge of the absolute signs $[x]_0$ of the variables. (See problem 1.) Thus, we begin by

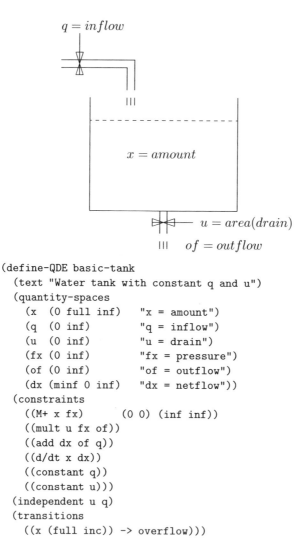

```
(define-QDE basic-tank
  (text "Water tank with constant q and u")
  (quantity-spaces
    (x  (0 full inf)    "x = amount")
    (q  (0 inf)         "q = inflow")
    (u  (0 inf)         "u = drain")
    (fx (0 inf)         "fx = pressure")
    (of (0 inf)         "of = outflow")
    (dx (minf 0 inf)    "dx = netflow"))
  (constraints
    ((M+ x fx)      (0 0) (inf inf))
    ((mult u fx of))
    ((add dx of q))
    ((d/dt x dx))
    ((constant q))
    ((constant u)))
  (independent u q)
  (transitions
    ((x (full inc)) -> overflow)))
```

Figure 7.1
Water tank model: $\dot{x} = q - u \cdot f(x)$.

determining the basic qualitative states of the system: the states characterized by the qualitative magnitudes of the variables with respect to their pre-existing landmark values. When 0 is the only landmark of interest, we can use the $\{+, 0, -\}$ quantity space and confluences over $[x]_0$ terms to solve for the basic qualitative states.

Since the M^+ constraint in this QDE has corresponding values at $(0,0)$, we can translate the constraints to magnitude confluences:

$$
\begin{aligned}
fx &= M^+(x) & & & [fx]_0 &= [x]_0 \\
of &= fx \cdot u & &\Longrightarrow & [of]_0 &= [fx]_0 \cdot [u]_0 \\
q - of &= dx = 0 & & & [q]_0 &- [of]_0 = 0
\end{aligned}
$$

Using `Cfilter` (chapter 4) to solve the qualitative constraints, and taking into account that none of the variables may be negative, we can determine that the four basic qualitative states consistent with the equilibrium equations are the following:

	(1)	(2)	(3)	(4)
u	+	+	0	0
q	+	0	0	0
of	+	0	0	0
fx	+	0	0	+
x	+	0	0	+

1. There is water in the tank, the drain is open, and inflow and outflow are in balance.

2. The drain is open, but there is no inflow and no water in the tank.

3. The drain is closed, but there is no inflow and no water in the tank.

4. The drain is closed, there is water in the tank, but there is no inflow.

If it is necessary to take into account the non-zero landmark **full** in the quantity space of **x**, then we can no longer use the $\{+, 0, -\}$ quantity space and the confluence representation for constraints. The full quantity space representation lets us make finer distinctions among basic qualitative states, but also requires a less compact notation. The following table assumes that we can recognize that values of $x > full$ are outside of the current operating region.

	(1a)	(1b)	(2)	(3)	(4a)	(4b)
u	$(0, \infty)$	$(0, \infty)$	$(0, \infty)$	0	0	0
q	$(0, \infty)$	$(0, \infty)$	0	0	0	0
of	$(0, \infty)$	$(0, \infty)$	0	0	0	0
fx	$(0, \infty)$	$(0, \infty)$	0	0	$(0, \infty)$	$(0, \infty)$
x	$(0, full)$	$full$	0	0	$(0, full)$	$full$

In most comparative statics problems, a small perturbation leaves the system in the same basic qualitative state. However, from certain states, even a small perturbation moves the system to another basic qualitative state.

• Starting in state (2), where $[q]_0 = 0$, any perturbation $[q]_* = [+]$ must bring the system into state (1).

• Starting in states (3) or (4), where $[u]_0 = [q]_0 = 0$, and applying the perturbation $[q]_* = [+]$ while keeping $[u]_* = 0$, there is no corresponding equilibrium solution at all! (See problem 2.)

We will focus our attention here on comparative statics problems that have solutions within the same basic qualitative state, in this case state (1) (or under the richer description, state (1a)).

7.3.2 Solve a Comparative Statics Problem

Within the first basic qualitative state — where all variables are positive — suppose we want to determine the effect of a perturbation on the system. We posit a reference state in this region, and reason with confluences in terms of the $[x]_*$ qualitative value description with respect to this equilibrium value.

Notice that the multiplication constraint translates to an additive confluence, since we know that fx and u are both positive.

$$
\begin{aligned}
fx &= M^+(x) & & [fx]_* = [x]_* \\
of &= fx \cdot u & \implies & [of]_* = [fx]_* + [u]_* \\
q - of &= dx = 0 & & [q]_* - [of]_* = 0
\end{aligned}
\qquad (7.1)
$$

We will solve three different perturbation problems, starting in this state:

1. Suppose we impose a perturbation on this equilibrium by increasing q suddenly: $[q]_* = [+]$. The confluences (7.1) can be solved to determine which perturbations

of the entire system are consistent with a given input change. It is easy to see that
if $[q]_* = [+]$ and $[u]_* = 0$, the only solution is

$$[of]_* = [fx]_* = [x]_* = [+].$$

2. Suppose that q remains constant but we open the drain somewhat. Since $[q]_* = 0$
and $[u]_* = [+]$, we can conclude that $[of]_* = 0$ and $[fx]_* = [x]_* = [-]$. That is, an
initially increased outflow of is a transient effect, leading to a lower level of water
in the tank, where q and of are in equilibrium again.

3. If we superimpose two perturbations, $[q]_* = [+]$ and $[u]_* = [+]$, we can conclude
with certainty that $[of]_* = [+]$, but there are three possible solutions for the rest
of the parameters:

   (a) $[fx]_* = [x]_* = [+]$
   (b) $[fx]_* = [x]_* = [0]$
   (c) $[fx]_* = [x]_* = [-]$

Just as with dynamic qualitative simulation, the qualitative information given is
not specific enough to select a unique new equilibrium state.

7.3.3 Solving for Initial and Final Response

Comparative statics gives us the long-term response of a system to a perturbation.
The immediate direction of change responding to the perturbation can be obtained
by solving for the initial states under the usual dynamic simulation assumptions.

This combination of short-term and long-term response, without the intermediate
transient behavior, can be a useful tool while avoiding some of the costs of dynamic
simulation (Rose and Kramer, 1991).

Given a perturbation at t_0, we define the initial response in terms of the values
of the variables in the immediately following open interval (t_0, t_1). This is because
a variable whose first- or higher-order derivative is influenced by the perturbation
could have magnitude equal to its reference value at t_0, but move off the reference
value at (t_0, t_1).

1. For the perturbation $[q]_* = [+]$ while $[u]_* = 0$, the following table shows the
initial QSIM state (at t_0), the initial response (at (t_0, t_1)), and the final equilibrium
response (at $t = \infty$).

		initial	*final*
	t_0	(t_0, t_1)	$t = \infty$
u	$\langle 0, std \rangle$	0	0
q	$\langle +, std \rangle$	+	+
of	$\langle 0, inc \rangle$	+	+
fx	$\langle 0, inc \rangle$	+	+
x	$\langle 0, inc \rangle$	+	+
dx	$\langle +, dec \rangle$	+	0

Notice that the initial response of the variables x, fx, and of to the perturbation is only visible in the magnitude at (t_0, t_1).

2. The perturbation $[u]_* = [-]$ while $[q]_* = 0$ gives us the following initial and final response:

		initial	*final*
	t_0	(t_0, t_1)	$t = \infty$
u	$\langle +, std \rangle$	+	+
q	$\langle 0, std \rangle$	0	0
of	$\langle +, dec \rangle$	+	0
fx	$\langle 0, dec \rangle$	−	−
x	$\langle 0, dec \rangle$	−	−
dx	$\langle -, inc \rangle$	−	0

Notice that the perturbation has a transient effect on outflow, $[of(t_0, t_1)]_* = [+]$, but no long-term effect: $[of(t = \infty)]_* = 0$. There are also systems that exhibit "inverse response," where the initial and final responses have opposite signs.

3. The perturbation $[u]_* = [+]$ with $[q]_* = [+]$ has an ambiguous effect at both initial and final states. The ambiguity can be recognized and controlled, but not by using the methods we have seen here.

7.3.4   Generalize to Slowly Moving Equilibrium

Once we have abstracted away the fast dynamic behavior between equilibrium states, we can reason not just about static states but about the motion of the abstracted system through a trajectory of equilibrium states. This reasoning depends on maintaining the validity of the time-scale abstraction underlying the quasi-equilibrium assumption: that is, the system must restore itself to equilibrium much more quickly than it is forced to move.

This type of reasoning is properly done using the methods of time-scale abstraction discussed in chapter 12. However, it may also possible to solve for the behavior of slowly moving equilibria by solving a set of confluences in derivative terms such as $[dx/dt]$. (See problem 5.)

7.4   Equilibrium Must Be Stable

7.4.1   The Locus of Equilibrium States

Consider the set of all possible states of the water tank, given that q and u are constant at some positive values. The variable x can vary from 0 to $+\infty$, and its value determines the values of all the other variables. We can say that this system has a one-dimensional *phase space*, corresponding to the possible values for x, in which a single point represents the entire state of the system (figure 7.2a).

Within this phase space, assuming that $q = q^*$, there is a single stable equilibrium point $x = x^*$, and all other points are non-equilibrium points, from which the system moves toward its equilibrium state.

We have seen that, starting from this equilibrium state and with $[u]_* = 0$, $[q]_* = [+]$ implies $[x]_* = [+]$. This can be visualized by making q an explicit dimension, expanding from a one-dimensional to a two-dimensional phase space, and observing that the set of equilibrium states obeys a monotonically increasing relationship between q and x (figure 7.2b).

Since q is constant, the system moves directly upward or downward from the non-equilibrium points to the locus of equilibrium values. The effect of a small perturbation to q is to move the system slightly off the equilibrium locus, from which the natural dynamics of the system returns it to equilibrium. Thus, if the perturbations are small enough or slow enough, the system essentially moves up and down along the locus of equilibrium points.

If we can ignore the small or fast dynamic changes from one equilibrium to the next, and if all other variables influencing the state of the system (e.g., u) are held constant, we can abstract this relationship to a monotonic function constraint, describing the locus of equilibrium states:

$$x = M^+(q).$$

This is a form of time-scale abstraction, allowing us to abstract a property of the *behavior* of a fast system into a constraint that can be considered part of the *structure* of a slower system. (See chapter 12.)

The phase-space view of comparative statics reasoning makes it easy to see why the assumption of stability is critical. We can construct a similar system, with a similar locus of equilibrium states, but representing an *unstable* equilibrium.

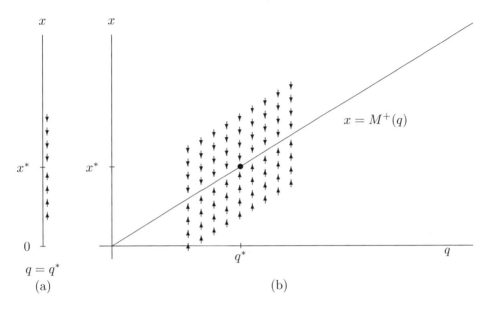

$x = M^+(q)$

x^*

q^*

$q = q^*$

(a)

(b)

- (a) For a given constant value of q, the system moves to a corresponding stable value of x.
- (b) The quasi-equilibrium assumption says that slow changes to q move the system along the line of equilibrium states, $x = M^+(q)$. (Dynamic simulation traces the path the system takes as it returns to the stable value.)

The locus of equilibrium states is not, in general, a straight line.

Figure 7.2
The locus of equilibrium states.

To illustrate this, imagine a one-tank system with water pumped *out* at a constant rate, and with an inflow rate that increases monotonically with the amount in the tank.

$$\dot{x} \;=\; M^+(x) - of$$
$$of \;=\; \text{constant}$$

This system will have an equilibrium state, where inflow exactly balances outflow, but any small perturbation from that state will be self-reinforcing, driving the system either to overflow or to empty.

In the phase-space view, non-equilibrium states flow *away* from the equilibrium locus (figure 7.3). A perturbation to one variable, no matter how small, will move the system away from equilibrium, and it will be unable to return.

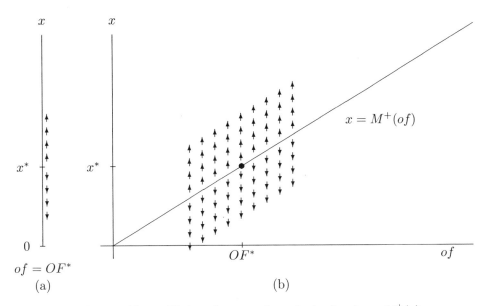

The system is in unstable equilibrium, because of constant of and $q = M^+(x)$.

- (a) For some value OF^* of of, the system is at an unstable equilibrium value x^* of x.
- (b) In such a case, after a small perturbation, the dynamics of the system will take it far from its locus of equilibrium states, $x = M^+(of)$.

Figure 7.3
Failure of comparative statics at an unstable equilibrium.

The problem is that the comparative statics problem-solving procedure QSEA will return a value just as before, representing motion along the locus of equilibrium states. Unfortunately, that solution represents a physically impossible behavior.

Thus, before applying the comparative statics method (or trusting its results), we need to assure ourselves that the system is stable.

7.4.2 Testing Stability by Simulation

Even when a system is incompletely known and described by a QDE, one can test stability of a fixed point by testing whether it is possible to simulate forward from the fixed point. (This requires temporarily suspending the quiescence filter (section 5.4.3).) Intuitively, taking the phase-space view as in figures 7.2 and 7.3, a point is stable if all nearby flows point inward. If there is an outward flow, the point is unstable.

The normal QSIM successor table (table 5.1 on page 100) proposes all ways that each variable could depart from a fixed point:

$v(t_i)$	$\Rightarrow$	$v(t_i, t_{i+1})$
$\langle l_j, std \rangle$		$\langle l_j, std \rangle$
$\langle l_j, std \rangle$		$\langle (l_j, l_{j+1}), inc \rangle$
$\langle l_j, std \rangle$		$\langle (l_{j-1}, l_j), dec \rangle$

QSIM successor generation then determines whether there are any consistent successor states departing from the fixed point, corresponding to outward trajectories.

- If there are none, the fixed point is labeled as stable. Because QSIM is guaranteed to find all real behaviors, this labeling should be correct. (But see problem 9.)

- If some consistent successor states exist, the point is labeled as unstable. Because QSIM is incomplete, it is possible that all such successors are spurious, and the label is incorrect.

For purposes of testing stability, the important question is simply existence or non-existence of outward trajectories. However, for purposes such as composing qualitative phase portraits of dynamical systems, the outgoing trajectories from saddle points describe separatrices, which are qualitatively important boundaries in the phase portrait (Lee and Kuipers, 1993; Lee, 1993; section 11.7).

7.4.3 Testing Stability Algebraically

Algebraic methods can also be used on a QDE to determine stability in the immediate neighborhood of a fixed point.

Suppose the QDE can be simplified to the form

$$\dot{x} = -f(x), \text{ where } f \in M_0^+.$$

Then the QDE represents a first-order negative feedback system, and the point $x = 0$ represents a stable equilibrium.

More generally, for higher-order systems, we can form the Jacobian matrix and determine the eigenvalues of a linear approximation to the system, valid in the immediate neighborhood of a fixed point. If the real parts of all the eigenvalues are negative, the fixed point is stable.

This method will be illustrated by example. Your favorite differential equations text will provide more detailed treatment. Consider the two-tank cascade (section 10.3.1), represented as a system of two coupled first-order differential equations.

$$\begin{aligned}
\dot{x} &= F_1(x,y) = q - f(x) \\
\dot{y} &= F_2(x,y) = f(x) - g(y)
\end{aligned} \quad \text{where } f, g \in M_0^+.$$

The Jacobian matrix J for this QDE is partially known because of the presence of $f, g \in M_0^+$ in the equation, and may vary with (x,y) because f and g may be non-linear.

$$J(x,y) = \begin{bmatrix} \frac{\partial F_1}{\partial x} & \frac{\partial F_1}{\partial y} \\ \frac{\partial F_2}{\partial x} & \frac{\partial F_2}{\partial y} \end{bmatrix} = \begin{bmatrix} -f'(x) & 0 \\ f'(x) & -g'(y) \end{bmatrix}.$$

Its eigenvalues are the solutions λ to $Det(J - \lambda I) = 0$.

$$\begin{aligned}
0 &= Det(J - \lambda I) \\
&= Det \begin{bmatrix} -f'(x) - \lambda & 0 \\ f'(x) & -g'(y) - \lambda \end{bmatrix} \\
&= (\lambda + f'(x))(\lambda + g'(y))
\end{aligned}$$

Therefore, in this case, the eigenvalues are

$$\begin{aligned}
\lambda &= -f'(x) \\
\lambda &= -g'(y),
\end{aligned}$$

which are both negative real values, for any $f, g \in M_0^+$ and for any $x, y > 0$, so the equilibrium states of the cascade are necessarily stable. (See problem 8.)

A much more extensive discussion of comparative statics problem solving with numerous examples and local stability criteria for complex systems is provided by Puccia and Levins (1985). Ishida (1989) also provides methods for determining the stability and observability of qualitatively modeled systems.

7.5 Case Study: Supply and Demand Curves

A paradigm comparative statics problem in economics involves reasoning about the intersection between Supply and Demand curves, as shown in figure 7.4. The horizontal axis of the graph represents the price paid per unit of some commodity (say, "goodies"), and the vertical axis represents the quantity produced or consumed. The Supply and Demand curves represent the loci of equilibrium states of the Supply and Demand processes, respectively.

The Supply curve is monotonically increasing because, as the price of goodies increases, producers will tend to increase the supply in order to increase profit.

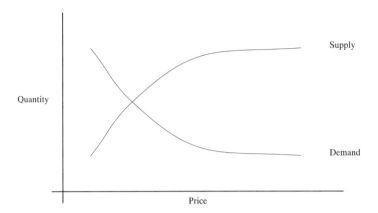

Figure 7.4
A producer-consumer system will tend toward equilibrium at the intersection of the Supply and Demand curves.

The Demand curve, on the other hand, is monotonically decreasing because, as the price increases, consumers will tend to buy fewer goodies.[1]

The locations of the equilibrium curves are influenced by exogenous factors, such as cost of raw material to the producer, or perceived desirability of goodies to the consumer. A sudden change in exogenous factors can move the system off one or both equilibrium curves. Each process independently changes price and/or quantity bought or sold, in order to return to equilibrium. Their joint effect will be to return the state of the system to the intersection of the Supply and Demand curves.

We can express this model as two qualitative equations:

- **Supply**: $quantity = M^+(price/XSF)$,
- **Demand**: $quantity = M^-(price/XDF)$,

where XSF represents the aggregate "external supply factors" and XDF represents "external demand factors."

Figure 7.5 gives the QDE implementation of this model, and figure 7.6 shows the response of this system to a sudden increase in exogenous supply factors (XSF):

$$[XSF]_* = [+] \quad \Rightarrow \quad [price]_* = [+] \text{ and } [quantity]_* = [-].$$

---

[1]This is a highly idealized model. Real markets for real commodities are often much more complex.

```
(define-QDE supply+demand
  (quantity-spaces
    (price     (0 inf))
    (quantity  (0 inf))
    (XSF       (0 inf))        ; "external supply factors"
    (XDF       (0 inf))        ; "external demand factors"
    (Sterm     (0 inf))        ; price/XSF
    (Dterm     (0 inf))        ; price/XDF
    )
  (constraints
    ((constant XSF))
    ((constant XDF))
    ((mult Sterm XSF price))
    ((mult Dterm XDF price))
    ((M+ Sterm quantity)   (0 0) (inf inf))  ; supply curve:  upward
    ((M- Dterm quantity)   (0 inf) (inf 0))  ; demand curve:  downward
    )
  (independent XSF XDF))

(defun increase-XSF ()
  (let* ((result (QSEA :from-qde        supply+demand
                       :initial-values '((price    ((0 inf) std))
                                         (quantity ((0 inf) std))
                                         (XSF      ((0 inf) std))
                                         (XDF      ((0 inf) std)))
                       :perturb        '((XSF +))
                       ))
         (R (car result))            ; reference state
         (S (cadr result)))          ; perturbed state
    (QSEA-table S :reference R)
    (qsim-display S :reference-states '((R ,R)))))
```

Figure 7.5
Defining and perturbing the Supply and Demand curve equations.

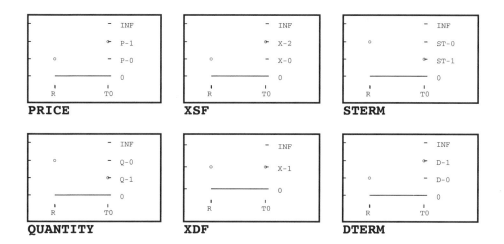

> (increase-xsf)

```
QSEA of SUPPLY+DEMAND.  [var]* values wrt S-0.
  var               S-2
 PRICE:              +
 QUANTITY:           −
 XSF:                +
 XDF:                0
 STERM:              −
 DTERM:              +
```

Figure 7.6
The reference state (R) and the perturbed solution (T0) for the Supply and Demand curves,
responding to increased XSF.

7.6   Case Study: The Pressure Regulator

The pressure regulator example discussed by de Kleer and Brown (1984) is one of the best-known examples in qualitative reasoning. The pressure regulator and a simplified version of the model, expressed in QSIM constraints, are shown in figures 7.7 and 7.8.

QSEA uses constraint satisfaction to determine unique solutions to two perturbation problems:

$$[P_{in}]_* = [+] \quad \Rightarrow \quad [P]_* = [Q]_* = [P_{out}]_* = [R]_* = [+]$$
$$[P_{in}]_* = [-] \quad \Rightarrow \quad [P]_* = [Q]_* = [P_{out}]_* = [R]_* = [-]$$

7.7   Case Study: Recycle Tank

Figure 7.9 shows a gravity-driven cascade of two tanks, with a pump-driven recycle flow, inflow, outflow, and two possible leaks (from Rose and Kramer, 1991).

Figure 7.10 shows the solutions to eight comparative statics problems, in which an exogenous variable was perturbed in the positive direction, while the other exogenous variables were left constant. The resulting perturbations are shown for each QSIM variable in the QDE model, which includes variables for a number of the subexpressions in the original model.

7.8   Problems

1. Show that, as long as the perturbation to x and y is small, and $[x]_0 = [y]_0 = [+]$, then $[xy]_* = [x]_* + [y]_*$.

2. In the example in section 7.3.1, we observed that if we start in state (3), where $[u]_0 = [q]_0 = [0]$, and apply the perturbation $[q]_* = [+]$, while keeping $[u]_* = [0]$, there is no corresponding equilibrium solution. Why not?

3. Implement the dependency-tracing algorithm in Iwasaki, 1988, based on prior algorithms in Simon, 1952, and Iwasaki and Simon, 1986a, to identify the exogenous variables from the structure of the QDE.

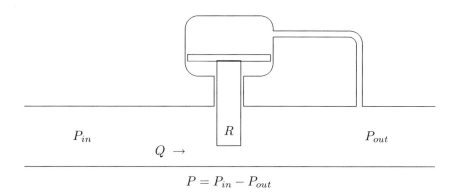

$$P = P_{in} - P_{out}$$

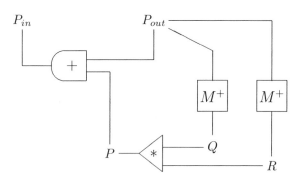

Figure 7.7
The de Kleer and Brown pressure regulator.

```
(define-QDE Pressure-Regulator
  (quantity-spaces
    (Pin   (0 inf))
    (Pout  (0 inf))
    (P     (minf 0 inf))
    (Q     (minf 0 inf))
    (R     (0 inf)))
  (constraints
    ((add P Pout Pin))
    ((mult Q R P))
    ((M+ Q Pout) (0 0) (inf inf))
    ((M+ R Pout) (0 0) (inf inf))
    ((constant Pin)))
  (independent Pin))

(defun p-reg (perturbation)
  (let* ((pair (QSEA :from-qde Pressure-Regulator
                     :initial-values '((Pin  ((0 inf) std))
                                       (Pout ((0 inf) std))
                                       (P    ((0 inf) std))
                                       (Q    ((0 inf) std))
                                       (R    ((0 inf) std)))
                     :perturb perturbation
                     :text "Perturb pressure regulator"))
         (R (car pair))
         (S (cadr pair)))
    (QSEA-table S :reference R)))
```

Figure 7.8
QDE and comparative statics code for the pressure regulator.

• The recycle tank consists of a cascade of two tanks, pump-driven recycle, inflow, outflow, and two possible leaks.

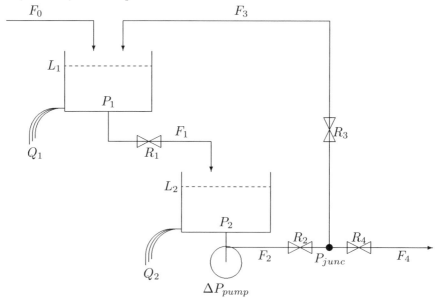

• The recycle tank is modeled with the following equations.

$$dL_1/dt = F_0 + F_3 - F_1 - Q_1$$
$$P_1 = M^+(L_1)$$
$$F_1 = (P_1)^{1/2}/R_1$$
$$dL_2/dt = F_1 + F_2 - Q_2$$
$$P_2 = M^+(L_2)$$
$$F_2 = (P_2 + \Delta P_{pump} - P_{junc})^{1/2}/R_2$$
$$F_3 = (P_{junc})^{1/2}/R_3$$
$$F_4 = (P_{junc})^{1/2}/R_4$$
$$F_2 = F_3 + F_4$$

Figure 7.9
The recycle tank and its model.

perturbed variable	F_0	Q_1	R_1	Q_2	R_2	ΔP	R_3	R_4
F_0	+	0	0	0	0	0	0	0
L_1	+	−	+	−	0	0	−	+
Q_1	0	+	0	0	0	0	0	0
P_1	+	−	+	−	0	0	−	+
R_1	0	0	+	0	0	0	0	0
F_1	+	−	0	−	0	0	−	+
L_2	+	−	0	−	+	−	−	+
Q_2	0	0	0	+	0	0	0	0
P_2	+	−	0	−	+	−	−	+
R_2	0	0	0	0	+	0	0	0
ΔP	0	0	0	0	0	+	0	0
F_2	+	−	0	−	0	0	−	+
R_3	0	0	0	0	0	0	+	0
F_3	+	−	0	−	0	0	−	+
R_4	0	0	0	0	0	0	0	+
F_4	+	−	0	−	0	0	0	0
P_{junc}	+	−	0	−	0	0	0	+
$F_0 + F_3$	+	−	0	−	0	0	−	+
$F_1 + Q_1$	+	−	0	−	0	0	−	+
$F_2 + Q_2$	+	−	0	−	0	0	−	+
dL_1/dt	0	0	0	0	0	0	0	0
dL_2/dt	0	0	0	0	0	0	0	0
$P_2 + \Delta P$	+	−	0	−	+	0	−	+
$P_2 + \Delta P - P_{junc}$	+	−	0	−	+	0	−	+
$(P_1)^{1/2}$	+	−	+	−	0	0	−	+
$(P_2 + \Delta P - P_{junc})^{1/2}$	+	−	0	−	+	0	−	+
$(P_{junc})^{1/2}$	+	−	0	−	0	0	0	+
$d(L_1 + L_2)/dt$	0	0	0	0	0	0	0	0
$Q_1 + Q_2$	0	+	0	+	0	0	0	0
$Q_1 + Q_2 + F_4$	+	0	0	0	0	0	0	0

Figure 7.10
Unique solutions to eight comparative statics problems on the recycle tank.

4. (Research Problem.) In section 7.3.2, we relied on the fact that perturbations are small, confining the solutions to comparative statics problems to the same or adjacent basic qualitative states. Using the full quantity-space representation instead of just $[x]_*$ values, show how to solve for the effects of non-small perturbations. Note that the behavior of a system can change dramatically within the same operating region, or across region boundaries.

5. (Research Problem.) Generalize the method in section 7.3.2 to handle slowly moving equilibria. This requires relaxing the constraint that $[\dot{x}] = 0$ for all variables x, to the weaker constraint that ((d/dt x y)) implies that $[\dot{x}] = [y]_0 = 0$. Demonstrate this method on the water tank example with slowly increasing inflow.

The hard part of the problem is showing that your method gives valid results, since the QSIM stability test can't be applied to changing states.

6. Using the code for the functions QSEA and QSIM in the QSIM system as a guide, implement a function that solves for the initial and final responses to a perturbation from an equilibrium state (section 7.3.3). You will need to combine initial-state generation, successor generation, and comparative statics.

7. (Research Problem.) Find an example where comparative statics returns a solution that is not the final state of any dynamic trajectory responding to the same perturbation. Is it possible for this to occur where the state found by comparative statics is not spurious, but is dynamically unreachable?

8. (Research Problem.) Using an auxiliary algebraic manipulation utility, develop a method for automatically analyzing a given QDE to determine its fixed points and their stability by finding and evaluating the Jacobian matrix at each fixed point. Where appropriate, identify any additional constraints on monotonic functions required to guarantee stability. Demonstrate your method on QDEs of interest to control engineers.

9. (Research Problem.) Modulo the consequence of incompleteness, the simulation-based stability test works correctly. However, the justification needs to be improved.

- A potential problem arises with the *unstable spiral* fixed point. There is no immediate successor to the fixed point itself, since the behavior leading away *starts* with an infinite sequence of tiny but growing oscillations. (This behavior is not a *reasonable* function in the sense of QSIM.) Thus, one might worry that

QSIM would determine that this state has no immediate successor state, and would incorrectly label it as stable!

• However, it turns out that a stable spiral attractor, simulated in QSIM, is accompanied by an infinite family of nodal behaviors that converge directly to the attractor after a finite number of cycles (section 11.4.3). By symmetry, the unstable attractor will have a similar family of departing nodal behaviors, which are therefore detectable by the successor test and will lead to the correct labeling of the state as unstable.

• In order to prove this, we need to show that a spiral is *necessarily* accompanied by the nodal family, under the qualitative description.

Provide the appropriate guarantee for testing stability by qualitative simulation.

10. (Research Problem.) Under what circumstances can the stability criteria for complex loop models (Puccia and Levins, 1985) be applied automatically to qualitative or semi-quantitative QDE models?

8 Region Transitions

8.1 Introduction

A model is valid within some domain or *operating region*. If the system departs from the domain of the current model, simulation within that model must cease. If there is a model for the new operating region, then simulation may resume within the new model.

Suppose we wish to model a ball, bouncing without energy loss. The primary variables are y, v, and a. While the ball is in flight, a "gravity" model is appropriate, and is valid as long as $y \geq 0$. Once the ball strikes the floor, the gravity model is no longer appropriate, and a "spring" model takes over. The spring model applies as long as $y \leq 0$. The transitional state when $y = 0$ is a boundary state, with a valid description under each model. We exploit this double description of boundary states to describe operating region transitions.

8.1.1 Moving from One Region to Another

There are several ways to represent regions and their boundaries.

In QSIM, a region is represented by its boundary. The boundary is represented by landmark values of particular variables, or more generally by boolean combinations of qualitative value descriptions of variables, specified in the antecedents of transition rules in the QDE.

DEFINITION 18   A *transition* is a rule of the form

condition → *transition function*

where

• The *condition* is a pattern of the form $(\langle variable \rangle (\langle qmag \rangle \langle qdir \rangle))$, or a boolean combination of such patterns. It succeeds at a state when the values of the specified variables match the corresponding description.

• The *transition function* is a function of one variable that is applied to the current state if the condition succeeds. It returns a new qualitative state, perhaps defined with respect to a new QDE, from which simulation can resume.

If the state of the system is on the boundary of the current operating region and moving outward, the transition-mapping function (if any) may provide a post-transition state from which simulation can be continued.

A region can also be represented by a logical condition, which can be evaluated on a given set of variables and values, and returns true if the values represent a state within the region. Qualitative physics using confluences (de Kleer and Brown, 1984) and qualitative process theory (Forbus, 1984) both define regions in this way. From the QSIM perspective, the two representations are equivalent, with the condition-based definition of a region compiled into a boundary-based definition during model building (see chapter 14; Crawford *et al.*, 1990; and Farquhar, 1993). However, the proper interpretation of models at operating region boundaries requires some care (section 8.1.3).

The third approach represents regions as fuzzy sets (Zadeh, 1965). Since the characteristic function of such a set can vary continuously over $[0, 1]$, the boundary of such a region does not occur at a specific landmark, and adjacent regions may overlap. A transition between fuzzy operating regions may be simulated qualitatively as a continuous change. This approach has been exploited by Kuipers and Åström (1991; 1994) to provide validity proofs for a type of heterogeneous (fuzzy) control law.

8.1.2   The Transition Mapping

The transition mapping, $S(t) \rightarrow S'(t)$, creates a correspondence between the final state, $S(t)$, in the old operating region, and one or more initial states $S'(t)$ in the new operating region. The transition-mapping function specifies several types of information required to define $S'(t)$:

- the QDE for the new operating region;
- the variables in $S(t)$ whose magnitudes should be inherited by variables in $S'(t)$;
- the variables in $S(t)$ whose directions of change should be inherited by variables in $S'(t)$; and
- the variables in $S'(t)$ for which qualitative values are explicitly asserted.

Once the new state $S'(t)$ is created, the relation *transition_identity*$(S(t), S'(t))$ is asserted to link the two states.

When a variable is shared between two operating regions, the quantity space for that variable in $S'(t)$ becomes the union of the quantity space at $S(t)$ and the quantity space as specified by the new region. Similarly, if a constraint is shared, its corresponding values are mapped to $S'(t)$.

If the information provided is not sufficient to specify $S'(t)$ uniquely, the simulation will branch on the consistent completions of $S'(t)$. Simulation then continues normally, predicting the qualitative successors of $S'(t)$, within the new operating region.

8.1.3   Interpretations of Region Transitions

There are several distinct interpretations of region transitions. First, the two operating regions are closed regions where different descriptions are appropriate and different constraints hold. The boundary state, being in both regions, may be described in both ways. As we move from one region to another, the region transition corresponds to a change in point of view as we describe the mechanism, not to an actual change in the state of the mechanism. This interpretation of operating regions is most appropriate when we switch viewpoint on the bouncing ball from a gravity model to a spring model.

The second interpretation is that a region transition corresponds to a discontinuous change in the actual state of the mechanism. This interpretation is more appropriate if we model the bouncing ball as simply reflecting off the floor, changing its velocity instantaneously from negative to positive. Similar fast changes accompany such "instantaneous" events as a string breaking, a balloon bursting, a latch releasing, a switch closing, etc. As these examples illustrate, a discontinuous change is often a description of the net effect of a continuous process taking place at a much faster time-scale, which we wish to treat as below the temporal granularity of the current model. In this case, the endpoints of the region transition do not represent redescriptions of the same state of the world, but the initial and final states of a fast process being treated as an instantaneous change.

In addition to elaborating on the second interpretation, Nishida and Doshita (1987) present a third interpretation, in which a causal explanation of discontinuous change is given by a sequence of intermediate "mythical states." These states may be inconsistent with the device model, but they satisfy certain region adjacency and causal locality constraints. QSIM does not take this approach, for reasons discussed in section 5.8. However, the basic approach taken by Nishida and Doshita (1987) — that discontinuous change should be viewed as a limiting case of very rapid continuous change — appears to be sound and productive.

8.2   Case: The Bouncing Ball

The gravity and spring models for the bouncing ball follow. The models include constraints for kinetic, potential, and total energy to eliminate spurious branches.[1] Figure 8.3 shows the behaviors predicted for two different models of the bouncing ball.

8.2.1   Bounce Viewed as Spring

In the example of the bouncing ball, the bounce takes place at time-point t_2. The state of the ball according to the gravity model follows:

$$Gravity(t_2) \Longrightarrow \boxed{\begin{array}{lcl} Y & = & \langle 0, dec \rangle \\ V & = & \langle v_1, dec \rangle \\ A & = & \langle g, std \rangle \\ vsq & = & \langle vsq_0, std \rangle \\ KE & = & \langle KE_0, std \rangle \\ PE & = & \langle 0, std \rangle \\ TE & = & \langle TE_0, std \rangle \end{array}}$$

The spring model's view of the same instant, renamed t_2', is obtained by inheriting the magnitudes of Y, V, and TE, and propagating their consequences within the spring model to reach a complete qualitative description.

$$Spring(t_2') \Longrightarrow \boxed{\begin{array}{lcl} Y & = & \langle 0, nil \rangle \\ V & = & \langle v_1, nil \rangle \\ TE & = & \langle TE_0, nil \rangle \end{array}} \Longrightarrow \boxed{\begin{array}{lcl} Y & = & \langle 0, dec \rangle \\ V & = & \langle v_1, std \rangle \\ A & = & \langle 0, inc \rangle \\ vsq & = & \langle vsq_0, std \rangle \\ KE & = & \langle KE_0, std \rangle \\ PE & = & \langle 0, std \rangle \\ TE & = & \langle TE_0, std \rangle \end{array}}$$

Although this transition can generally be regarded as a re-description of the same state of the world with respect to a new model, the difference in modeling assumptions results in a discontinuous change as $a(t_2) \rightarrow a(t_2')$. In the gravity model, gravity is considered a significant force; in the spring model, gravity is considered insignificant compared to the spring force, so the spring model assumes that $a(t_2') = 0$. The resulting behavior is shown in figure 8.3(a).

---

[1]This example uses a $U^+(y)$ expression for potential energy in the spring model. This is discussed in more detail in section 8.4 and problem 9.

$$y'' = g < 0; \qquad TE = KE + PE = M^+(v^2) + M^+(y) = constant.$$

```
(define-QDE Gravity
   (quantity-spaces
      (y        (0 inf))
      (v        (minf 0 inf))
      (a        (minf g 0 inf))
      (vsq      (0 inf)))
     (KE        (0 inf))
     (PE        (0 inf))
     (TE        (0 inf))
   (constraints
      ((d/dt y v))
      ((d/dt v a))
      ((constant a))
      ((mult v v vsq))
      ((M+ vsq KE)          (0 0) (inf inf))
      ((M+ y PE)            (0 0) (inf inf))
      ((add KE PE TE)))
      ((constant TE))
   (transitions
      ((y (0 dec)) -> transition-to-spring)))


(defun transition-to-spring (ball-state)
   (create-transition-state :from-state  ball-state
                            :to-qde      spring
                            :inherit-qmag '(y v te)))
```

Figure 8.1
The gravity region in the bouncing ball model.

8.2.2   Bounce Viewed as Reflection

The spring phase of the ball's behavior is very short compared with the gravity phase. We can build a model to neglect the spring behavior entirely, and view the bounce as a simple reflection off the floor. In this view, the gravity model holds both before and after the transition, and the qualitative values of position, acceleration, and energy are inherited across the transition, but we discontinuously reverse the sign of velocity.

$$y'' = M^-(y); \qquad TE = KE + PE = M^+(v^2) + U^+(y) = constant.$$

```
(define-QDE Spring
   (quantity-spaces
       (y       (minf 0))
       (v       (minf 0 inf))
       (a       (0 inf))
       (vsq     (0 inf)))
       (KE      (0 inf))
       (PE      (0 inf))
       (TE      (0 inf))
   (constraints
       ((d/dt y v))
       ((d/dt v a))
       ((M- y a)              (0 0) (minf inf))
       ((U+ y PE (0 0))       (minf inf))
       ((mult v v vsq))
       ((M+ vsq KE)           (0 0) (inf inf))
       ((add KE PE TE)))
       ((constant TE))
   (transitions
       ((y (0 inc)) -> transition-to-gravity)))


(defun transition-to-gravity (spring-state)
   (create-transition-state :from-state   spring-state
                            :to-qde       gravity
                            :assert       '((a (g std)))
                            :inherit-qmag '(y v te)))
```

Figure 8.2
The spring region in the bouncing ball model.

```
(defun reflect-velocity (ball-state)
   (create-transition-state :from-state   ball-state
                            :to-qde       Gravity
                            :inherit-qmag '(a te)
                            :assert       '((y (0 inc)))))
```

(a) Bouncing ball viewed as spring.

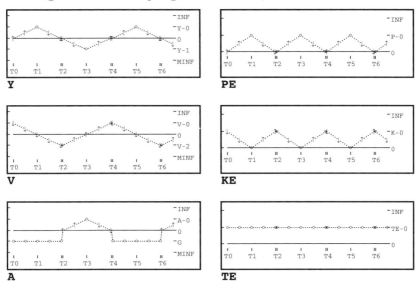

(b) Bouncing ball viewed as reflection.

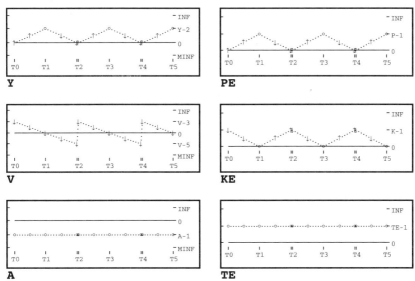

Figure 8.3
Two views of the bouncing ball (unique behavior predictions).

The QDE for the gravity model is the same as that in figure 8.1 except that the transition rule is replaced by

```
((y (0 dec)) -> reflect-velocity).
```

The effect of this mapping on the states $Gravity(t_2)$ and $Gravity(t_2')$ linked by the transition is illustrated here.

$$Gravity(t_2) \Longrightarrow \boxed{\begin{aligned} y &= \langle 0, dec \rangle \\ v &= \langle v_1, dec \rangle \\ a &= \langle g, std \rangle \\ vsq &= \langle vsq_0, dec \rangle \\ KE &= \langle KE_0, std \rangle \\ PE &= \langle 0, std \rangle \\ TE &= \langle TE_0, std \rangle \end{aligned}}$$

$$Gravity(t_2') \Longrightarrow \boxed{\begin{aligned} y &= \langle 0, inc \rangle \\ a &= \langle g, nil \rangle \\ TE &= \langle TE_0, nil \rangle \end{aligned}} \Longrightarrow \boxed{\begin{aligned} y &= \langle 0, inc \rangle \\ v &= \langle v_0, dec \rangle \\ a &= \langle g, std \rangle \\ vsq &= \langle vsq_0, dec \rangle \\ KE &= \langle KE_0, std \rangle \\ PE &= \langle 0, std \rangle \\ TE &= \langle TE_0, std \rangle \end{aligned}}$$

Notice that $v(t_2) = v_1 < 0$, and the transition mapping implies that $v(t_2') > 0$. Then corresponding values from $TE(t_2')$ to $KE(t_2')$ to $vsq(t_2')$ to $v(t_2')$ ensure that $v(t_2') = v_0 = -v_1$. The behavior of this model is shown in figure 8.3(b).

8.3   Representing Saturation: S^+ and S^- Constraints

Many functional relationships *saturate*. For example, a patient's response to a drug may increase monotonically with dosage up to a certain threshold, then remain constant. A transistor permits current flow proportional to the voltage between source and drain up to a certain threshold. Beyond that threshold, current is unaffected by increases in voltage.

In these and many other situations, there are functional relationships that are monotonic within a certain range of values, but constant outside that range (figure 8.4). This behavior can be expressed by region transitions in the overall model, but

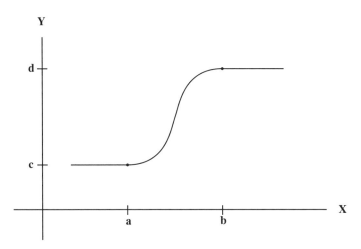

Figure 8.4
The constraint `(S+ x y (a c) (b d))`.

The relationship is monotonic within the interval (a, b), and constant elsewhere.

the change in response is most naturally associated with an individual functional relationship. It motivates the definition of a new class of constraints that make it easy to describe threshold effects.

Threshold-type curves are often called "S-shaped" or "sigmoid" curves, so we define the constraint `((S+ x y (a c) (b d))`, which means that $y = f(x)$, where f is continuously differentiable, and $f(x) = c$ for $x \leq a$, $f(x) = d$ for $x \geq b$, and $f'(x) > 0$ for $x \in (a, b)$. (Note that this definition implies that $f'(a) = f'(b) = 0$.) In addition to the "turning points" (a, c) and (b, d), corresponding value pairs may be asserted about an `S+` constraint, just like the `M+` constraint. An `S-` constraint is defined in the obvious way, with a monotonically decreasing section between constant regions.

8.3.1   Case: Drug Metabolism

Consider a drug that has a minimum and a maximum effective concentration (but without toxic reaction to an above-maximum dose).

`(S+ serum-level effect (min 0) (max full))`

If we give an initial dose above the maximum effective level, we will get the following prediction about the effect on the patient as the drug is excreted from the body (figure 8.5).

```
(define-QDE drug-dosage
  (quantity-spaces
    (serum-level    (0 min max inf))
    (effect         (0 full inf))
    (inflow         (0 inf))
    (outflow        (0 inf))
    (netflow        (minf 0 inf)))
  (constraints
    ((S+ serum-level effect (min 0) (max full)))
    ((M+ serum-level outflow)              (0 0) (inf inf))
    ((add netflow outflow inflow))
    ((constant inflow))
    ((d/dt serum-level netflow))))
```

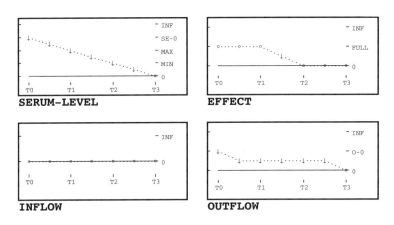

Figure 8.5
Drug dosage model and unique behavior on crossing thresholds.

1. The full effect remains constant while the drug is initially being excreted, since the serum level is above the maximum threshold.

2. The effect drops steadily as the drug is excreted.

3. When the serum level reaches the minimum threshold, effect becomes constant again at zero, while the remaining drug is excreted.

8.3.2   Example: Irreversible Population Change

We can easily make a model in which population rises and falls according to the availability of resources. However, populations such as nerve cells decrease irreversibly. A given population has a certain requirement for resources. If insufficient resources are available, the population will decrease until the needs of the survivors can be met by the available resources. If more resources later become available, the population cannot grow to take advantage of them and recover to its previous state.

In order to describe such a situation, we can use an S^+ constraint:

```
(S+ surplus change (minf minf) (0 0))
```

This constraint asserts that when surplus is negative, change will vary with it, so the population will fall. However, when surplus is positive, change will remain constant at 0.

```
(define-QDE Population
  (quantity-spaces
    (population      (0 inf))
    (food-needed     (0 inf))
    (food-supply     (0 inf))
    (surplus         (minf 0 inf))
    (change          (minf 0 inf)))
  (constraints
    ((M+ population food-needed)               (0 0) (inf inf))
    ((add surplus food-needed food-supply))
    ((constant food-supply))
    ((S+ surplus change (minf minf) (0 0)))
    ((d/dt population change))))
```

Figure 8.6 shows the effect of a temporary shortage of food on such a population. This example is motivated by Weiss *et al.*'s (1978) CASNET model of glaucoma, in which increased pressure within the eye restricts the flow of blood to the optic nerve, resulting in irreversible damage to the nerve, and narrowing of the optic field. A QSIM model of this phenomenon is presented in section 8.7.

8.4 U^+ and U^- Constraints

Another important type of functional relation that changes qualitative mode is the U^+ (and U^-) constraint. A functional relation f satisfies the constraint

1. Food shortage causes population drop. (One of three behaviors, branching on the sign of $surplus(t_0)$.)

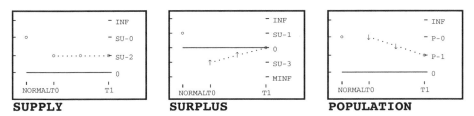

SUPPLY   **SURPLUS**   **POPULATION**

2. Restored food supply has no effect on population. (Unique behavior.)

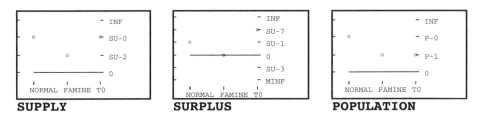

SUPPLY   **SURPLUS**   **POPULATION**

Figure 8.6
Irreversible population change.

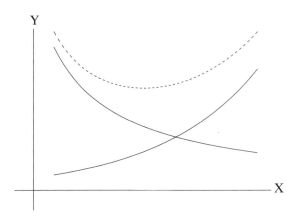

Figure 8.7
$y = M^+(x) + M^-(x) = U^+(x)$.

```
(U+ x y (a b))
```

if $y = f(x)$ decreases monotonically to (a, b), then increases monotonically after. More precisely, f is a reasonable function, $f(a) = b$, $f'(x) < 0$ for $x < a$, and $f'(x) > 0$ for $x > a$.

There are several ways we might encounter U^+ or U^- constraints. Suppose that two variables x and y are related along two different paths, so $y = M^+(x) + M^-(x)$. Depending on the actual shapes of the M^+ and M^- functions, it may be that $y = U^+(x)$; in other cases, perhaps $y = U^-(x)$. (See figure 8.7.) As the figure illustrates, the assertion that $y = M^+(x) + M^-(x)$ also satisfies $y = U^+(x)$ provides a new and useful piece of information about the relationship among the unknown monotonic functions.

The U^+ constraint also appears in the spring model (figure 8.2). Potential energy is defined as

$$PE(y) = \int_0^y f(\bar{y}) \, d\bar{y},$$

where $f \in M_0^+$ is the restoring force on the spring. From this definition, it is not hard to prove that $PE(y) = U^+(y)$. (Problem 9.) Since $f \in M_0^+$ need not be symmetrical, $PE \in U^+$ need not be symmetrical either.

8.5   Example: On-Off Control

The familiar home thermostat controls temperature by turning the furnace on or off when certain thresholds are crossed. Our thermostat model has two aspects:

1. The general structure of the home, as a container for heat, with heat flows to the environment and from a furnace, affected by exogenous variables such as the outside temperature, the insulation factor, the thermal mass of the house, the heating capacity of the furnace, and the desired setpoint temperature.[2]

2. The controller model, which determines the rate of heatflow from the furnace as a function of the error between setpoint and inside temperature.

In this model, the on-off controller switches the heatflow between 0 and *On* as the error term crosses certain thresholds. These discontinuous changes are modeled as region transitions, changing the value of a constant variable, but otherwise leaving the QDE the same (figure 8.8).

---

[2]This structural model is shared by several different thermal control models. In other models, we replace the on-off controller with a proportional controller (section 6.2), or a proportional-integral (PI) controller (section 11.6).

```
(define-QDE Thermostat-On-Off
  (quantity-spaces
    (heat    (0 inf))
    (mass    (0 inf))
    (TempIn  (0 RoomTemp inf))
    (TempOut (0 RoomTemp inf))
    (TempSet (0 RoomTemp inf))
    (dTemp   (minf 0 inf))
    (error   (minf Lo 0 Hi inf))
    (R       (0 inf))
    (HFout   (minf 0 inf))
    (HFin    (0 On))
    (netHF   (minf 0 inf)))
  (constraints
    ((mult TempIn Mass Heat))
    ((add TempOut dTemp TempIn)         (RoomTemp 0 RoomTemp) )
    ((add TempSet error TempIn)         (RoomTemp 0 RoomTemp) )
    ((mult R HFout dTemp))
    ((add HFout netHF HFin))
    ((d/dt Heat netHF))
    ((constant HFin))
    ((constant Mass))
    ((constant TempOut))
    ((constant TempSet))
    ((constant R)))
  (transitions
    ((error (Lo dec)) -> turn-furnace-on)
    ((error (Hi inc)) -> turn-furnace-off)))


(defun turn-furnace-on (heater-state)
  (create-transition-state :from-state  heater-state
                           :to-qde      Thermostat-On-Off
                           :assert      '((HFin  (On std))
                                          (netHF ((0 inf) nil)))
                           :inherit-qmag :rest))

(defun turn-furnace-off (heater-state)
  (create-transition-state :from-state  heater-state
                           :to-qde      Thermostat-On-Off
                           :assert      '((HFin  (0 std))
                                          (netHF ((minf 0) nil)))
                           :inherit-qmag :rest))
```

Figure 8.8
QDE for the on-off thermostat model.

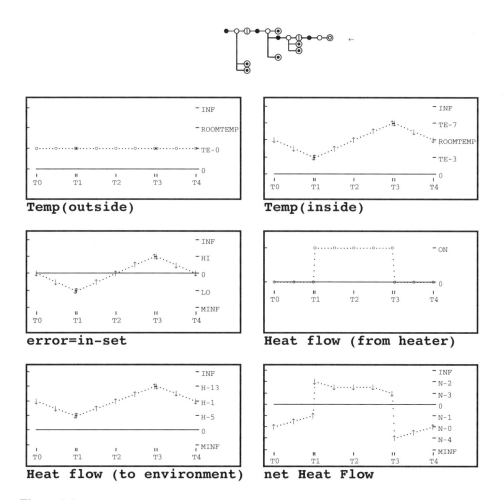

Figure 8.9
One of seven behaviors predicted for the on-off thermostat model.

The on-off thermostat model, responding to a sudden drop in outside temperature, predicts seven behaviors, which fall into three qualitative classes:

1. Figure 8.9 shows the usual behavior: inside temperature drops, turning the
furnace on, so temperature rises until the furnace turns off again, so temperature
drops again, and the cycle continues. (Behavior 2.)

2. The temperature drop may be so small (or the threshold so low) that the system
reaches equilibrium at a lower temperature, but without turning the furnace on.
(Behaviors 6 and 7.)

3. The temperature drop may be so large (or the threshold so high, or the furnace so
weak) that the furnace turns on, but can never raise the temperature high enough to
turn the furnace back off again. Equilibrium is reached with the furnace continually
on. (Behaviors 1, 3, 4, and 5.)

8.6   Example: Linear and Rotary Motion

Sinusoidal motion is a common type of non-monotonic change. The spring examples
demonstrate how sinusoidal behavior can arise as a function of time, from monotonic
and derivative constraints alone. But how should we model the piston in a four-
cycle gasoline engine, where linear and rotary motion are structurally linked? We
will study this issue in simplified form with a slider and crank.

   In this simplified model, motion is driven by the crank, which has an angular
position θ, measured counter-clockwise from the positive x-axis, and a constant
angular velocity, $\theta' > 0$. The end of the crank is linked to the slider, which moves
back and forth between A and B on a linear track. There are several tricks to
making a reasonable model of this mechanism.

• In order to capture the cyclic range of angles θ, we include region transitions on
the variable θ: $\langle 360, inc \rangle \rightarrow \langle 0, inc \rangle$ and $\langle 0, dec \rangle \rightarrow \langle 360, dec \rangle$, leaving the rest of
the model unchanged.

• The relation $x = \cos \theta$ is expressed in terms of two separate monotonic regions,
decreasing for $\theta \in [0, 180]$ and increasing for $\theta \in [180, 360]$. S^+ and S^- constraints,
rather than M^+ and M^-, are used to capture the fact that $x' = 0$ even though
$\theta' > 0$, where $\theta = 0$ or 180. This decomposition is also expressed as operating
region transitions.

```
(define-QDE Slider-Crank-A
  (text "Rotary crank drives linear slider (0..180)")
  (quantity-spaces
    (slider         (A B))
    (x              (-1 0 +1))
    (theta          (0 90 180))
    (dtheta         (0 DT* inf)))
  (constraints
    ((d/dt theta dtheta))
    ((constant dtheta))
    ((S- theta x (0 1) (180 -1))  (90 0))
    ((M+ x slider)                (-1 A) (+1 B)))
  (transitions
    ((theta (180 inc)) -> inc-180)
    ((theta (0 dec))   -> dec-0)))

(defun dec-0 (ostate)
  (create-transition-state :from-state  ostate
                           :to-qde      slider-crank-B
                           :assert      '((theta (360 dec)))
                           :inherit-qmag :rest
                           :inherit-qdir :rest))

(defun inc-180 (ostate)
  (create-transition-state :from-state  ostate
                           :to-qde      slider-crank-B
                           :inherit-qmag :all
                           :inherit-qdir :all))

(defun rotate-crank ()
  (let* ((sim (make-sim :state-limit 25
                        :cycle-detection nil))
         (initial (make-new-state :from-qde slider-crank-A
                                  :sim        sim
                                  :assert-values '((theta  (0   nil))
                                                   (dtheta (dt* std)))))))
    (qsim initial)
    (qsim-display initial)))
```

Figure 8.10
QDE for the slider-crank mechanism (segment A).

```
(define-QDE Slider-Crank-B
  (text "Rotary crank drives linear slider (180..360)")
  (quantity-spaces
    (slider       (A B))
    (x            (-1 0 +1))
    (theta        (180 270 360))
    (dtheta       (0 DT* inf)))
  (constraints
    ((d/dt theta dtheta))
    ((constant dtheta))
    ((S+ theta x (180 -1) (360 1))  (270 0))
    ((M+ x slider)                  (-1 A) (+1 B)))
  (transitions
    ((theta (180 dec)) -> dec-180)
    ((theta (360 inc)) -> inc-360)))

(defun dec-180 (ostate)
  (create-transition-state :from-state   ostate
                           :to-qde       slider-crank-A
                           :inherit-qmag :all
                           :inherit-qdir :all))

(defun inc-360 (ostate)
  (create-transition-state :from-state   ostate
                           :to-qde       slider-crank-A
                           :assert       '((theta (0 inc)))
                           :inherit-qmag :rest
                           :inherit-qdir :rest))
```

Figure 8.11
QDE for the slider-crank mechanism (segment B).

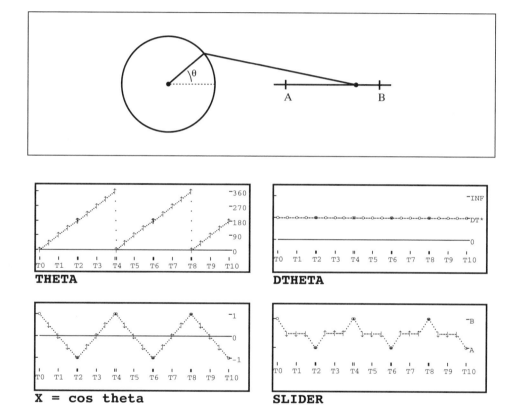

Figure 8.12
The behavior of the slider-crank mechanism.

• The slider position, $slider = M^+(x)$, corresponds to a relatively complex function of $\cos\theta$, $\sin\theta$, and the lengths of the crank and the link. Fortunately, we can abstract all of this complexity into the M^+ constraint.

• The quantity space for slider position does not include any of the usual landmark values, $-\infty$, 0, or ∞. Omitting them is not normally recommended, but they are neither necessary nor useful here, and this example demonstrates that it is legal to leave them out of a model on occasion. (They are *necessary* for any variable that participates in a MULT or MINUS constraint, or is the *rate* argument to a d/dt constraint.)

• For this example, we disable the cycle-detection filter, so the qualitative behavior plot shows several cycles of the system.

The QDE model of the slider-crank is in figures 8.10 and 8.11, and the unique predicted behavior is in figure 8.12.

8.7   Example: Glaucoma

CASNET (Weiss *et al.*, 1978) was one of the earliest AI projects to exploit a causal model of the mechanisms underlying a diagnostic problem. CASNET was applied to problems of diagnosing glaucoma, and achieved near-perfect levels of performance, due in part to a detailed causal model of disease progression, showing how states of the disease evolve with time (figure 8.13).

In this case, we construct a QSIM model of a key portion of the CASNET/Glaucoma causal network, which explains how glaucoma is caused. The intra-ocular fluid is produced within the eye and flows out through a drainage system; the amount of fluid, and hence the pressure within the eye, is controlled by the balance between production and outflow rates. Glaucoma arises when the outflow (*flow facility* in the causal net) is restricted, so pressure rises. Intra-ocular pressure then compresses the blood vessels in the eye, restricting the flow of blood to the optic nerve. With insufficient blood supply, nerve cells begin to die. Since nerve cells do not regenerate, this effect is modeled by the "irreversible population change" model of section 8.3.2. With fewer cells, the optic nerve begins to "cup," and the visual angle decreases. Eventually, total blindness can result.

The QSIM QDE model (figure 8.14) is a relatively straightforward cascade of a "water tank" model of intra-ocular pressure with an "irreversible population change" model of the optic nerve. The balance between production and outflow of intra-ocular fluid reaches equilibrium at a point that determines intra-ocular

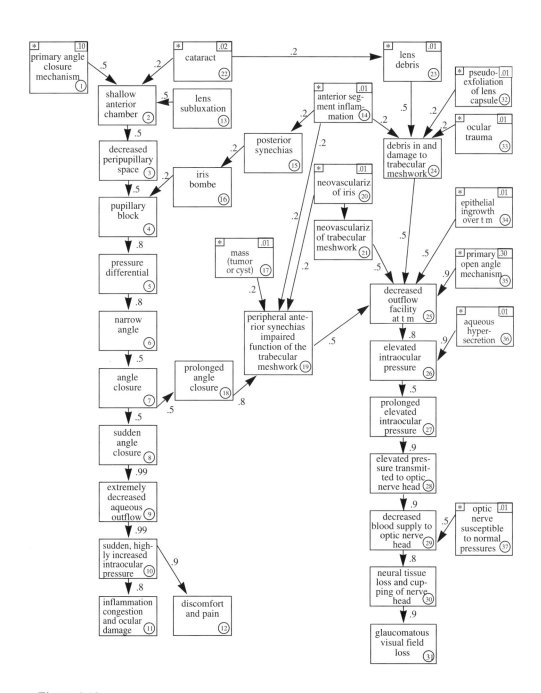

Figure 8.13
CASNET causal network model of glaucoma. The QSIM model addresses only the vertical chain of states on the lower right.

Source: Weiss *et al.*, 1978, figure 2, p. 147.

```
(define-QDE Glaucoma
  (quantity-spaces
     (amt  (minf 0 inf)  "amt(fluid,eye)")
     (iop  (minf 0 inf)  "intraocular pressure")
     (ffac (minf 0 inf)  "flow facility (const)")
     (prod (minf 0 inf)  "fluid production")
     (of   (minf 0 inf)  "fluid outflow")
     (nf   (minf 0 inf)  "net flow")
     (bp   (0 inf)       "blood pressure")
     (nbs  (0 inf)       "neural blood flow")
     (os   (minf 0 inf)  "O2 supply")
     (on   (minf 0 inf)  "O2 need")
     (om   (minf 0 inf)  "O2 margin")
     (cp   (0 inf)       "cell population")
     (cpr  (minf 0 inf)  "rate of cell pop change"))
  (constraints
     ((m+ amt iop)  (0 0) (inf inf))     ; intra-ocular pressure
     ((mult iop ffac of))
     ((constant ffac))
     ((add nf of prod))
     ((constant prod))
     ((d/dt amt nf))
     ((mult nbs iop bp))                 ; iop = resistance
     ((constant bp))
     ((m+ nbs os)   (0 0) (inf inf))
     ((m+ cp on)    (0 0) (inf inf))
     ((add on om os))
     ((s+ om cpr (minf minf) (0 0)))     ; nerve cell population
     ((d/dt cp cpr)))
  (independent prod ffac bp))

(defun low-flow-facility ()
  (let* ((normal (make-new-state :from-qde Glaucoma
                                 :assert-values '((ffac ((0 inf) std))
                                                  (prod ((0 inf) std))
                                                  (bp   ((0 inf) std))
                                                  (amt  ((0 inf) std))
                                                  (cp   ((0 inf) std))
                                                  (om   ((0 inf) std)))))
         (init (make-new-state :from-state normal
                               :inherit '(amt cp prod bp)
                               :perturb '((ffac -)))))
    (qsim init)
    (qsim-display init :reference-states '((normal ,normal)))))
```

Figure 8.14
QDE for the glaucoma model.

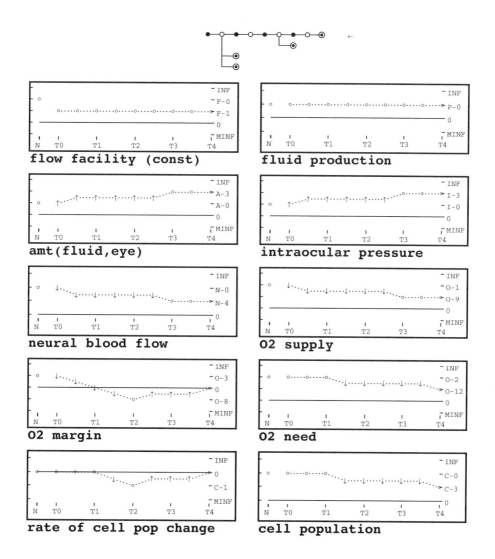

Figure 8.15

Behavior derived from the glaucoma QDE.

Decreased flow facility for intra-ocular fluid, with constant production rate, causes increased amount of fluid and hence intra-ocular pressure, which causes a decreased neural blood supply and O_2 supply to the optic nerve. If supply falls below minimum need for the current population, the population decreases until need matches supply.

pressure. Intra-ocular pressure is then linked directly to resistance to blood flow, which determines the oxygen supply for the nerve cell population. There is a potential for intractable "chatter" on the derivative of the nerve cell population, but automatic derivation of higher-order derivative constraints (chapter 10) is adequate to handle the situation.

Four behaviors are predicted as a result of simulation:

• Two predict a decrease in blood supply to the optic nerve, but without causing a deficit resulting in nerve cell death.

• The other two predict nerve cell death, irreversibly decreasing the population of the optic nerve. They differ according to whether the intra-ocular pressure reaches equilibrium before, or at the same time, as the nerve cell population. The behavior shown in figure 8.15 represents the first of these two cases.

8.8   Problems

1. Create two models of overflow in the bathtub:

(a) Model overflow as a region transition, into a new region where water level is constant, in spite of increases in inflow. Don't forget to handle the reverse transition, where inflow decreases again.

(b) Use the S+ constraint to model the equilibrium level of water in the tub as a function of inflow. Build this into a larger model.

2. Build a model of a ball bouncing around within a well, under the influence of gravity. Assume perfectly elastic collisions with the walls, and either (a) perfectly elastic or (b) perfectly inelastic (i.e., "sticky") collisions with the floor.

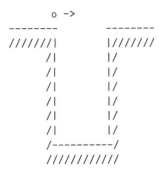

```
        o  ->
--------        --------
////////\       \////////
       /|       |/
       /|       |/
       /|       |/
       /|       |/
       /|       |/
       /|       |/
      /----------/
      ////////////
```

3. Create a sequence of models linked by region transitions, illustrating the following scenario and the other behaviors branching off from it:

- Inflate a balloon from a constant-pressure source of helium.
- Upon reaching equilibrium, seal and release it to rise into the air.
- It will accelerate upward until it reaches terminal velocity.
- It expands as it rises and the air becomes thinner.
- If it bursts, it falls back to earth.
- If it does not burst, it slowly loses helium and drifts back to earth.

4. Create a sequence of models for the toaster:

- Push the carrying rack and toast down into the toaster, against spring pressure.
- Heat source heats up the interior of the toaster, including the bread. Bread approaches the burn point, latch approaches the release point.
- Once the latch releases, the carrying rack and toast accelerate upward.
- After the rack stops, the toast continues upward, perhaps flying out of the toaster.

5. In some cases, the boundary between operating regions is hard to express by a simple landmark value of a variable in the QDE. For example, the boundaries between the solid, liquid, and gas phases of a substance are normally functions of both pressure and temperature.

In such a case, the boundary can be considered a *hypersurface* in the product space of the variables (Kokar, 1987). Such a transition can be represented in this framework by defining an auxiliary function, say $h(x, y, \ldots)$, with a landmark value c in the quantity space for h, such that the region transition occurs when $h(t) = \langle c, inc \rangle$ or $h(t) = \langle c, dec \rangle$.

For example, the dimensionless *Reynold's number*,

$$R = \frac{\rho \cdot v \cdot D}{\eta},$$

where ρ is density, v is average velocity, D is pipe diameter, and η is viscosity, captures important qualitative properties of fluid flow within a pipe. When $R < 2000$, flow is laminar; when $R > 3000$, flow is turbulent; when $2000 < R < 3000$, flow is unstable, changing from one form to the other. Therefore, the hypersurfaces defined by $R = 2000$ and $R = 3000$ define boundaries between regions for laminar flow and turbulent flow.

Make the simplifying assumption that the flow regime changes from laminar to turbulent at a landmark value R^* in $[2000, 3000]$. Look up the dependence of flow on pressure in each regime, and build a model of flow within a pipe that exhibits transitions between laminar and turbulent flow.

6. Build a two-compartment pharmaco-kinetic model of drug metabolism. This is a two-tank cascade (figure 10.5), with the upstream tank representing the gut, which receives a bolus (an instantaneous increment) of drug. The drug is absorbed into the bloodstream from the gut, and eventually excreted from the blood. An S^+ constraint describes the relationship between the serum concentration and the therapeutic effect. Use the "ignore-qdir" method of section 10.6 to avoid intractable branching.

7. An MOS transistor (Mead and Conway, 1980, section 1.1) has three terminals, the *gate*, the *source*, and the *drain*. The gate controls the rate that current can flow between the source and the drain. For a fixed, positive voltage V_{gs} between the gate and the source, the current I_{ds} to the drain from the source is proportional to the voltage V_{ds}, but only up to a threshold value. Beyond that point, the transistor is said to be *saturated*, and I_{ds} remains constant, independent of V_{ds}.

(a) For fixed V_{gs}, use the S^+ constraint to model the behavior of the MOS transistor.

(b) As V_{gs} varies, the behavior of the MOS transistor is given by the following figure (taken from Mead and Conway, 1980, figure 1.4, p. 3). Extend your model to incorporate the qualitative properties of this figure.

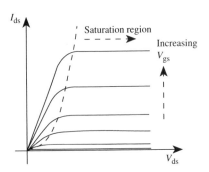

8. Use a U^- constraint to represent the Laffer curve,

$$revenue = U^-(taxrate),$$

which was used as the basis of "supply-side economics." Create a QSIM model that predicts the possible effects of reducing taxes. What is the critical ambiguity in this model?

9. If $f \in M_0^+$, and we define

$$PE(y) = \int_0^y f(x)dx,$$

prove that $PE(y) = U^+(y)$.

10. Use region transitions to model the effect of actions taken by an agent in a dynamic environment. Implement QDE models of the following scenarios.

    (a) A chemical engineer first opens the inflow valve on a water tank (section 6.1), later opens the drain valve, and finally closes the inflow valve.

    (b) A trapeze artist waits while the trapeze swings toward him, then leaps toward it from a platform, either catching it or falling into the net.

Extend these examples to planning and plan refinement, as well as prediction. Semi-quantitative reasoning methods (chapter 9) will be useful for this task. You will probably also find it helpful to use the qualitative modeling methods illustrated by the example in section 9.6.

11. (Research Problem.) Combine qualitative simulation and the situation calculus to address the problem of reasoning about action in a continuous world. Reasoning about action in the situation calculus has been a very active research area, but typically represents time as a sequence of discrete points. See McCarthy and Hayes, 1969; Allen, 1984; Lifschitz, 1987; Baker, 1991; and Gelfond *et al.*, 1991, among many others.

    Sandewall (1989), Shoham and McDermott (1988), and Rayner (1991) engage in an interesting argument about how to reason about continuous time. As we have seen, the qualitative simulation perspective provides a very different viewpoint on this topic, which I believe can be very productive. Forbus (1989) addresses some aspects of this issue, but much remains to be done.

9 Semi-Quantitative Reasoning

Semi-quantitative reasoning is the task of combining incomplete quantitative and qualitative knowledge.

Semi-quantitative reasoning is important to model-based reasoning tasks such as diagnosis, monitoring, and design. By their nature, these tasks involve incomplete knowledge in both qualitative and quantitative forms. The use of qualitative behaviors to define a framework for quantitative reasoning has been important from the beginning of qualitative reasoning in AI (de Kleer, 1977).

There are a number of different representations for incomplete knowledge of quantities, including bounding intervals, probability distribution functions, fuzzy sets, and order-of-magnitude relations. In this chapter, we will focus on the use of bounding intervals $[lb, ub]$ where $lb, ub \in \Re^*$, to represent partial knowledge of a real number $x_0 \in \Re$:

$$range(x_0) = [lb, ub] \quad \equiv \quad x_0 \in [lb, ub] \quad \equiv \quad lb \le x_0 \le ub.$$

Fortunately, the qualitative behavior description generated by QSIM provides exactly the right framework for semi-quantitative reasoning. Landmark values are symbolic names for unknown real values: i.e., they can be viewed as algebraic variables. There are a few other terms implied by the qualitative behavior description that also denote real numbers, and so have the same role. The QDE and the behavior description imply constraints which can be expressed as algebraic equations over these value-denoting terms.

Given interval bounds on the values of some landmarks, a behavior description and its QDE define a constraint-satisfaction problem: its variables are the landmarks and related terms; the domain of each variable is the set of intervals with bounds in $\Re^*$; and the constraints are the implied algebraic equations. A solution to this CSP is an assignment of an interval to each landmark (and related term) consistent with the constraints (Davis, 1987). If no solution exists, the constraints and given interval bounds are inconsistent, so the behavior is refuted. If there are solutions, we want to find the solution for which the interval bounds are as tight as possible.

Q2 (for **Q**ualitative + **Q**uantitative) is the basic semi-quantitative reasoner implemented as an extension to QSIM (Kuipers and Berleant, 1988). Functionally, it acts as a global filter on behaviors (cf. section 5.4), inferring bounds on value-denoting terms and refuting behaviors when possible. Q2 uses constraint propagation (section 4.2) and interval arithmetic (Moore, 1966; 1979) to tighten interval bounds on value-denoting terms. Figure 9.1 shows the representations used in QSIM + Q2 for qualitative and quantitative information, and the processes that generate each from its predecessors.

Like QSIM, Q2 does conservative inference, ruling out values or behaviors only when they are genuinely inconsistent (section 9.4). This extends QSIM's guaranteed coverage to semi-quantitative reasoning.

Section 9.5.4 describes recent advances building on QSIM + Q2 to provide tighter bounds in the semi-quantitative prediction, and a guarantee that the semi-quantitative prediction converges to the real trajectory as uncertainty in the given intervals shrinks to zero.

9.1   Example: The Water Tank

We illustrate QSIM + Q2 with a simple example exhibiting first-order dynamic behavior: a water tank of finite size, moving from empty toward a steady state where outflow balances inflow (figure 9.2). Q2 has been applied to many larger qualitative models, especially in the domain of chemical engineering (Dalle Molle, 1989; Dalle Molle and Edgar, 1989).

• Figure 9.2 describes a state of very incomplete quantitative knowledge about the structure of a water tank: its capacity is between 80 and 100 gallons, and the inflow rate is between 4 and 8 gallons per minute.[1]

• Figure 9.3 shows the computable *static envelopes* bounding the region which contains the actual monotonic function described by the constraint *outflow* = $M^+(amount)$. Engineering handbooks in many domains often contain tables and graphs specifying envelopes similar to these.

• Figure 9.4 shows two of the three qualitative behaviors (equilibrium and overflow) predicted by QSIM for the water tank. The third behavior (equilibrium at the brim of the tank) is the boundary case between the other two, and is treated much like the overflow behavior in this example.

Each qualitative behavior serves as a framework for semi-quantitative reasoning by providing a set of landmarks (and other terms not visible in the plot) that can be annotated with interval bounds. A few qualitative behaviors cover a wide range of real possibilities. A contradiction refutes a qualitative behavior and all the real possibilities it describes. And the descriptions of the survivors are strengthened by semi-quantitative annotations.

---

[1] We do not address the important issues of units and unit conversion. In all examples, all quantities are assumed to have appropriate and compatible units.

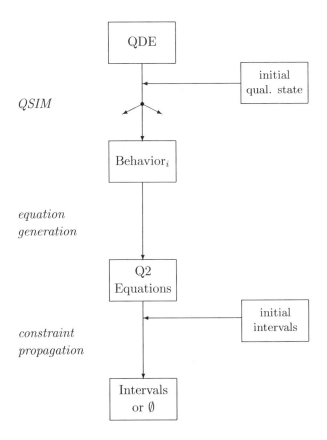

Figure 9.1
Overview of qualitative and quantitative reasoning in Q2.

QSIM predicts one or more qualitative behaviors from a given QDE and initial state. Each behavior implies a set of algebraic equations relating value- and set-denoting terms to each other. Incomplete knowledge about values associated with these terms can be propagated across the equations, either refuting the behavior or producing a stronger semi-quantitative description.

9.2 Generating Equations from a Behavior

Given a qualitative behavior, we can systematically generate a set of terms denoting specific but unknown real values, terms denoting sets or ranges of values, and equations and inequalities among those terms. We will refer to them as the *Q2 equations*. The Q2 equations can support a variety of different types of numerical

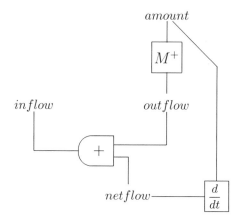

```
(define-QDE Water-tank
  (quantity-spaces
    (amount    (0 full inf))
    (outflow   (0 inf))
    (inflow    (0 if* inf))
    (netflow   (minf 0 inf)))
  (constraints
    ((M+ amount outflow)    (0 0) (inf inf))
    ((add netflow outflow inflow))
    ((d/dt amount netflow))
    ((constant inflow)))
  (transitions ((amount (full inc)) -> t))
  (envelopes
    ((M+ amount outflow) (upper ue)    ; ue, ui, le, and li
                         (u-inv ui)    ; are the names of the
                         (lower le)    ; envelope functions
                         (l-inv li)))
  (initial-ranges ((amount full) (80 100))
                  ((inflow if*)  (4 8))
                  ((time t0)     (0 0)))))
```

Figure 9.2
Qualitative and semi-quantitative water tank model.

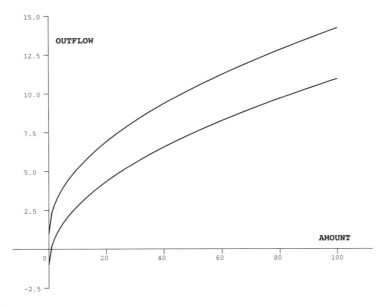

Figure 9.3
Static envelope for $outflow = M^+(amount)$.

$$y = e_u(x) \quad = \quad k\sqrt{\alpha_u x} + \beta_u$$

$$y = e_l(x) \quad = \quad k\sqrt{\alpha_l x} + \beta_l$$

where $k = 1.26$, $\alpha_u = 1.1$, $\alpha_l = 0.9$, $\beta_u = +1.0$, and $\beta_l = -1.0$.

and symbolic inference about the implications of qualitative behaviors.

A qualitative behavior is a set of qualitative states representing a sequence of alternating time-points and time-intervals.

$$Behavior = [Qstate(t_0), Qstate(t_0, t_1), Qstate(t_1), \ldots, Qstate(t_n)].$$

At each qualitative state, each variable has a qualitative value.

Equations are derived from the values the variables take on at a state, the constraints among the variables, the corresponding values, and the values of variables at time-points adjacent to each time-interval. Equation generation depends on the fact that the behavior of each variable is qualitatively uniform between adjacent time-points.

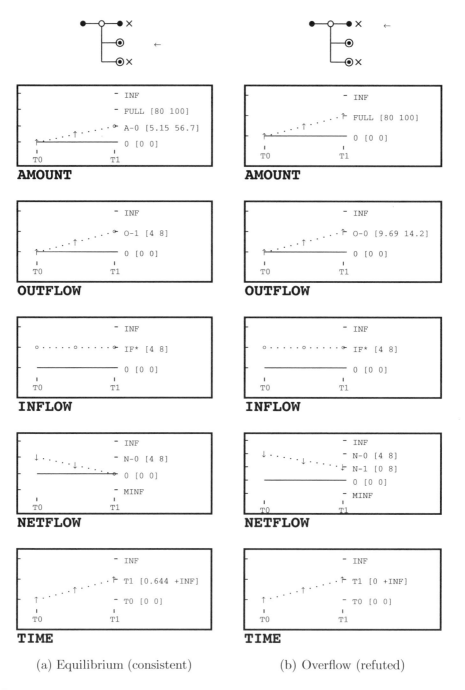

(a) Equilibrium (consistent) (b) Overflow (refuted)

Figure 9.4
Water tank behaviors with quantitative interval information.

In the overflow behavior, the constraint $netflow(t_1) = inflow(t_1) - outflow(t_1)$ implies the equation $if^* = n_1 + o_0$, which implies a contradiction: $[4, 8] = [0, 8] + [9.69, 14.2]$.

9.2.1 Value-Denoting Terms

There are four kinds of terms denoting specific but unknown real values that arise from the qualitative behavior description.

- **Landmarks.** The landmark value p in the quantity space of the variable $x(t)$ is represented internally as (x p). The time-point t_i is represented as (time ti).

- **Non-landmark point values.** If, at some time-point t_i, described by qualitative state s_i, $x(t_i)$ is not equal to a landmark value, it is represented internally as (x (at si)). In such a case, $x(t_i)$ falls within some interval (p, q), so we can assert the inequalities $p < x(t_i) < q$.

- **Difference terms.** The difference $q - p$ between two landmarks $p < q$ of the variable $x(t)$ is written as $d(p, q)$, and represented internally as (x (d p q)). The qualitative behavior description contains enough information to determine whether $p < q$ or $q < p$, so the difference between p and q is always positive, and can always be written correctly as $d(p, q)$ or $d(q, p)$, respectively.

  Difference terms are created as needed by equations following from the Mean Value Theorem, at which time appropriate defining equations are asserted. For example,

$$d(p, q) \;=\; q - p$$
$$d(t_{i-1}, t_i) \;=\; t_i - t_{i-1}.$$

- **Monotonic functions.** The QSIM constraint ((M+ x y) ...(p q) ...) asserts that there is some function $f \in M^+$ such that $y = f(x)$, and $q = f(p)$. (The M- constraint is treated similarly.)

  In order to express the equations $q = f(p)$ and $p = f^{-1}(q)$, we need terms denoting the value resulting from applying a function to an argument.

term	internal representation
$f(p)$	(function (M+ x y) (x p))
$f^{-1}(q)$	(inverse (M+ x y) (y q))

9.2.2 Set-Denoting Terms

In addition to terms denoting real numbers, there is need for terms denoting sets or ranges of real values.

- **Indefinite values.** In Q2, the Mean Value Theorem asserts equations that refer to the value of $x(t^*)$ for some unspecified $t^* \in (t_{i-1}, t_i)$, between two adjacent time-points. If the state of the system over the time-interval (t_{i-1}, t_i) is described by

the qualitative state s_i, then the indefinite value term is represented internally as
(x (at si)).

An indefinite value is constrained by the "span" of its defining interval. Where
p and q are any two qualitative values, not necessarily landmarks, define the term
$span(p, q)$ to denote the smallest landmark-bounded interval including both p and
q. When reasoning about $x(t^*)$, where $t^* \in (t_{i-1}, t_i)$, we know that $x(t^*) \in$
$span(x(t_{i-1}), x(t_i))$, because the behavior of x must be qualitatively uniform between the adjacent time-points t_{i-1} and t_i, so $x(t)$ is monotonic within (t_{i-1}, t_i).

The assertion $x(t^*) \in span(p, q)$ is translated into inequalities of the form $p <$
$x(t^*) < q$, if $p < q$ and p and q are both landmark values. If $p > q$, the senses of
the inequalities are reversed. If either p or q is not a landmark value, the form of
the inequality remains the same, but the appropriate landmark bounds are derived
from the quantity space of x.

- **Properties of functions**. There are several semi-quantitative ways to describe
the graph of a partially known monotonic function $f \in M^+$. The term $slope(f)$ denotes the smallest interval containing all values of $f'(x)$, and $curvature(f)$ denotes
the smallest interval containing all values of $f''(x)$. Figure 9.3 shows an example
of bounding envelope functions.

9.2.3   Arithmetic Constraints

Arithmetic constraints imply corresponding Q2 equations relating values of the
variables appearing in the constraints. Each equation is derived either from corresponding value tuples, or from the values taken on by the variables at a particular
time-point.

- ((ADD x y z) ...(p q r) ...).
  Each corresponding value tuple (p q r) implies $p + q = r$.
  At each time-point t, $x(t) + y(t) = z(t)$.

- ((MULT x y z) ...(p q r) ...).
  Each corresponding value tuple (p q r) implies $p \cdot q = r$.
  At each time-point t, $x(t) \cdot y(t) = z(t)$.

- ((MINUS x y) ...(p q) ...).
  Each corresponding value tuple (p q) implies $p = -q$.
  At each time-point t, $x(t) = -y(t)$.

9.2.4   Quantity Spaces

A pair of adjacent landmarks p and q in the quantity space ($\cdots$ p q $\cdots$) implies the inequality $p < q$. Time is also a quantity space, so adjacent time-points ($\cdots t_{i-1}\ t_i\ \cdots$) are adjacent landmarks, and imply that $t_{i-1} < t_i$.

In the current implementation of Q2, these inequalities are not generated explicitly but are enforced by a more efficient special-purpose algorithm. Non-landmark point values are handled similarly.

9.2.5   Derivative Constraints: (d/dt x y)

Given $y = dx/dt$, the Fundamental Theorem of the Calculus says that, for each time-interval (t_{i-1}, t_i),

$$x(t_i) - x(t_{i-1}) = \int_{t_{i-1}}^{t_i} y(t)\ dt. \tag{9.1}$$

(See Spivak, 1967, or any other good calculus text.) Then, the Mean Value Theorem for Integrals says that

$$\int_{t_{i-1}}^{t_i} y(t)\ dt = (t_i - t_{i-1}) \cdot y(t^*) \tag{9.2}$$

for some t^* in $[t_{i-1}, t_i]$. Finally, as previously discussed,

$$y(t^*) \in span(y(t_{i-1}), y(t_i)). \tag{9.3}$$

We can therefore conclude

$$d(x(t_{i-1}), x(t_i)) \ \in \ d(t_{i-1}, t_i) \cdot span(y(t_{i-1}), y(t_i)). \tag{9.4}$$

In Q2, this is expressed as an inclusion between interval-valued expressions:

$$\frac{range(d(x(t_{i-1}), x(t_i)))}{range(d(t_{i-1}, t_i))} \ \subseteq \ span(y(t_{i-1}), y(t_i)). \tag{9.5}$$

It is worth noting that the longer chain of three equations introduces a potentially useful value-denoting term, the definite integral:

$$\int_{t_{i-1}}^{t_i} y(t)\ dt. \tag{9.6}$$

While Q2 does not make significant use of this term, the derivation of dynamic envelopes (Kay and Kuipers, 1993) exploits the definite integral and the structure of the QDE to derive tighter bounds on the behavior prediction than is possible with the Mean Value Theorem alone. (See section 9.5.4.)

Since the behavior of $x(t)$ must be qualitatively uniform between adjacent time-points, if we know $qdir(x)$ over the interval (t_{i-1}, t_i), we also know the sign of $x(t_i) - x(t_{i-1})$, so the range associated with $d(x(t_i), x(t_{i-1}))$ cannot straddle zero.

9.2.6 Monotonic Function Constraints: (M+ x y)

The QSIM constraint ((M+ x y) ...(p q) ...) asserts that there is some function $f \in M^+$ such that $y = f(x)$, and $q = f(p)$. (The M- constraint is treated similarly.)

The user can specify numerical *envelope functions* $\overline{f}$ and $\underline{f}$ providing bounds on f, such that

$$\underline{f}(x) \leq f(x) \leq \overline{f}(x) \text{ for all } x.$$

These externally provided bounds on monotonic functions in the QDE are sometimes referred to as *static envelopes*, to distinguish them from derived *dynamic envelopes* that provide semi-quantitative bounds on predicted behaviors (Kay and Kuipers, 1993).

- **Constraints on the function.** Each corresponding value pair (p q) implies the equations $q = f(p)$ and $p = f^{-1}(q)$.

equation	internal representation
$q = f(p)$	(= (y q) (function (M+ x y) (x p)))
$p = f^{-1}(q)$	(= (x p) (inverse (M+ x y) (y q)))

Similarly, at any time-point t_i, we may assert the equations $y(t_i) = f(x(t_i))$ and $x(t_i) = f^{-1}(y(t_i))$. If both $x(t_i)$ and $y(t_i)$ take on landmark values, this relationship is already expressed by the corresponding value pair.

Propagation of quantitative intervals over an equation such as $q = f(p)$ requires user-supplied numerical envelopes that provide upper and lower bounds on f and f^{-1}. (See section 9.3.4.)

- **Constraints on the function's derivative.** If we know that $f \in M^+$, and no quantitative bounds are known for $f'(x)$, then the Mean Value Theorem does not imply any useful conclusions. However, quantitative bounds frequently *are* known for $f'(x)$. In such a case, just as with the derivative constraint, the Mean Value Theorem asserts that, for each time-interval (t_{i-1}, t_i), $\exists x^* \in span(x(t_{i-1}), x(t_i))$ such that

$$\frac{y(t_i) - y(t_{i-1})}{x(t_i) - x(t_{i-1})} = \frac{d(y(t_{i-1}), y(t_i))}{d(x(t_{i-1}), x(t_i))} = f'(x^*) \in slope(f).$$

In Q2, this is expressed as an inclusion among interval-valued expressions, similar to equation (9.5).

9.2.7 Indexing the Equations

We have seen how a variety of Q2 equations can be derived from a given qualitative behavior. Suppose we have an equation $E(p, q, r, s, \ldots)$ expressing a relationship among the value- and set-denoting terms $\{p, q, r, s, \ldots\}$. In order to use this equation for propagation, we need to rearrange it to obtain an expression for each term as a function of the others:

$$
\begin{aligned}
p &= f_1(q, r, s, \ldots) \\
q &= f_2(p, r, s, \ldots) \\
r &= f_3(p, q, s, \ldots) \\
&\cdots
\end{aligned}
$$

Depending on the structure of $E(p, q, r, s, \ldots)$, it may not always be possible to solve for each term.

We will update the value for p by evaluating $f_1(q, r, s, \ldots)$ using interval arithmetic, and intersecting the new and the old values.

For example, consider the equation $p + q = r$.

1. The equation $p + q = r$ has three different forms, useful under different circumstances, depending on what information has been changed.

$$
\begin{aligned}
r &= p + q \qquad \text{if } changed(p) \text{ or } changed(q) \\
p &= r - q \qquad \text{if } changed(r) \text{ or } changed(q) \\
q &= r - p \qquad \text{if } changed(r) \text{ or } changed(p)
\end{aligned}
$$

2. Index the equations for efficient retrieval.

$$
\begin{aligned}
changed(p) \;&\rightarrow\; r = p + q \\
&\rightarrow\; q = r - p \\
changed(q) \;&\rightarrow\; r = p + q \\
&\rightarrow\; p = r - q \\
changed(r) \;&\rightarrow\; p = r - q \\
&\rightarrow\; q = r - p
\end{aligned}
$$

This indexing is done for each of the Q2 equations derived from a given qualitative behavior.

$o_1 = f(a_0)$	$a_0 = f^{-1}(o_1)$
$if^* = n_0 + 0$	$n_0 = if^* - 0$
	$0 = if^* - n_0$
$if^* = 0 + o_1$	$o_1 = if^* - 0$
	$0 = if^* - o_1$
$span(n_0, 0) = d(0, a_0)/d(t_0, t_1)$	$d(0, a_0) = d(t_0, t_1) \cdot span(n_0, 0)$
	$d(t_0, t_1) = d(0, a_0)/span(n_0, 0)$
$slope(f) = d(0, o_1)/d(0, a_0)$	$d(0, o_1) = slope(f) \cdot d(0, a_0)$
	$d(0, a_0) = d(0, o_1)/slope(f)$
	$d(0, a_0) = a_0 - 0$
	$a_0 = d(0, a_0) - 0$
	$0 = a_0 - d(0, a_0)$
	$d(t_0, t_1) = t_1 - t_0$
	$t_1 = d(t_0, t_1) - t_0$
	$t_0 = t_1 - d(t_0, t_1)$
	$d(0, o_1) = o_1 - 0$
	$o_1 = d(0, o_1) - 0$
	$0 = o_1 - d(0, o_1)$

Figure 9.5
Q2 equations implied by the equilibrium behavior of the water tank.

The basic equations are on the left. The right column contains derived forms of the equation and defining equations for $d(p, q)$ terms.

Figure 9.5 shows the set of Q2 equations generated from the equilibrium qualitative behavior of the water tank. Problem 1 asks you to derive these equations and the corresponding set for the overflow behavior.

9.3   Interval Constraint Propagation

We treat the value- and set-denoting terms, and the Q2 equations relating them, as defining a constraint-satisfaction problem over domains of interval values. This section describes how Q2 uses constraint-propagation methods to find a solution or a contradiction.

9.3.1 Representation: Intervals around Values

A landmark value is a symbol representing a unique but unknown real number. The incompletely known value of a landmark value p can be described by a closed interval on the real line:

$$range(p) = [lb, ub] = \{x \in \Re \mid lb \leq x \leq ub\}.$$

We allow $+\infty$ to be an upper bound, and $-\infty$ to be a lower bound, even though $\pm\infty$ are not actual values in $\Re$, and so cannot be elements of $range(p)$. Where $range(p) = [a, b]$, we may use the selector functions $lb(p) = a$ and $ub(p) = b$.

The interval representation is well understood, widely used, and quite powerful (Moore, 1966; 1979; Alefeld and Herzberger, 1983). Many researchers in AI have developed and applied methods for combined algebraic, ordinal, and interval reasoning (Brooks, 1981; Brown et $al.$, 1982; McDermott, 1983; McDermott and Davis, 1984; Simmons, 1986; Davis, 1987; Dean and McDermott, 1987; Karp and Friedland, 1989; Ward et $al.$, 1989).

As Ward et $al.$ (1989) point out, there are multiple interpretations for interval descriptions of quantities, with different computational implications. In Q2, we interpret each interval as describing the set of possible values of an incompletely known, but constant, real number or range that is an attribute of an individual physical system.

Quantitative knowledge expressed as intervals complements qualitative knowledge expressed as ordinal relations, each description providing information difficult or impossible to express in the other form. Figure 9.6 illustrates this. Landmarks A and B may appear anywhere in the range $[0, 1]$, but must also obey constraints on their order and distance from each other.

9.3.2 Representation: Envelopes around Functions

Describing an unknown monotonic function $f \in M^+$ is more complex than describing a single value. However, we can follow the same philosophy by specifying bounding "envelope" functions (e.g., figure 9.3). In addition to using envelopes to constrain the values a function f can take on, it is possible to assert bounds on its derivatives f' and f''.

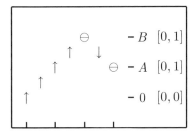

Independent assertions:

$$range(A) = [0, 1]$$
$$range(B) = [0, 1]$$
$$range(d(A, B)) = [0, .2]$$

Figure 9.6
Complementary qualitative and quantitative descriptions.

- The constraint that $A < B$ is in the qualitative description, but not in the quantitive description.

- The constraint that $B - A \leq .2$ is in the quantitative description, but not in the qualitative description.

1. *Envelopes* are numerically computable partial functions $\underline{f}$ and $\overline{f}$, with numerically computable partial inverses $\underline{f}^{-1}$ and $\overline{f}^{-1}$, such that

$$\forall x, \ \underline{f}(x) \leq f(x) \leq \overline{f}(x).$$

2. *Derivative bounds*, $[m_l, m_u]$, assert that $\forall x, f'(x) \in [m_l, m_u]$.

3. *Curvature bounds*, $[c_l, c_u]$, assert that $\forall x, f''(x) \in [c_l, c_u]$.

The envelopes need only be *partial* functions. Where they are undefined, they are treated as providing no constraint. The use of partial functions is required to handle cases where an M^+ or M^- function has a finite vertical or horizontal asymptote, in which case either an envelope function or its inverse may only be defined over part of the real line.

The derivative bounds are useful for equations involving an $f'(x^*)$ term, derived from M+/M– constraints (section 9.2.6). Curvature bounds are not currently used, but may eventually be useful for evaluating higher-order derivative constraints (chapter 10).

9.3.3   Interval Arithmetic

We define the range resulting from evaluating an expression as the smallest closed interval including all values of the expression, wherever it is defined, for any values in the ranges of the variables in the expression. Thus, we may evaluate the expression num/den even if $range(den)$ includes the value 0. In Q2, no interval involved in a quotient can straddle zero, though it may have zero as an endpoint, because QSIM requires that any qualitative variable participating in a multiplication constraint must have the landmark 0 in its quantity space.

Suppose we have a multiplicative relation such as

$$quo = num/den,$$

where we know that $range(num) = [1,1]$. Then we can draw conclusions like the following:

$$
\begin{aligned}
range(den) = [1,2] \quad &\Rightarrow \quad range(quo) = [0.5, 1] \\
range(den) = [0,2] \quad &\Rightarrow \quad range(quo) = [0.5, +\infty] \\
range(den) = [-2,0] \quad &\Rightarrow \quad range(quo) = [-\infty, -0.5] \\
range(den) = [2,\infty] \quad &\Rightarrow \quad range(quo) = [0, 0.5] \\
range(den) = [-\infty, -2] \quad &\Rightarrow \quad range(quo) = [-0.5, 0] \\
range(den) = [-2, +2] \quad &\Rightarrow \quad range(quo) = [-\infty, +\infty] \\
range(den) = [-\infty, +\infty] \quad &\Rightarrow \quad range(quo) = [-\infty, +\infty] \\
range(den) = [0,0] \quad &\Rightarrow \quad range(quo) = \emptyset
\end{aligned}
$$

Note that $num/den = [1,1]/[0,0] = \emptyset$ because there is no $x \in num$ and $y \in den$ such that x/y is defined. Also, $[1,1]/[-2,+2] = [-\infty,+\infty]$, even though values in the open interval $(-0.5,+0.5)$ are not possible values for quo. It is possible to extend the interval representation to accept unions (i.e., disjunctions) of disjoint intervals. We do not do so in Q2 because of the possibility of explosively increasing numbers of disjoint intervals in each union.

9.3.4   Expression Evaluation

A recursive expression-evaluator computes the interval value of an expression in terms of the interval values of its parts. A real number evaluates to an interval of zero width, and a primitive value- or set-denoting term is evaluated by looking up its stored value.

- Base cases: x is a primitive term or constant.

$$x \in \Re \quad \rightarrow \quad range(x) = [x, x]$$
$$primitive(x) \quad \rightarrow \quad lookup(x)$$

- Decomposing expressions: x and y are expressions evaluating to intervals, and $f \in M^+$.

$$
\begin{aligned}
range(x + y) &= [lb(x) + lb(y), ub(x) + ub(y)] \\
range(x - y) &= [lb(x) - ub(y), ub(x) - lb(y)] \\
range(span(x, y)) &= [min(lb(x), lb(y)), max(ub(x), ub(y))] \\
range(|x|) &= \begin{cases} [lb(x), ub(x)] & \text{if } lb(x) \geq 0 \\ [-ub(x), -lb(x)] & \text{if } ub(x) \leq 0 \\ [0, max(ub(x), -lb(x))] & \text{otherwise} \end{cases} \\
range(x \cdot y) &= [lb(x) \cdot lb(y), ub(x) \cdot ub(y)] \\
& \quad \text{if } lb(x) \geq 0 \text{ and } lb(y) \geq 0 \\
range(1/x) &= [1/ub(x), 1/lb(x)], \text{ if } lb(x) > 0 \\
range(x/y) &= range(x \cdot (1/y)) \\
range(f(x)) &= [\underline{f}(lb(x)), \overline{f}(ub(x))] \\
range(f^{-1}(y)) &= [\overline{f}^{-1}(lb(y)), \underline{f}^{-1}(ub(y))]
\end{aligned}
$$

The entries in this table for $x \cdot y$ and $1/x$ handle only the cases where $x, y \geq 0$. The full case split on possible conbinations of signs, and the extension to handle $\pm\infty$ as bounds, are straightforward (problem 4).

9.3.5   Intersecting New Intervals with Old

The equations derived from a behavior are of the form $p = f(q, r, s, \ldots)$, where f is an arithmetic expression. We retrieve the known values associated with $q, r, s, \cdots$, and use interval arithmetic to compute a revised value for p,

$$p_{new} = f(q, r, s, \cdots).$$

However, we always have some *a priori* knowledge, $range(p) = p_{old}$, about the value of p, even if only that $range(p) = [-\infty, +\infty]$. Therefore, the stored value of $range(p)$ must be updated to

$$range(p) = p_{old} \cap p_{new}.$$

Because new and old values are intersected, $range(p)$ always shrinks monotonically, so the quantitative precision of the belief can never decrease.

If $p_{old} \cap p_{new} = \emptyset$, there is a contradiction between the qualitative behavior description (the source of the equations) and the quantitative information (the given intervals). In the context of a qualitative simulation, a contradiction refutes the current behavior. This, in turn, increases our confidence in the alternate behaviors or makes it possible to refute an entire model (section 9.5.1).

9.3.6   Benefits of the Interval Representation

As simple as it is, the interval representation gives us a number of important benefits. Its simplicity means that descriptions of incomplete knowledge of quantities in the form of bounding intervals are easy to obtain. Furthermore, the consequence of two interval descriptions of the same quantity is easy to compute by intersecting the intervals.

One well-known limitation of interval-based simulation is the uncertainty explosion that results from repeated operations on interval values. Q2 avoids the uncertainty explosion because there is a fixed set of terms with interval values, determined by the qualitative behavior, rather than an indefinitely increasing set of terms as in a traditional time-stepped numerical simulation. A newly inferred interval is *intersected* with the previous interval associated with a given term, so uncertainty decreases monotonically as the computation progresses.[2]

9.3.7   Inference: Propagation

Local propagation of intervals across equations and inequalities is a simple and reasonably powerful inference method. Inclusions (e.g., equation (9.5)) are treated identically to equations, except that the range on an including interval is not updated.

Conceptually, propagation of quantitative ranges takes place after qualitative simulation has produced a set of complete behavior descriptions. However, for efficiency, Q2 runs as a global filter after each time-point state is created. This interleaves semi-quantitative range propagation with qualitative simulation to prune impossible branches earlier in the simulation process.

Interval propagation in Q2 can be implemented as a simple agenda-driven loop.

---

[2]In the extended algorithm Q3 (section 9.5.4; Berleant and Kuipers, 1991; 1992), an indefinitely large number of new terms can be created, but only when bounded by existing terms, so the uncertainty explosion is still prevented.

Algorithm **Q2 Propagation**:

Given a time-point state $S(t_i)$ and initial bounds on the value-denoting and set-denoting terms in the behavior segment $[S(t_0), \ldots, S(t_i)]$.

1. Generate the Q2 equations implied by the behavior segment and place them on the agenda.

2. Select an equation $p = f(q, r, s, \ldots)$ from the agenda.

  • If the agenda is empty, stop.

Let $p_{old} = range(p)$, the current range stored for the value-denoting term p.

3. Use interval arithmetic to compute $p_{new} = f(q, r, s, \ldots)$.

4. If $p_{old} \cap p_{new} = \emptyset$, the current behavior is refuted.

5. Update the stored value of $range(p)$ to $p_{old} \cap p_{new}$.

  • If $p_{old} \neq p_{old} \cap p_{new}$, then $changed(p)$.

6. Retrieve equations indexed under $changed(p)$, and add them to the agenda. Go to step 2.

It is possible for a local propagation algorithm such as this to enter a theoretically infinite loop converging to a value or interval. Such a loop cannot diverge, because the size of $range(p)$ is non-increasing.

In practice, exponential convergence to a value, as in problem 3, halts quickly due to the finite precision of floating point arithmetic. If need be, the definition of $changed(p)$ could require a change to $lb(p)$ or $ub(p)$ more than some minimum $\epsilon > 0$ (Davis, 1987).

Figure 9.7 shows the propagation steps by which Q2 derived the intervals associated with terms in the equilibrium qualitative behavior of the water tank. Problem 2 asks you to replicate this process for both the equilibrium and overflow behaviors in figure 9.4.

9.4   Soundness

In this section, we provide a guarantee that the conclusions derived by Q2 are sound. That is, if Q2 derives a contradiction, then the qualitative behavior is inconsistent with the given QDE, initial qualitative state, and initial quantitative ranges. Every real solution to an ODE consistent with the given QDE, initial qualitative state

Variable:Landmark			
$amount : full$	$[-\infty, +\infty]$	$\rightarrow$	$[80, 100]$
$inflow : if^*$	$[-\infty, +\infty]$	$\rightarrow$	$[4, 8]$
$amount : a_0$	$[-\infty, +\infty]$	$\rightarrow$	$[-\infty, 100]$
$amount : a_0$	$[-\infty, 100]$	$\rightarrow$	$[0, 100]$
$outflow : o_1$	$[-\infty, +\infty]$	$\rightarrow$	$[0, +\infty]$
$outflow : o_1$	$[0, +\infty]$	$\rightarrow$	$[0, 14.2]$
$amount : d(0, a_0)$	$[-\infty, +\infty]$	$\rightarrow$	$[0, 100]$
$outflow : d(0, o_1)$	$[-\infty, +\infty]$	$\rightarrow$	$[0, 14.2]$
$time : t_1$	$[-\infty, +\infty]$	$\rightarrow$	$[0, +\infty]$
$time : d(t_0, t_1)$	$[-\infty, +\infty]$	$\rightarrow$	$[0, +\infty]$
$netflow : at(t_0, t_1)$	$[-\infty, +\infty]$	$\rightarrow$	$[0, +\infty]$
$netflow : at(t_0, t_1)$	$[0, +\infty]$	$\rightarrow$	$[0, 8]$
$outflow : o_1$	$[0, 14.2]$	$\rightarrow$	$[4, 8]$
$outflow : d(0, o_1)$	$[0, 14.2]$	$\rightarrow$	$[4, 8]$
$amount : a_0$	$[0, 100]$	$\rightarrow$	$[5.15, 56.7]$
$amount : d(0, a_0)$	$[0, 100]$	$\rightarrow$	$[5.15, 56.7]$
$time : d(t_0, t_1)$	$[0, +\infty]$	$\rightarrow$	$[0.644, +\infty]$
$time : t_1$	$[0, +\infty]$	$\rightarrow$	$[0.644, +\infty]$

Figure 9.7
Q2 propagation of intervals through equations representing the equilibrium behavior.

and initial quantitative ranges must be included among the predictions from QSIM + Q2.

QSIM takes as input a QDE and a description of its state at time t_0. It then predicts the possible behaviors of the QDE as a (possibly branching) tree of states. A behavior is a sequence of qualitative descriptions of states:

$Behavior = [Qstate(t_0), Qstate(t_0, t_1), Qstate(t_1), \ldots, Qstate(t_n)]$.

QSIM can be viewed as a set of axioms about inequalities and continuous functions, along with a specialized theorem prover that proves theorems of the following form:

$QSIM \vdash (QDE \wedge Qstate(t_0)) \longrightarrow or(B_1, \ldots B_k)$,

where $\{B_1, \ldots B_k\}$ is the set of possible behaviors. That is, given a QDE, and starting in $Qstate(t_0)$, QSIM predicts that one of the behaviors $B_1, \ldots B_k$ will describe the actual behavior of the system.

- **QSIM is sound.** We have already shown (theorem 6, page 118) that, given a QDE and a qualitative description of an initial state, the set $\{B_1, \ldots B_k\}$ of predicted qualitative behaviors is guaranteed to contain all behaviors consistent with the given QDE and initial state. Soundness is proved because the QSIM algorithm implicitly defines a product space guaranteed to include all valid behaviors, and filters out impossible behaviors with provably correct filters. We follow this technique in proving the soundness of our semi-quantitative reasoning.

- **Equation derivation is sound.** Given a particular qualitative behavior description B_i, each equation derived from B_i is logically implied by B_i (by inspection of section 9.2). Therefore, if the derived equations are shown to be inconsistent with known quantitative information, B_i is refuted.

- **Interval arithmetic is sound.** An interval arithmetic expression evaluator can be constructed (Moore, 1966) so that, given an expression $f(x_1, \ldots, x_k)$ defined over landmark values $x_1, \ldots, x_k$, and given an interval $range(x_i)$ for each $i = 1, \ldots, k$, if $[lb, ub]$ is the value returned by the evaluator applied to $f(x_1, \ldots, x_k)$, then

$$\forall i, a_i \in range(x_i), \quad f(a_1, \ldots, a_k) \in [lb, ub].$$

The imprecision of machine arithmetic is accounted for by incrementing the upper bound and decrementing the lower bound of each new interval by a small amount at each operation.

Every landmark x_i is initially assigned the range $[-\infty, \infty]$. Ranges are updated by intersection, so $range(x_i)$ is always a closed interval or $\emptyset$.

- **Interval updating by intersection is sound.** If we know that $range(x_i) = [a, b]$, and later deduce that $range(x_i) = [c, d]$, then we can conclude that $range(x_i) = [a, b] \cap [c, d] = [max(a, c), min(b, d)]$. If $max(a, c) > min(b, d)$, then $range(x_i) = \emptyset$, and there is no possible value for x_i. The behavior within which this variable occurs must therefore be inconsistent.

We summarize this discussion as the following theorem.

THEOREM 7 (SOUNDNESS OF Q2)   Suppose we are given a QDE, $Qstate(t_0)$, and a set of interval ranges, $range(x_i)$, associated with value- and set-denoting terms in each behavior B_j in the QSIM prediction from QDE and $Qstate(t_0)$.

Then any real-valued solution to any ODE consistent with the given QDE, its initial qualitative state, and the quantitative ranges must also be consistent with the ranges derived by Q2 for one of the behaviors B_j.

The contrapositive of this theorem is sufficiently useful to state as an obvious corollary.

COROLLARY 1   Suppose we are given a QDE, $Qstate(t_0)$, and a set of interval ranges, $range(x_i)$, associated with landmarks in each behavior B_j in the QSIM prediction from QDE and $Qstate(t_0)$.

If Q2 derives $range(x_i) = \emptyset$ for any landmark x_i in a behavior B_j, then B_j does not describe any solution to any ODE consistent with the given qualitative and quantitative information. If *every* behavior predicted from QDE and $state(t_0)$ is thus excluded, then no ODE is consistent with the given qualitative and quantitative information.

That is, a refutation derived by Q2 is a sound consequence of the given information.

9.5   Discussion

9.5.1   Applications to Diagnosis

The water tank examples suggests a generate-and-test model for diagnosis, somewhat in the spirit of GTD (Simmons and Davis, 1987), in which Q2 serves as the *test* component.

1. A set of normal and fault models of a device is proposed. These models could be explicitly enumerated in advance, selected by an associative reasoner (Buchanan and Shortliffe, 1984), or generated automatically by a dependency-tracing algorithm that identifies and analyzes conflict sets (Reiter, 1987; de Kleer and Williams, 1987; Struss and Dressler, 1989).

2. QSIM predicts the possible behaviors for each model.

$$QDE \wedge Qstate(t_0) \rightarrow QBeh_1 \vee \cdots \vee QBeh_n.$$

3. Q2 uses quantitative information from observations or *a priori* knowlege to refine or refute each predicted behavior.

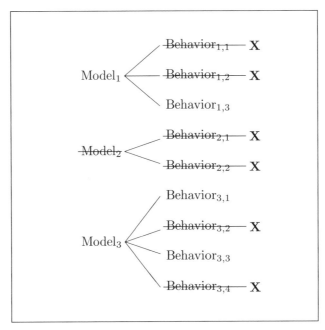

4. If all behaviors of a model are refuted, the model itself is rejected (e.g., Model$_2$ above).

$$Qstate(t_0) \wedge \neg QBeh_1 \wedge \cdots \wedge \neg QBeh_n \quad \rightarrow \quad \neg QDE$$

5. Analyze the remaining predictions (e.g., Behavior$_{1,3}$, Behavior$_{3,1}$, and Behavior$_{3,3}$) to select the most useful observation for further quantitative inference (step 3), or to propose new models (step 1).

This is the basis for the MIMIC approach to monitoring and diagnosis of continuous dynamic systems (Dvorak and Kuipers, 1989; Dvorak and Kuipers, 1991; Dvorak, 1992; Vinson and Ungar, 1993). An important issue in monitoring is finding a suitable qualitative or semi-quantitative description of an observed data stream (Cheung and Stephanopoulos, 1990). Another important issue is analyzing the observation stream to acquire static envelopes bounding monotonic functions (Hellerstein, 1990; Kay and Ungar, 1993).

Measurement interpretation via ATMI (Forbus, 1983; Forbus, 1986) and DATMI (DeCoste, 1991) is another approach to using qualitative behaviors to explain the qualitative properties of a stream of quantitative data. DATMI maps a quantitative observation stream into a stream of qualitative descriptors, then uses a total envisionment graph to "parse" the stream of qualitative descriptors. DATMI annotates the envisionment graph with transition probabilities to yield the most likely interpretation, and provides other facilities to handle missing or erroneous data. Q2 focuses on the task of unifying a given set of quantitative assertions with a given qualitative behavior, relying on MIMIC (Dvorak and Kuipers, 1989; Dvorak and Kuipers, 1991; Dvorak, 1992) to manage the set of possible interpretations. Q2 assimilates quantitative information directly to the behavior description, and thereby avoids the potential loss of information from mapping quantitative observations to a qualitative description prior to interpretation. DeCoste (1991) makes the plausible suggestion of a multi-level approach, using DATMI as a first filter on possible behaviors, followed by Q2.

9.5.2   Applications to Design

While designing an artifact, the partially specified model may be consistent with several qualitative behaviors, some desirable, some not. We can use semi-quantitative reasoning to derive bounds on controllable parameters adequate to guarantee, or prevent, particular behaviors.

For example, in the water tank, suppose we know that $amount : full = [80, 100]$, and that $outflow = M^+(amount)$ lies within the envelopes described in figure 9.3. We apply QSIM and Q2 to the model with the controllable parameter $inflow : if^* = [0, +\infty]$. No behavior is refuted, of course, but the different behaviors imply different ranges for if^*.

Equilibrium		
Variable	Landmark	Interval
$amount$	$full$	$[80, 100]$
	a_0	$[0, 100]$
	$d(0, a_0)$	$[0, 100]$
$outflow$	o_1	$[0, 14.2]$
	$d(0, o_1)$	$[0, 14.2]$
$inflow$	if^*	$[0, 14.2]$
$netflow$	n_0	$[0, 14.2]$
	$at(t_0, t_1)$	$[0, 14.2]$
$time$	t_0	$[0, 0]$
	t_1	$[0, +\infty]$
	$d(t_0, t_1)$	$[0, +\infty]$

Overflow		
Variable	Landmark	Interval
$amount$	$full$	$[80, 100]$
	$d(0, full)$	$[80, 100]$
$outflow$	o_0	$[9.69, 14.2]$
	$d(0, o_0)$	$[9.69, 14.2]$
$inflow$	if^*	$[9.69, +\infty]$
$netflow$	n_0	$[9.69, +\infty]$
	n_1	$[0, +\infty]$
	$at(t_0, t_1)$	$[0, +\infty]$
$time$	t_0	$[0, 0]$
	t_1	$[0, +\infty]$
	$d(t_0, t_1)$	$[0, +\infty]$

Within the context of the other quantitative knowledge in the model, Q2 infers the dependency between $inflow$ and the qualitative behaviors.

Overflow $\rightarrow$ $if^* \geq 9.69$

Equilibrium $\rightarrow$ $if^* \leq 14.2$.

These relations imply quantitative constraints for guaranteeing or preventing a particular qualitative behavior.

$if^* < 9.69$ $\rightarrow$ Equilibrium

$if^* > 14.2$ $\rightarrow$ Overflow

$9.69 \leq if^* \leq 14.2$ $\rightarrow$ or(Equilibrium,Overflow)

This type of inference is a significant aspect of computer-assisted design. Q2 makes it possible to draw these conclusions in spite of substantially incomplete knowledge.

9.5.3 Other Representations

We can contrast semi-quantitative reasoning with traditional numerical simulation methods. Q2 does simulation by progressive refinement: define a set of possible solutions, and shrink it while maintaining the guarantee that the solution lies within the set. By contrast, a numerical simulation is a one-point sample of the set of solutions.

Monte Carlo simulation takes many more samples of this set, but still a finite number. The cost of Monte Carlo simulation, and the chance of missing important behaviors, increases rapidly with the dimension of the parameter space. The cost of semi-quantitative inference with Q2 is not dependent on the size of the parameter space, but is a function of the number of distinct qualitative behaviors predicted by QSIM. Clearly, these methods have very different strengths and weaknesses, and so are likely to complement each other.

A sophisticated calculus for semi-quantitative reasoning based on order-of-magnitude relations has also been developed (Raiman, 1986; 1991; Mavrovouniotis and Stephanopoulos, 1987; 1988; Murthy, 1988; Nayak, 1993; Dague, 1993a; 1993b). The diagnostic system DEDALE (Dague $et\ al.$, 1987) applies knowledge of order-of-magnitude relations exactly as discussed in section 9.5.1. Both observed and $a\ priori$ order of magnitude relations are unified with each hypothesized model of a device. New relations are propagated through each model, and a contradiction results in a model and its hypothesis being discarded. Yip (1993) applies order-of-magnitude reasoning to simplify complex partial differential equation models.

Fuzzy representations for incomplete knowledge of quantities can also be used in conjunction with qualitative behaviors (D'Ambrosio, 1987; 1989; Shen and Leitch, 1992; 1993; Vescovi and Robles, 1992; Bousson and Travé-Massuyès, 1993).

Qualitative and semi-quantitative knowledge about probability distributions have been investigated by Wellman, 1990; Berleant, 1990; and Druzdzel and Henrion, 1993.

9.5.4   Tighter Bounds Building on QSIM + Q2

One important limitation of Q2 is that the quantitative information inferred remains very coarse. For example, in the equilibrium behavior in figure 9.4(a), $d(t_0, t_1) = [0.644, +\infty]$. This weak quantitative conclusion is due to the weakness of the Mean Value Theorem and the large grain-size of the qualitative behavior, with landmark time-points only for the initial and final states of the system.

Two recent advances build on QSIM + Q2 to greatly strengthen the semi-quantitative conclusions that can be drawn from incomplete information, and the kinds of guarantees that can be provided.

- Q3 (Berleant, 1990; Berleant and Kuipers, 1991; 1992) extends Q2 with *step-size refinement*, adaptively inserting landmarks into qualitative intervals to decrease the effective step-size and strengthen semi-quantitative inference. In addition to providing tighter predictions and more refutations, Q3 provides the important new guarantee that the uncertainty in the semi-quantitative behavior prediction converges to zero as the uncertainty in initial conditions and the maximum step-size converge to zero. Along with the Q2 soundness guarantee, this means that semi-quantitative reasoning smoothly spans the gap from purely qualitative simulation on the one hand to numerical simulation on the other. Figure 9.10 in section 9.6 demonstrates the application of Q3 to a problem where Q2 gives relatively weak bounds, and illustrates convergence to the true behavior when there is no uncertainty in the initial conditions.

- Dynamic envelopes are used by the semi-quantitative reasoning program NSIM (Kay and Kuipers, 1993) to improve on Q2 by providing much tighter bounds over qualitative intervals. In Q2, behavior over an interval is only bounded by the rectangle defined by bounds on landmarks at the endpoints of the interval. Dynamic envelopes are numerically defined solutions to an *extremal system* of ODEs that can be derived from the QDE and Q2 bounds, and proved to bound its solutions. Dynamic envelope bounds are therefore curvilinear, and take advantage of stronger properties of the QDE than the Mean Value Theorem. Figure 9.11 demonstrates the application of NSIM to the water tank and clocked acceleration examples.

Q3 and dynamic envelopes have different strengths and weaknesses, and appear to be synergistic when applied to the same problem. There are clearly more opportunities to strengthen semi-quantitative reasoning within the framework provided by QSIM + Q2, and many of them lie quite close to the surface.

9.6 Example: An Autonomous Clock

Some mechanisms have elements that are autonomously clocked. For example, the pump that circulates and filters the solvent in a chemical process tank may be on a fixed duty cycle, independent of the rest of the system.

We can model such a system by including a variable to represent the state of the clock, and assert that it changes at a constant rate. A region transition represents a "tick" at regular intervals.

```
(define-QDE Timer
  (quantity-spaces
    (clock   (0 tick inf))
    (dclock  (0 rate inf)))
  (constraints
    ((d/dt clock dclock))
    ((constant dclock)))
  (transitions
    ((clock (tick inc)) -> tock))))

(defun tock (ostate)
  (create-transition-state :from-state  ostate
                           :to-qde      Timer
                           :assert      '((clock (0 inc)))
                           :inherit-qmag '(dclock)))
```

Unfortunately, in a purely qualitative simulation, this provides little help. Without quantitative constraints on the rate of the clock, or the distance between ticks, a simulation that included other events would branch indefinitely according to the number of ticks that could take place between events.

Fortunately, Q2 allows us to incorporate quantitative constraints. Furthermore, when a rate, like *dclock*, is constant, the Mean Value Theorem allows us to draw a strong conclusion about the time required to cover a known distance. Thus, we can assert quantitative information about the landmarks *clock* : *tick* and *dclock* : *rate*, and get useful constraints on the times at which the ticks take place.

```
(define-QDE Timer
  (quantity-spaces
    (clock     (0 tick inf))
    (dclock    (0 rate inf))
    (X         (minf 0 inf))
    (V         (minf 0 inf))
    (A         (0 inf)))
  (constraints
    ((d/dt clock dclock))
    ((constant dclock))
    ((d/dt X V))
    ((d/dt V A))
    ((constant A)))
  (transitions
    ((clock (tick inc)) -> tock)))

(defun tock (ostate)
  (create-transition-state :from-state    ostate
                           :to-qde        Timer
                           :assert        '((clock (0 inc)))
                           :inherit-qmag  '(dclock X V A)
                           :inherit-ranges :all))

(defun start-clock ()
  (let* ((sim (make-sim :state-limit 10
                        :Q2-constraints t))
         (init (make-new-state :from-qde timer
                               :sim       sim
                 :assert-values '((clock  (0 inc))
                                  (dclock (rate std))
                                  (X      (0  nil))
                                  (V      (0  nil))
                                  (A      ((0 inf) std)))
                 :assert-ranges '(((clock tick)  (10 10))
                                  ((dclock rate) (1 1))
                                  ((A (at t0))   (1 1))
                                  ((time t0)     (0 0))))))
    (qsim init)
    (qsim-display init)))
```

Figure 9.8
QDE representing clock and motion under constant acceleration.

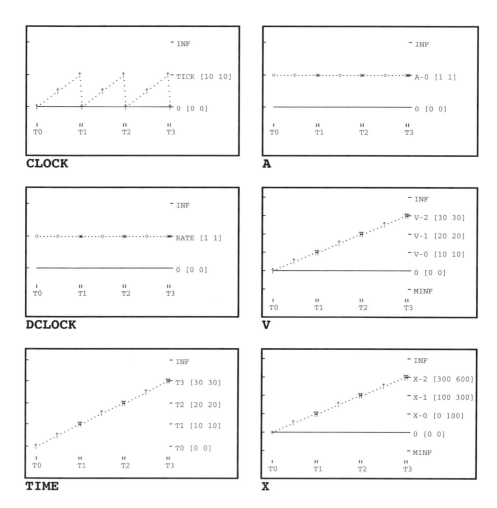

Figure 9.9
Clocked motion under constant acceleration.

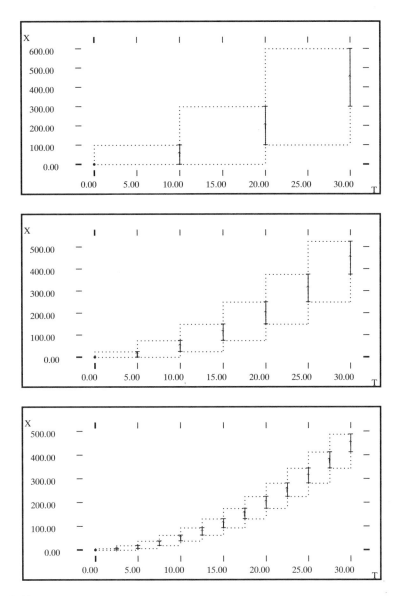

Figure 9.10
Step-size refinement in Q3 converges to the true behavior.

The first plot redisplays the qualitative plot of $X(t)$ from figure 9.9, using solid rectangles to represent quantitative uncertainty at time-points, and dotted rectangles for time-intervals. The second and third plots show the uncertainty remaining after Q3 interpolates a new time-point into the middle of each time-interval in the preceding plot and applies Q2 to propagate ranges.

(a) Dynamic envelopes for *amount*(*t*) and *outflow*(*t*) in figure 9.4(a) for the water tank model.

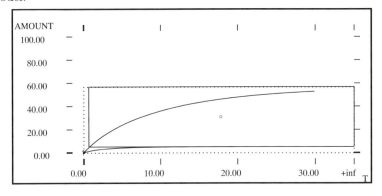

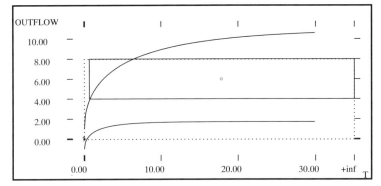

(b) Dynamic envelopes for $X(t)$ in the clock example from section 9.6, but initialized with 20% uncertainty about acceleration: $A(t) = [1.0, 1.2]$.

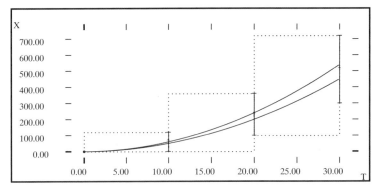

Figure 9.11
NSIM derives and predicts dynamic envelopes.

Dynamic envelopes are numerical trajectories, so they can have curvilinear bounds, in contrast with the rectangular bounds derived by Q2 and Q3. Neither source of constraint dominates the other, as shown by *outflow*(*t*), so the two types of bounds should be intersected.

Figure 9.8 shows the clock model extended to include additional qualitative constraints representing motion under constant acceleration. The resulting unique qualitative behavior is shown in figure 9.9. Given perfect quantitative knowledge of the clock rate and distance between ticks, Q2 infers perfect knowledge of the times of the ticks, and hence the period of the clock. Then, since $A(t)$ is constant, the value of $V(t)$ at each time-point is known exactly. However, since $V(t)$ varies over each time-interval, the equations in Q2, based on the Mean Value Theorem, draw weaker conclusions about the values of $X(t)$ at the time-points. Figure 9.10 shows how Q3 is able to give stronger results for this problem. Since there is no quantitative uncertainty in this problem, NSIM can predict the exact numerical trajectory of the system. However, if we introduce 20% numerical uncertainty in the acceleration, figure 9.11(b) shows the numerical envelopes that NSIM predicts, bounding all possible real trajectories.

9.7 Problems

1. By hand, apply the rules in section 9.2 to derive all value-denoting terms and equations corresponding to the behaviors (a) Equilibrium and (b) Overflow in figure 9.4. Compare with figure 9.5.

2. By hand, apply the propagation algorithm in section 9.3 to the equations in figure 9.5 (or the equations you derived in problem 1) corresponding to the behaviors (a) Equilibrium and (b) Overflow. Compare with figure 9.7 and figure 9.4.

3. The following set of equations has the unique solution $(x = 2, y = 1)$.

$$x \ = \ 2 \cdot y$$
$$x \ = \ y + 1$$

Since these are simultaneous equations, local propagation through single equations cannot solve for the variable values directly. By hand, trace the Q2 Propagation algorithm, starting with the initial values $x = [0, 10]$ and $y = [0, 5]$.

4. In the description of the interval-based expression evaluator, the entries for $1/x$ and $x \cdot y$ cover only the cases where $x, y > 0$, and the symbolic values $+\infty$ and $-\infty$ are not covered. Extend the table to complete these specifications.

5. The one-constraint-at-a-time Q2 Propagation algorithm does not draw the strongest possible conclusion on a model of gravity:

$$V = \frac{d}{dt}X; \qquad A = \frac{d}{dt}V; \qquad constant(A)$$

where we know $range(A(t)) = [9.8, 9.8] \ m/s^2$.

Trace the propagation inferences and demonstrate what the problem is. Add a mechanism that can identify these situations and can assert and use a Q2 equation of the form

$$X(t_i) - X(t_{i-1}) = \frac{1}{2}A(t) \cdot (t_i - t_{i-1})^2 + V(t_{i-1}) \cdot (t_i - t_{i-1}).$$

6. Is it possible to generate an interval propagation example in which "convergence" does not terminate? For example, a variable might take on a sequence of values such as

$$[1, \infty] \to [2, \infty] \to \cdots$$

When can this happen? If it cannot, why not?

7. Is it possible for a propagation process, converging to a single point value, to reach a spurious contradiction due to roundoff error? Is the following argument valid?

Since roundoff replaces an actual value with the nearest value on a finite grid, it is not possible to have $lb \leq ub$, but $round(lb) > round(ub)$. It is, however, possible for $[lb, ub] \cap [round(lb), round(ub)] = \emptyset$. Therefore, we will not get a spurious contradiction, but the rounded interval might fail to contain the true value.

8. (Research Problem.) Read the literature on inequality inference and interval constraint satisfaction, and improve on the local propagation algorithm currently used in Q2. Methods for reasoning explicitly with algebraic equations and inequalities (Sacks, 1987a; Bledsoe et al., 1985) are capable of recognizing and solving sets of simultaneous equations, and therefore obtaining exact values for certain variables without propagation. Under what circumstances do the improved bounds justify the added computational costs?

9. (Research Problem.) Since quantitative information propagates in any direction across the Q2 equations, use Q2 to assert quantitative ranges about landmarks defined at both the initial and final states of the behavior, thereby providing a

semi-quantitative solution to a two-point boundary value problem. What leverage is obtained on this problem, from QSIM providing a qualitative description of the entire trajectory, from beginning to end, before any quantitative inference takes place? Does it simplify the application of "shooting methods"?

10. Build a QSIM model to predict what will happen when the three billiard balls below are set in motion at the same time and at the same rate. Use QSIM to predict all qualitative possibilities, then add exact quantitative information and use Q2 predict all quantitatively consistent futures. Define region transitions so that the simulation is terminated when the distance between any two balls becomes zero.

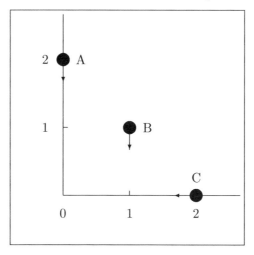

This example illustrates a discussion between Manny Rayner (1991), Erik Sandewall (1989), and Yoav Shoham and Drew McDermott (1988) on the applicability of non-monotonic logic to formal reasoning about continuous time. Since a QSIM prediction is a deductive consequence of the model and initial conditions, how does your result speak to this controversy? (This question sparked an email discussion that grew into an enormously stimulating workshop (IFIP, 1992).)

10 Higher-Order Derivatives

10.1   Introduction

As we have seen, dynamic qualitative simulation predicts a set of possible behaviors, which is interpreted as a disjunction:

$$QDE \wedge Qstate(t_0) \longrightarrow or(B_1, \ldots B_k).$$

That is, given a system described by QDE and starting in $Qstate(t_0)$, QSIM predicts that one of the behaviors $B_1, \ldots B_k$ will describe the actual behavior of the system.

The success of diagnostic, design, and other applications of qualitative simulation rests on the ability to produce a tractably small set of predictions including all real possible behaviors of the mechanism. In some cases, simulation of a QDE produces a small set of behaviors, all representing real possibilities consistent with the available knowledge. However, in other cases, the result may be an intractably branching tree of predicted behaviors. A few real solutions may be obscured by a forest of non-solutions, or all solutions may be real but not interestingly distinct.

This problem arises from the incomplete qualitative descriptions of variable values: an ordinal description of the magnitude with respect to landmark values, the sign of the first derivative, and no information about higher derivatives. With such sparse information, circumstances arise where certain variables *chatter*: their behavior is unconstrained except by continuity. Qualitative simulation must then branch on every possible number, magnitude, and timing of changes of the chattering variables, resulting in an intractably branching, and hence useless, set of predictions. Figure 10.1 shows one behavior in an intractably branching tree of predictions for a system of two cascaded tanks. The behaviors are distinguished only by the behavior of the variable $netflowB(t)$, representing the rate of change of the amount in the second tank.

The presence of an infinite family of uninteresting behaviors is particularly striking when the set of possible behaviors is represented as a tree (figure 10.1). The same problem arises, however, in the finite envisionment representation of qualitative behavior (section 5.7). Once one attempts to interpret the envisionment as predicting specific behaviors, loops in the transition graph give rise to infinite families of paths, and the same problem of chatter arises.

This chapter describes two solutions to the problem of chatter. The first exploits higher-order derivative information implicit in the QDE, to *eliminate* certain predicted behaviors. We discuss the methods required to extract higher-order derivative information in the face of incomplete knowledge of a mechanism, and their costs and benefits. The second solution method changes the granularity of the qualitative description, to *abstract* many behaviors into a few.

These methods are fundamentally local, constraining branching at particular time-points. Qualitative simulation of complex mechanisms also requires non-local constraints such as energy constraints and analysis of the qualitative phase plane

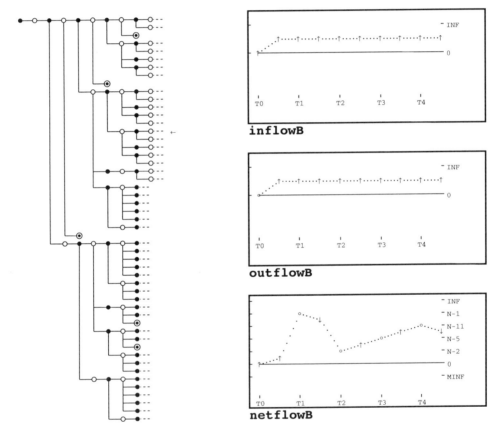

Figure 10.1
Intractable branching due to chatter.

In a qualitative model of two cascaded tanks (A and B), $NetflowB(t) = InflowB(t) - OutflowB(t)$ is constrained only by continuity as long as $NetflowB(t)$ remains in the interval $(0, \infty)$. Thus, the simulation branches on all possible trajectories of $NetflowB(t)$, while all other variables are completely uniform. (The ellipses on the fringe of the QSIM behavior tree represent states whose successors have not yet been computed, due to a resource cut-off.)

(chapter 11), and decomposition of large-scale mechanisms into weakly interacting components by time-scale abstraction (chapter 12).

10.2 Higher-Order Derivatives

The first method for eliminating chatter is based on knowledge of higher-order derivatives implicit in the QDE.

Suppose that a variable $v(t)$ reaches a critical point: $v'(t_i) = 0$. According to the qualitative successor rules (table 5.1 on page 100), $v'(t)$ could be positive, negative, or zero over the following qualitatively uniform interval (t_i, t_{i+1}). That is, the direction of change $qdir(v)$ could be inc, dec, or std during the time-interval (t_i, t_{i+1}).

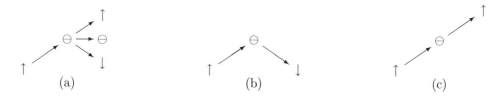

(a) $v(t_i)$ has a three-way branch from a critical point: $v'(t_i) = 0$.

(b) In case we know that $v''(t_i) < 0$, only one of three branches is consistent.

(c) If $v''(t_i) = v'(t_i) = 0$, and $v'''(t_i) > 0$, then only one branch is consistent.

Figure 10.2
Three-way and one-way branches.

If the derivative of $v(t)$ is not adequately constrained, directly or indirectly, none of the three possibilities in figure 10.2a can be excluded, so a branch is required. However (figure 10.2b), if we have reason to know that $v''(t_i) < 0$, then two of these possibilities can be excluded, leading to a unique description of the qualitative state over (t_i, t_{i+1}).

More generally, at any time-point t_i, the sign of the first non-zero derivative of v at t_i determines the direction of change of v over (t_i, t_{i+1}). In figure 10.2c the third derivative controls the qualitative transition.

DEFINITION 19 Just as $qdir(v)$ represents the sign of the first derivative of v, we define the abbreviations $sd2$ and $sd3$ for the signs of the second and third derivatives of v.

$$qdir(v,t) = \left[\frac{dv}{dt}(t)\right]; \quad sd2(v,t) = \left[\frac{d^2v}{dt^2}(t)\right]; \quad sd3(v,t) = \left[\frac{d^3v}{dt^3}(t)\right].$$

The value *nil* represents an ambiguous sign. The second argument, t, to *qdir*, *sd2*, and *sd3*, may be suppressed when the current time-point is clearly specified by context.

We will use the term *higher-order derivative (HOD) constraint* to refer to the use of the first non-zero derivative to filter out impossible behaviors as in figure 10.2(b,c). In the usual case, it is the second derivative $v''(t_i)$ that provides the necessary information (figure 10.2b), and we may then refer to the HOD constraint as a *curvature constraint*. In more complex situations (e.g., figure 10.2c and section 3.2), third-order derivatives may be required. We do not extend our analysis beyond third-order derivatives, for reasons that will be discussed in section 10.4.

There are three steps to applying the higher-order derivative constraint:

1. Identify variables in the QDE likely to chatter.

2. Derive algebraic expressions and evaluate them to obtain the signs of the second- or third-order derivatives of chattering variables.

3. Use the sign of the higher-order derivative to constrain branching.

The methods described in this chapter build on work by Williams (1984b; 1984a) who showed how to exploit knowledge of higher-order derivatives of exogenous input; by de Kleer and Bobrow (1984) who showed how to derive qualitative confluences for higher-order derivatives from an ODE; and by Kuipers and Chiu (1987) and Kuipers, *et al.* (1991) who extended the higher-order derivative analysis to QDEs.

In the following sections, we will discuss steps 1 and 3 before step 2.

10.2.1   Identifying Chattering Variables

DEFINITION 20   A variable v appearing in a QDE *chatters*, starting at a qualitative time-point t_i, if the constraints in the QDE are consistent with any qualitative value of $qdir(v,t)$, for every t in some open interval (t_i, t_j).

It is possible to propose candidate variables that are likely to chatter during simulation by analysis of the structure of the QDE. We observe, first, that if two variables x and y are related by a monotonic function constraint, either both chatter or neither does. Second, if the derivative x' of a variable x is explicitly represented in the QDE, then the variable x will not chatter.[1]

The algorithm for proposing candidate variables is as follows:

1. Group the variables in the QDE into equivalence classes according to the following criteria:

$$equiv(x,y) \quad \leftarrow \quad M^+(x,y)$$
$$equiv(x,y) \quad \leftarrow \quad M^-(x,y)$$

We may exploit the fact that other explicit constraints in the QDE imply the weaker M^+ or M^- constraints. For example,

$$equiv(x,y) \quad \leftarrow \quad MINUS(x,y)$$
$$equiv(y,z) \quad \leftarrow \quad ADD(x,y,z) \text{ and } constant(x)$$
$$equiv(x,z) \quad \leftarrow \quad ADD(x,y,z) \text{ and } constant(y)$$
$$equiv(x,y) \quad \leftarrow \quad ADD(x,y,z) \text{ and } constant(z)$$
$$equiv(y,z) \quad \leftarrow \quad MULT(x,y,z) \text{ and } constant(x)$$
$$equiv(x,z) \quad \leftarrow \quad MULT(x,y,z) \text{ and } constant(y)$$
$$equiv(x,y) \quad \leftarrow \quad MULT(x,y,z) \text{ and } constant(z)$$
$$equiv(w,z) \quad \leftarrow \quad ADD(x,y,z) \text{ and } M^+(w,x) \text{ and } M^+(w,y)$$
$$equiv(w,x) \quad \leftarrow \quad ADD(x,y,z) \text{ and } M^+(w,z) \text{ and } M^-(w,y)$$

2. Eliminate the equivalence class containing a variable x if the QDE contains one of the constraints:

- $constant(x)$
- $\frac{d}{dt}x = x'$.

3. Variables in the remaining equivalence classes may chatter.

Only one variable in each equivalence class needs a HOD constraint.

The ability of this algorithm to identify exactly the chattering variables is limited by the ability of an algebraic manipulator to recognize expressions that imply monotonic function constraints. If some complex expression implying $equiv(x,y)$ goes unrecognized, then the algorithm might determine that x does not chatter, but leave y unnecessarily on the list of potentially chattering variables. It is also

---

[1]Suppose we have the pathological situation that both x and its derivative x' appear explicitly in a QDE, but both variables are otherwise unconstrained. According to definition 20, x' will chatter while x will not. Although QSIM will eventually predict all possible qualitative behaviors for x, $qdir(x)$ is always constrained by the sign of x'.

possible for the QSIM model builder to assert explicitly which variables require higher-order derivative constraints.

10.2.2   Applying the Higher-Order Derivative Constraint

The QSIM qualitative simulation algorithm operates by proposing all possible qualitative state transitions, then filtering out those that are inconsistent with available information.

DEFINITION 21   A filter on a set of candidates is *conservative* if it only filters out candidates that are provably inconsistent.

As long as each filter is conservative, the algorithm preserves the guarantee that all real behaviors are predicted. The higher-order derivative constraint is applied within this framework to filter out certain sequences of qualitative states. As we shall see (section 10.4), the HOD constraint may fail to be conservative in the presence of M^+ or M^- constraints.

Figure 10.3 shows which sequences of states are consistent, and which can be filtered out, given signs for $v''(t)$ and $v'''(t)$. The HOD constraint is implemented as a global filter. It applies at two distinct times around a critical point in the behavior: when the critical point is being generated (the pre-filter), and when its successors are being generated (the post-filter).

The behavior in figure 10.2a in which $v(t)$ becomes constant over an interval is filtered out by the analytic-function constraint (section 10.5): if $v(t)$ is constant over any interval, it must be constant everywhere.

PROPOSITION 4   If $v(t)$ is a non-constant analytic function in the neighborhood of $t = t_i$, and $v'(t_i) = 0$, then figure 10.3 shows which sequences of qualitative directions of change are consistent (or inconsistent) with knowledge of the signs of $v''(t_i)$ and $v'''(t_i)$.

Proof   Since we are assuming that a variable $v(t)$ is analytic around a critical point t_i, in the neighborhood of t_i, the qualitative properties of v are determined by the first non-zero terms of the Taylor series:

$$v(t) \approx v(t_i) + v'(t_i)(t - t_i) + \frac{v''(t_i)}{2}(t - t_i)^2 + \frac{v'''(t_i)}{3!}(t - t_i)^3.$$

At a critical point, $v'(t_i) = 0$, if $v''(t_i) \neq 0$,

$$v(t) \approx v(t_i) + \frac{v''(t_i)}{2}(t - t_i)^2.$$

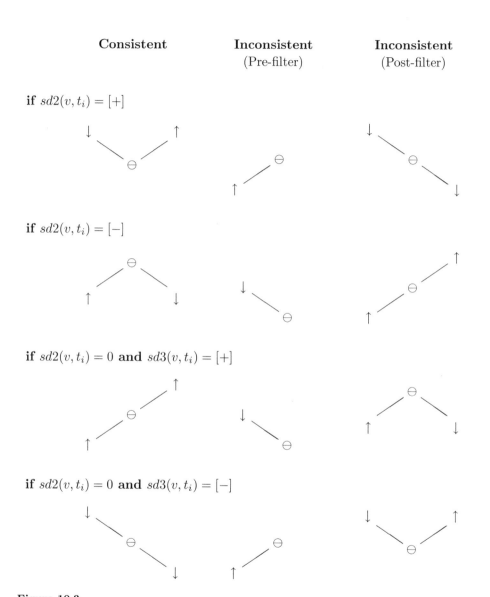

Figure 10.3
Consistent and inconsistent sequences of qualitative values.

In the neighborhood of a time-point t_i such that $v'(t_i) = 0$, knowledge of the signs of $v''(t_i)$ and $v'''(t_i)$ can be used to determine sequences of qualitative states that are inconsistent, and can therefore be filtered out.

In this case, the qualitative behavior of $v(t)$ is that of t^2; that is, $dec \to std \to inc$ or $inc \to std \to dec$.

Where $v''(t_i) = v'(t_i) = 0$, but $v'''(t_i) \neq 0$,

$$v(t) \approx v(t_i) + \frac{v'''(t_i)}{3!}(t - t_i)^3,$$

so the qualitative behavior of $v(t)$ is that of t^3; that is, $inc \to std \to inc$ or $dec \to std \to dec$. ∎

This leaves us with the problem of determining the sign of $v''(t_i)$, and perhaps $v'''(t_i)$, from information in the QDE and the qualitative behavior up to t_i. If v is a variable appearing in an *ordinary* differential equation, its higher-order derivatives can be derived by repeatedly differentiating the original equation (de Kleer and Bobrow, 1984). However, when we are dealing with incomplete knowledge, as represented by a *qualitative* differential equation, the problem becomes more difficult. Because of the assumptions required to derive higher-order derivatives in the presence of incompletely known monotonic function constraints (discussed in more detail in section 10.4), our implementation of the HOD constraint is restricted to second- and third-order derivatives.

10.2.3   Deriving an Expression for $sd2(v, t)$

As we have seen, chattering arises because the qualitative representation explicitly describes the magnitude of $v(t)$ and the sign of its first derivative, $qdir(v, t)$, but not the signs of its higher derivatives. However, the QDE provides a set of algebraic and differential constraints that can be used to solve for $sd2(v, t)$ in terms of values that *are* explicitly represented.

An explicit expression for $sd2(x)$ is found using a limited algebraic manipulator that searches a space of expressions generated by equivalence-preserving transformation rules. The following list illustrates the essential rules; the complete set is given in figure 10.4.

$$sd2(x) \text{ where } M^+(x, y) \;\; \to \;\; sd2(y)$$
$$sd2(x) \text{ where } x = y + z \;\; \to \;\; sd2(y) + sd2(z)$$
$$sd2(x) \text{ where } constant(x) \;\; \to \;\; 0$$
$$sd2(x) \text{ where } y = \frac{d}{dt}x \;\; \to \;\; qdir(y)$$
$$qdir(z) \text{ where } chattering\_variable(z) \;\; \to \;\; 0$$

PROPOSITION 5   Suppose a chattering variable z has a critical point at t_i, i.e. $qdir(z, t_i) = 0$. If we assume that, for any variables x and y,

$$M^+(x, y) \;\Rightarrow\; sd2(x, t_i) = sd2(y, t_i), \tag{10.1}$$

then each transformation in figure 10.4 is validity preserving when applied at t_i.

Using this proposition, we derive an expression for $sd2(z, t_i)$ by searching a space of expressions produced by sequences of transformations from figure 10.4 (along with validity-preserving algebraic simplification rules). The goal of the search is an expression that can be evaluated using the QSIM description of $Qstate(t_i)$; i.e., it contains no $sd2$ terms. Even then, of course, the value of the expression may be qualitatively ambiguous, in which case the HOD constraint is unable to filter out any behaviors.

The "sign-equality" assumption (10.1) embedded in this proposition is critical to higher-order derivative reasoning in the face of unknown monotonic function constraints. In section 10.4, we will examine this assumption in more detail, showing how to prove it is valid, and the circumstances under which it is violated.

Proof of the Proposition   The transformations involving monotonic function constraints are a restatement of the sign-equality assumption. The rule that, where z is the chattering variable, $qdir(z) \to 0$, is valid because the rules are only applied at a critical point of the chattering variable.

The addition transformation requires a bit of reflection. In the algebra of signs, the transformation $[A + B] \to [A] + [B]$ preserves validity, but may yield a weaker description when $[A] = -[B]$, because $[A + B]$ has some definite sign, while $[A] + [B] = [?]$. This allows us to conclude

$$sd2(x, t) = [x''(t)] = [y''(t) + z''(t)] \to [y''(t)] + [z''(t)] = sd2(y, t) + sd2(z, t).$$

The remainder of the transformation rules are straightforward consequences of the addition transformation, the identity $[A \cdot B] = [A] \cdot [B]$, and the rules for differentiation. ∎

The complex expressions resulting from the `mult` constraint are the result of applying only the real algebra. If we apply the axioms of the hybrid sign-real algebra SR1 (section 3.4.4), the expressions become considerably simpler (problem 3).

10.2.4   Determining the Value of $sd3(v, t)$

Consideration of the second derivative allows many mechanisms, such as the two-tank cascade, to be simulated that would otherwise have been intractable. However,

```
(defparameter *transformation-rules*
  '(((sd2 ?x) (M+ ?x ?y) -> (sd2 ?y))
    ((sd2 ?y) (M+ ?x ?y) -> (sd2 ?x))

    ((sd2 ?x) (M- ?x ?y) -> (- 0 (sd2 ?y)))
    ((sd2 ?y) (M- ?x ?y) -> (- 0 (sd2 ?x)))

    ((sd2 ?z) (add ?x ?y ?z) -> (+ (sd2 ?x) (sd2 ?y)))
    ((sd2 ?x) (add ?x ?y ?z) -> (- (sd2 ?z) (sd2 ?y)))
    ((sd2 ?y) (add ?x ?y ?z) -> (- (sd2 ?z) (sd2 ?x)))

    ((sd2 ?z) (mult ?x ?y ?z) -> (+ (* ?y (sd2 ?x))
                                     (+ (* ?x (sd2 ?y))
                                        (* 2 (* (qdir ?x) (qdir ?y))))))
    ((sd2 ?x) (mult ?x ?y ?z) -> (- (/ (sd2 ?z) ?y)
                                     (- (* 2 (* (qdir ?z)
                                                (/ (qdir ?y) (^ ?y 2))))
                                        (- (* 2 (* ?z (/ (^ (qdir ?y) 2)
                                                         (^ ?y 3))))
                                           (* ?z (/ (sd2 ?z) (^ ?y 2)))))))
    ((sd2 ?y) (mult ?x ?y ?z) -> (- (/ (sd2 ?z) ?x)
                                     (- (* 2 (* (qdir ?z)
                                                (/ (qdir ?x) (^ ?x 2))))
                                        (- (* 2 (* ?z (/ (^ (qdir ?x) 2)
                                                         (^ ?x 3))))
                                           (* ?z (/ (sd2 ?z) (^ ?x 2)))))))

    ((sd2 ?x) (minus ?x ?y) -> (- 0 (sd2 ?y)))
    ((sd2 ?y) (minus ?x ?y) -> (- 0 (sd2 ?x)))

    ((sd2 ?x) (d/dt ?x ?y) -> (qdir ?y))
    ((sd2 ?x) (independent ?x) -> 0)
    ((qdir ?x) (chattering-variable ?x) -> 0)
    ))
```

Figure 10.4
Rules for deriving an expression for $sd2(x)$.

The first clause in the rule is matched against the sd2 expression. Additional clauses before ->
are matched against QDE constraints, after substitutions. The clause after the -> has bindings
substituted, and is returned. Note that there are no explicit derivative or monotonic function
constraints in the resulting expression, and a subexpression may only be raised to a constant
power.

there are also situations where $sd2(v, t) = 0$, so a third- or higher-order derivative is necessary to apply the HOD constraint. Important examples of this are the cascaded systems of three or more tanks, for which spurious behaviors are generated when only the second-order derivative is considered, but which yield unique predictions when third-order derivatives are taken into account.

While it would be possible to construct a table of transformations for $sd3(v, t)$ analogous to the one for $sd2(v, t)$, this table would be quite complex, and turns out to be unnecessary. We may exploit the fact that $sd3(v, t)$ is only needed when $sd2(v, t) = qdir(v, t) = 0$. $sd3(v, t)$ can be evaluated as the derivative of the expression derived and stored for $sd2(v, t)$:

$$sd3(v, t) = \frac{d}{dt} sd2(v, t).$$

Inspection of the algebraic transformations in figure 10.4 reveals that the expressions that can be derived for $sd2(v, t)$ have a very restricted form. This allows us to evaluate the derivative of the expression stored for $sd2(x)$ using the following transformations:

$$\frac{d}{dt}\langle number \rangle = 0$$

$$\frac{d}{dt}x = qdir(x)$$

$$\frac{d}{dt}(x + y) = \frac{dx}{dt} + \frac{dy}{dt}$$

$$\frac{d}{dt}(x - y) = \frac{dx}{dt} - \frac{dy}{dt}$$

$$\frac{d}{dt}(x \cdot y) = y\frac{dx}{dt} + x\frac{dy}{dt}$$

$$\frac{d}{dt}(x/y) = \frac{1}{y}\frac{dx}{dt} - \frac{1}{y^2}\frac{dy}{dt}$$

$$\frac{d}{dt}qdir(x) = sd2(x)$$

There are two ways to evaluate terms of the form $sd2(x)$ resulting from these transformations. If the derivative x' of such a variable x is explicitly represented in the QDE, then $sd2(x) = qdir(x')$. Otherwise, if the curvature expression $sd2(x)$ was previously asserted or derived for x, it can simply be retrieved.

The rationale for the last rule is somewhat subtle, since the expression stored for $sd2(x)$ is based on the assumption that $qdir(x) = 0$. When evaluating $sd3(y)$, where x and y are different variables, we may assume that $sd2(y) = qdir(y) = 0$, but it is not clear that we may safely assume that $qdir(x) = 0$.

- Suppose we are attempting to evaluate

$$sd3(y) = \frac{d}{dt} sd2(y)$$

and we encounter the term $qdir(x)$ in the expression stored for $sd2(y)$, where x and y stand for different variables in the QDE.

- We only evaluate $sd3(y)$ under circumstances where the expression stored for $sd2(y)$ evaluated to zero. This will let us draw conclusions about the signs of terms embedded in the expression for $sd2(y)$.

- Since curvature expressions are evaluated using the algebra of signs, if the expression $[A] + [B]$ evaluates to 0, it must be because $[A] = 0$ and $[B] = 0$. (In the algebra of signs it is consistent to have $[A + B] = 0$ when $[A] = [+]$ and $[B] = [-]$, but in that case the value of $[A + B]$ would have been indeterminate, not zero.)

- The same rationale applies to $A - B$ and A/B, since inspection of the rules in figure 10.4 reveals that a $qdir(x)$ term can only appear in the numerator of a quotient, and not at all in an exponential A^n. (Exponentials only arise in the quotient rules.)

- If a product $A \cdot qdir(x)$ evaluates to zero, either $A = 0$ or $qdir(x) = 0$. Recall that the value of $qdir(x, t)$ is explicitly available in the QSIM representation of $Qstate(t)$. The product rule gives us

$$\frac{d}{dt}(A \cdot qdir(x)) = qdir(x) \cdot \frac{d}{dt} A + A \cdot \frac{d}{dt} qdir(x).$$

  - If $qdir(x) = 0$, this is the assumption under which $sd2(x)$ was derived, so the rule $\frac{d}{dt} qdir(x) = sd2(x)$ is legitimate.
  - If $qdir(x) \neq 0$ then $A = 0$, so the value (and validity) of the $\frac{d}{dt} qdir(x)$ term resulting from the product rule is irrelevant.

The same reasoning applies to a product $A \cdot B$, where $qdir(x)$ is embedded within A or B.

We summarize this discussion as the following Proposition.

PROPOSITION 6   Under the assumption that $M^+(x, y)$ implies that $sd2(x) = sd2(y)$ and $sd3(x) = sd3(y)$, the transformations applied in evaluating $sd3(x, t)$ are all validity preserving.

Thus, the previous set of rules will give us a legitimate value for $sd3(x)$, modulo the sign-equality assumption, to be discussed in section 10.4.

10.3   Examples: Cascades

10.3.1   The Two-Tank Cascade

The system of two cascaded tanks (figure 10.5) is one of the simplest to exhibit chatter.

$$
\begin{aligned}
A' &= in - f(A) \\
B' &= f(A) - g(B) \\
&\quad f, g \in M^+
\end{aligned}
$$

Figure 10.1 shows one behavior of this system simulated without the HOD constraint.

Identifying Chattering Variables   The variables in the QDE for the two-tank cascade form equivalence classes as shown. If any variable in an equivalence class has an explicit derivative in the QDE, none of the variables in the class exhibit chatter.

$\{in\}$	no chatter, because $constant(in)$.
$\{A, f(A), A'\}$	no chatter, because $A' = dA/dt$.
$\{B, g(B)\}$	no chatter, because $B' = dB/dt$.
$\{B'\}$	chatters.

Therefore, the variable B' (named `netflowB` in the QSIM code) chatters, so we need to apply the HOD constraint.

Deriving the Curvature Constraint   The derivation of the curvature constraint is the following. Recall that we only apply the value of $sd2(B')$ when $qdir(B') = 0$.

$$
\begin{aligned}
sd2(B') &= sd2(f(A)) - sd2(g(B)) \\
&= sd2(A) - sd2(B) \\
&= qdir(A') - qdir(B') \\
&= qdir(A')
\end{aligned}
$$

In terms of the QSIM variables, $sd2(netflowB) = qdir(netflowA)$.

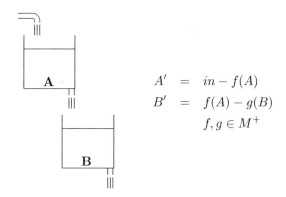

$$A' = in - f(A)$$
$$B' = f(A) - g(B)$$
$$f, g \in M^+$$

```
(define-QDE Two-Tank-Cascade
  (quantity-spaces
    (inflowa    (0 inf))                        ; in
    (amounta    (0 inf))                        ; A
    (outflowa   (0 inf))                        ; f(A)
    (netflowa   (minf 0 inf))                   ; A'
    (amountb    (0 inf))                        ; B
    (outflowb   (0 inf))                        ; g(B)
    (netflowb   (minf 0 inf)))                  ; B'
  (constraints
    ((constant inflowA))
    ((M+ amounta outflowa)          (0 0) (inf inf))
    ((add outflowa netflowa inflowa))
    ((d/dt amounta netflowa))
    ((M+ amountb outflowb)          (0 0) (inf inf))
    ((add outflowb netflowb outflowa))
    ((d/dt amountb netflowb))))
```

Figure 10.5
The two-tank cascade, and its QDE model, in both algebraic and QSIM forms.

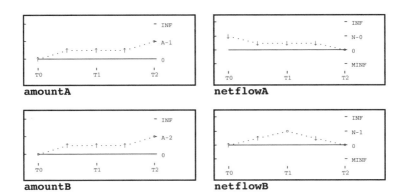

Figure 10.6
With the curvature constraint, a unique behavior is predicted for the two-tank cascade.

Applying the Curvature Constraint Consider the behavior of $netflowB$ illustrated in figure 10.1. Consider the critical points at t_1 and t_2, where $qdir(netflowB, t) = 0$.

- At t_1, we know that $sd2(netflowB, t_1) = qdir(netflowA, t_1) = [-]$, so the concave-down behavior at $netflowB(t_1)$ is acceptable (figure 10.3).

- At t_2, we know that $sd2(netflowB, t_2) = qdir(netflowA, t_2) = [-]$, but the predicted behavior of $netflowB(t_2)$ is concave up, so this behavior is inconsistent (figure 10.3, pre-filter).

With the curvature constraint, instead of the intractable branching of figure 10.1, the two-tank cascade is predicted to have a unique qualitative behavior (figure 10.6).

10.3.2   The Three-Tank Cascade

The three-tank cascade is structurally similar to the two-tank cascade, but it is no longer possible to eliminate all spurious behaviors with the second-order derivative alone. We will require a third-order derivative. Fortunately, second- and third-order derivatives are adequate for cascades of any length.

In algebraic form, the QDE for the three-tank cascade is

$$A' = in - f(A)$$
$$B' = f(A) - g(B)$$
$$C' = g(B) - h(C)$$
$$f, g, h \in M^+.$$

Identifying Chattering Variables   The equivalence classes for the variables in the three-tank cascade are the following.

$\{in\}$ no chatter because $constant(in)$.
$\{A, f(A), A'\}$ no chatter, because $A' = dA/dt$.
$\{B, g(B)\}$ no chatter, because $B' = dB/dt$.
$\{B'\}$ chatters.
$\{C, g(C)\}$ no chatter, because $C' = dC/dt$.
$\{C'\}$ chatters.

Thus, we will need expressions for higher-order derivatives of B' and C'.

Deriving and Applying Curvature Constraints   Using the same method as for the two-tank cascade, we derive expressions for $sd2(B')$ and $sd2(C')$:

$$sd2(netflowB) \quad = \quad qdir(netflowA)$$
$$sd2(netflowC) \quad = \quad qdir(netflowB)$$

Application of these constraints eliminates many branches, but still leaves two spurious behaviors. For example, in the two behaviors shown in figure 10.7, the critical points at $netflowC(t_1)$ are not possible in actual behaviors, but could not be eliminated by $sd2$ alone, because

$$sd2(netflowC, t_1) = qdir(netflowB, t_1) = 0.$$

Evaluating the $sd3$ Constraint   We determine $sd3(netflowC, t)$ by differentiating the expression stored for $sd2(netflowC, t)$.

$$
\begin{aligned}
sd3(netflowC) \quad &= \quad \frac{d}{dt} sd2(netflowC) \\
&= \quad \frac{d}{dt} qdir(netflowB) \\
&= \quad sd2(netflowB) \\
&= \quad qdir(netflowA)
\end{aligned}
$$

Thus, in the two spurious behaviors shown in figure 10.7, $sd3(netflowC, t_1) = qdir(netflowA, t_1) = [-]$. Consulting the table of acceptable qualitative transitions in figure 10.3, we demonstrate that both behaviors in figure 10.7 will be filtered out by the pre-filter. Figure 10.8 then shows the single behavior resulting from simulation using both $sd2$ and $sd3$ constraints.

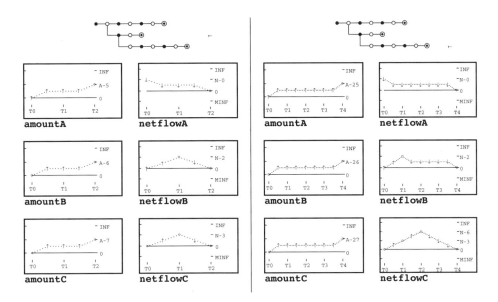

Figure 10.7
With *sd2* expression alone, two spurious predictions for the three-tank cascade survive.

10.4 Monotonic Function Constraints

A major strength of qualitative reasoning is the ability to obtain useful predictions in the face of incomplete knowledge of the structure of a mechanism. The monotonic function constraint is a key method for expressing this knowledge. For example, the following constraints could appear in QDE models of a water tank or a spring, respectively.

$M^+(water\text{-}level, outflow\text{-}rate)$

$M^-(spring\text{-}displacement, restoring\text{-}force)$

When it is useful to have a name for a monotonic function, we will use the alternate notation.

$outflow\text{-}rate = f(water\text{-}level), \ f \in M^+$

$restoring\text{-}force = -g(spring\text{-}displacement), \ g \in M^+$

A function $f \in M^+$ is known to satisfy $f' > 0$ everywhere on the interior of its domain, so it is strictly monotonically increasing (section 3.3). However, f'' is

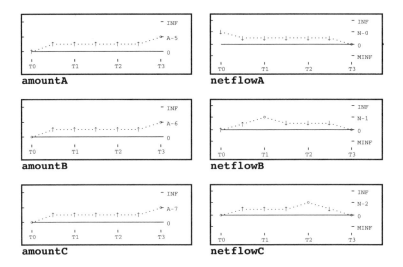

Figure 10.8
Unique qualitative behavior for the three-tank cascade.

Using both *sd2* and *sd3* expressions for the higher-order derivative constraint, the three-tank cascade predicts a single behavior.

unspecified. Monotonic function constraints are useful for expressing incomplete knowledge, but they raise important problems when reasoning about higher-order derivatives.

10.4.1 The Sign-Equality Assumption

The constraint $M^+(x, y)$ means that there is some $f \in M^+$ such that for all t, $y(t) = f(x(t))$. We can differentiate this equation to get

$$y'(t) = f'(x(t)) \cdot x'(t)$$
$$y''(t) = f'(x(t)) \cdot x''(t) + f''(x(t)) \cdot (x'(t))^2.$$

Since $f' > 0$, we know that $[y'(t)] = [x'(t)]$, or $qdir(y, t) = qdir(x, t)$. However, f'' is unspecified, so the second-derivative relationship is weaker.

The rule for solving for $sd2(v, t)$ in the presence of monotonic function constraints relies on the *sign-equality assumption*, that

$$[y''(t)] = [x''(t)].$$

The sign-equality assumption is correct whenever $x''(t)$ and f'' have the same sign, or when $f \in M^+$ is linear, so $f'' = 0$. Because of the role of the sign-equality assumption, the higher-order derivative constraint is potentially not a conservative filter, when the QDE includes monotonic function constraints.

PROPOSITION 7   If every monotonic function constraint $M^+(x, y)$ in a QDE satisfies $sd2(x, t_i) = sd2(y, t_i)$ at a qualitative time-point t_i, then filtering according to the $sd2$ constraint is conservative at t_i.

Proof   Follows directly from propositions 4 and 5.   ∎

PROPOSITION 8   Suppose that a QDE contains a monotonic function constraint $M^+(x, y)$ representing an unknown function $f \in M^+$ such that $y = f(x)$, and suppose the $sd2$ constraint is being applied at qualitative time-point t_i. Then $sd2(x, t_i) = sd2(y, t_i)$ in case *any* of the following conditions hold:

1. The function $f \in M^+$ is linear;
2. $x'(t_i) = 0$;
3. $[x''(t_i)]_0 = [f''(x(t_i))]_0$;
4. $[y''(t_i)]_0 = -[f''(x(t_i))]_0$;
5. $[x''(t_i)]_0 = -[f''(x(t_i))]_0$ and $|f''(x(t_i))(x'(t_i))^2| < |f'(x(t_i))x''(t_i)|$.

Proof   Differentiate $y = f(x)$ twice and map to the domain of signs.

$$
\begin{aligned}
[y''(t)] &= [f'(x(t))] \cdot [x''(t)] + [f''(x(t))] \cdot [(x'(t))^2] \\
&= [x''(t)] + [f''(x(t))] \cdot [(x'(t))^2]. \quad \blacksquare
\end{aligned}
$$

The first four conditions in this proposition rely on the availability of additional qualitative knowledge, such as the sign of f''. The fifth condition is a quantitative criterion, and cannot be established using a purely qualitative description of a system. Using semi-quantitative reasoning methods (chapter 9), it can be possible to evaluate such a criterion, even in the presence of incomplete knowledge.

One can, however, construct examples where the $f''(x(t)) \cdot (x'(t))^2$ term makes a significant contribution to the sign relationship, so the sign-equality assumption is violated.

10.4.2   Example: Violating the Sign-Equality Assumption

We have already seen, in figure 10.6, the predicted qualitative behavior of a two-tank cascade. Notice that $netflowB(t)$ rises monotonically from zero to its maximum

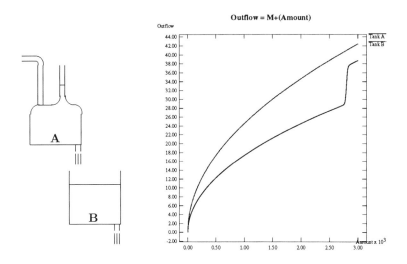

Figure 10.9
Two cascaded tanks where $outflowA = M^+(amountA)$ has a sharp bend.

value, then falls monotonically back to zero. However, suppose we consider an actual pair of tanks such that the upper tank has a tall thin stack, so that the monotonic relationship

$$outflowA = f(amountA) \tag{10.2}$$

has a sharp bend (figure 10.9). If we fill the cascade at a constant rate of inflow, when the level in tank A reaches the stack, $amountA(t)$ will be concave down, but since f'' is large and positive, $outflowA(t)$ will be concave up. Numerical simulation of a model of this situation gives the behavior shown in figure 10.10. All variables are consistent with the qualitative prediction except for $netflowB(t)$, which includes a dip followed by a significant rise before decreasing to zero.

Figure 10.11 shows a numerical sensitivity analysis on the curvature of the monotonic function f in equation (10.2). It may be possible to use traditional Taylor series methods to estimate the magnitude of the error as a function of the magnitudes of the derivatives of the monotonic function (problem 8).

10.4.3   Avoiding Prediction Failure

One of the important features of qualitative simulation is the ability to predict all possible behaviors consistent with incomplete knowledge. Thus, the prospect of

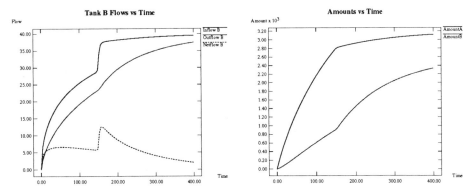

Figure 10.10
Numerical simulation of the two-tank cascade.

Contrary to the qualitative prediction in figure 10.6, $netflowB(t)$ includes a pronounced dip and rise. If the assumption of a single maximum for $netflowB(t)$ were used at $t = 150$ to predict the minimum time until $amountB = 2000$, a significant error would result.

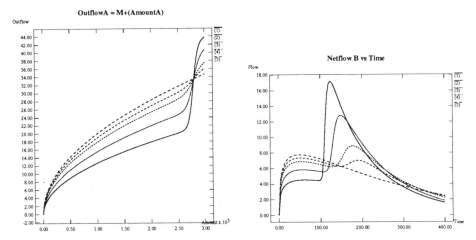

Figure 10.11
Sensitivity to curvature of $outflowA = M^+(amountA)$.

As the curvature in $M^+(amountA, outflowA)$ becomes smoother, the unpredicted dip and rise in $netflowB(t)$ becomes smaller, and the actual behavior converges to the qualitative prediction in figure 10.6.

failing to predict actual behaviors due to the use of a non-conservative filter is quite troubling. However, a deeper analysis of these prediction failures demonstrates that, while the phenomenon is real, there are a number of effective strategies for avoiding or minimizing problems due to it.

• Prediction failures arise because the derived higher-order derivative constraint eliminates a genuine behavior of a chattering variable. The qualitative predictions about non-chattering variables are completely reliable. If a variable $v(t)$ is important, one may include an explicit variable for its derivative $v'(t)$, along with derived constraints on that variable. The problem of chatter will still need to be solved for $v'(t)$, but predictions about the behavior of $v(t)$ will be reliable.

• These prediction failures only occur in the presence of monotonic function constraints. Although avoiding monotonic function constraints sacrifices an important part of the expressive power for incomplete knowledge, qualitative simulation of *ordinary* differential equations can still provide valuable insight into the set of all possible behaviors of a system.

• The representation for higher-order derivative expressions could be extended to record their dependency on monotonic functions. When enough information is available about the slopes and curvatures of monotonic functions, the possibility and magnitude of violations of the sign-equality assumption can be determined by semi-quantitative reasoning (chapter 9).

An alternate method of eliminating the phenomenon of chatter is to change the level of qualitative description, accepting a weaker description of the predicted behaviors and a lesser degree of filtering of spurious predictions, to preserve the guarantee that all real behaviors are predicted. We will discuss this behavior abstraction method in section 10.6.

10.5   The Analytic-Function Constraint

Qualitative simulation requires that variables be continuously differentiable functions of time. Higher-order derivative constraints impose stronger requirements on the differentiability of the underlying functions of time described by qualitative variables. However, since HOD constraints are only applied at isolated critical points of the behavior, strictly speaking such a variable $v(t)$ needs only to be differentiable to the degree necessary to determine its first non-zero derivative, and then only at the isolated critical point.

Under many circumstances in analysis, for example whenever using Taylor series, one restricts one's attention to *analytic* functions: functions whose higher-order derivatives exist for all orders over the entire domain of interest. Fortunately, most of the familiar mathematical functions — polynomials, exponentials, trigonometric functions, etc. — are analytic at all points where they are defined. However, an important fact is that if a function is analytic over an interval and is constant over any open subinterval, it must be constant over the entire interval.

In the examples in this chapter, we restrict our attention to analytic functions, by filtering out any behavior that is constant over an interval without being constant everywhere. This is implemented in QSIM as an optional (switch-controlled) global filter called the *analytic-function constraint*. Using this constraint, the only consistent behavior for the two-tank cascade (figures 10.6 and 10.13) has both tanks reaching their final values simultaneously at $t = \infty$.

However, if we allow non-analytic solutions, we obtain additional intuitively plausible solutions (figure 10.12). This prediction corresponds intuitively with real-world observations of processes acting at different time-scales: the faster one apparently reaches its limit significantly before the slower one. Two variables may be approaching their limits exponentially and asymptotically, but the more rapidly converging of two exponentials will pass below the level of observability very swiftly, and thereafter appear constant. While this method provides an indication of the possible time-scale relations in a mechanism, more rigorous methods are available (chapter 12) for expressing time-scale abstraction in complex mechanisms.

10.6   Behavior Abstraction

In this section, we develop an alternate solution to the problem of unconstrained, chattering variables. Each of the two solutions has its own strengths and weaknesses, and each technique suggests a direction for further developments in qualitative reasoning methods.

Consider the two cascaded tanks (figure 10.5). As we have seen, the chattering variable

$$netflowB(t) = inflowB(t) - outflowB(t)$$

is the difference between two other variables, both of which are increasing monotonically with time in this situation (figure 10.1b). Thus, the direction of change, $qdir(netflowB, t)$, is constrained only by continuity. In a particular instance of this model, the details of how $netflowB(t)$ behaves are determined by the detailed

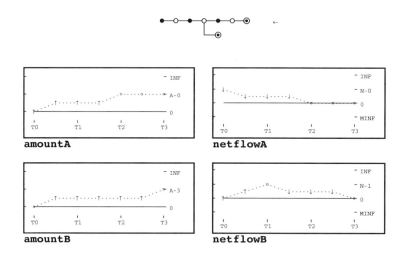

Figure 10.12
Non-analytic behavior for the two-tank cascade.

$amountA(t)$ is non-analytic because it reaches its final value at finite time and remains constant while $amountB(t)$ approaches its limit. The second behavior is identical to that in figure 10.6.

behavior of $inflowB(t) = outflowA(t)$ and $outflowB(t)$. These, in turn, are determined by the particular monotonic functions described by the constraints

$$outflowA(t) = M^+(amountA(t))$$
$$outflowB(t) = M^+(amountB(t)).$$

Depending on how the two monotonic functions interact, the actual behavior of $netflowB(t)$ may rise and fall any number of times. I.e., the undesirable prediction in figure 10.1b accurately describes a behavior like that in figure 10.10 of a real system. Therefore, we must accept the conclusion that the intractably branching tree of predicted behaviors represents an infinite collection of *real* possibilities: the set of all possible behaviors violating the sign-equality assumption.

10.6.1   Collapsing Descriptions

However, even though the behaviors are genuine and qualitatively distinct, the distinctions between them may be uninteresting to a problem solver. An effective approach in this situation is to adopt an alternate level of description that abstracts an infinite set of possible behaviors into a single description, while preserving validity.

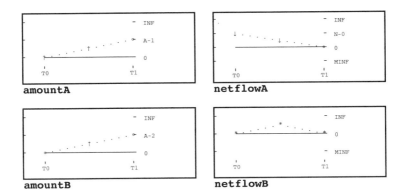

Figure 10.13
The unique behavior of the two-tank cascade, ignoring $qdir(netflowB)$, using * to represent the
ign qdir.

In the case of the two-tank cascade, $netflowB(t)$ is the chattering variable, and
the distinctions among behaviors can be attributed to changes in $qdir(netflowB, t)$.
If we replace the distinctions between inc, std, and dec when describing the direction of change of $netflowB$, with a single value ign (for "ignore"), then the infinite,
intractably branching tree of behaviors collapses into a single finite behavior (figure 10.13). Essentially, this means that the qualitative values of $netflowB(t)$,
instead of being described by $\langle qmag, qdir \rangle$ pairs, are described by $\langle qmag \rangle$ alone.

In order to eliminate chattering, this "ignore-qdir" description must be applied
to *every* variable in the chattering equivalence classes identified in section 10.2.1.

Comparing figure 10.13 with figure 10.6, we see that the description captures
many of the same qualitative features. However, figure 10.13 represents a weaker
description of the behavior of $netflowB(t)$ than figure 10.6 does. The qualitative
description that $netflowB(t) = \langle (0, \infty), ign \rangle$ for $t \in (t_0, t_1)$ is consistent with any
number of dips and oscillations, as long as they don't reach the endpoints of the
interval. The prediction in figure 10.6 is significantly stronger.

Figure 10.14 uses a simplified $\{+, 0, -\}$ quantity space with a single landmark at 0
to illustrate the qualitative transitions possible during chatter. Abstracting behavior by ignoring qdirs collapses an infinite family of behaviors wandering among the
states $\langle +, inc \rangle$, $\langle +, std \rangle$, and $\langle +, dec \rangle$, into the single qualitative state description
$\langle +, ign \rangle$.

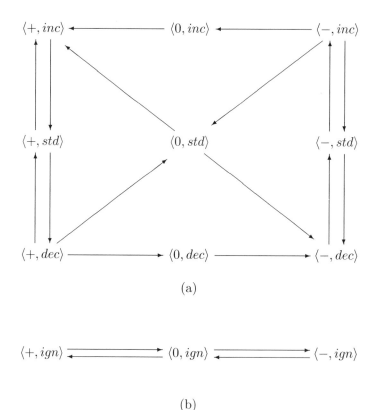

(a)

$\langle +, ign \rangle \rightleftarrows \langle 0, ign \rangle \rightleftarrows \langle -, ign \rangle$

(b)

- (a) The full qualitative transition graph is adequate to capture continuity constraints, but permits "chattering" behaviors.
- (b) The collapsed transition graph, ignoring direction of change, eliminates chatter, but fails to detect discontinuous change.

Figure 10.14
Transition graphs for a single unconstrained qualitative variable around the landmark 0.

10.6.2   Verifying Viability

Unfortunately, if we simply collapse the transitions in figure 10.14a to the simpler set in figure 10.14b, we lose an important source of constraint: the derivatives of variables must change continuously. For example, although the transition

$$\langle +, ign \rangle \longrightarrow \langle 0, ign \rangle$$

is apparently consistent (figure 10.14b), the more specific transition

$$\langle +, ign \rangle \longrightarrow \langle 0, inc \rangle$$

is inconsistent with the requirement that variables in QDEs be continuously differentiable.

To recapture the constraint that the derivative of a variable must change continuously, we apply a global *satisfiability filter* to each state where the *ign* direction of change was used. The satisfiability filter determines whether there is a complete, consistent state in which each occurrence of *ign* is replaced by one of $\{inc, std, dec\}$, and which is a consistent successor of the previous state. The satisfiability filter is clearly conservative.

PROPOSITION 9   The set of behaviors predicted by QSIM, applying the "ignore-qdir" description to any subset of variables in the QDE, includes every consistent behavior predicted by QSIM using the standard qualitative description.

Proof Sketch   We know that the table of qualitative successor rules (table 5.1) includes every possible transition. As illustrated by figure 10.14, the set of possible transitions under the ignore-qdir description encompasses each of those transitions, so all possible qualitative state changes are proposed. Since the satisfiability filter eliminates only inconsistent states, every actual behavior must remain.   ∎

The satisfiability filter is a weaker constraint than simulation with the larger set of distinctions, $\{inc, std, dec\}$. For example, it may be possible for a sequence of qualitative states

$$S1 \longrightarrow S2 \longrightarrow S3$$

to survive the satisfiability filter because one set of substitutions is consistent with $S1 \rightarrow S2$, while another is consistent with $S2 \rightarrow S3$, although no one set of substitutions is consistent with both transitions.

10.6.3   Discussion

The choice of method for handling chatter depends on which variables must be described to what degree of detail. In complex models, it may be appropriate to determine higher-order derivative constraints for certain variables, while ignoring qdirs on others (Dalle Molle, 1989). Changing level of description has two advantages over the explicit higher-order derivative constraint:

• It makes no assumptions about the M^+/M^- functions, and thus preserves the desirable property that all real behaviors are predicted.

- It can be implemented within the existing constraint-filtering computational framework, rather than requiring a possibly elaborate algebraic manipulation package.

However, there are two significant disadvantages as well.

- The coarser level of description makes it impossible to derive information about higher-order derivatives that could be used to filter out genuinely spurious behaviors. Figure 10.15 shows such an example.

- The coarser level of description produces a weaker prediction, and hence is less useful for semi-quantitative reasoning, explaining observations, or for hypothesis testing.

More generally, a number of researchers have investigated a variety of approaches to behavioral abstraction. Weld (1986) and Yeh (1990) have studied methods for aggregating the net effect of repetitive behaviors over time. Schaefer (1991) explores methods for finding closed-form solutions to qualitative differential equations. Coiera (1992) generalizes the superposition property of linear ODEs to a class of QDEs, to decompose complex simulation problems into simpler ones. Bhaskar and Nigam (1990) have used dimensional analysis of the variables in the model to derive certain behavioral relationships without any simulation at all.

Ideally, qualitative simulation should be controlled so that only those distinctions (and therefore branches) that are significant to the modeler are made explicit. This requires the simulator to take into account the purpose of the model, and perhaps search through a space of levels of abstraction. Initial explorations into this approach have been taken by Fouché (1992), DeCoste and Collins (1991), and Clancy and Kuipers (1993).

10.7   Conclusions

As we have seen, an important source of intractable branching in qualitative simulation is lack of constraint on the direction of change of certain variables, due to lack of information about the higher-order derivatives of those variables.

One method for eliminating this type of branching is to derive and apply the required information about higher-order derivatives: the *HOD constraint*. It is possible to do this while focusing attention on the higher-order derivatives only at those isolated points where branching takes place. The disadvantage of this approach is that it requires certain assumptions about the behavior of monotonic function constraints which may not, in general, be warranted. This sign-equality

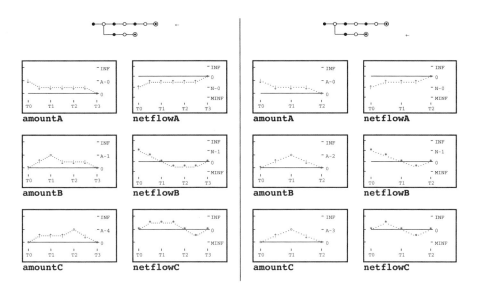

Figure 10.15

Behavior 1 is genuine, but behavior 2 is impossible.

Consider the three-tank cascade, initialized with tank A filled, and draining through tanks B and C until all tanks are empty. It is not possible for $B(t)$ and $C(t)$ to have their critical points at the same time, but the information required to filter this possibility is not available when ignoring qdirs.

assumption means that certain qualitative behaviors may be filtered out, in spite of being genuine possibilities.

A second method for eliminating this branching is to abstract the descriptions of certain directions of change, to avoid representing unimportant distinctions. This method avoids reliance on added assumptions about monotonic function constraints. However, this conservative approach produces a slightly weaker description of the predicted behavior, and the ability to filter out spurious predictions is reduced.

Thus, we observe another instance of the classic trade-off between generality and power (or false-negative versus false-positive error rates). The decision of which method is appropriate depends on the details of the pragmatic context within which the simulation is being used. For example, one must ask which predictions are actually important, how much knowledge is actually available to bound the curvature of unknown monotonic functions, and how serious a deviation between prediction and observation (e.g., the "dip" in figure 10.10) can be tolerated at what cost.

These higher-order derivative constraint methods have been sufficient to allow
tractable predictions of the possible behaviors of open and closed two-tank systems,
cascades of any number of tanks, and numerous other mechanisms drawn from
chemical engineering (Dalle Molle, 1989).

10.8   Problems

1. Build and simulate a QDE model of the open-ended U-tube, an important generic
two-compartment system.

The interaction between the two compartments is closer than in the cascade,
since increasing pressure in the downstream tank can affect the upstream tank. The
equations follow:

$$
\begin{aligned}
\Delta p &= p_a(A) - p_b(B) \\
\dot{A} &= in - f(\Delta p) \\
\dot{B} &= f(\Delta p) - g(B) \\
& \quad p_a, p_b, f, g \in M^+ \\
& \quad constant(in)
\end{aligned}
$$

Derive the necessary HOD constraints and simulate this model from a variety
of initial states.

2. In micro-economics, the dynamic state of a firm can be modeled as a network of
compartments connected by flows of money (Hart *et al.*, 1986). For example, in the
problem of cash management, the manager of a firm must select a policy according
to which some of the firm's available cash is used to pay its liabilities. What are
the effects of a particular choice of policy?

We will use a very simplified two-compartment model of the firm (Bailey *et al.*,
1991). *Sales* is a constant exogenous input, and compartments represent *Cash* and
Liabilities. (Eventually, *Inventory* should be added as a third compartment, but
that does not appear in our current model.) Unlike the fluid-flow models, a flow
from *Cash* to *Liabilities* reduces both levels! The qualitative model equations are
the following.

$$
\begin{aligned}
CashPmtRate &= f(Cash) \cdot g(Liabilities) \\
\frac{d}{dt} Cash &= Revenues(Sales) - CashPmtRate \\
\frac{d}{dt} Liabilities &= Costs(Sales) - CashPmtRate \\
&\quad f, g, Revenues, Costs \in M^+ \\
&\quad constant(Sales)
\end{aligned}
$$

The first equation in the model represents the chosen policy governing flow from *Cash* to *Liabilities*. The effect of this policy is that *CashPmtRate* is positively influenced by both the amount of cash and the amount of liabilities, but neither level is allowed to fall to zero unless the other becomes infinite. The availability of credit is not included in the model, and bankruptcy is only modeled as *Cash* = 0 or *Liabilities* = *MAX*.

Implement this model as a QDE in QSIM, derive the necessary HOD constraints, define a reference equilibrium state, and obtain a single behavior predicting the effect of an increase in *Sales*.

For further research, experiment with variations on the initial state, the cash management policy, the overall model of the firm, and the incorporation of semi-quantitative constraints into the model.

3. Apply the axioms of the hybrid sign-real algebra SR1 (section 3.4.4) to simplify the expressions in figure 10.4 associated with the `mult` constraint.

4. (Research Problem.) Find and formalize an improved method for identifying chattering variables. To what extent can this be done statically, by algebraic analysis of the QDE as in section 10.2.1, and to what extent must it rely on analysis of the predicted behavior tree or envisionment graph (e.g., figure 10.1)? Among chattering variables in the same equivalence class, are some better candidates for HOD constraints than others?

5. (Research Problem.) Specify and implement a general-purpose algebraic manipulation interface for QSIM, to serve the higher-order derivative constraint (this chapter), the energy constraint (chapter 11), and other purposes (chapter 3). Demonstrate programs satisfying this interface based on simple internal algorithms (e.g., figure 10.4), and on sophisticated externally provided utilities such as Macsyma (Macsyma, 1988), Bounder (Sacks, 1987a), or Mathematica (Wolfram, 1988).

6. (Research Problem.) The open-ended "W-tube"

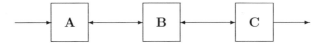

raises more difficult problems of chatter, especially on the variable $\dot{B}$. Explore methods of structural and behavioral abstraction to get a tractable prediction from this model.

7. (Research Problem.) Extend the method for automatic derivation of HOD expressions to handle $S^{\pm}$ and $U^{\pm}$ constraints. In the current implementation of QSIM, the expression derived for $sd2(x)$ is stored as a property of the QDE, and is assumed to apply to any state with that QDE as its operating region. However, if we permit the S^{+}/S^{-} and U^{+}/U^{-} constraints to appear in the QDE, this assumption no larger holds. Extend the representation and the implementation to record the dependency of the HOD expresssion on the qualitative state. Nonetheless, ensure that HOD expressions are rederived only when necessary.

8. (Research Problem.) In general, the sign-equality assumption might be violated whenever a monotonic function is non-linear. However, in many cases these violations will be small (cf. figure 10.11). Suppose semi-quantitative information is available on the slopes and curvatures of monotonic functions in a QDE. How can we assure ourselves that the violations of the sign-equality assumption are "small enough" for a given purpose, so we are justified in considering only the behaviors consistent with the derived HOD constraint?

11 Global Dynamical Constraints

11.1 Introduction

Local consistency of an individual state, or of a state and its immediate neighbors, has been the basis of most of the filtering methods we have considered in qualitative simulation, so far. However, some important properties of qualitative behaviors are only visible from a more global perspective.

There is a very rich mathematical theory of the qualitative properties of *ordinary* differential equations that provides us with useful algebraic and geometric constraints on possible behaviors. These constraints are necessary to obtain tractable sets of predicted behaviors for many second- and higher-order systems with periodic or weakly periodic behavior.

We will illustrate these methods in the context of two very simple models: the spring-mass oscillator, with and without damping friction.

- Simple spring: without friction.

$$
\begin{aligned}
\dot{x} &= v \\
\dot{v} &= -f(x) \\
& \quad f \in M_0^+
\end{aligned}
$$

- Damped spring: with friction.

$$
\begin{aligned}
\dot{x} &= v \\
\dot{v} &= -f(x) - g(v) \\
& \quad f, g \in M_0^+
\end{aligned}
$$

Consider the simple spring system, without friction. Start at t_0 with $x(t_0) = x_0 > 0$, and $v(t_0) = 0$. The predicted behavior evolves without branching, creating new landmark values to represent extreme values of the variables, until time-point t_4. At t_4, the behavior branches three ways according to whether $v(t) = 0$ before, after, or at the same time as $x(t) = x_0$. Figure 11.1 shows the three predicted behaviors of this system.

Since the spring model contains an unknown monotonic function $f \in M^+$, which could be non-linear or even asymmetrical, could it be that all three behaviors are real possibilities? No, as it turns out. Suppose we define the total energy of the spring system as the sum of the kinetic and potential energies:

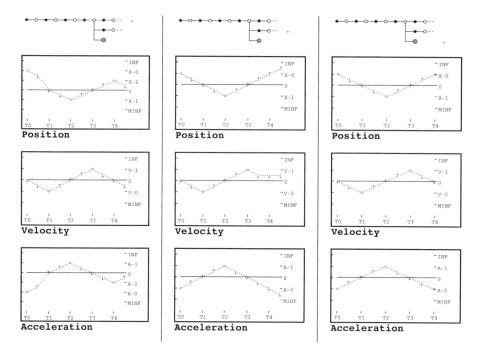

Figure 11.1
Qualitative behaviors of the undamped spring.

$$E(t) = KE + PE = \frac{1}{2}\, v^2 + \int_0^x f(\bar{x})\, d\bar{x}. \tag{11.1}$$

Then we can show (problem 1) that the QDE for the simple spring implies that $E(t)$ is constant, and therefore, the only consistent behavior has $x(t_4) = x_0$ and $v(t_4) = 0$. The other two behaviors are *spurious*: not consistent with any ODE that is abstracted to this QDE.

Even though this problem is manifested as a branch at time-point t_4, the underlying problem begins at the first time-interval, (t_0, t_1), where we lose any connection between the qualitative state of the system and the implicit invariant $E(t)$.

In section 5.6, we discussed the general implications of this type of problem for our confidence in the results and guarantees of qualitative simulation. In this chapter, we explore methods for solving many particular cases of the problem. First, we can explicitly assert the implicit invariant. Second, a more sophisticated generalized energy constraint can handle cases where energy is not, in fact, constant. Third, a topological constraint on trajectories in phase space provides additional filtering.

11.2   Solution 1: Make the Invariant Explicit

In the case of the simple spring and other conservative systems, we can explicitly assert the invariant as constraints in the QDE.

$$
\begin{aligned}
E(t) &= KE(t) + PE(t) \\
&= \frac{1}{2}m\,v^2 + m\int_0^x f(\bar{x})\,d\bar{x} \\
&= M_0^+(v^2) + U_0^+(x).
\end{aligned}
$$

This eliminates the spurious behaviors (figure 11.2). See problems 2 and 3.

Elastic collisions can also be represented using an explicit conservation-of-energy constraint, where the region transition representing the collision explicitly inherits the value of $E(t)$ across the transition (figure 11.3). This method works even when the expression for $E(t)$ is different on the two sides of the transition, such as when modeling a bouncing ball in terms of transitions between a gravity model and a spring model (section 8.2).

Thus, for systems where energy is conserved, such as undamped oscillations or elastic collisions, making the implicit invariant explicit solves the problem and eliminates the spurious behaviors. However, for damped oscillations, or partially inelastic collisions, we lack such a convenient invariant. Nonetheless, under suitable circumstances, we can exploit qualitative constraints on the energy in the system and the way it changes.

11.3   Example: Predator-Prey Ecology

Suppose we have a population y of predators, whose food supply is a population x of prey. Foxes and rabbits are one classic example. How will the sizes of these populations evolve over time?

By abstracting the sizes of these populations of discrete individuals to continuous variables x and y, we can model this situation with a dynamical system.[1] We will develop a linear model, and leave its generalization to a qualitative model to problem 7.

---

[1]This discussion is adapted from Hirsch and Smale, 1974, pages 258–265.

$$\begin{aligned}
\dot{x} &= v \\
\dot{v} &= -f(x), \text{ where } f \in M^+ \\
E &= M_0^+(v^2) + U_0^+(x) \\
&\quad constant(E)
\end{aligned}$$

```
(define-QDE Spring-with-energy-conservation
   (quantity-spaces
        (a      (minf 0 inf))
        (v      (minf 0 inf))
        (x      (minf 0 inf))
        (vsq    (minf 0 inf))
        (KE     (minf 0 inf))
        (PE     (minf 0 inf))
        (E      (minf 0 inf)))
   (constraints
        ((d/dt x v))
        ((d/dt v a))
        ((M- a x)          (0 0) (minf inf) (inf minf))
        ((mult v v vsq))
        ((M+ vsq KE)       (0 0) (inf inf))
        ((U+ x PE (0 0))   (minf inf) (inf inf))
        ((add KE PE E))
        ((constant E))))
```

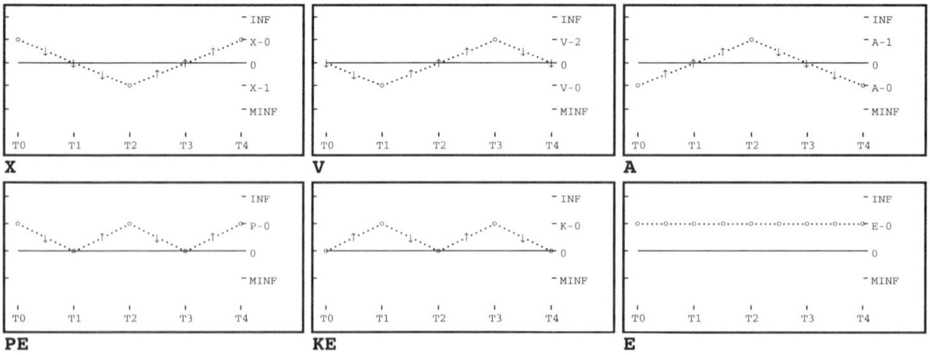

Figure 11.2
The simple spring with explicit invariant $E(t)$ produces a single cyclic behavior.

```
(define-QDE Simple-bounce
    (text "Simple bouncing ball, reflecting off Y=0")
    (quantity-spaces
        (y       (minf 0 inf))
        (v       (minf 0 inf))
        (a       (minf 0 inf))
        (vsq     (0 inf))
        (KE      (0 inf))
        (PE      (0 inf))
        (E       (0 inf)))
    (constraints
        ((d/dt y v))
        ((d/dt v a))
        ((constant a))
        ((mult v v vsq))
        ((M+ vsq KE)       (0 0) (inf inf))
        ((M+ y PE)         (0 0) (inf inf))
        ((add KE PE E))
        ((constant E)))
    (transitions
        ((y (0 dec)) -> reflect-velocity)))

(defun reflect-velocity (ball-state)
    (create-transition-state :from-state    ball-state
                             :to-qde        simple-bounce
                             :inherit-qmag  '(a E)
                             :assert        '((y (0 inc))))))
```

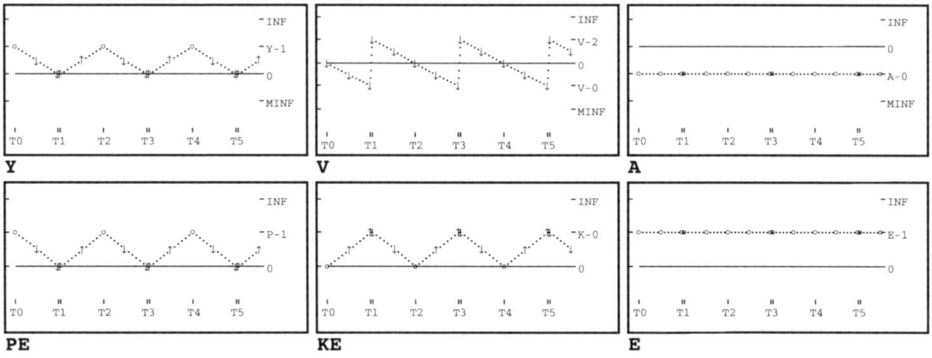

Figure 11.3
Bouncing ball with elastic collisions.

Energy is conserved by an explicit constraint within each region, and by inheriting $E(t)$ across region transitions.

The rate of change of the predator population is proportional to the population, and to the average food supply available to an individual predator, compared with the minimal requirement σ for survival:

$$\dot{y} = a\left(\frac{kxy}{y} - \sigma\right) = a(kx - \sigma)y = (Cx - D)y$$

where kxy, the total food consumption of the population, is assumed to be proportional to the number of predator-prey encounters.

The prey population is assumed to have enough food for unlimited growth, but of course its growth is limited by predation:

$$\dot{x} = Ax - Bxy = (A - By)x.$$

The resulting linear model of predator-prey interaction

$$\begin{aligned} \dot{x} &= (A - By)x \\ \dot{y} &= (Cx - D)y \end{aligned} \tag{11.2}$$

is also known as the *Volterra-Lotka* equation.

First, we note that the model has fixed points at $(0,0)$ and $(D/C, A/B)$. By solving the QDE for points where $\dot{x} = \dot{y} = 0$, QSIM can find both of these points and classify $(D/C, A/B)$ as stable and $(0,0)$ as unstable.

Next, we augment the QDE with landmark values $(x^*, y^*) = (D/C, A/B)$ representing the stable fixed point, and with the Lyapunov function

$$H(x, y) = F(x) + G(y) = Cx - D\log x + By - A\log y.$$

Hirsch and Smale (1974) derive $H(x, y)$ and show that it is constant along every trajectory of the sytem. We observe that $F \in U^+_{(x^*, 0)}$ and $G \in U^+_{(y^*, 0)}$, and that both F and G have corresponding values $(0, +\infty)$ and $(+\infty, +\infty)$.

With this information, QSIM predicts a unique qualitative behavior resulting from a perturbation from (x^*, y^*). Figure 11.4 shows the cyclic behavior following from the initial state $x(t_0) > x^*$, $y(t_0) = y^*$. (Since this model ignores qdirs on $\dot{x}$ and $\dot{y}$, the strong state match does not detect the cycle, but a weak state match would.)

In a more realistic model, it is possible for either the predator or prey species to become extinct. Equation (11.2) excludes this possibility for two reasons. First, $H(x, y) \to +\infty$ as x or y approach zero, so no trajectory that startes at a finite point can intersect an axis. Second, the abstraction from discrete to continuous

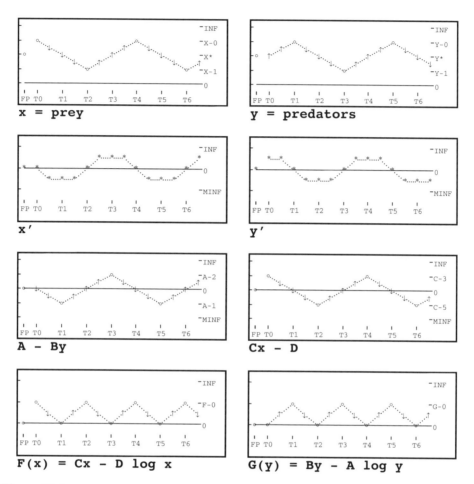

Figure 11.4
Unique behavior of the Volterra-Lotka (predator-prey) system.

variables breaks down and the model becomes invalid as the population becomes very small (certainly if $x < 2$ or $y < 2$!).

If we explore this possibility with a slight modification to the Lyapunov function so that $F(0)$ and $G(0)$ have finite values, we get two additional behaviors from the same initial conditions, predicting extinction of either predator or prey species (figure 11.5).

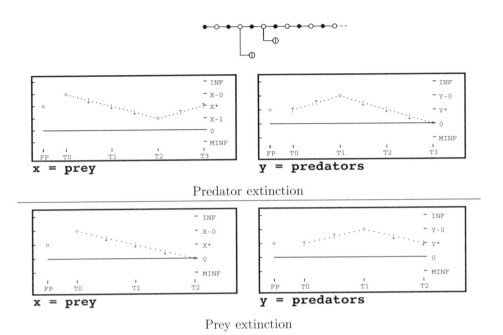

Predator extinction

Prey extinction

Figure 11.5
Extinction of either predators or prey is possible.

11.4   Solution 2: The Kinetic Energy Theorem

When energy is conserved, as in the simple spring, we can think of energy as flowing
back and forth between one container holding kinetic energy and another holding
potential energy, with no loss. More generally, even if energy is not conserved, we
can consider flows of energy into or out of the system.

Work is the flow of energy from one form to another. The work done by a system
can be decomposed into *conservative work* (flow of kinetic energy into potential energy and back) and *non-conservative work* (other energy flows, including irreversible
dissipation into the environment).

Under some circumstances, this decomposition can be identified from the structure of the QDE, and the terms in the energy flow balance equation can be evaluated
qualitatively from the information in the qualitative behavior. As we shall see, this
balance can provide a very effective constraint on the set of possible behaviors.

Suppose a system includes three variables x, v, and a such that

$$v = \frac{dx}{dt} \text{ and } a = \frac{dv}{dt},$$

and suppose that a can be decomposed into the sum of two terms

$$a(t) = C(x(t)) + N(t)$$

where the *conservative* term, $C(x(t))$, is dependent only on the value of x. Consider a segment of behavior between time-points t_i and t_j, and use the notation

$$x_i = x(t_i), \ v_i = v(t_i), \ x_j = x(t_j), \ v_j = v(t_j).$$

We can decompose the change in kinetic energy[2] into the sum of the *conservative work* and the *non-conservative work*:

$$\Delta KE(t_i, t_j) = W_C(t_i, t_j) + W_N(t_i, t_j), \tag{11.3}$$

where

$$\begin{aligned} \Delta KE(t_i, t_j) &= \frac{1}{2}(v_j^2 - v_i^2) \\ W_C(t_i, t_j) &= \int_{x_i}^{x_j} C(x)\, dx \\ W_N(t_i, t_j) &= \int_{t_i}^{t_j} N(t)v(t)\, dt. \end{aligned}$$

This claim, the Kinetic Energy Theorem, is proved in section 11.4.4. For now, we will simply apply equation (11.3) as a constraint on behaviors.

11.4.1   Determining Signs of Terms

It is frequently possible to determine the signs of the terms in equation (11.3) from the information in a qualitative behavior description. If the signs are not consistent with the qualitative addition constraint, the behavior can be filtered out.

- The sign of ΔKE depends on the variation in absolute value of v between t_i and t_j.

$$[\Delta KE(t_i, t_j)]_0 = [|v_j| - |v_i|]_0 = [|v_j|]_{|v_i|}.$$

This sign can be determined if v_i and v_j have the same sign, or if either of the terms $|v(t)|$ or $v(t)^2$ is explicitly represented.

---

[2]The physical terms "energy" and "work" are used only metaphorically in this discussion. The result depends only on the equations relating x, v, a, C, and N, and applies equally well to physical and non-physical domains. Therefore, the constant mass m is omitted from the equations.

- If $C(x)$ does not change sign on the interval between x_i and x_j, then

$$[W_C(t_i, t_j)]_0 = [x_j - x_i]_0 \, [C(x_j)]_0.$$

- The sign of $W_N(t_i, t_j)$ can be determined from the qualitative behavior if the product $N(t)v(t)$ has constant sign (except for isolated zeroes) from t_i to t_j. Fortunately this is often true, since $N(t)$ frequently represents frictional or motor forces, in the same or opposite direction to the velocity. In this case,

$$[W_N(t_i, t_j)]_0 = [N(t)v(t)]_0, \text{ for all but isolated } t \in (t_i, t_j).$$

Thus $[N(t)\,v(t)]_0$ can be determined from its value on the qualitative time-intervals within (t_i, t_j).

- The signs of the terms in equation (11.3) can be determined in a few other special cases, such as where it is known that $C(-x) = -C(x)$, or where numerical range information is available about x_i, x_j, v_i, and v_j.

The kinetic energy constraint is applied as a global behavior filter. For each new state at a time-point t_j, each earlier time-point t_i is considered. If the signs of the terms in equation (11.3) can be determined over the interval (t_i, t_j), and if they violate the qualitative addition constraint, the proposed state at t_j is inconsistent and can be filtered out.

11.4.2   Example: Undamped Spring

For the simple, undamped spring-mass system, we can decompose $a(t)$ into $C(x) = -M_0^+(x)$ and $N(t) = 0$, indicating conservative forces only. Now we can compute the signs of the terms in equation (11.3) for the three behaviors of the system (figure 11.1) over the interval (t_0, t_4).

	(1)	(2)	(3)
$x(t)$	$0 < x(t_4) < x(t_0)$	$x(t_4) = x(t_0) > 0$	$x(t_4) = x(t_0) > 0$
$v(t)$	$v(t_4) = v(t_0) = 0$	$v(t_4) > v(t_0) = 0$	$v(t_4) = v(t_0) = 0$
$[\Delta KE(t_0, t_4)]_0$	0	+	0
$[W_C(t_0, t_4)]_0$	−	0	0
$[W_N(t_0, t_4)]_0$	0	0	0

Clearly, behaviors (1) and (2) are qualitatively inconsistent, and can be filtered out.

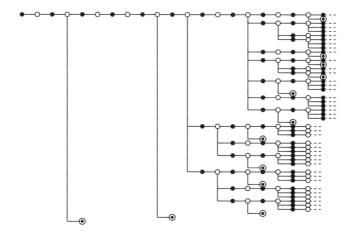

Figure 11.6
Behavior tree for the damped spring, ignoring $qdir(a(t))$.

11.4.3   Example: Damped Spring

For the damped spring, the $a(t)$ is decomposed into $C(x) = -M_0^+(x)$ and $N(t) = -M_0^+(v(t))$. The qualitative behavior of the damped spring is considerably more complex than that of the simple spring, and involves the potential for *chatter*, which we eliminate by ignoring the direction of change of $a(t)$, the highest-order derivative (chapter 10). This still leaves us with an intractably branching tree of behaviors (figure 11.6).

Applying the kinetic energy constraint to the damped spring filters out the spurious behaviors. Figure 11.7 shows three inconsistent behaviors and how they were detected by the kinetic energy constraint.

The result is an infinite, but completely regular, tree of behaviors (figure 11.8), representing decreasing oscillations toward the origin, with the possibility that the system can become overdamped after any finite number of half-cycles. For a *linear* spring, only the first branch is valid: the system is either always overdamped, or always underdamped. For a *non-linear* spring, however, all the behaviors are possible (see problem 4).

11.4.4   Proof of the Kinetic Energy Theorem

THEOREM 8 (KINETIC ENERGY)   Suppose we have a system with continuous variables x, v, and a such that

	(a)	(b)	(c)
$x(t_i), x(t_j)$	$x(t_6) = x(t_0) > 0$	$x(t_7) > x(t_2) = 0$	$x(t_6) = x(t_0) > 0$
$v(t_i), v(t_j)$	$v(t_6) > v(t_0) = 0$	$v(t_7) < v(t_2) < 0$	$v(t_6) = v(t_0) = 0$
$[\Delta KE(t_i, t_j)]_0$	$+$	$+$	0
$[W_C(t_i, t_j)]_0$	0	$-$	0
$[W_N(t_i, t_j)]_0$	$-$	$-$	$-$

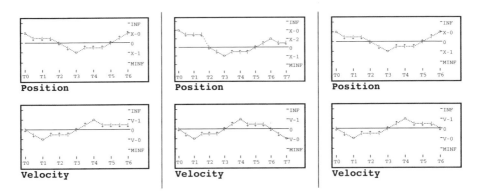

Figure 11.7
Three behaviors of the damped spring, inconsistent with the kinetic energy constraint.

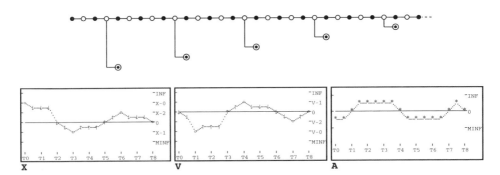

Figure 11.8
Tree of valid behaviors, and time-plot of behavior 4, for the monotonic damped spring, ignoring $qdir(a(t))$ and applying the kinetic energy constraint.

$$v = \frac{dx}{dt} \text{ and } a = \frac{dv}{dt}$$

and a can be written

$$a(t) = C(x(t)) + N(t).$$

Further, suppose the system moves, over the interval (t_i, t_j), from

$$x_i = x(t_i), v_i = v(t_i) \text{ to } x_j = x(t_j), v_j = v(t_j).$$

Then

$$\Delta KE(t_i, t_j) = W_C(t_i, t_j) + W_N(t_i, t_j) \tag{11.4}$$

where

$$
\begin{aligned}
\Delta KE(t_i, t_j) &= \frac{1}{2} \left(v_j^2 - v_i^2 \right) \\
W_C(t_i, t_j) &= \int_{x_i}^{x_j} C(x)\, dx \\
W_N(t_i, t_j) &= \int_{t_i}^{t_j} N(t)v(t)\, dt.
\end{aligned}
$$

Proof   The work done by the forces acting on the system from t_i to t_j is

$$W(t_i, t_j) = \int_{t_i}^{t_j} a(t)v(t)\, dt. \tag{11.5}$$

Replacing $a(t)$ by $v'(t)$ and changing the variable of integration lets us write

$$
\begin{aligned}
W(t_i, t_j) &= \int_{t_i}^{t_j} v(t)v'(t)\, dt \\
&= \int_{v_i}^{v_j} v\, dv \\
&= \frac{1}{2} \left(v_j^2 - v_i^2 \right).
\end{aligned}
$$

By defining

$$\Delta KE(t_i, t_j) = \frac{1}{2} \left(v_j^2 - v_i^2 \right) \tag{11.6}$$

to be the change in kinetic energy in the system, we get

$$W(t_i, t_j) = \Delta KE(t_i, t_j). \tag{11.7}$$

Now, suppose we can decompose $a(t)$ into two terms, one of which depends only on the value of x:

$a(t) = C(x(t)) + N(t)$.

Then we can rewrite (11.5) as

$$W(t_i, t_j) = W_C(t_i, t_j) + W_N(t_i, t_j),\qquad\qquad(11.8)$$

where

$$W_C(t_i, t_j) = \int_{t_i}^{t_j} C(x(t))v(t)\ dt\qquad\qquad(11.9)$$

and

$$W_N(t_i, t_j) = \int_{t_i}^{t_j} N(t)v(t)\ dt.\qquad\qquad(11.10)$$

Substituting $x'(t)$ for $v(t)$ in (11.9) and changing the variable of integration gives us

$$W_C(t_i, t_j) = \int_{x_i}^{x_j} C(x)\ dx.\qquad\qquad(11.11)$$

Combining equations (11.6), (11.7), (11.8), (11.10), and (11.11) gives us equation (11.4). ∎

11.4.5   Identifying the Kinetic Energy Constraint

In some cases, the kinetic energy constraint can be identified syntactically from the constraints in the QDE. Essentially, we search for the appropriate collection of constraints, using rules of the following form:

```
((d/dt ?x ?v)
 (d/dt ?v ?a)
 (add ?c ?n ?a)
 (depends-only-on ?c ?x)
 ->
 (kinetic-energy-constraint ?x ?v ?c ?n))
```

There are two problems with this search. First, the decomposition $a(t) = C(x(t)) + N(t)$ may exist, but not appear in the QDE in precisely this syntactic form. A substantial amount of algebraic manipulation could be required to derive the decomposition from the constraints in the QDE. Second, evaluation of the `depends-only-on` predicate could also involve substantial amounts of algebraic manipulation, attempting to eliminate other variables, on both successful and unsuccessful candidates for `?c`.

A syntactic search of this form is able to derive the kinetic energy constraint for small models like the simple spring or the damped spring, but is inadequate for more complex systems (Fouché and Kuipers, 1992). (See problem 6.)

11.5   Solution 3: The Phase-Space Representation

An alternate point of view on qualitative behaviors provides a constraint on global behaviors whose effect overlaps with, but is not identical to, the kinetic energy constraint. The Kinetic Energy Theorem gives us an *algebraic* criterion for consistency that we can evaluate qualitatively. The phase-space representation gives us *geometric* criteria for consistency, which can also be evaluated qualitatively in many cases.

The *phase space* for a system of differential equations is a space whose axes are defined by a complete set of state variables for the system, so that a point in phase space characterizes the state of the system. A behavior is thus represented as a trajectory through phase space. Qualitative properties of the behavior of a system over time are thus visible as geometric properties of the trajectory in phase space. This important insight was due to the great mathematician Henri Poincaré.

The geometric properties of the phase-space representation follow from the existence and uniqueness theorems for differential equations (Hirsch and Smale, 1974).

1. The existence theorem means that every point in a phase space lies on some trajectory of the system.

2. The uniqueness theorem says that, except for asymptotic limit points, no point can lie on more than one trajectory.

   - This also implies that any trajectory that includes non-limit points can only intersect *itself* if it is a simple closed curve, which represents a periodic behavior.

For second-order systems, where the phase space is two-dimensional, these constraints greatly restrict the possible patterns of flow of the trajectories representing solutions to a differential equation. For *linear* systems, there are only a few possible global patterns: saddle, spiral (underdamped), and nodal (overdamped), with boundary cases called centers (cyclic) and foci (critically damped) (figure 11.9). The patterns can also vary according to the direction of flow along the trajectories,

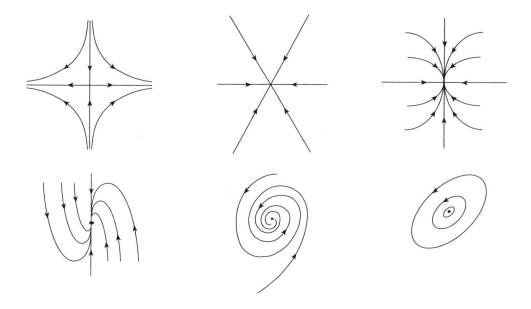

Figure 11.9
The possible phase portraits for second-order linear differential equations.
Based on Hirsch and Smale, 1974.

corresponding to the stability or instability of the behavior. *Non-linear* systems in the phase plane have the same types of local behavior, but their global patterns may be more complex, involving limit cycles and separatrices.

11.5.1   Qualitative Phase Space

A quantity space is a qualitative abstraction of the real line, divided by landmark values into points and intervals. Similarly, we can abstract the phase space to a *qualitative* phase space, divided into rectangles, boundary lines, and points by landmark values on the axes. A trajectory (i.e., a behavior) corresponds to a sequence of rectangles (counting boundaries as degenerate rectangles) and directions of change. Under the qualitative representation, of course, we typically do not know the actual position of the trajectory: only that it moves monotonically through a particular rectangle. Figure 11.10 shows qualitative plots of the x-v phase plane for several behaviors of the damped spring.

(a) Valid trajectories (cf. figure 11.8).

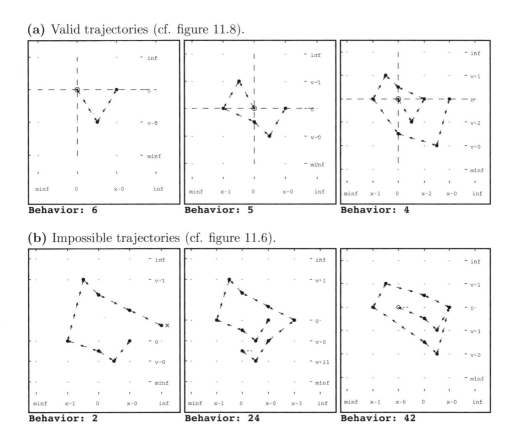

(b) Impossible trajectories (cf. figure 11.6).

Figure 11.10
Qualitative plots of the x-v phase plane for (a) valid and (b) invalid behaviors of the damped spring.

Certain behaviors can be identified as spurious in the qualitative phase-space representation because they correspond to self-intersecting trajectories (figure 11.12). If we can identify self-intersections, we can label those behaviors as inconsistent and filter them out. The problem is to identify intersections from the information in the qualitative behavior description, since it only weakly describes where the actual trajectory goes.

11.5.2   Identifying Intersections Qualitatively

How do we identify an intersection when we don't know where the trajectory goes? Suppose a curve passes diagonally through a rectangle, from one corner to the opposite corner; for example, from a to c in figure 11.11(a). If another curve (a later segment of the same trajectory) enters the rectangle at the third corner b and exits from the fourth d, then the two curves must have intersected somewhere within the rectangle.[3]

The intersection criterion must be cautiously stated, in case a curve enters the rectangle through a segment of a boundary line (defined by a landmark value on one axis and an interval on the other axis) rather than a corner (defined by landmarks on both axes). As shown in figure 11.11(b), if the first curve enters in segment (a, b) and leaves from (d, e), then we can only show an intersection if the second curve enters through $[b, c, d]$ and leaves through $[e, f, a]$, or vice versa. If the second curve passes through either (a, b) or (d, e), we don't have enough information to tell whether an intersection takes place or not.[4]

11.5.3   Limitations

There are several limitations on our ability to filter out behaviors by identifying trajectory intersections. First, the uniqueness theorem implies that *no* two trajectories can intersect, while we detect only *self*-intersections. This is because a qualitative differential equation may correspond to several different ordinary differential equations, so two distinct qualitative behaviors may describe solutions to different ODEs. In that case, their intersection in the qualitative phase-space representation is not inconsistent. Only recently (Lee and Kuipers, 1993; Lee, 1993) has it become possible to assemble the many behaviors predicted from a given QDE into a complete set of possible *qualitative phase portraits*. Section 11.7 gives an overview of this work.

Another limitation arises from the coarseness of the qualitative representation. In the theory of ordinary differential equations, any complete set of independent state variables defines a phase space which completely characterizes the properties of the system. For example, for the simple spring, either the x-v or the v-a phase plane represents the state of the system. (The variables x and a do not define a

---

[3] For rectangular regions and reasonable functions, this result is intuitively obvious, and follows immediately from the Intermediate Value Theorem. The more general theorem, the Jordan Curve Theorem, states that *any* simple closed curve in the plane divides the plane into exactly two regions. In full generality, this theorem is surprisingly deep (Spanier, 1966).

[4] More complex geometrical situations can arise, involving overlapping rectangles, where neither rectangle alone is sufficient, but taken together we have enough information to infer that an intersection exists.

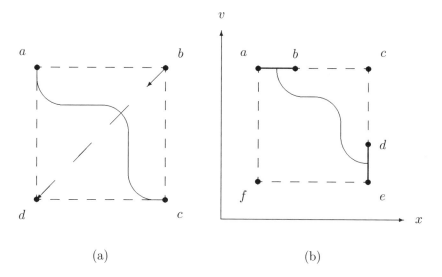

Figure 11.11
Qualitative intersection criteria.

phase space because they are related by $a = -f(x)$, and therefore cannot represent independent state variables.) However, under the qualitative representation, certain properties such as self-intersections may be visible in one phase plane but not in another. Furthermore, it is possible for the phase-plane trajectories to be individually consistent, but mutually inconsistent. Figure 11.12 shows a behavior exhibiting both of these phenomena.

11.6 Example: The PI Controller

A *proportional* (or P) controller is one whose action is proportional to the sensed error:

$$u = k_1 e.$$

A *proportional-integral* (or PI) controller is one whose action is a weighted sum of the sensed error and the integral of the error over time:

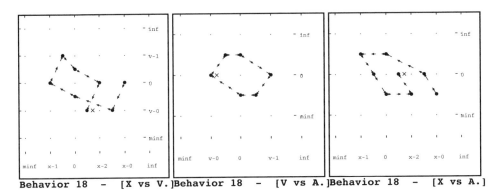

Behavior 18 – [X vs V.]Behavior 18 – [V vs A.]Behavior 18 – [X vs A.]

Figure 11.12
Inconsistent qualitative behavior of the damped spring showing (a) self-intersection in the x-v phase plane, (b) periodic behavior in the v-a phase plane, and (c) non-periodic behavior in the x-a phase plane.

$$u = k_1 e + k_2 I, \text{ where } I = \int e.$$

In section 6.2, we considered the example of a house whose temperature is controlled by a *qualitative* proportional controller: one whose action is a monotonic function of the error:

$$u = f(e), \text{ where } f \in M_0^+.$$

Here we will discuss a qualitative PI controller,

$$u = f(e) + g(I), \text{ where } I = \int e \text{ and } f, g \in M_0^+.$$

A proportional controller has the property that a continuing abnormal input (say, cold weather outside the house) must result in a non-zero steady-state error term. In the case of the house, cold weather causes increased heat loss, which must be balanced by increased heat input, which only happens if the error term is non-zero. This undesirable property is called *steady-state offset*. The advantage of the integral term is that it forces steady-state offset to be zero. (Because in steady state, $e = dI/dt = 0$.)

In order to formulate a qualitative model of the home thermostat with PI controller, we will need to do some algebra on the model. Let us start by restating the model for the proportionally controlled thermostat from section 6.2. In this model, H is the heat content of the house and $\dot{H} = dH/dt$. M is the thermal mass, T_{in} is the temperature inside the house, T_{out} is the outside temperature, T_{set} is the setpoint of the thermostat, and E is the error term. R is resistance to heat loss, and HF_{in} is the flow of heat from the furnace.

$$T_{in} = \frac{H}{M} \tag{11.12}$$

$$\dot{H} = HF_{in} - \frac{1}{R}(T_{in} - T_{out}) \tag{11.13}$$

$$E = T_{in} - T_{set} \tag{11.14}$$

$$HF_{in} = -f(E), \text{ where } f \in M_0^+. \tag{11.15}$$

We replace the qualitative proportional controller in equation (11.15) with a qualitative PI controller

$$HF_{in} = -f(E) - g(I), \text{ where } f, g \in M_0^+ \text{ and } I = \int E. \tag{11.16}$$

In order to apply the energy constraint, we will need a chain of three variables (I, E, and $\dot{E}$) linked by derivative constraints:

$$\frac{d}{dt}I = E, \quad \frac{d}{dt}E = \frac{d}{dt}\left(\frac{H}{M} - T_{set}\right) = \frac{1}{M}\dot{H} = \dot{E}.$$

Now we can rewrite equations (11.12), (11.13), (11.14), and (11.16) as the following:

$$\dot{E} = \frac{1}{M}\left[-f(E) - g(I) - \frac{1}{R}(E + T_{set} - T_{out})\right] \tag{11.17}$$

$$= -\left[\frac{1}{M}f(E) + \frac{1}{RM}E\right] + \left[\frac{1}{M}g(I) + \frac{1}{RM}(T_{set} - T_{out})\right] \tag{11.18}$$

$$= -F(E) - G(I) + k, \text{ where } F, G \in M_0^+. \tag{11.19}$$

To apply the energy constraint, we decompose $\dot{E}$ into conservative and non-conservative terms:

$$C(I) = -G(I) + k$$

$$N(t) = -F(E(t))$$

We can simulate this model successfully, obtaining the infinite but completely regular behavior tree in figure 11.13, by using the energy constraint, ignoring $qdir(\dot{E})$, and applying the non-intersection constraint to the C-E phase plane. Figure 11.14 shows an inconsistent behavior filtered out by the energy constraint, and figure 11.15 shows an inconsistent behavior filtered out by the non-intersection constraint.

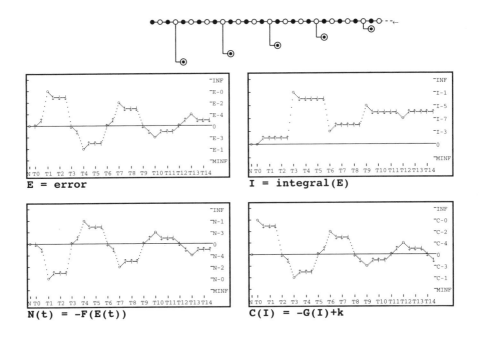

Figure 11.13
Behaviors of the PI-controlled thermostat.
Like the damped spring, we get an infinite underdamped behavior, plus an infinite family of
behaviors that converge in an overdamped fashion after a finite number of oscillations.

11.7 Qualitative Phase Portraits

Recent work has drawn together a number of these methods in a program called
QPORTRAIT that constructs phase portraits for qualitative differential equations
(Lee and Kuipers, 1993; Lee, 1993). QPORTRAIT applies to autonomous systems of
two coupled first-order qualitative differential equations with nondegenerate fixed
points. It generates qualitative descriptions of all possible phase portraits of the
given system.

Non-degeneracy of fixed points is checked by an algebraic criterion that can often
be evaluated qualitatively. Non-degeneracy allows us to assume that fixed points
are locally linearizable. In the phase plane, this gives us a simple finite classification
of possible behaviors near a fixed point. QPORTRAIT also relies heavily on the non-
intersection constraint, which applies in any dimension, but only provides a useful

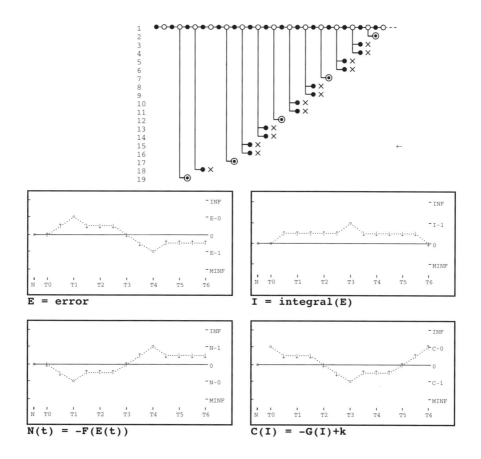

Figure 11.14
Inconsistent behavior detected by the energy constraint.

Behavior 15 violates the energy constraint over the interval (t_0, t_6), because $[\Delta KE] = [+]$, while $[W_C] = 0$ and $[W_N] = [-]$.

amount of filtering in the phase plane.

Like the real number line, the phase plane has its landmarks and its dividing boundaries. The landmarks are the fixed points, which can be classified as sources, sinks, saddles, and centers; and points at infinity, which can be sources or sinks for flows. Closed orbits and separatrices (trajectories that connect to saddle points) serve as dividing boundaries between qualitatively distinct flows. The basic strategy used by QPORTRAIT is to exhaustively enumerate and combine these landmarks,

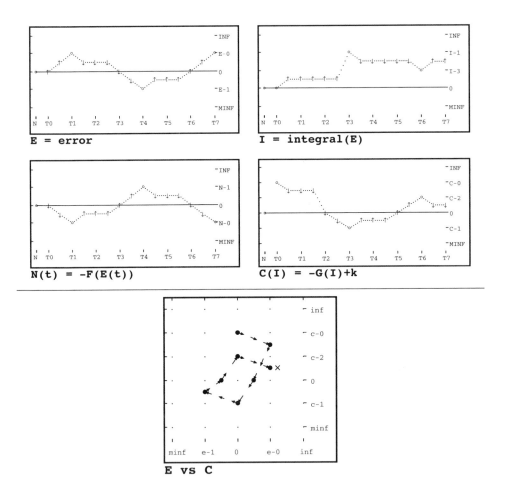

Figure 11.15
Inconsistent behavior detected by the non-intersection constraint.

Behavior 14 appears to be inconsistent because $N(t_7) = N(t_1)$, but this cannot be confirmed by the energy constraint because $C(t_1)$ and $C(t_7)$ have overlapping interval values. However, the non-intersection constraint on the E-C phase plane is able to detect the inconsistency and filter out this behavior.

boundaries, and flows, filtering out inconsistent combinations and abstracting away uninteresting distinctions.

The major steps of QPORTRAIT are the following. For a more complete presentation, see Lee and Kuipers, 1993; Lee, 1993.

1. **Total envisionment**.

   • Form a directed graph of all possible qualitative states and continuous transitions.

   • Collapse distinctions due to non-phase variables.

   • Identify fixed (quiescent) points. If necessary, create new landmarks to represent the fixed points and repeat the total envisionment.

   • Check fixed points for non-degeneracy using the eigenvalues of the Jacobian matrix.

2. **Identify all asymptotic limits**.

   • Classify fixed points:

   sink: trajectories only enter;

   source: trajectories only emerge;

   saddle: trajectories both enter and emerge;

   center: trajectories neither enter nor emerge.

   • Identify loops in the envisionment graph. These can correspond both to cyclic trajectories and to spirals. Small "chatter" loops are identified and abstracted away.

   • Identify loops consisting of unions of saddles and connecting separatrices.

   • Identify points at infinity on trajectories.

3. **Gather trajectories**.

   • Exhaustively trace all paths between asymptotic limits.

   • Abstract by unifying topologically equivalent (homotopic) paths.

   • Classify possible spiral trajectories corresponding to loops in the envisionment graph using the energy constraint and envisionment-guided behavior generation.[5]

   • Form complete trajectories from trajectory fragments terminating on loop paths, requiring compatibility with spiral characteristics just determined.

---

[5] An envisionment graph is generated without creating new landmarks, which prevents the energy constraint from being useful. Envisionment-guided simulation applies QSIM to an initial state and a path through the envisionment graph, and generates only behaviors that are consistent with (i.e., refinements of) the given path.

• Abstract bundles of nodal and spiral trajectories around sources and sinks (cf. figure 11.8). The nodal-spiral bundle factors out a localized distinction among intersecting trajectories that may not appear in the same phase portrait.

• Use envisionment-guided simulation and the energy constraint to verify that each trajectory is consistent.

4. **Compose phase portraits**.

• Form separatrix sets around each saddle: two separatrices entering, and two emerging, from opposite directions. The non-intersection constraint filters out inconsistent combinations.

• Combine separatrix sets between saddles, also filtering with the non-intersection constraint. This forms the possible skeletons for the phase portraits.

• Compose all remaining flows into the combinations of separatrix sets, filtering for non-intersection.

Since the algorithm has been carefully designed to generate all possibilities exhaustively and only discard impossible combinations, it provides guaranteed coverage of all possible qualitative phase portraits, just as QSIM guarantees coverage of all possible behaviors.

Although QPORTRAIT obviously has the potential to be intractably combinatoric, it has been applied to a number of non-trivial systems with good results.

• The qualitative Lienard equation

$$\ddot{x} + \dot{x} + U^+(x) = 0$$

gives a single qualitative phase portrait consistent with the known behavior of the traditional Lienard equation $\ddot{x} + \dot{x} + x^2 + x = 0$.

• The undamped pendulum

$$\ddot{\theta} + f(\sin \theta) = 0, \text{ where } f \in M_0^+$$

gives a single correct qualitative phase portrait. Note that this problem requires reasoning about a cylindrical phase space.

• The qualitative van der Pol equation

$$\ddot{x} + U^+(x)\dot{x} + x = 0$$

gives three qualitative phase portraits, one of which corresponds to the correct behavior of the familiar van der Pol equation, $\ddot{x} + (x^2 - 1)\dot{x} + x = 0$. All three portraits agree on the correct qualitative behavior within the limit cycle, but differ on possible behaviors outside the limit cycle. The additional portraits are probably spurious, but progress in qualitative reasoning will be required to filter them out (problem 8).

• A predator-prey model produced 22 distinct phase portraits, including the correct portrait for the fully specified model. The relatively large number of portraits is due to (1) lack of an implemented filter to refute a certain clear inconsistency, and (2) lack of an implemented abstraction operator to abstract a certain uninteresting distinction. Just as with qualitative simulation, progress in qualitative phase portrait generation will require the accumulation of an adequate set of constraints and abstraction operators.

The phase portrait describes the set of all possible behaviors of a system in a way that is grounded in the mathematics of dynamical systems and is directly useful to scientists, mathematicians, and engineers. By extending the total envisionment graph to describe all possible phase portraits of a qualitative differential equation, QPORTRAIT takes an important step toward automatically analyzing and proving the properties of dynamic physical systems. Naturally, the purely qualitative analysis in the current version of QPORTRAIT can be strengthened in combination with semi-quantitative and numerical simulation methods.

11.8   Discussion

Global constraints are needed because the consistency of a behavior cannot always be determined from a single qualitative state. Rather, it can depend on the history leading up to a given qualitative state. This contrasts with many simulation systems, which depend on the *Markov property*: that the future development of a system is determined by the current state, and not by its history.

We have looked at both *algebraic* and *geometric* ways to constrain the set of behaviors consistent with a qualitative differential equation. Some models (section 11.6) may require both types of constraints.

• Explicit conservation-of-energy invariants and the Kinetic Energy Theorem provide relatively powerful filters on qualitative behaviors, but derivation of the appropriate constraints may require more algebraic manipulation than the current QSIM program can do automatically.

• The qualitative phase-space representation can be created and examined, independent of prior knowledge of the system being modeled, but the self-intersection constraint alone provides a relatively weak constraint on possible behaviors.

11.8.1   From the Algebraic Point of View

Lyapunov functions generalize the concept of potential energy, and are very useful for proving qualitative properties of non-linear ordinary differential equations,
such as periodicity and asymptotic stability (Hirsch and Smale, 1974). It is also
possible to derive a Lyapunov function for a *qualitative* differential equation, in
which incompletely known monotonic function constraints appear. The exact form
of the Lyapunov function is then unknown, and dependent on the exact form of the
monotonic functions in the QDE, but its qualitative properties may be sufficient to
determine the qualitative properties of the solutions to the QDE.

There is no algorithm for determining a Lyapunov function for a given ordinary
or qualitative differential equation. However, solutions for special cases are known,
and there are heuristics for constructing plausible candidates. An algebraic manipulation problem solver for deriving Lyapunov functions would be very useful in this
context, as well as for deriving kinetic energy constraints, higher-order derivative
constraints, and other transformations of QDEs (problem 6).

In related work, Ishida (1989) shows how to identify an *invariant sign pattern*
in a qualitative description of a linear ODE. This pattern can be used to infer
qualitative versions of system-theoretic concepts such as stability and observability.
He discusses ways to extend this work to non-linear systems. Kalagnanam, *et
al.* (1991), also discuss qualitative reasoning methods in terms of sign stability,
comparative statics, and the qualitative theory of dynamical systems.

11.8.2   From the Geometric Point of View

The qualitative geometrical properties of the phase-space representation have been
the basis for the very productive *qualitative theory of ordinary differential equations* (Arnold, 1973; Hirsch and Smale, 1974). Within the artificial intelligence
community, Abelson *et al.* (1989); Sacks (1987b; 1990; 1991); Dordan (1992); Yip
(1988; 1991a; 1991b); Nishida *et al.* (1991); Nishida and Doshita (1991); Nishida
(1993); and Zhao (1991) have done pioneering work on intelligently guided numerical experimentation, exploring the phase space to determine the qualitative
properties of solutions to ordinary differential equations.

The use of qualitative phase space to detect trajectory self-intersection was developed independently by Lee and Kuipers (1988) and by Struss (1988a), who also
describes promising methods for reasoning with symmetries that are visible in the
phase-space representation.

There is clearly much more gold in this area, much of it near the surface. The
challenge is to import powerful methods from the qualitative theory of ordinary

differential equations, weakening the hypotheses of the theorems so they can be applied where knowledge is incomplete and qualitative.

11.9   Problems

1. Show that the QDE for the simple, undamped spring, and the definition of total energy,

$$E(t) = KE(t) + PE(t) = \frac{1}{2} m\, v^2 + m \int_0^x f(\bar{x})\, d\bar{x},$$

imply that $dE/dt = 0$ everywhere. Then use the fact that $E(t)$ is constant to refute two of the three predicted behaviors shown in figure 11.1.

2. When $f \in M_0^+$, and we define $g(x) = \int_0^x f(\bar{x})\, d\bar{x}$, show that $g \in U_0^+$. Note that neither f nor g needs to be symmetrical about zero.

3. Hand simulate the behavior of the simple spring with energy conservation from t_0 through t_4, to replicate the behavior in figure 11.2, and demonstrate how the effect of the invariant is applied through the corresponding values in the expression.

4. Construct and simulate a numerical model of a non-linear monotonic damped spring that oscillates a finite number of times around the origin before switching to overdamped behavior and converging directly to the origin. How does the number of oscillations depend on the shapes of the non-linear monotonic functions?

5. Prove that if one continuous monotonic curve crosses the rectangle in figure 11.11(a) from a to c, and another crosses from b to d, then the two curves must intersect in the interior of the rectangle.

6. (Research Problem.) Build a system that attempts to find a Lyapunov function for a given QDE. Express the result in a form usable by the kinetic energy constraint. This project will undoubtedly require a significant algebraic manipulation capability.

7. Generalize the Volterra-Lotka equation to a QDE by introducing monotonic function constraints representing plausible non-linearities and incomplete knowledge of the model. Derive a Lyapunov function for the QDE and demonstrate tractable simulation.

8. (Research Problem.) Develop an automatic method adequate to analyze the qualitative van der Pol equation,

$$\ddot{x} + U^+(x)\dot{x} + x = 0.$$

Focus on determining its possible behaviors or phase portraits *outside* of the limit cycle.

12 Time-Scale Abstraction

12.1 Hierarchical Structure

Many complex system models have too many state variables, and hence too many possible successor states, to be tractable by qualitative simulation. Fortunately, many of these systems can be made tractable because they have some sort of hierarchical structure that can be exploited to break a hard problem into easy problems. In this chapter, we discuss a hierarchical structuring method on dynamic models called *time-scale abstraction*, applied to a complex system made up of interacting equilibrium mechanisms.

Time-Scale Abstraction Principle: If a complex system can be decomposed into mechanisms that operate at widely separated time-scales, then a particular mechanism can view a faster one as being instantaneous, and a slower one as being constant.

Numerous examples throughout AI and computer science demonstrate the power of modular, hierarchical structure for handling complex problems. In order to apply such a method, we need to define a valid hierarchical structure that breaks a complex system into a collection of tractable mechanisms. The structure must also support a discipline for moving the focus of attention among the individual mechanisms in the hierarchy, and a mapping relation for communicating information meaningfully among the mechanisms.

When a faster mechanism in a time-scale hierarchy views a slower one as constant, the slower one can simply be treated as a source of values for exogenous parameters. When a slower mechanism views a faster one as instantaneous, a relation among shared variables may be treated by the slow mechanism as a functional relationship, and by the fast mechanism as the result of a process over time.

12.1.1 Communicating across Time-Scales

In order to use a hierarchical model linked by time-scale abstraction for qualitative simulation of a complex system, information must be transmitted through shared variables among mechanisms operating at different time-scales.

We need a discipline for shifting the focus of attention among different time-scales and for making valid use of previously derived information in subsequent computations. The two directions of shift in focus from a given mechanism require different methods.

- **Faster to Slower**. Given an initial perturbation to its environment, qualitative simulation predicts the resulting equilibrium state of the fastest mechanism, and

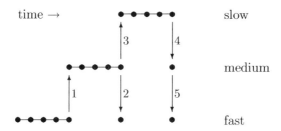

Figure 12.1
Control of focus of attention.
Each bead represents a qualitative state, so simulation produces a string of beads, and propagation of an equilibrium state produces a single bead. Changes in focus of attention take place in the sequence shown. (1) The equilibrium state of the fastest mechanism provides values for initializing a simulation of the next slower mechanism. (2) The final state of the second simulation is first used to propagate a new equilibrium state for the fastest mechanism. (3) Then values from both faster mechanisms are available to initialize the slowest mechanism. Values from the final state of the slowest mechanism are propagated to equilibrium states of (4) the intermediate and (5) the fastest mechanisms.

shifts attention to the next slower one. The final values of variables that are shared with the slower mechanism can be treated as part of the initial state of the slower mechanism. The final effect of the fast mechanism is abstracted to a monotonic function constraint, for use in the slow model.

• **Slower to Faster.** After a slower mechanism has reached equilibrium, the environment it provides for a faster mechanism may have changed. However, the faster mechanism, by definition, must have tracked the slower mechanism on its way to equilibrium. Thus, the fast mechanism is already in equilibrium, and its state can be derived from the values of shared variables by comparative statics.

Figure 12.1 shows the pattern of control for a three-level time-scale hierarchy, deriving the effect of an initial perturbation throughout the system. Upward arrows initiate dynamic simulation to a new equilibrium, and downward arrows initiate propagation to a more complete description of an existing equilibrium state. The algorithm is as follows. After simulating a mechanism, QSIM identifies the faster mechanisms that share variables with the current mechanism, and propagates the shared values to determine the equilibrium state of the faster mechanism. Once this is done, the slower mechanisms sharing variables are identified. The current values of variables shared with this mechanism are used to define the initial state from which it is simulated. The process repeats recursively.

In order for the abstraction hierarchy to support correct simulation, control of the focus of attention must be combined with an appropriate interpretation of information from one level of the hierarchy, as viewed from another.

12.2   Simulating at Multiple Time-Scales

Qualitative simulation of a mechanism described by several QDEs at different time-scales requires a small amount of additional information to be provided by the modeler, and several new types of inference.

• For a faster mechanism to be viewed by a slower one as instantaneous, its effect is abstracted to a multivariate monotonic function constraint (section 3.6.1).

• For models at different time-scales to be linked into a model of a complex mechanism, monotonic function constraints appearing in a slower model are linked to the faster model they abstract.

• For the effect of simulation of a faster model to be communicated to a slower one, landmarks and corresponding values in the faster model must be translated into the slower model.

• For the pattern of simulation in figure 12.1 to be achieved, initial-state information for each simulation step must be inherited from several sources.

12.2.1   Fast-to-Slow: Abstracting a Process to a Constraint

From a slower perspective, the effect of a fast mechanism should be viewed as instantaneous. We have already encountered this view in chapter 7, as the effect of the quasi-equilibrium assumption. In this section, we describe how the locus of equilibrium points defined by the quasi-equilibrium assumption is abstracted to a multivariate monotonic function constraint.

1. We assume that the set of exogenous variables $x_1, \ldots x_n$ in the QDE is known. In QSIM, the exogenous variables are specified by the user in the **independent** clause of the QDE, but they should also be automatically derivable using the causal dependency methods of Iwasaki and Simon (1986a).

2. The fast-to-slow abstraction step applies separately to each stable quiescent state that appears in the behavior tree. Each abstracted constraint therefore applies only to those states resulting from behaviors matching its path in the behavior tree. A behavior leading to an unstable equilibrium, cycle, or region transition will not have abstracted constraints.

3. Fast-to-slow abstraction takes a specified dependent variable y in the QDE, and derives a constraint describing the functional relationship

$$y = f(x_1, \ldots x_n)$$

that holds between the values of the dependent and exogenous variables in the equilibrium state. In QSIM, the dependent variable is specified in the `derive-M-constraint-for` clause of the QDE, and the resulting constraint is stored as an attribute of the equilibrium state.

4. Since the state being abstracted is a stable equilibrium, we can use comparative statics to determine the signs of the partial derivatives

$$s_i = \left[\frac{\partial f}{\partial x_i} \right]$$

for each exogenous variable x_i.

If s_i is unambiguous, i.e., $s_i \in \mathcal{S} = \{+, 0, -\}$, then the function f is monotonic in x_i in the neighborhood of the steady state. If $s_i = [?]$, then comparative statics found more than one consistent solution to its perturbation problem, and f may not be monotonic.

5. The resulting multivariate monotonic function constraint is

`((M s1 ...  sn) x1 ...  xn y) .`

6. Corresponding values for this constraint are obtained from the values of variables at equilibrium states where the constraint is known and valid. The obvious state is the one where the constraint is derived. However, additional corresponding values can come from reference states of the same mechanism, and corresponding value tuples learned by a faster mechanism may be communicated to a slower mechanism for use.

Figure 12.2 illustrates this abstraction using a simple model of the water tank,

$$\dot{x} = q - u \cdot f(x).$$

12.2.2   Linking Models at Different Time-Scales

• A slower model points to a faster model by including a monotonic function constraint that is abstracted from the faster model. In QSIM, this is represented by the form (*constraint* <- *qde*) in the `abstracted-from` clause of the QDE.

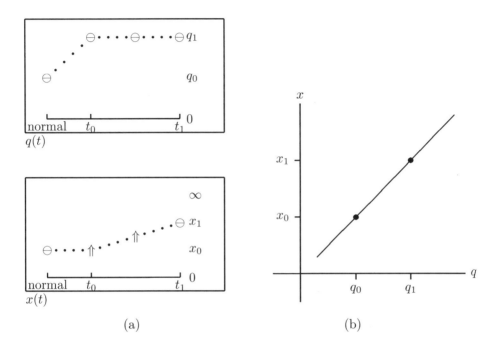

Figure 12.2
The relationship between $q(t)$ and $x(t)$.

- (a) From the point of view of the dynamic model $\dot{x} = q - u \cdot f(x)$, a change to q *causes* a subsequent change to x.
- (b) The locus of equilibrium states of the dynamic model is represented by the functional relation $x = F(q, u)$, where $F \in$ (M + -). Graph (b) shows how x and q change together if u is constant.

For example, a slow controller model might abstract the faster behavior of a tank as

`((M + -) q u x).`

- A faster model indicates which of its dependent variables should have monotonic function constraints derived by listing those variables in the `derive-M-constraint-for` clause of the QDE.

12.2.3 Translation from One Model to Another

For the effect of simulation of a faster model to be communicated to a slower one, landmarks and corresponding values in the faster model must be translated into the slower model. In particular, corresponding value tuples of the abstracted monotonic function constraint represent information about its shape. Unfortunately, these corresponding value tuples are expressed in terms of landmarks appearing in the quantity spaces of the faster model, and they are needed in the slower model. Since the quantity spaces of a model define a descriptive language of distinctions that can be expressed within that model, we face a problem of translation from one descriptive language to another.

Mapping Landmarks   Fortunately, we have some information about what the variables and landmarks in the two models can denote. We know that faster and slower models are attempting to describe the same thing, albeit at different time-scales.

• Variables with the same names in different models are assumed to denote the same variables. Similarly, landmarks of the same variable, with the same name, are assumed to denote the same values.

• We currently assume that all independent variables in the faster model, which are the arguments to the abstracted function f, also appear as variables in the slower model. A useful generalization will be for certain variables in the fast model, which do not vary in the slower models, to be invisible to slower models.

• Two states, one from each model, are *corresponding* if they describe the same situation. For example, two descriptions of a normal equilibrium reference state are corresponding. Also, the final equilibrium state of the faster model and the initial perturbed state of the slower model describe the same situation. If a variable appears in two corresponding states, the values of that variable in those states denote the same value, and hence are *corresponding landmarks*.

• If a variable is shared between two models, and a landmark of that variable in one model corresponds to an open interval between two landmarks in the other model, then a new landmark may be created in the second model, corresponding to the landmark in the first model.

Using these methods, a corresponding value tuple can be mapped from one model to another, if all of its variables are shared, by mapping each of its landmarks to corresponding landmarks.

Mapping Monotonic Function Constraints A faster model produces a monotonic function constraint, and a slower model uses it. Translating information about monotonic functions from a faster model to a slower model involves the following steps.

1. Determine which abstracted monotonic functions are used in the slower model. There may be other abstractions of the faster model that are not of interest in this situation.

2. Identify an abstracted monotonic function constraint in the final equilibrium state of the faster model that matches the monotonic function constraint used in the slower model.

3. Map each of its corresponding value tuples from the faster model to the slower model.

There is a bit of subtlety in the matching of monotonic function constraints. It is possible to map a constraint from one model to another even if the signs of one of the partial derivatives do not match, as long as the exogenous variable in question remains at a single constant value across both models. An example of this appears in section 12.3.5.

Inheriting Values for Initial States Whether following the upward or downward arrows in figure 12.1, the values for variables at an initial state are inherited from one of several states, defined with respect to different QDE models.

• The state of a system is determined by the values of its independent and its history variables. The history variables are either explicitly specified by the modeler (in the `history` clause of the QDE), or are assumed to be the set of explicitly integrated variables. These variables are the ones whose values must be asserted or inherited.

• Other than variables with explicitly asserted values, any independent or history variables that are shared with the most recently simulated model at a faster or slower time-scale are given values inherited from the final state of that model.

• Any remaining independent or history variables inherit their values from the most recent (or reference) state of the same model.

12.3   Example: Adaptive Controllers

12.3.1   The Basic Tank and Controller

The fast system is a tank and proportional controller.

- The basic tank model is

$$x' = q - u \cdot f(x), \tag{12.1}$$

where x is the amount of water in the tank, q is the constant inflow, $f \in M^+$ represents the dependence of outflow on amount via pressure, u is the area of the valve, so outflow is $u \cdot f(x)$.

- The basic proportional controller for the tank is

$$u = k_1(x - x_s) + u_s, \tag{12.2}$$

where x_s is the setpoint, k_1 is the controller gain, and u_s is a bias term set so that $x = x_s$ when q has its nominal value.[1]

Together, these two equations make a straightforward first-order equilibrium system (figure 12.3). We can test the equilibrium states for stability, and use comparative statics to abstract the behavior to multivariate monotonic function constraints representing the locus of equilibrium states.

$$x = g(k_1, x_s, u_s, q), \text{ where } g \in (\text{M} - + - +) \tag{12.3}$$

$$u = h(k_1, x_s, u_s, q), \text{ where } h \in (\text{M} + - + +) \tag{12.4}$$

12.3.2   Adaptive Control

At a slower time-scale, we can impose a second proportional controller to adapt the constants governing the system, in order to achieve more sophisticated behavior.

- Zero-offset proportional-integral control can be achieved by controlling the bias term u_s at a slower time-scale:

$$u_s' = k_2(x - x_s) \tag{12.5}$$

---

[1]This example is written with linear controllers, with constant, easily compared gains. It could be generalized to monotonic fuctions (problem 4).

```
(define-QDE tank+P
  (quantity-spaces
    (x  (0 full inf)       "x = amount")
    (q  (0 on inf)         "q = inflow")
    (u  (0 inf)            "u = drain")
    (fx (0 inf)            "fx = pressure")
    (of (0 inf)            "of = outflow")
    (dx (minf 0 inf)       "dx = netflow")
    ;
    (xs (0 x* full inf)    "xs:  setpoint")
    (e  (minf 0 inf)       "error:  x - xs")
    (k  (0 inf)            "k:  gain")
    (us (0 inf)            "us:  bias")
    (ua (minf 0 inf)       "ua: k(x-xs)")
    )
  (constraints
    ;  the basic tank
    ((m+ x fx) (0 0) (inf inf))
    ((mult u fx of))
    ((add dx of q))
    ((constant q))
    ((d/dt x dx))
    ;  the controller
    ((add e xs x)   (0 full full))
    ((mult k e ua))
    ((add ua us u))
    ((constant k))
    ((constant xs))
    ((constant us))
    )
  (independent k xs us q)
  (derive-M-constraint-for x u)
  (transitions
    ((x (full inc)) -> t)))
```

Figure 12.3
The fast model: basic tank and P-controller.
This model encodes equations (12.1) and (12.2).

$$x' = q - u \cdot f(x)$$
$$u = k_1(x - x_s) + u_s.$$

where $k_2 \ll k_1$ to ensure the time-scale separation.

Clearly, the fixed point of this equation is only reached when $x = x_s$. This model is shown in figure 12.4.

- Habituation, where the response to a perturbation decreases with time, is important in physiological systems such as blood-pressure control. This is achieved by applying a slow ($k_3 \ll k_1$) adaptive controller to the *setpoint*.

$$x'_s = k_3(u - u_s). \tag{12.6}$$

This system reaches its fixed point only when the control action u returns to its nominal value u_s. The fast system responds quickly to a disturbance, but then slowly adjusts the setpoint (which reduces the error signal) to eliminate the abnormal control action.

Habituation is important to physiological systems because the cost of the control response may, over the long run, be greater than the cost of the original deviation. The blood-pressure regulation system (Guyton, 1991) applies a series of different regulatory mechanisms at relatively short time-scales, each habituating away, but keeping blood pressure sufficiently regulated until the slow, zero-offset fluid balance system can solve the problem completely.

12.3.3 Simulation with Time-Scale Abstraction

The scenario is run by specifying the fast and slow models, variable values representing the normal state of the system, and a perturbation. QSIM decides how to initialize and run each model.

```
(defun tt2 (change)
  (tsa2 :fast tank+P
        :slow adaptive-controller
        :normal '((q  (on std))
                  (us ((0 inf) std))
                  (k  ((0 inf) std))
                  (k2 ((0 inf) std))
                  (xs (x* std))
                  (e  (0 std))
                  (x  ((0 full) std)))
        :perturb '((q ,change)))))
```

In the first step, we create equilibrium states representing the normal states of the fast and slow systems, and an initial perturbed state for simulation of the fast behavior.

```
(define-QDE adaptive-controller
  (quantity-spaces
    (x   (0 full inf))
    (q   (0 on inf))
    ;
    (xs  (0 x* full inf)   "xs:  setpoint")
    (e   (minf 0 inf)      "error:  x - xs")
    (k   (0 inf)           "k:  gain")
    (k2  (0 inf)           "k2:  adaptive gain")         ; k2 << k
    (us  (0 inf)           "us:  bias")
    (dus (minf 0 inf)      "us'")
    )
  (constraints
    ;  the basic controlled tank
    (((M - + - +) K XS US Q X))
    ((constant q))
    ((constant k))
    ((constant xs))
    ;  the controller
    ((d/dt us dus))
    ((constant k2))
    ((mult k2 e dus))
    ((add e xs x))
    )
  (independent k k2 xs q)
  (abstracted-from
   ((((M - + - +) k xs us q x) <- tank+P)))
  (transitions
    ((x (full inc)) -> t)))
```

Figure 12.4

The slow model: abstraction of fast model and adaptive controller.

The slow model encodes the abstraction of the tank model (12.3), and the adaptive controller (12.5).

$$x = g(k_1, x_s, u_s, q), \text{ where } g \in (\texttt{M - + - +})$$

$$u_s' = k_2(x - x_s)$$

```
> (tt2 '-)
Derived abstracted constraint ((M 0 + - +) K XS US Q X) at state S-0.
Derived abstracted constraint ((M 0 - + +) K XS US Q U) at state S-0.
 Abstracted constraint ((M 0 - + +) K XS US Q U) at state S-0
        getting cvals (k-0 x* u-1 on u-0).
 Abstracted constraint ((M 0 + - +) K XS US Q X) at state S-0
        getting cvals (k-0 x* u-1 on x-0).

Fast system TANK+P with slow system ADAPTIVE-CONTROLLER.
 Normal fast state S-0, status = (COMPLETE STABLE QUIESCENT).
 Normal slow state S-28, status = (COMPLETE STABLE QUIESCENT).
 Initial fast state S-30, status = (COMPLETE).
```

12.3.4 Simulating the Fast Model

Then we simulate the fast system, getting a single behavior, and abstract the final stable equilibrium state to a monotonic function relation.

```
Simulating fast system TANK+P from S-30.
Derived abstracted constraint ((M + + - +) K XS US Q X) at state S-32.
Derived abstracted constraint ((M - - + +) K XS US Q U) at state S-32.
 Abstracted constraint ((M - - + +) K XS US Q U) at state S-32
        getting cvals (k-0 x* u-1 q-6 u-25).
 Abstracted constraint ((M + + - +) K XS US Q X) at state S-32
        getting cvals (k-0 x* u-1 q-6 x-12).
Run time: 2.050 seconds to simulate 3 states.
     (S-30 S-31 S-32)
```

It is interesting to note that the functions abstracted from S_0 and S_{32} differ in the signs derived for $\partial x/\partial k$ and $\partial u/\partial k$. This is because the normal state S_0 is defined to be exactly *at* the setpoint $x = x^*$, in which case variation in controller gain k has no effect on the system.

The resulting behavior of the fast system is plotted in figure 12.5.

12.3.5 Simulating the Slow Model

The slow model is initialized with values from the final state of the fast model, with any remaining necessary values inherited from the normal state of the slow model. Simulation of the slow model gives three behaviors, only one of which (the second) will turn out to be viable. We will follow that behavior here, and discuss the others later, in section 12.3.7.

```
Initializing S-70 with (US K E XS Q X TIME) from S-32, and (K2) from S-28.
```

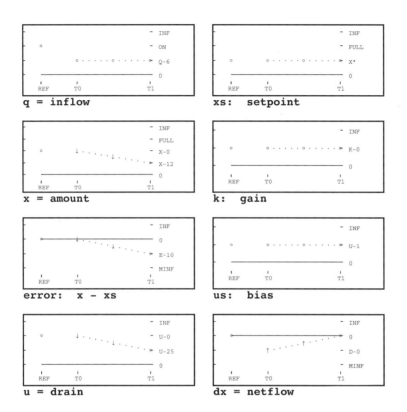

Figure 12.5
The single behavior of the fast system, with decreased inflow.

Reference state = S-0; Behavior = (S-30 S-31 S-32).


```
State S-70 is looking for (((M - + - +) K XS US Q X) <- TANK+P)
State S-32 can provide:
    (((M - - + +) K XS US Q U) (k-0 x* u-1 q-6 u-25))
    (((M + + - +) K XS US Q X) (k-0 x* u-1 q-6 x-12))
 Matching ((M + + - +) K XS US Q X)
        to ((M - + - +) K XS US Q X)
 because (K) doesn't vary.
Translating (((M + + - +) K XS US Q X) (k-0 x* u-1 q-6 x-12))
            from S-32 to S-70.
Translated cvtuple (K XS US Q X):
    (k-0 x* u-1 q-6 x-12) -> (k-3 x* u-24 q-9 x-33).


Simulating slow system ADAPTIVE-CONTROLLER from S-70.
```

```
Run time: 0.120 seconds to simulate 4 states.
    (S-70 S-71 S-72)
    (S-70 S-71 S-73)
    (S-70 S-71 S-74)
```

The successful slow behavior is plotted in figure 12.6.

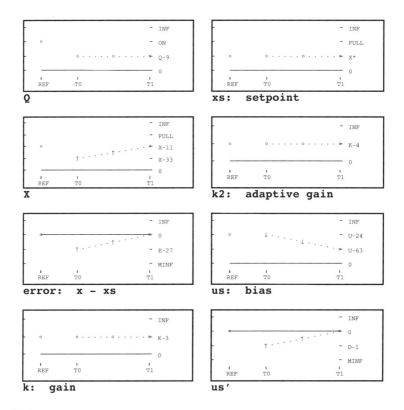

Figure 12.6
Behavior 2 of the slow system; no boundaries are reached.

Reference state = S-28; Behavior = (S-70 S-71 S-73).

12.3.6   Completing the State of the Fast Model

Once the final equilibrium state of the slow model has been reached, we must find
the corresponding complete equilibrium state of the fast model.

```
Mapping final state of slow behavior (S-70 S-71 S-73) down to fast system
```

TANK+P.

Initializing S-77 with (US K E XS Q X TIME) from S-73, and NIL from S-32.
Derived abstracted constraint ((M 0 + - +) K XS US Q X) at state S-77.
Derived abstracted constraint ((M 0 - + +) K XS US Q U) at state S-77.
 Abstracted constraint ((M 0 - + +) K XS US Q U) at state S-77
        getting cvals (k-0 x* u-64 q-6 u-65).
· Abstracted constraint ((M 0 + - +) K XS US Q X) at state S-77
        getting cvals (k-0 x* u-64 q-6 x-0).

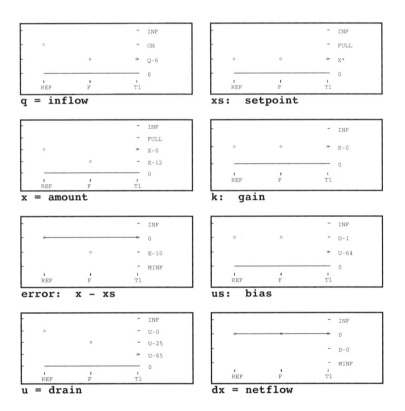

Figure 12.7
Unique completion of the fast system, from the final state of slow behavior 2.

Reference state = S-0; Final state of fast behavior = S-32; Completion after slow behavior =
S-77.

To clarify the meaning of these predictions, figure 12.8 compares the plots of
variables appearing in figures 12.5, 12.6, and 12.7.

- $x(t)$ drops rapidly, then returns slowly to normal.

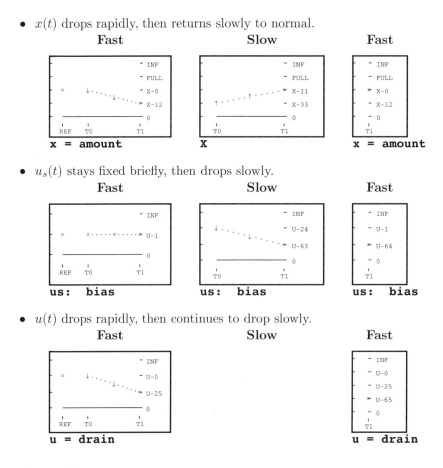

Figure 12.8
Combine predictions at different time-scales.

12.3.7   Inconsistent Completion Refutes Slow Behaviors

Behaviors 1 and 3 of the slow mechanism reach the region boundary defined by $u_s = 0$. (Behavior 1 attempts a region transition, while behavior 3 represents equilibrium exactly on the boundary.)

Consider the final state of behavior 3, shown in figure 12.9. In that state, $e = x - x_s = 0$ and $u_s = 0$. Therefore, the constraints in the fast model imply that $u = 0$ and outflow is zero. At the same time, however, inflow is positive and steady, so it is a contradiction for the fast system to be in equilibrium. The same argument refutes the fast completion of slow behavior 1.

Since final states of slow behaviors 1 and 3 cannot be extended to describe the corresponding equilibrium states of the fast mechanism, they are inconsistent and the two behaviors are refuted.

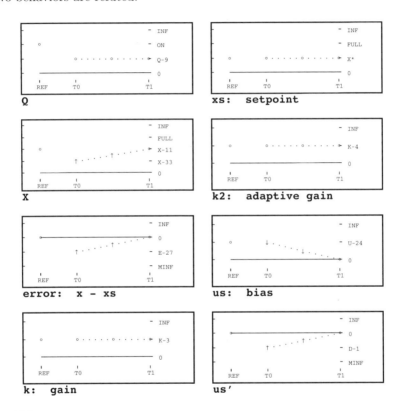

Figure 12.9
The slow system reaches equilibrium exactly at the region boundary.
Reference state = S-28; Behavior = (S-70 S-71 S-74).

12.4 Case Study: Aristotelean Physics

In modern Newtonian physics, the fundamental law of motion is $F = ma$, or in terms that suggest the visible causality of the world,

$$a = M^+(F). \tag{12.7}$$

However, for two thousand years, motion was explained by the laws of Aristotelean physics, essentially,

$$v = M^+(F). \tag{12.8}$$

The strange thing is that, although Newton's law is a more fundamental truth of the universe, Aristotle's law is a far better explanation for most observed uniform motion. These apparently contradictory views can be reconciled by observing that Aristotle's law is a quasi-equilibrium abstraction of uniform motion with damping friction.

The genius of Aristotle was to see structure in the forces and motions of the world, and to describe them accurately. The genius of Newton was to see the deeper, simpler structure that is hidden by the complex relation between force and motion in a "friction-dominated" world.

To see this relation more clearly, let us rewrite equation (12.7) as a dynamical system relating the position x and velocity v of an object to its mass m and the force F on it.

$$\dot{x} = v$$
$$\dot{v} = F/m$$

When F is used to represent the net force on the object, it implicitly sums both forces actively exerted and frictional resistive forces. However, from the point of view of commonsense causal reasoning, it seems more useful to distinguish an externally applied force F — e.g., the motor on a car, the wind on a sailboat, or gravity on a skydiver — from a resistive force $R(v, c)$. $R(v, c)$ increases monotonically with velocity, but opposes it in direction, and increases monotonically with a parameter c that represents the "cross-section" of the object to the resistive force.

With this revised notation, our equation of motion becomes

$$\dot{x} = v$$
$$\dot{v} = \frac{F}{m} - \frac{R(v, c)}{m}.$$

For constant F, m, and c, the second equation

$$\dot{v} = \frac{F}{m} - \frac{R(v, c)}{m} \tag{12.9}$$

is a stable system that will move quickly to equilibrium, $\dot{v} = 0$. When $\dot{x} = v \neq 0$, x is not constant, of course, describing uniform motion such as a skydiver falling at terminal velocity.

At equilibrium, we can abstract equation (12.9) to get $R(v, c) = F$, or equivalently,

$$v = f(F, m, c), \quad \text{where } f \in (\text{M} + \text{O} -). \tag{12.10}$$

This is the same as equation (12.8) if m and c are constant.

12.5 Related Work

It is not a new idea, of course, that mechanisms may operate on multiple time-scales and can profitably be analyzed from that perspective (Lynch, 1986).

Simon and Ando (1961), and later, Iwasaki and Bhandari (1988), show how to analyze the relative magnitudes of coefficients in an influence matrix to determine the time-scale structure of an "almost decomposable" system of linear ordinary differential equations.

Research in mathematics and control theory investigates the conditions under which the solution to a system

$$\begin{aligned} x' &= f(t, x, y, \epsilon) \\ \epsilon y' &= g(t, x, y, \epsilon) \end{aligned}$$

approaches the solutions to a pair of simpler time-scale abstracted mechanisms as the time-scales diverge (i.e., as $\epsilon \to 0$). The "slow" mechanism is obtained by formally setting ϵ to 0.

$$\begin{aligned} x' &= f(t, x, y, 0) \\ 0 &= g(t, x, y, 0). \end{aligned}$$

The "fast" or "boundary layer" model at $t = \alpha$ is obtained by transforming the independent variable to $s = (t - \alpha)/\epsilon$ and setting $\epsilon = 0$ in the result, giving

$$\begin{aligned} x' &= 0 \\ y' &= g(\alpha, \beta, y, 0) \end{aligned}$$

where β represents the constant value of x. See Hoppensteadt, 1966; Kokotovic et al., 1976; Saksena et al., 1984; and Marino and Kokotovic, 1988. This area is referred to as *singular perturbation theory* because the parameter ϵ is perturbed to zero, a singular value.

Chin, Hedstrom, and Howes (1985) and Kreiss (1985) discuss a variety of analytic and numerical methods applying to ordinary and partial differential equations to determine and exploit knowledge of relative time-scales. Compared with these numerical and analytical approaches, the contribution of our work is to show how time-scale relations can be exploited in the context of incomplete knowledge of a complex system, where qualitative relations are available and reliable while quantitative knowledge may be unavailable or unreliable.

De Kleer and Brown's (1984) qualitative physics with confluences is based on a quasi-equilibrium assumption: that a system can be considered to be at, or infinitely close to, equilibrium at all times. Under this assumption, true transient behavior can be ignored, and the only changes are shifts of equilibrium in response to perturbations. This is a special case of time-scale abstraction, looking at fast mechanisms from the point of view of a slower time-scale.

Weld (1986) developed a method called *aggregation*, whereby the discrete net effect of one cycle of a repetitive process can be viewed from a different scale as an incremental change in a continuous process. For example, if a catalyst causes a reaction that consumes one molecule of a substance, and the catalyst is then freed to repeat the cycle, we can step back to view the amount of the substance as a continuously decreasing quantity, amenable to the usual limit analysis methods. Aggregation is another important type of time-scale reasoning, relating discrete and continuous descriptions of a repetitive process.

12.6 Problems

1. Use the concepts in section 12.4 to build qualitative models of

   - the effect of spreading his arms, or opening his parachute, on a falling skydiver;
   - the effect of changing the accelerator position in a car.

2. (Research Problem.) Prove that the result of the abstraction process described in section 12.2.1 is a *reasonable* function. How should we extend the definition of *reasonable function* to multivariate functions?

3. (Research Problem.) Apply the mathematical methods from Marino and Kokotovic, 1988, and related work to derive a suitable guarantee for the results of qualitative simulation under time-scale abstraction.

4. (Research Problem.) Generalize the linear adaptive controller example of section 12.3 to *qualitative* proportional controllers at both time-scales. What exten-

sions or assumptions are required to ensure that the time-scales of the controllers are genuinely separated? What happens if they are not?

5. Select a suitable domain and build a time-scale hierarchy of qualitative models to capture its essential properties. Human physiology has many phenomena that operate at multiple time-scales, for example,

A. C. Guyton. 1991. Blood pressure control — special role of the kidneys and body fluids. *Science* **252**: 1813–1816.

6. Abstract the Starling equilibrium (section 6.3.1) to get ((M - +) PP PI AFP). Build a time-scale hierarchy to show the effect of this perturbation on the water balance model (section 6.3.2), and hence on the sodium balance model (section 6.3.3).

13 Component-Connection Models

13.1 Model Building and Model Simulation

Our overall framework for qualitative reasoning (figure 13.1, reproducing figure 1.1) distinguishes the tasks of model building and model simulation. The two tasks communicate via the qualitative representation for QDE models and initial states. Although the two tasks interact intimately, they tend to draw on different inference methods and different mathematical foundations. Pragmatically, this modularity means that research on the two tasks uses different methods, and the qualitative reasoner can benefit from independent research advances in each area.

A *model* is a description of some phenomenon, created for some purpose. It embodies a *closed-world assumption* (CWA): that the set of objects and relations in the model includes everything necessary for that purpose. Simulation depends on the closed-world assumption. It is impossible to predict the next value of a variable in a set of equations without assuming that all the influences on that variable are known. It is impossible to predict the behavior of an electrical circuit without assuming that all the components and connections in the circuit are known.

Model *building*, on the other hand, draws on background knowledge of the domain contained in a library. Since the elements of this library may be composed in unanticipated ways, they *cannot* embody a closed-world assumption. We refer to an element of such a library as a *model fragment*. It is not a model, since its world is not closed.[1]

The task of the model builder is to assemble a collection of model fragments, impose a closed-world assumption, and transform the set of fragments into a model capable of supporting simulation. Different approaches to model building differ on all these steps, but the handling of the closed-world assumption is the key.

- When a human modeler specifies a model as an ordinary or qualitative differential equation, he or she provides the closed-world assumption explicitly.

- As we shall see in this chapter, component-connection modeling draws on a library of component definitions. Because a component may be connected to other components through its terminals, it is only a fragment of a model, and its world is not closed. When a modeler specifies a complete device, the set of components is complete and every terminal is connected to other known terminals. The modeler therefore provides the CWA, and a model can be built.

---

[1] In a slight abuse of terminology, we may call this an "open-world assumption."

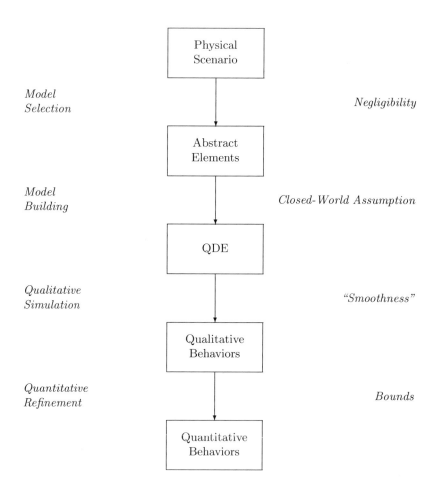

Figure 13.1
The central framework for qualitative modeling and simulation.

Model building and model simulation are largely distinct, though they interact via the QDE representation.

• In chapter 14, we will discuss *compositional modeling*, in which an automated reasoner builds models of a given scenario, drawing on the model fragments in a domain theory. To build a model, the *algorithm* collects a set of active model fragment instances, decides when to close the world, and transforms the collection of model fragments into a model.

13.2   A Component Ontology for Model Building

13.2.1   Part and Whole

The relation between *part* and *whole* is critical to describing the structure of a mechanism. Different modeling methods have different concepts of what should count as a "part" of a system, and how the parts should relate to each other.

In the equation-based approach to modeling, the "parts" of a mechanism are the continuous variables that characterize its state, and the relations among them are expressed as mathematical constraints.

However, a physical mechanism can often be described as a set of physical parts whose relationships determine which variables are relevant and which equations apply. Frequently, the parts of a system are *components* that interact through explicitly specified *connections*. Electrical circuits are paradigm examples of systems with an appropriate component-connection level of description (cf. figure 13.2).

• A *component* is a mechanism, described in terms of variables and constraints, that can interact with other components only through variables associated with explicitly specified *terminals*.

• A *connection* is an explicitly specified identity relation among component terminals. It implies constraints on the variables associated with the terminals.

Qualitative simulation focuses on deriving the set of all possible behaviors of a device. Component-connection models decompose the task of determining all possible behaviors according to the following principle.

The behavioral repertoire of a mechanism is determined by the behavioral repertoires of its components, constrained by their connections.

The part-whole relation supports a hierarchical decomposition of the structure of a system. A component is itself a mechanism, and its behavior may be explained by its own components and their connections.

The *level of granularity* of a model is the depth to which the parts of a mechanism and their relationships are made explicit (Hobbs, 1985). This modeling decision includes ontological choices between lumped and distributed parameters, and between qualitative and quantitative value domains, as well as choice of level of detail for component decomposition. Level of granularity helps specify the *content* of a model, in contrast with the closed-world assumption, which is a structural requirement for *being* a model.

In some instances of the component-connection modeling methodology, the components and their connections are less directly tied to the physical structure of the mechanism than in the electrical domain.

• Compartmental modeling (Jacquez, 1985) is used in physiology and biology, for example to describe the storage and flow of ions among abstract compartments representing fluid in the cells and fluid in the blood plasma.

• System dynamics (Forrester, 1961) can be used in the social sciences, for example to model large-scale economic and political phenomena in terms of levels and rates of accumulation of various abstract substances (Forrester, 1969).

Frequently, we see *emergent* behavior: a mechanism exhibits behavior — oscillation, for example — that was not a behavior of any of its components. This is often what is meant by saying "the whole is more than the sum of its parts."

13.2.2   The Closed-World Assumption

For a component-connection model, the closed-world assumption means that the only objects in the model are the explicitly specified components, and their only interactions take place via explicitly specified connections. Using this CWA, we can compile the component-connection model of a device into the variables and constraints of a QDE.

1. The variables from the component instances provide the variables of the QDE.

2. The constraints from the component instances provide constraints for the QDE.

3. The connections provide certain additional constraints.

A proposed model can be an incorrect description of the world, of course. For example, objects or relations that turn out to be necessary for achieving the model's purpose could have been omitted. In such a case, the CWA was incorrect, so the problem solver must find an alternate model, or simply fail to achieve its purpose. Davis (1984) gives a particularly compelling and influential description of a diagnostic problem solver that first considers models under a restrictive CWA, but if all such models fail, falls back to consider a larger set of models consistent with a less restrictive closed-world assumption. We return to this topic in section 13.6.

13.2.3   Generic Quantities and Bond Graphs

A widely useful modeling methodology applies when the primary variables describe amount-like, pressure-like, and flow-like properties of some conserved quantity. The theory of *bond graphs* (Karnopp *et al.*, 1990) builds on the familiar analogy between fluids and electricity, to exploit a structural isomorphism among the variables and constraints that describe the flow of power and energy across a range of domains. For example, the generic variable types *displacement*, *effort*, and *flow* express common properties of variable types across domains.

- **Displacement**: amount of fluid, electrical charge, or heat energy;
- **Effort**: pressure, voltage, or temperature difference;
- **Flow**: fluid flow, electrical current, or heatflow.

In the electrical and hydraulic domains discussed in this chapter, we have the following special properties that imply useful constraints on effort and flow variables at connections.

- Kirchhoff's Voltage Law (KVL): An effort quantity has a well-defined value at every connection point in the network. This implies that differences between the values of an effort quantity at adjacent connections can be defined, and the sum of those differences around any loop must be zero. This property justifies identifying component variables for effort quantities at a connection point.

- Kirchhoff's Current Law (KCL): A connection point cannot store substance, and amounts are conserved, so the flows in and out of a connection point must balance. Adopting the convention that positive flows along a terminal are directed toward the component (away from the connection), this principle justifies asserting the constraint that the flows at a connection must sum to zero.

In the full theory of bond graphs, there are Type 0 junctions, at which effort variables are shared and flow variables sum to zero, and Type 1 junctions, at which flow variables are shared and effort variables sum to zero. Bond graphs also include several other generic types (most importantly, *power*, *energy*, and *momentum*), and an elaborate formalism for expressing and manipulating the common structure of sets of constraints, applicable across domains.

A major strength of the bond graph representation is that it localizes certain relationships that may be distributed globally in the component-connection description. An important and active research direction is to improve on component-connection modeling methods by using bond graphs (problem 7).

13.2.4 "No Function in Structure"

De Kleer and Brown (1981) proposed a modeling principle to guide the construction of useful and reusable component definitions.

The **"No Function in Structure" Principle**: The behavioral repertoire of a component must be specified independently of the contexts in which instances of that component may appear.[2]

This principle attempts to ensure locality in the definition of the component. For example, it would be incorrect to define a switch by stating that current flows when the switch is closed:

$$closed(switch) \quad \rightarrow \quad i > 0$$
$$open(switch) \quad \rightarrow \quad i = 0.$$

This definition presumes that the switch is built into a complete circuit with a current source and no other breaks (e.g., it assumes that the fuse in the basement is not blown, and the electric bill has been paid). The problem with global dependencies in a component model is that the component can violate its specifications when its global assumptions are false, and hence be diagnosed as broken even when it is working correctly.

A better, and more local, definition of the switch remains correct and useful whether the basement fuse is working or not.

$$closed(switch) \quad \rightarrow \quad \Delta v = 0$$
$$open(switch) \quad \rightarrow \quad i = 0$$

Although "no function in structure" is useful as a goal for the modeler, it is also unachievable in principle. A model, by definition, is simpler than the reality it describes. Certain attributes of the world are negligible in the current context of use, and so are omitted from the model. In another context, those features may be critical. For example, our improved model of the switch still assumes that voltages and currents are sufficiently small, and the environment is sufficiently benign, that arcing when the switch is opened or closed is a negligible phenomenon. These and other "class-wide assumptions" are embedded in the component library, and are applied to every model constructed from that library. (See Davis 1984 and section 13.6 in this chapter.)

---

[2]This rephrases their original, "The rules for specifying the behavior of any constituent part of the overall system can in no way refer, even implicitly, to how the overall system functions."

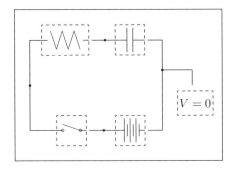

```
(define-component RC electrical
  "Resistor-Capacitor Circuit"
  (components (B battery)
              (R resistor)
              (C capacitor)
              (S switch)
              (V reference-voltage))
  (connections (n1 (R t1) (S t1))
               (n2 (R t2) (C t1))
               (n3 (C t2) (B t2) (V t))
               (n4 (B t1) (S t2))))

(define-component Resistor electrical
  "Resistor:  V = IR"
  (terminal-variables (t1 (v1 voltage)
                          (i  current))
                      (t2 (v2 voltage)
                          (-i current)))
  (component-variables (v voltage)
                       (r resistance))
  (constraints ((add v v2 v1))
               ((mult i r v))
               ((minus i -i))
               ((constant r))))
```

Figure 13.2
Component-connection models of resistor and RC circuit.

13.3   A Model-Building Language

The component-connection approach to device modeling has long been used in a
variety of fields. Our approach draws most heavily on the work of Sussman and
Stallman (1975) and de Kleer and Brown (1984). CC, the device-modeling language we use here, was developed by David Franke and Daniel Dvorak (Franke,
1989; Franke and Dvorak, 1990), and refined by numerous contributors since then
(cf. (Biswas *et al.*, 1993)). CC is designed for simple, clear representation of hi-
erarchically structured device models, and straightforward compilation into QSIM
QDEs.

13.3.1   CC: A Language for Component-Connection Models

This section provides a brief overview of the CC language, adequate for understanding the examples in figure 13.2 and the rest of the chapter.

In CC, every device is specified as a component. A component without terminals
is a fully specified device description, and can be compiled to a QSIM QDE by the
function `build-qde`.

• The `define-component` macro defines a component *type*. Component *instances*
are created when referenced as subcomponents of a device, and when a fully specified device description is compiled using `build-qde`.[3]

• The `define-component` form specifies a component name, a default domain for
variables of that component, a documentation string, and a number of clauses that
specify the properties of the component type.

• The `components` clause of a `define-component` form specifies the names and
types of embedded component instances that appear in the device.

• The `connections` clause specifies which terminals of the embedded components
are identified, and optionally a name for each connection.

• The `terminal-variables` clause defines the terminals of a component type, and
the variables that are bundled into each terminal. A terminal may not contain two
variables with the same domain and generic type.[4] Since a terminal represents
a logical connection, and cannot store substance, no terminal variable can have

---

[3]The distinction between component type and instance, although useful, is not as clear-cut as
it may seem. A component instance appearing as a subcomponent in a component definition will
be further instantiated when the containing component is used in a model.

[4]Domain-specific type terms such as `voltage` and `current` are abbreviations for the domain
`electrical` and generic types `effort` and `flow`, respectively.

generic type *displacement*. By convention, the positive direction for flow variables at a terminal is *inward*, toward the component and away from the node.

- The `component-variables` clause specifies variables that represent the state variables or parameters of the component itself.

- Both terminal and component variables may be annotated with `quantity-space` subclauses, specifying landmarks to augment the default quantity space, (`minf 0 inf`).

- The `mode-variables` clause specifies discrete variables and their sets of possible values, representing the operating modes (or fault modes) of an individual component instance. A mode value may be *static* (only settable by the user), or it may be associated with a condition implying that the component has that mode value.

- The `constraints` clause specifies QSIM constraints among the terminal and component variables of this component and its embedded subcomponent instances. Some or all of the constraints may be conditional on the values of mode variables.

The syntax and semantics of the CC modeling language are described more completely in Franke and Dvorak, 1990, and are illustrated by the examples appearing later in this chapter. Mode variables and mode-conditional constraints are illustrated by the `Switch` and `Resistor+` component definitions in the electrical component library (section 13.4.2).

13.3.2 Compiling a CC Model to a QSIM QDE

We can predict the possible behaviors consistent with a CC device description by compiling it to a QSIM QDE and simulating the behaviors of the QDE with QSIM.

- `build-qde`: takes the name of a CC component without terminals, and optional initial values for mode variables, and returns a QSIM QDE representing the same device.

The compilation process involves several steps.

1. Propose as the initial sets of variables and constraints in the QDE the union of the variables and constraints appearing in the CC model. The variables may be terminal or component variables of the device itself, or of its subcomponents to any degree of nesting. Similarly, constraints are identified by recursively expanding all embedded subcomponents.

2. A connection identifies several terminals, and a terminal bundles several variables of generic type *effort* and *flow*, perhaps in different domains. At each connection,

- all effort variables from the same domain are identified with each other and replaced by a generated effort variable for that node (KVL);

- all flow variables from the same domain must sum to zero, so a MINUS or SUM-ZERO constraint is asserted (KCL).

3. Any variables that do not appear in any of the constraints in the QDE are deleted. This can arise when terminal variables are unconstrained by the component, or do not completely match at connections.

4. Each variable receives the default quantity space (minf 0 inf), unified with any explicitly asserted quantity spaces. This unification must give a total order on all landmarks.

5. Conditions on mode variables or constraints are compiled into QSIM region transitions.[5]

6. The resulting set of variables, quantity spaces, constraints, and region transitions is asserted as a QDE.

13.3.3 Mapping CC Names to QSIM Variables

CC provides a hierarchical language of names, in terms of components, embedded components, and variables, for referring to the QSIM variables that result from model compilation. For example, in figure 13.2, the voltage v2 at the terminal t2 of resistor R in device RC has the CC name (RC R v2). In context, the leading name of the entire device (here, RC) may be omitted. CC names are used by the human modeler to specify the initial state and control the simulation. The next section provides an example.

- CC-name: translates a CC name, list of names, or a list indexed by names into the corresponding structure, but with QSIM variables from a given QDE.

- make-CC-state: calls make-new-state after appropriate translation of names to variables.

- CC-display: calls qsim-display after translating the layout description.

---

[5] In fact, the implementation of CC compiles mode variables into discrete variables, and mode-conditional constraints into moded constraints in QSIM. Neither of these QSIM features is discussed in this book. Dynamic conditions on mode variable values are compiled into region transitions. Additional issues raised by these features are discussed by Biswas, Manganaris, and Yu (1993).

13.4   Example: The Electrical Domain

13.4.1   The RC Circuit

In this section, we compile the CC model of the RC circuit in figure 13.2 into a QSIM QDE. This model includes instances of five different component types, drawn from a general-purpose electrical component library (section 13.4.2).

The initial QDE is created under certain assumptions about the values of mode variables. Initial values (and the display layout) can be specified using CC names for variables.

```
(defun test-RC ()
  (setq qde (build-qde 'RC :initial-values '(((R mode) (working std))
                                             ((S mode) (closed  std)))))
  (let* ((init (make-CC-state  :from-qde qde
                               :assert-values '(((B v) ((0 inf) std))
                                                ((C c) ((0 inf) std))
                                                ((C q) (0        nil)))
                               :text "Charge a capacitor"))
         (cc-layout '(((b v1)  (b v2)  (b i)  (b v))
                      ((r v1)  (r v2)  (r i)  (r r) (r v))
                      ((c v1)  (c v2)  (c i)  (c c) (c q))
                      ((s v1)  (s v2)  (s i)  (s mode))
                      ((V v)   (V i)))))
    (qsim init)
    (CC-display init :layout cc-layout) ))
```

Section 13.4.3 traces the model compilation done by `build-qde`, and figure 13.3 shows the unique behavior obtained by QSIM from the resulting QDE.

13.4.2   Electrical Component Library

The components for the electrical circuit domain are defined as follows.[6]

• The **Battery** maintains constant voltage: $v_{bat} = v_1 - v_2$. (A battery viewed as an exhaustible reservoir of charge is qualitatively identical to the capacitor model below.)

---

[6]The current implemented system does not make use of generic variable type information about component variables.

```
(define-component Battery electrical
  "Battery:  constant voltage source"
  (terminal-variables (t1 (v1 voltage)
                          (i  current))
                      (t2 (v2 voltage)
                          (-i current)))
  (component-variables (v voltage (quantity-space (0 vbat inf))))
  (constraints ((add v v2 v1))
               ((minus i -i))
               ((constant v vbat))))
```

- The **Resistor** obeys Ohm's law, $v_1 - v_2 = I \cdot R$. If it is working properly, R is finite. If it is burned out, $R = \infty$.

```
(define-component Resistor electrical
  "Resistor:  Ohm's law"
  (terminal-variables (t1 (v1 voltage)
                          (i  current))
                      (t2 (v2 voltage)
                          (-i current)))
  (component-variables (v voltage)
                       (r resistance (quantity-space (0 R* inf))))
  (mode-variables
   (mode working burnout))
  (constraints ((add v v2 v1))
               ((mult i r v))
               ((minus i -i))
               ((mode working) -> ((constant r R*)))
               ((mode burnout) -> ((constant r inf)))))
```

- The extended **Resistor+** component is augmented with the variable p representing power, and the constraint $p = v \cdot i$, in order to be able to express the resistor's capacity limit. Explicit conditions on the values of the mode variable allow the simulator to determine the component's mode and how it changes. (This model would also be appropriate for the **Wire**, when it is modeled as a component rather than an ideal connection.)

```
(define-component Resistor+ electrical
  "Resistor+:  Ohm's law plus maximum power limit"
  (terminal-variables (t1 (v1 voltage)
                          (i  current))
                      (t2 (v2 voltage)
                          (-i current)))
  (component-variables (v voltage)
```

```
                          (p power (quantity-space (0 max-power inf)))
                          (r resistance (quantity-space (0 R* inf)))))
     (mode-variables
       (mode (working <- (and (p ((0 max-power) nil))
                              (r ((0 inf) nil))))
             (burnout <- (p ((max-power inf) nil)))))
     (constraints ((add v v2 v1))
                  ((mult i r v))
                  ((minus i -i))
                  ((mult v i p))
                  ((mode working) -> ((constant r R*)))
                  ((mode burnout) -> ((constant r inf))) ))
```

- The **Capacitor** is described by the equation $I = C \cdot \frac{d}{dt}(v_1 - v_2)$.

```
(define-component Capacitor electrical
  "Capacitor:  container for charge"
  (terminal-variables (t1 (v1 voltage)
                          (i  current))
                      (t2 (v2 voltage)
                          (-i current)))
  (component-variables (v voltage)
                       (c capacitance (quantity-space (0 C* inf)))
                       (q charge))
  (constraints ((add v v2 v1))
               ((mult v c q))
               ((d/dt q i))
               ((minus i -i))
               ((constant c C*))))
```

- The **Inductor** is described by the equation $v_1 - v_2 = L \cdot \frac{d}{dt}I$. The variable type flux-linkage in the electrical domain belongs to the generic type *momentum*.

```
(define-component Inductor electrical
  "Inductor:  container for flux"
  (terminal-variables (t1 (v1 voltage)
                          (i  current))
                      (t2 (v2 voltage)
                          (-i current)))
  (component-variables (v voltage)
                       (L inductance (quantity-space (0 L* inf)))
                       (f flux-linkage))
  (constraints ((add v v2 v1))
               ((mult L i f))
               ((d/dt f v))
```

```
                   ((minus i -i))
                   ((constant L L*))))
```

• **Ground** is a component that acts as a reference voltage, $v = 0$, and a current sink. Any number of components can be connected to ground.

```
(define-component Ground electrical
  "Ground:  constant voltage (current sink)"
  (terminal-variables (t (v voltage)
                         (i current)))
  (constraints ((constant v 0))))
```

• A **Reference Voltage** does nothing, but establishes the voltage at the current point to be $v = 0$.

```
(define-component Reference-Voltage electrical
  "Reference Voltage:  v=0"
  (terminal-variables (t (v voltage)
                         (i current)))
  (constraints ((constant v 0))
               ((constant i 0))))
```

• A **Measurement Point** is a component that does nothing, but allows voltage to be measured.

```
(define-component Measurement-Point electrical
  "Measurement point:  test-point for voltage; zero current"
  (terminal-variables (t (v voltage)
                         (i current)))
  (constraints ((constant i 0))))
```

• The **Switch** has two states, and guarantees either that current does not flow, or that two voltages are identical.

```
(define-component Switch electrical
  "Switch:  externally opened or closed"
  (mode-variables (mode open closed))
  (terminal-variables (t1 (v1 voltage)
                          (i  current))
                      (t2 (v2 voltage)
                          (-i current)))
  (component-variables (v voltage))
  (constraints ((add v v2 v1))
               ((minus i -i))
               ((mode open)    ->  ((constant i 0)))
               ((mode closed)  ->  ((constant v 0)))))
```

13.4.3   Compiling the Model

This section traces in detail the process of compiling the component-connection model of the RC circuit to a QSIM QDE model. For each step of the compilation process, we describe the variables and constraints being created, followed by the actual trace of CC doing the compilation.[7]

```
(define-component RC electrical
  "Resistor-Capacitor Circuit"
  (components (B battery)
              (R resistor)
              (C capacitor)
              (S switch)
              (V reference-voltage))
  (connections (n1 (R t1) (S t1))
               (n2 (R t2) (C t1))
               (n3 (C t2) (B t2) (V t))
               (n4 (B t1) (S t2))))
```

Create Component Instances An instance of a component creates instances of its variables by concatenating the instance name with the local variable name. Thus, the voltage V1 of resistor R is represented first by the place holder structure (R V1), which is later transformed to the QSIM variable R.V1.

• The battery is modeled as a constant voltage source.

```
Interpreting component B of type BATTERY.
  Identified terminal T1
    Identified terminal variable (B V1)
    Identified terminal variable (B I)
  Identified terminal T2
    Identified terminal variable (B V2)
    Identified terminal variable (B -I)
  Created model variable B.V with qspace (0 VBAT INF)
  Created constraint ((ADD (B V) (B V2) (B V1)))
  Created constraint ((MINUS (B I) (B -I)))
  Created constraint ((CONSTANT (B V) VBAT))
```

• The resistor provides Ohm's law but may be either working or burned out.

```
Interpreting component R of type RESISTOR.
  Identified terminal T1
```

---

[7]To obtain this trace while running CC examples in the QSIM program, set the variable *CC-trace* to T.

```
    Identified terminal variable (R V1)
    Identified terminal variable (R I)
  Identified terminal T2
    Identified terminal variable (R V2)
    Identified terminal variable (R -I)
  Created model variable R.V with qspace (MINF 0 INF)
  Created model variable R.R with qspace (0 R* INF)
  Created model mode variable R.MODE with qspace (WORKING BURNOUT)
  Created constraint ((ADD (R V) (R V2) (R V1)))
  Created constraint ((MULT (R I) (R R) (R V)))
  Created constraint ((MINUS (R I) (R -I)))
  Created moded constraint (R.MODE BURNOUT) -> ((CONSTANT (R R) INF))
  Created moded constraint (R.MODE WORKING) -> ((CONSTANT (R R) R*))
```

• The capacitor is a container for charge. Current is flow of charge, and accumulating charge determines voltage, which provides a back pressure to flow.

```
Interpreting component C of type CAPACITOR.
  Identified terminal T1
    Identified terminal variable (C V1)
    Identified terminal variable (C I)
  Identified terminal T2
    Identified terminal variable (C V2)
    Identified terminal variable (C -I)
  Created model variable C.V with qspace (MINF 0 INF)
  Created model variable C.C with qspace (0 C* INF)
  Created model variable C.Q with qspace (MINF 0 INF)
  Created constraint ((ADD (C V) (C V2) (C V1)))
  Created constraint ((MULT (C V) (C C) (C Q)))
  Created constraint ((D/DT (C Q) (C I)))
  Created constraint ((MINUS (C I) (C -I)))
  Created constraint ((CONSTANT (C C) C*))
```

• The switch can be in one of two states: open, which requires current flow to be zero; or closed, which requires voltage drop to be zero.

```
Interpreting component S of type SWITCH.
  Identified terminal T1
    Identified terminal variable (S V1)
    Identified terminal variable (S I)
  Identified terminal T2
    Identified terminal variable (S V2)
    Identified terminal variable (S -I)
  Created model variable S.V with qspace (MINF 0 INF)
  Created model mode variable S.MODE with qspace (OPEN CLOSED)
```

```
Created constraint ((ADD (S V) (S V2) (S V1)))
Created constraint ((MINUS (S I) (S -I)))
Created moded constraint (S.MODE CLOSED) -> ((CONSTANT (S V) 0))
Created moded constraint (S.MODE OPEN) -> ((CONSTANT (S I) 0))
```

- The reference voltage defines one connection point as representing $V = 0$, which avoids needless branching by the simulator on choice of coordinate system.

```
Interpreting component V of type REFERENCE-VOLTAGE.
  Identified terminal T
    Identified terminal variable (V V)
    Identified terminal variable (V I)
  Created constraint ((CONSTANT (V V) 0))
  Created constraint ((CONSTANT (V I) 0))
```

Connections Define Identities and Constraints   Terminals are connected together at nodes. A terminal bundles a voltage variable and a current variable, but when these are translated into constraints they are treated differently.

- Kirchhoff's Voltage Law (KVL): The voltage variables at a node are identified with each other, allowing us to create a new variable standing for the voltage at that node.

- Kirchhoff's Current Law (KCL): The current variables at a node must sum to zero, since a node has no storage. In the special case where two variables sum to zero, we rewrite X + Y = 0 as (MINUS X Y).

connections	KVL	KCL
(n1 (R t1) (S t1))	R.V1 ≡ S.V1	R.I + S.I = 0
(n2 (R t2) (C t1))	R.V2 ≡ C.V1	R.-I + C.I = 0
(n3 (C t2) (B t2) (V t))	C.V2 ≡ B.V2 ≡ V.V	C.-I + B.-I + V.I = 0
(n4 (B t1) (S t2)))	B.V1 ≡ S.V2	B.I + S.-I = 0

```
Interpreting connection (N1 (R T1) (S T1))
  For domain ELECTRICAL, CC variables are:
    Effort variables:  (R V1) (S V1)
    Flow variables:  (R I) (S I)
  Created variable N1.EFFORT_ELECTRICAL for shared terminal variables:
      R.V1 S.V1
  Created model variable R.I with qspace (MINF 0 INF)
  Created model variable S.I with qspace (MINF 0 INF)
  Applying KCL constraint to variables: R.I S.I
    Created KCL constraint: ((MINUS R.I S.I))
```

```
Interpreting connection (N2 (R T2) (C T1))
  For domain ELECTRICAL, CC variables are:
    Effort variables:  (R V2) (C V1)
    Flow variables:  (R -I) (C I)
  Created variable N2.EFFORT_ELECTRICAL for shared terminal variables:
      R.V2 C.V1
  Created model variable R.-I with qspace (MINF 0 INF)
  Created model variable C.I with qspace (MINF 0 INF)
  Applying KCL constraint to variables: R.-I C.I
    Created KCL constraint: ((MINUS R.-I C.I))

Interpreting connection (N3 (C T2) (B T2) (V T))
  For domain ELECTRICAL, CC variables are:
    Effort variables:  (C V2) (B V2) (V V)
    Flow variables:  (C -I) (B -I) (V I)
  Created variable N3.EFFORT_ELECTRICAL for shared terminal variables:
      C.V2 B.V2 V.V
  Created model variable C.-I with qspace (MINF 0 INF)
  Created model variable B.-I with qspace (MINF 0 INF)
  Created model variable V.I with qspace (MINF 0 INF)
  Applying KCL constraint to variables: C.-I B.-I V.I
    Created KCL constraint: ((SUM-ZERO C.-I B.-I V.I))

Interpreting connection (N4 (B T1) (S T2))
  For domain ELECTRICAL, CC variables are:
    Effort variables:  (B V1) (S V2)
    Flow variables:  (B I) (S -I)
  Created variable N4.EFFORT_ELECTRICAL for shared terminal variables:
      B.V1 S.V2
  Created model variable B.I with qspace (MINF 0 INF)
  Created model variable S.-I with qspace (MINF 0 INF)
  Applying KCL constraint to variables: B.I S.-I
    Created KCL constraint: ((MINUS B.I S.-I))
```

Delete Unconstrained Variables   After all variables and constraints have been generated, there may be some variables that have no constraints. These are deleted from the model. No unconstrained variables occur in this example.

Create the QDE Model   As shown in previous sections of the trace, the variables, quantity spaces, mode variables, and constraints are provided by the components and connection. Here they are assembled into a QDE.

```
Completed specification for model RC_UNIQUE:
```

```
Variables and quantity-spaces:
  B.V                               (O VBAT INF)
  R.V                               (MINF O INF)
  R.R                               (O R* INF)
  C.V                               (MINF O INF)
  C.C                               (O C* INF)
  C.Q                               (MINF O INF)
  S.V                               (MINF O INF)
  N1.EFFORT_ELECTRICAL              (MINF O INF)
  R.I                               (MINF O INF)
  S.I                               (MINF O INF)
  N2.EFFORT_ELECTRICAL              (MINF O INF)
  R.-I                              (MINF O INF)
  C.I                               (MINF O INF)
  N3.EFFORT_ELECTRICAL              (MINF O INF)
  C.-I                              (MINF O INF)
  B.-I                              (MINF O INF)
  V.I                               (MINF O INF)
  N4.EFFORT_ELECTRICAL              (MINF O INF)
  B.I                               (MINF O INF)
  S.-I                              (MINF O INF)

Mode variables and quantity-spaces:
  S.MODE                            (OPEN CLOSED)
  R.MODE                            (WORKING BURNOUT)

Constraints:
  For mode (S.MODE OPEN):
    ((CONSTANT S.I 0))
  For mode (S.MODE CLOSED):
    ((CONSTANT S.V 0))
  For mode (R.MODE WORKING):
    ((CONSTANT R.R R*))
  For mode (R.MODE BURNOUT):
    ((CONSTANT R.R INF))
  For mode NIL:
    ((ADD B.V N3.EFFORT_ELECTRICAL N4.EFFORT_ELECTRICAL))
    ((MINUS B.I B.-I))
    ((CONSTANT B.V VBAT))
    ((ADD R.V N2.EFFORT_ELECTRICAL N1.EFFORT_ELECTRICAL))
    ((MULT R.I R.R R.V))
    ((MINUS R.I R.-I))
    ((ADD C.V N3.EFFORT_ELECTRICAL N2.EFFORT_ELECTRICAL))
    ((MULT C.V C.C C.Q))
```

```
((D/DT C.Q C.I))
((MINUS C.I C.-I))
((CONSTANT C.C C*))
((ADD S.V N4.EFFORT_ELECTRICAL N1.EFFORT_ELECTRICAL))
((MINUS S.I S.-I))
((CONSTANT N3.EFFORT_ELECTRICAL 0))
((CONSTANT V.I 0))
((MINUS R.I S.I))
((MINUS R.-I C.I))
((SUM-ZERO C.-I B.-I V.I))
((MINUS B.I S.-I))
```

Simulating the QDE Model   Simulating the resulting QDE model for the RC circuit gives the single behavior in figure 13.3.

13.5   Example: The Hydraulic Domain

Hydraulic systems — consisting of pipes, tanks, pumps, and valves — are naturally modeled much like electrical systems, using very similar components and connections, following the strong analogy between variables of the same generic type in the two domains.

hydraulic	electrical	generic
pressure	voltage	effort
flow	current	flow
resistance	resistance	resistance
amount	charge	displacement

13.5.1   Hydraulic Component Library

The component definitions for the hydraulic domain include the following:

• A **Compartment** is a tank, with inflow at the top (no backpressure) and flow at the bottom (dependent on pressure, which depends on the amount in the tank).

```
(define-component Compartment hydraulic
  "Compartmental modeling tank"
  (terminal-variables (in (inflow flow)
                           (Pin pressure))
                       (out (outflow flow)
                            (Pout pressure)))
  (component-variables (netflow flow)
                       (amount amount))
```

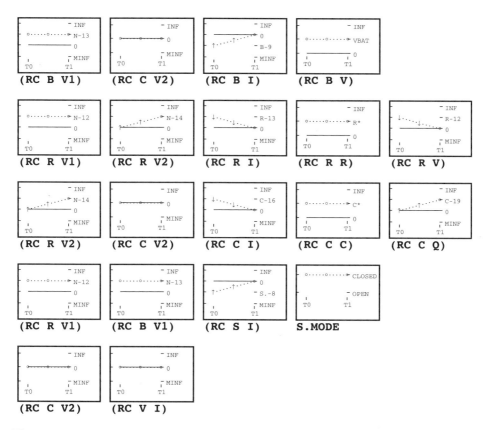

Figure 13.3
Unique behavior of the CC-generated RC circuit model.

The rows are the components (B, R, C, S, V); the columns are mostly corresponding variables of the components (V1, V2, I, and others). A variable shared between two components is labeled with only one name (though it can be retrieved by either), so it may look misplaced in this array.

```
(constraints ((M+ amount Pout) (minf minf) (0 0) (inf inf))
             ((add inflow outflow netflow))
             ((d/dt amount netflow))
             ((constant Pin 0))))
```

- The **Pipe** is essentially a resistor: $p_1 - p_2 = q \cdot k$.

```
(define-component Pipe hydraulic
  "bidirectional flow, with single resistance"
  (terminal-variables (in (q  flow)
```

```
                          (p1 pressure))
                   (out (-q flow)
                        (p2 pressure)))
    (component-variables (k resistance (quantity-space (0 inf)))
                         (dp pressure))
    (constraints ((minus q -q))
                 ((add dp p2 p1))
                 ((mult k q dp))
                 ((constant k))))
```

- The **Arrow** is a one-way flow, without backpressure. In a hydraulic system, it can be used to model an open pipe, for example in a cascade of tanks. In compartmental analysis (Jacquez, 1985), it describes a directed flow from one compartment to another, and k is a *fractional transfer coefficient*, specifying the fraction of the contents of the upstream compartment that flows to the downstream compartment per unit time. A pair of opposed **Arrows** is equivalent to a **Pipe**.

```
(define-component Arrow hydraulic
   "flow with fractional transfer coefficient"
   (terminal-variables (in (q   flow)
                            (Pin pressure))
                   (out (-q flow)
                        ))
   (component-variables (k conductance (quantity-space (0 inf))))
   (constraints ((minus q -q))
                ((mult Pin k q))
                ((constant k))))
```

- **QPump** establishes a constant flow rate.

```
(define-component QPump hydraulic
   "one-directional pumped flow, with constant flow rate"
   (terminal-variables (in  (q flow))
                   (out (-q flow)))
   (constraints ((constant q))
                ((minus q -q))))
```

- A **PPump** establishes a constant pressure head: $p_2 = p_1 + head$.

```
(define-component PPump hydraulic
   "bidirectional pumped flow, with resistance and pressure head"
   (terminal-variables (in (q flow)
                           (p1 pressure))
                   (out (-q flow)
                        (p2 pressure)))
```

```
(component-variables (k resistance  (quantity-space (0 inf)))
                     (head pressure (quantity-space (0 inf)))
                     (ep pressure)
                     (dp pressure))
(constraints ((minus q -q))
             ((add p1 head ep))
             ((add dp p2 ep))              ; dp = p1 + h - p2
             ((mult k q dp))
             ((constant head))
             ((constant k))))
```

- A **Valve** component permits no flow when closed, and flow governed by resistance and pressure drop when open. Thus, the **Valve** component is a bit more complex than the electrical domain **Switch**.

```
(define-component Valve hydraulic
  "Valve may only be open or closed"
  (terminal-variables (in  (Pin  pressure)
                           (q    flow))
                      (out (Pout pressure)
                           (-q   flow)))
  (mode-variables
   (mode open closed))
  (component-variables (dp pressure)
                       (k  resistance (quantity-space (0 inf))))
  (constraints ((add dp Pout Pin))
               ((constant k))
               ((minus q -q))
               ((mode open)   -> ((mult q k dp)))
               ((mode closed) -> ((constant q 0)))))
```

- A **Source** provides a constant inflow.

```
(define-component Source hydraulic
  "Infinite tank for source of flow"
  (terminal-variables (out (P pressure)))
  (constraints ((constant P))))
```

- A **Sink** receives any outflow at any pressure.

```
(define-component Sink hydraulic
  "Infinite tank for destination of flow"
  (terminal-variables (in  (P pressure)))
  (constraints))
```

- A **Stopper** occupies a terminal and constrains flow to be zero.

```
(define-component Stopper hydraulic
  "Attach to a compartment terminal to prevent flow"
  (terminal-variables (in  (q flow)))
  (constraints ((constant q 0))))
```

13.5.2   The Two-Tank Pumped Loop

This model is a simplified version of the model in section 7.7 (which, in turn, is taken from Rose and Kramer, 1991). It illustrates how to combine constraints representing conservation of mass with components and connections representing the overall structure of the system.

The top-level component draws on definitions in the hydraulic component library. The resulting QDE model is shown here. Figure 13.4 shows the behaviors resulting from changes, not necessarily small, to the pressure head provided by the pump.

```
(define-component PLoop hydraulic "Two-compartment pumped loop"
  (components (A compartment)
              (B compartment)
              (F arrow)
              (P Ppump))
  (component-variables (total amount))
  (connections (n1 (P out) (A in))
               (n2 (A out) (F in))
               (n3 (F out) (B in))
               (n4 (B out) (P in)))
  (constraints ((constant total))
               ((add (A amount) (B amount) total))
               ((minus (A netflow) (B netflow)))))
```

The completed QDE model for the pumped loop is the following.

```
Completed specification for model PLOOP_UNIQUE:

  Variables and quantity-spaces:
    .TOTAL                          (MINF 0 INF)
    A.NETFLOW                       (MINF 0 INF)
    A.AMOUNT                        (0 INF)
    B.NETFLOW                       (MINF 0 INF)
    B.AMOUNT                        (0 INF)
    F.K                             (0 INF)
    P.K                             (0 INF)
    P.HEAD                          (0 INF)
    P.EP                            (MINF 0 INF)
    P.DP                            (MINF 0 INF)
```

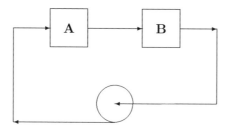

(a) Tanks A and B are a two-tank cascade, and the PPump provides a pressure head allowing the output of B to cascade into A as well.

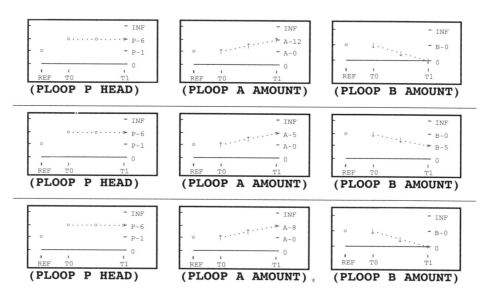

(b) Increased pump head gives three behaviors, varying according to whether tank B becomes empty.

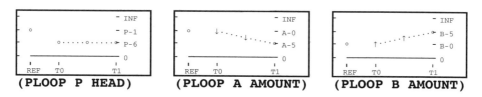

(c) Decreased pump head gives a single behavior.

Figure 13.4
CC pumped loop model responding to perturbations.

```
N1.EFFORT_HYDRAULIC                     (MINF 0 INF)
P.-Q                                    (MINF 0 INF)
A.INFLOW                                (MINF 0 INF)
N2.EFFORT_HYDRAULIC                     (MINF 0 INF)
A.OUTFLOW                               (MINF 0 INF)
F.Q                                     (MINF 0 INF)
N3.EFFORT_HYDRAULIC                     (MINF 0 INF)
F.-Q                                    (MINF 0 INF)
B.INFLOW                                (MINF 0 INF)
N4.EFFORT_HYDRAULIC                     (MINF 0 INF)
B.OUTFLOW                               (MINF 0 INF)
P.Q                                     (MINF 0 INF)
```

Mode variables and quantity-spaces:

Constraints:
  For mode NIL:
```
    ((M+ A.AMOUNT N2.EFFORT_HYDRAULIC) (0 0) (INF INF))
    ((CONSTANT N1.EFFORT_HYDRAULIC 0))
    ((ADD A.INFLOW A.OUTFLOW A.NETFLOW))
    ((D/DT A.AMOUNT A.NETFLOW))
    ((M+ B.AMOUNT N4.EFFORT_HYDRAULIC) (0 0) (INF INF))
    ((CONSTANT N3.EFFORT_HYDRAULIC 0))
    ((ADD B.INFLOW B.OUTFLOW B.NETFLOW))
    ((D/DT B.AMOUNT B.NETFLOW))
    ((MINUS F.Q F.-Q))
    ((MULT N2.EFFORT_HYDRAULIC F.K F.Q))
    ((CONSTANT F.K))
    ((MINUS P.Q P.-Q))
    ((ADD N4.EFFORT_HYDRAULIC P.HEAD P.EP))
    ((ADD P.DP N1.EFFORT_HYDRAULIC P.EP))
    ((MULT P.DP P.K P.Q))
    ((CONSTANT P.HEAD))
    ((CONSTANT P.K))
    ((CONSTANT .TOTAL))
    ((ADD A.AMOUNT B.AMOUNT .TOTAL))
    ((MINUS A.NETFLOW B.NETFLOW))
    ((MINUS P.-Q A.INFLOW))
    ((MINUS A.OUTFLOW F.Q))
    ((MINUS F.-Q B.INFLOW))
    ((MINUS B.OUTFLOW P.Q))
```

Generated QDE model PLOOP_UNIQUE
  under mode assumptions NIL

13.6 Discussion

13.6.1 Diagnosis from First Principles

The component-connection modeling paradigm is the basis for the "reasoning from first principles" approach to model-based diagnosis (Davis, 1984; Genesereth, 1984; de Kleer and Williams, 1987; Reiter, 1987; Struss and Dressler, 1989). This approach to diagnosis relies on tracing dependencies upstream from an observed discrepancy between prediction and observation to identify a *conflict set* of components that cannot all be functioning correctly. The conflict sets from several observations can then be analyzed to determine *minimal candidates*: hypothesized sets of failing components adequate to make predictions and observations consistent. The basic algorithm can be augmented with failure modes and probabilities to further focus diagnosis and probe selection. Most of this work has dealt with static, combinatorial circuits, but Hamscher (1989; 1991) and Ng (1991) have applied these methods to time-varying and dynamic systems.

In most applications of the "first principles" approach, dependency tracing takes place at the level of granularity of the component-connection model of the device, rather than at the level of the qualitative differential equation or the logical inference steps used to reason about the device.[8] Therefore, it relies on exactly the closed-world assumption for component-connection models: that the only significant parts of the device are the explicitly specified components, and that their only significant interactions take place over the explicitly specified connections. Problem 8 asks you to implement dependency tracing and "first principles" diagnosis in CC.

13.6.2 Relaxation of Assumptions

Diagnosis from "first principles" gets its power from the explicit enumeration of interaction paths in the component-connection representation for a device. However, any given component library embodies class-wide assumptions about which phenomena and interactions are significant and which are negligible (section 13.2.4). If the correct answer to a diagnostic problem violates one of these assumptions, it will not appear in the search space used by the "first principles" algorithm. The algorithm will not even be able to express the correct answer and may either refute all possible hypotheses or continually pursue ever more improbable hypotheses.

Davis (1984) observed this problem in the diagnosis of electronic circuits. His algorithm correctly diagnosed faulty components. However, a "bridge fault" (an

[8]In its most abstract form (Reiter, 1987), "first principles" diagnosis is applicable at any of these levels of granularity.

added connection, often due to an accidental blob of solder between adjacent pins of a component) would defeat the basic algorithm. Davis's solution was to generate a hierarchy of diagnostic problems, starting with a strong closed-world assumption providing a great deal of focus, then progressively relaxing the assumption when the initial problem formulation failed to find a solution. The different problems would typically require different representations. For example, to diagnose bridge faults, the representation used geometric layout information to identify added-connection hypotheses involving adjacent pins.

How is the hierarchy of diagnostic problems created? This is not yet known (problem 9), but it clearly requires a model-building methodology stronger than the component-connection methodology with its user-provided closed-world assumption and component library embodying class-wide assumptions. This is one reason we turn our attention to the more difficult but potentially more powerful methodology of *compositional modeling*.

13.7 Problems

1. Build a CC model of the two-tank cascade (figure 10.5), using the hydraulic component library (section 13.5.1). Hint: a constant inflow can be modeled as a `Source` and a `QPump`.

2. Define a `Diode` component for the electrical domain library, permitting current flow in one direction but not in the other.

3. Define a `Transistor` component for the electrical domain library.

4. Build CC component libraries for other domains such as

- heat flow;
- physiological modeling of acid, base, and electrolyte transport among fluid compartments;
- macro-economics.

Build a variety of models to demonstrate your domain library.

5. Form equivalence classes of flow variables during compilation.

Effort variables at a node are considered equivalent, by KVL, and replaced by a single variable, as shown in section 13.4.3.

Another opportunity for identifying equivalent variables arises from MINUS constraints relating two flow variables. These appear most frequently at two-component nodes and at two-terminal components.

(MINUS A B) & (MINUS B C) $\Rightarrow$ A $\equiv$ C

For example, in the RC circuit model, we get the following equivalence classes:

QSIM variable	equivalence class
IA	S.I $\equiv$ R.I2 $\equiv$ C.I2 $\equiv$ B.I
IB	S.I2 $\equiv$ R.I $\equiv$ C.I $\equiv$ B.I2

Define an equivalence relation on flow variables, and extend the CC model-compilation process to exploit these equivalence relations to simplify the generated model.

6. Evaluate the following claim: "*Information* is not usefully described as a substance, since pressure is not meaningful and the lack of conservation of mass means that KCL does not hold."

7. (Research Problem.) Study the use of bond graphs in engineering modeling (Karnopp *et al.*, 1990), and the growing AI literature on the application of bond graphs for modeling physical systems (Top and Akkermans, 1990; 1991; Söderman and Strömberg, 1991; Biswas and Yu, 1993). Implement a model builder that (1) builds a bond graph representation from a given component-connection description of a physical device, and (2) builds a QDE for simulation from the bond graph. Analyze the advantages and disadvantages of the bond graph approach over the approach taken in this chapter.

8. (Research Problem.) Dependency tracing for "first principles" diagnosis may be done in a number of ways, including tracking propagation order (de Kleer and Brown, 1984), analysis of ATMS labels (de Kleer and Brown, 1986; de Kleer and Williams, 1987), causal ordering (Iwasaki and Simon, 1986a; Iwasaki, 1988), or bond graphs (Top and Akkermans, 1991). Analyze the advantages and disadvantages of these methods, extend the CC representation as needed, and demonstrate "first principles" diagnosis for a class of devices based on their CC models.

9. (Research Problem.) Select a domain and example devices with component-connection models suitable for diagnosis from "first principles." Analyze the class-

wide assumptions embedded in the component library for this domain. Create, by hand, a hierarchy (or lattice) of models of the example devices, progressively relaxing the class-wide assumptions. Determine what sort of model-based diagnosis algorithm is appropriate for each model in the hierarchy. Can you devise a way to generate this hierarchy of models automatically from a background library of domain knowledge?

14 Compositional Modeling

14.1 What to Leave In, What to Leave Out?

The essence of model building is to decide which aspects of the world should be explicitly described in the model, and which should be omitted. Paraphrasing Einstein, a model should be as simple as possible, but no simpler; as complicated as necessary, but no more.

Compositional modeling addresses the problem of building a model by selecting an appropriate set of model fragments from a potentially vast background knowledge base, imposing the closed-world assumption on that set of fragments, and transforming them into a model.

It is helpful to distinguish between several elements of the model-building process:

- The world itself (infinite);
- The question (the purpose for building a model);
- The scenario (a small initial description of a set of objects and relations in the world);
- The modeler's knowledge base (vast);
- The model (the resulting small description of the world, capable of answering the question).

In component-connection modeling (chapter 13), the human modeler explicitly specifies the set of components to be considered, and their complete set of connections. The component library specifies how each component is to be modeled. A well-constructed library, appropriate to its domain and the modeler's purposes, gives the human modeler a powerful tool for conveniently constructing complex models. However, it is the human, not the automated reasoning system, that makes the modeling decisions and decides when to impose the closed-world assumption.

In compositional modeling, a larger portion of the model-building process is explicitly formalized and automated, and the model fragments in the knowledge base are not necessarily mutually consistent.

Research on model building has focused on two questions.

1. How is a model built from a set of model fragments?
2. How does the model builder decide which model fragments to include?

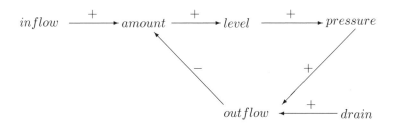

Figure 14.1
Signed influence diagram for a water tank model.

The field is approaching consensus on a set of methods to answer the first question. The second question is the focus of an active research area, exploring a range of alternative solutions, reviewed in section 14.4.

14.2 Composing Models

14.2.1 Signed Directed Influence Graphs

There is a long tradition of building models of mechanisms by collecting all of the influences that have a significant effect on variables of interest. These influences can be represented by directed graphs ("digraphs") such as figure 14.1, in which each node represents a continuous variable, and each directed edge is characterized by a sign, or sign and magnitude. Even with signs alone, global qualitative properties of the system can be determined by analysis of the graph. For example, the loop in figure 14.1 with a net negative effect denotes a negative feedback mechanism.

Puccia and Levins (1985) give a clear overview of methods for qualitative "loop analysis" of signed digraph models, applying even to quite complex systems such as multiple predator-prey models in ecology or producer-consumer models in economics. These methods employ the quasi-static equilibrium assumption and focus on determining the stability of the system in the region of interest and the direction of change due to a perturbation. (See chapter 7.)

14.2.2 Qualitative Process Theory

Qualitative process theory (or "QP theory") (Forbus, 1984) was the first method in AI for assembling influence models automatically from a substantial knowledge base of model fragments. GIZMO, Forbus's original implementation, was later replaced by QPE (Forbus, 1990; 1992). QP theory was originally designed as a theory of human commonsense reasoning about physical systems, with an emphasis on the generation of causal explanations (Forbus and Gentner, 1983). However, it has also been applied to the thermodynamic modeling of large engineered systems (Hollan *et al.*, 1984; LeClair and Abrams, 1988; Collins, 1989), to geometric and kinematic reasoning (Forbus *et al.*, 1991), and to the creation of self-explanatory numerical simulations (Forbus and Falkenhainer, 1990a; 1990b).

QP theory extends the concept of influence graph in a number of important ways, all contributing to automating the process of modeling and simulation.

• The knowledge base includes two kinds of model fragments, which can be automatically instantiated with objects from the given scenario, and which have explicit conditions for activation. *Individual views* describe subsets of the given scenario from particular perspectives, and *processes* describe interactions among objects and causes of change.

• The magnitudes of quantities are described in terms of quantity spaces and landmark values, rather than simply signs.

• Influences may be of two distinct types: *direct* influences, which affect the rate of change of a quantity; and *indirect* influences, which describe functional relationships among magnitudes.

• The resulting model consists of the continuous quantities, quantity spaces, and influences collected from the active model fragments.

• The behavioral prediction is in the form of a total envisionment. Since changes in the values of quantities during a behavior can affect the activation conditions of model fragments, the sets of quantities and influences can vary during a behavior.[1]

14.2.3   Influences and Constraints

A particularly significant contribution of qualitative process theory is the use of *influences*, as distinct from *constraints*, to represent partial, and composable, descriptions of functional relationships.

A signed influence $Q^+(y, x_i)$ is a directed relationship from x_i to y. It tells us how y will change as a result of a change in x_i, *all else being equal*. The qualification is critical: it means that an influence embodies an "open-world assumption." We cannot conclude from the fact that x_i is increasing that y is increasing, nor can we conclude from an observation that x_i is increasing and y is decreasing that our

---

[1] From the perspective we take in this book, the lasting contribution of QP theory is in its approach to model building. As described in section 14.2.4, we attempt to clarify this contribution by combining it with the QSIM approach to model simulation.

model is inconsistent. In each case, there may be another influence on y whose effect dominates that of x_i.

In contrast, a constraint $M^+(y, x_i)$ between x_i and y embodies a limited and local closed-world assumption. Regardless of the presence of other constraints on x_i or y, we *can* conclude from the fact that x_i is increasing that y must be increasing, or from the simultaneous observation that x_i is increasing while y is decreasing that the model must be inconsistent. In order to support simulation, a model can contain only constraints.

In order for the model fragments in a general-purpose knowledge base to be compositional, it is very useful for them to be able to assert influences rather than constraints. They can then be combined with other influences that may have been created independently.

- **Indirect Influences.** The indirect influence $Q^+(y, x_i)$ means that there is some functional relationship f between x_i and y such that

$$Q^+(y, x_i) \quad \equiv \quad y = f(\ldots, x_i, \ldots) \text{ and } \frac{\partial f}{\partial x_i} > 0.$$

This relationship is sometimes called "qualitative proportionality."[2]

The ellipses ($\ldots$) in the definition are critical. An indirect influence asserts that a functional relationship exists without specifying the number and nature of arguments to the function. Only after applying the closed-world assumption to the set of influences can we determine the complete set of arguments $x_1 \ldots x_n$ to each functional relation.

- **Direct Influences.** The direct influence $I^+(y, x_i)$ also represents a directed relationship between x_i and y, but the influence applies to the derivative of y (and therefore only changes the magnitude of y when integrated over time), and multiple direct influences are combined additively.

$$I^+(y, x_i) \quad \equiv \quad \frac{dy}{dt} = sum(\ldots, x_i, \ldots).$$

The restricted combination rule for direct influences does not reduce the expressive power of the language, since indirect influences can be applied to the directly influencing variables.

Influence resolution is the process of transforming the complete sets of influences on each variable to constraints, once the closed-world assumption has been imposed,

---

[2]The notation $Q^+(y, x_i)$ for the indirect influence from x_i to y replaces the typographically challenging notation $y \, \alpha_{Q+} \, x_i$ from Forbus, 1984.

so the resulting model will support simulation. In QP theory, a variable can have only direct, or only indirect, influences on it. If $\{x_1, \ldots, x_n\}$ is the complete set of variables influencing y, with corresponding signs $\{s_1, \ldots, s_n\}$, the complete set of arguments to a constraint is determined.

- A set of indirect influences is transformed into a multivariate monotonic function constraint.

```
((M s1 ...  sn) x1 ...  xn y)
```

- A set of direct influences is transformed into a multivariate signed sum constraint

```
((ssum s1 ...  sn) x1 ...  xn y')
```

where `(d/dt y y')`.

(See section 3.6.) Forbus and Falkenhainer (1990a; 1990b) and Woods (1991) add the ability to retrieve fully quantified multivariate functions from a library, given the assembled qualitative constraints.

If a variable is not influenced, it is assumed to be constant. In qualitative process theory, this is called the *sole mechanism assumption*, and means that any change is directly or indirectly caused by some process.

14.2.4   QPC

QPC (Crawford *et al.*, 1990; Farquhar, 1993) is a model builder that builds on, clarifies, and extends the ideas of qualitative process theory within the QSIM framework (figure 13.1). The discussion and examples in this chapter are based on QPC, which is described much more completely in Farquhar, 1993.

The principal contributions of QPC to compositional modeling are the following.

- Qualitative reasoning is clearly separated into distinct model-building and model-simulation tasks, interacting through the QSIM QDE representation. This clarifies the different representation and inference methods used before and after the closed-world assumption is imposed (cf. section 14.2.3).

- The separation of tasks allows numerous technical issues in the design of a compositional modeling system to be clarified. Two of the most visible follow:

  - QPC clarifies the precise meaning of influences, the criteria for coherence of sets of influences, and the method for translating sets of influences into constraints.

- The model builder and the simulator interact as coroutines, allowing modeling and simulation to be done incrementally as required by the evolving behaviors predicted by the model, rather than requiring an initial enumeration of all possible models and states of the system.

- The clarified representation and inference method makes it possible to prove a "guaranteed coverage" theorem analogous to that of QSIM.

If a QDE model of a given scenario exists, and the knowledge required to build the model exists within the knowledge base, then the QPC model-building algorithm will identify the appropriate model fragments and build that model.

Naturally, this guarantee is conditional on a scenario having a model in a form that qualitative simulation can apply to, and on the modeler having the necessary background knowledge. Combined with the guaranteed coverage theorem for QSIM (theorem 6 on page 118), this means that the real behavior will be predicted as well.

The importance of the coverage guarantee is that the model builder can have confidence in the soundness of the underlying model-building algorithm. In practice, search for models must be guided by explicit modeling assumptions that eliminate large portions of a potentially vast search space of model fragments (section 14.4). If a model cannot be found for a given purpose, it is valuable for the modeler to know that the responsibility must lie with the selection of modeling assumptions or the coverage of the knowledge base, and not with the underlying model-building algorithm.

14.2.5   Axiomatizing Compositional Modeling

Qualitative reasoning generally, and especially compositional modeling, has posed interesting and difficult problems for the logic-based knowledge representation (KR) community (Rayner, 1991; IFIP, 1992). Compositional modeling raises particular problems because of the way the "open-world assumption" is embedded in the definition of influences.[3]

Davis (1991; 1992) takes a step toward solving this problem by exhibiting an axiomatization in first-order logic of a small domain theory and model stated in qualitative process theory. He shows how the qualitative state transitions in a total envisionment of this model can be proved as first-order theorems from his

---

[3] Although their concern is with axiomatizing continuous change rather than than model building, there is a fascinating discussion between Sandewall (1989), Shoham and McDermott (1988), and Rayner (1991). Problem 2 in chapter 8 and problem 10 in chapter 9 describe QSIM models for the examples discussed in these papers.

axiomatization. This work significantly clarifies the relation between the QR and KR views of reasoning about physical systems.

The critical axioms in this work, however, enumerate the set of all possible influences on each variable. Essentially, they explicitly represent the coverage of the entire knowledge base. Therefore, they represent the *result* of applying a closed-world assumption to the knowledge base as a whole. The identification of active model fragments, and the use of modeling assumptions to focus on a smaller set of model fragments, can then be expressed as first-order axioms applying to this closed set of possibilities.

As Davis points out, these closed-world axioms could plausibly be derived as consequences of a simpler and clearer non-monotonic theory. Such a non-monotonic theory would preserve the important property of *additivity* for the knowledge base as a whole: if a new model fragment is added, existing axioms should not become false.

Crawford and Etherington (1992) argue that a non-monotonic approach incorporating the separation between model building and model simulation solves a number of problems with defeasible inference about physical situations, including the Yale Shooting Problem and more plausible physical scenarios. In particular, there is a critical distinction between defeasible inference during simulation (e.g., any influence overrides the default assumption that variables remain constant), and defeasible inference during model building (e.g., the assumption when modeling a filling bathtub that bulk fluid flows are significant while evaporation is negligible).

14.3   Building Models

This section describes how a set of model fragments is identified from the knowledge base, and how the fragments are composed into a model. This is a simplified description of the QPC model-building algorithm (Farquhar, 1993).

14.3.1   The Participants

The *scenario* is a given description of a small set of objects and relations in the world. The *knowledge base* includes a large number of *model fragments*. Each abstract model-fragment definition specifies

- a set of *individuals*: objects described by the model fragment;

- a set of *structural conditions*: attributes of, and relations among, the individuals, not including conditions on continuous quantities;

- a set of *operating conditions*: relations among continuous attributes of individuals, or between continuous attributes and constants; and

- a set of *consequents*: assertions of the existence of objects in the world,[4] attributes of and relations among individuals and continuous quantities.

An abstract model fragment in the knowledge base goes through two stages on its way to participating in a model of a scenario.

1. A model fragment (MF) *instance* is created for each substitution of objects in the scenario for individuals in the model-fragment definition satisfying the structural conditions of the model fragment.

2. A model-fragment instance is *active* if its operating conditions are known to be true. It is *inactive* if they are known to be false, and *ambiguous* otherwise.

An active model-fragment instance asserts its consequents into the knowledge base, augmenting the scenario description. It may assert the existence of new objects in the scenario, their attributes and relations, continuous quantities, and their relations. This, in turn, may cause new model-fragment instances to be created and possibly become active.

14.3.2   The QPC Model-Building Algorithm

The model-building and simulation algorithm works as follows. The basic algorithm is exhaustive, providing the coverage guarantee. Annotations in italics show where modeling assumptions can be applied to prune the search space.

1. Start with the initial scenario, which describes a set of objects and relations in the world.

2. For each model fragment in the knowledge base, create a model fragment instance for each substitution of objects in the scenario for individuals satisfying the structural conditions.

Modeling assumptions can be applied at this stage to create instances only of those abstract model fragments most likely to be relevant.

3. For each model-fragment instance, evaluate the truth of its operating conditions to determine whether it is active, inactive, or ambiguous.

---

[4]Actually, QPC includes a distinct type of model fragment called an *entity definition*, which asserts new entity descriptions on demand under specified circumstances (section 14.5.3). The two are collapsed here for pedagogical simplicity.

- For each condition resulting in ambiguous model-fragment instances, branch on the truth value of that condition, so that on each branch, every MF instance is either active or inactive.

  Modeling assumptions at this point may heuristically prune or suspend consideration of some branches.

4. For each active model-fragment instance, assert its consequents into the scenario description.

   - Repeat from Step 2 until no new model fragment instances become active.

     Modeling assumptions can be applied at this stage to eliminate active model-fragment instances that are negligible.

At this point, the complete set of active model-fragment instances has been identified, and the closed-world assumption is imposed.

5. Build a QDE model for the current scenario:

   - collect the complete set of continuous variables appearing in the MF instances;

   - collect the complete sets of inequality relations among landmarks to build quantity spaces (branching if necessary to achieve a totally ordered quantity space for each variable); and

   - resolve the complete set of influences into constraints (section 14.2.3).

6. Define operating region boundaries for the QDE from the operating conditions of the active *and inactive* model fragment instances. If the truth values of any of these conditions changes, the set of active model-fragment instances may change, and the model may need to be rebuilt.[5]

7. Apply QSIM to simulate the behavior of this QDE model, starting with an initial qualitative state derived from inequalities in the initial scenario description.

8. If a predicted qualitative behavior terminates at an operating region transition, create a new scenario description representing the known state of the world after the transition.

The current version of QPC assumes that existing objects continue to exist, and that the magnitudes (but not necessarily the derivatives) of quantities are continuous across region transitions.[6]

---

[5] Region boundaries depend only on the operating conditions, since simulation alone cannot change the truth value of structural conditions and hence cannot change the set of MF instances.

[6] These assumptions could be weakened if the domain theory were able to specify which objects and values persist across region transitions.

• Return to step 2 to apply the model builder to the post-transition scenario. The activation of model-fragment instances at a region transition can create new objects, assert new structural conditions, create new MF instances, and change the set of active influences.

9. Stop when all behaviors terminate at quiescent or cyclic states.

This will produce a tree of models and behaviors analogous to the QSIM behavior tree, but including scenario descriptions prior to the initial state of each QSIM behavior and following each transition state.

This high-level description has omitted a number of important theoretical and practical aspects of QPC. See Farquhar, 1993 for the full story.

14.4   Modeling Assumptions and Negligibility

Q: Which valid model fragments should be included, and which omitted as negligible, when the closed-world assumption is imposed?

Once all invalid model fragments have been filtered out, there may be inconsistent combinations, or simply too many, valid model fragments remaining. For example, steady-state and dynamic models of a phenomenon may be equally valid individually, but inconsistent together. Since the world is (effectively) infinitely complex, even the set of mutually consistent model fragments from a realistically large knowledge base would almost certainly give a uselessly complex model.

Any model builder decides that certain aspects of the phenomenon being modeled can be treated as negligible[7] for the purpose for which the model is being constructed. The corresponding model fragments can then be omitted from the model.

In some cases, a theorem is available to prove that certain factors can be neglected, for example the fact that inverse-square forces among distant extended bodies can be treated as applying to point masses located at the centers of mass of the bodies. In other cases, order-of-magnitude reasoning justifies neglecting certain model fragments (e.g., relativistic effects at low speeds). Alternatively, causal dependency analysis can show that one feature of a situation (e.g., color of container) is causally irrelevant for a given purpose (e.g., estimation of volume). (In a particular context, color may be relevant as *evidence*, however.)

---

[7]Negligible. *a.* Capable of being neglected or disregarded. OED.

Therefore, in deciding which valid model fragments to omit, the model builder is making a set of *modeling assumptions* about the significance or negligibility of different aspects of the world, for the purpose of answering the given question. When a model fails to describe the real world, it does not necessarily mean that the model represents a false hypothesis about the state of the world. The failure can also be due to a failure in the modeling assumptions embodied in the model.

14.4.1   Types of Modeling Decisions

An exciting body of research has recently emerged, focused on automated methods for making different types of modeling decisions. Each decision selects a modeling assumption, and so determines one aspect of what is included and what is excluded from the model.

The following list of modeling decisions draws on the work of Falkenhainer and Forbus (1988; 1991) and, most directly, Weld (1992). The selection of assumptions for a particular model is only partially decomposable into separate decisions since the assumptions interact in important ways. These are informal descriptions of categories that seem intuitively meaningful, but have not yet been fully formalized. (Problem 6.)

• The *scope* of a model specifies the boundary between the system being modeled and the environment it reacts to. It is represented by a set of variables considered internal to the model, and those considered exogenous. For example, one model of the thermal properties of a house may draw its boundary at surface temperatures at the walls and roof of the house, while another may consider the surrounding trees, sun motion, and wind patterns.

• The *coverage* of a model specifies the phenomena within its scope that should be explicitly described. For example, in one model of fluid flow through a pipe the thermal properties of the fluid and the pipe may be irrelevant, while in flow through a heat exchanger the thermal properties are critical.

• The *detail* (or sometimes "granularity") of a model specifies which substructures of the system are represented explicitly, which are described with substructures of their own, and which are described as "black boxes." For example, a model of the physiology of water balance may describe the kidney as a black box controller of fluids and electrolytes; or it may explicitly represent the structure of the nephron and the flow of fluid along its tubule; or it may take an intermediate view.

• The *domain* of a model specifies ranges or other constraints on the values of variables (both internal and exogenous) for which the model applies. For example, one model may apply only at non-relativistic speeds; another only in regions where flow through a pipe is turbulent.

• The *accuracy* of a model represents the quality of the approximation between the predictions of the model and observations of the corresponding system in the world. For example, two otherwise equivalent models could differ in accuracy according to how many terms of a Taylor series are explicitly used to calculate a function.

• The *resolution* of a model specifies the precision with which values are described in their domains. In the presence of incomplete knowledge (i.e., always), resolution and accuracy trade off against each other. For example, a qualitative model of a ball thrown upward in a constant gravitational field gives an answer that is perfectly accurate but of very low resolution. A numerical model gives much higher resolution, but other modeling assumptions will necessarily reduce accuracy.

• The *time-scale* of a model determines, out of a hierarchy of ongoing processes taking place at different rates, which are modeled as

  • *Fast*: essentially instantaneous, modeled with the quasi-static equilibrium assumption or as a discontinuous change;

  • *Dynamic*: non-equilibrium states visible at the time-scale of interest;

  • *Slow*: essentially constant, dynamic changes too slow to be visible.

• The *micro vs. macro* decision determines whether a system is modeled in terms of the trajectory of an individual through a state-space, or in terms of the aggregate properties of one or more populations. This decision corresponds to the relationship between micro- and macro-economics; between classical and statistical mechanics of gases; and between the molecular-collection and contained-stuff ontologies in qualitative reasoning (Collins and Forbus, 1987; Amador and Weld, 1990; Liu and Farley, 1990; Rajamoney and Koo, 1990; 1991; Skorstad, 1992; Kiriyama and Tomiyama, 1993).

The list of modeling decisions is certainly incomplete, and we have a limited understanding of how these decisions interact.

14.4.2   Selecting Modeling Assumptions

Within the compositional modeling framework, the task of building a model from a given knowledge base of model fragments reduces to selecting a set of modeling assumptions giving the simplest coherent model capable of achieving its purpose. Not surprisingly, considered as a combinatorial problem, this task is intractable in general. Much of the subsequent research has concentrated on providing additional focus to the search for appropriate sets of modeling assumptions.

Falkenhainer and Forbus (1988; 1991) use the ATMS assumption-labeling mechanism to identify sets of assumptions relevant to the given question. Then they apply coherence tests and simplicity-ranking criteria to those sets to select the best one. While their approach provides a useful framework for organizing knowledge relevant to the search, it remains intractable in many cases.

The graph of models (Addanki *et al.*, 1989; Addanki *et al.*, 1991) avoids the search problem by explicitly enumerating a collection of coherent models under alternate assumptions, with transition links specifying when and how to replace a simpler model with a more complex one. (This up-front cost can, of course, be very large.) Given a question, a relevant graph of models is chosen, and the reasoner starts with the simplest model. If a conflict is detected between the predictions of the model and observations of the world, the conflict is analyzed to determine which variables must be differently constrained to eliminate the conflict. Then transition links within the graph of models show how to select a more complex model.

In order to clarify the nature of these transition links, Weld (1990) and Nayak (1992b) formalize behavioral and structural criteria, respectively, for when one model can be viewed as a simplified approximation of another. In addition, Weld (1992) analyzes the content of the query to determine when a simplified bounding abstraction model will be adequate to answer the given question.

Nayak (1992a), Nayak, Joskowicz and Addanki (1992), and Iwasaki and Levy (1993) describe similar methods for decomposing the search for modeling assumptions into several more focused searches. Suppose the space of modeling assumptions is divided into assumption classes, each of which can be ordered (perhaps partially) by simplicity. If the desired global model can be found by moving monotonically up the lattice of models in each assumption class independently, then the global search will be tractable. The approach is similar to component-connection modeling in that the given device description specifies the components and their connections. However, assumption classes can provide alternate models for each component, or assumptions applying to aggregates cutting across components.

Looking more generally at the problem of selecting modeling assumptions, and building on work on meta-reasoning by Subramanian and Genesereth (1987), Levy, Iwasaki, and Motoda (1992) argue for an explicit, declarative approach to reasoning about the relevance or irrelevance of model fragments for a given purpose. They demonstrate that a relevance logic can express in a natural way heuristics developed and encoded procedurally by a number of other researchers.

.

Shirley and Falkenhainer (1990) and Falkenhainer (1992a; 1992b) observe that experienced engineers rarely seem to search for appropriate models, but rather use knowledge of the "credibility domains" of different modeling assumptions to select the appropriate model first. Falkenhainer (1992a) shows how idealized models can be constructed from order-of-magnitude reasoning and simple algebraic manipulation using two reduction rules to eliminate negligable terms from a complex domain theory.

$$A + B \approx A \quad \text{when} \quad |A| \gg |B|$$
$$\frac{dy}{dx} = 0 \quad \text{when} \quad \frac{dy}{dx} \approx 0.$$

The expected accuracy of the resulting idealized model, and the credibility domains for the order-of-magnitude assumptions, are assessed by further algebraic reasoning, or by experience modeling other domains (Falkenhainer, 1992b).

Raiman and Williams (1992) present a method of "caricatural reasoning" that also uses order-of-magnitude assumptions and algebraic reasoning to identify negligible aspects of a complex domain theory. Furthermore, they demonstrate the creation of a "patchwork" of different order-of-magnitude assumptions and corresponding simplified theories to cover the entire state-space of a non-trivial problem in acid-base chemistry.[8]

Rickel and Porter (1992) demonstrate a method for selecting model fragments from a large knowledge base in the domain of plant physiology constructed for a number of different purposes clustered around the tasks of explanation and tutoring (Porter *et al.*, 1988). The model has the purpose of answering a particular simulation or "what if" question. The question describes properties of a set of given quantities, and asks about the behavior of one or more quantities of interest. Their goal is to find the slowest time-scale at which the question has a useful answer. Their algorithm first searches the space of interaction paths defined by the model fragments in the knowledge base to find the slowest time-scale at which every quantity of interest is linked to some given quantity. The choice of time-scale determines which processes are modeled dynamically, which quasi-statically, and which variables can be treated as exogenous, for purposes of the current explanation. Finally, the scope of the model is increased to include all influences into the selected interaction paths at the chosen time-scale.

---

[8]For more on order-of-magnitude reasoning, see section 9.5.3.

14.5   A Simple Domain Theory for Fluids

In this section, we present a simple QPC knowledge base for describing fluids, containers, and flows (Farquhar, 1993).[9] Many of the constructs in the QPC syntax reflect its implementation language, Algernon (Crawford and Kuipers, 1989; 1991b; 1991a).

14.5.1   Ontology: Objects and Relations

The *ontology* of a domain theory consists of the types of objects that can be described, and the relations that can be represented among those objects. The domain theory for fluids presented here rests on a more basic domain theory including `sets`, `booleans`, `scopes`, and other concepts, defined in much the same way.

The `deftaxonomy` form creates a taxonomic hierarchy of sets and subsets corresponding to the named lists and sublists in its argument. By convention, the names of sets are plural nouns.

```
(deftaxonomy (objects
                (physobs
                  (contained-stuff
                    (contained-liquids)
                    (contained-gases)))
                (containers)
                (fluid-sources)
                (drains)
                (paths
                  (heat-paths)
                  (fluid-paths))
                (surfaces)))
```

A relation is defined by specifying a name and the tuple of domains over which the relation is defined. Scopes are used to represent reasoning contexts, including temporal contexts. Relations whose truth value can vary with context are represented by including the set `scopes` among its domains.

```
(defrelation container          (contained-stuff containers))
(defrelation contents           (containers contained-stuff)
(defrelation aligned            (scopes paths booleans))
(defrelation fluid-connection (scopes containers fluid-paths containers))
(defrelation flows-into         (scopes fluid-sources containers))
(defrelation drains-outof       (scopes drains containers))
```

---

[9]This example domain theory is based on one developed by Adam Farquhar.

Quantity types are real-valued attributes of members of certain sets. The only continuous variables QPC can reason about are those that arise from these attributes of known individual objects. Since QPC builds qualitative models, it reasons with qualitative descriptions of the real values of quantity attributes. The same methods can be used to build semi-quantitative or numerical models (problem 8).

```
(quantity-type mass                physobs)
(quantity-type height              containers)
(quantity-type fluid-level         containers)
(quantity-type interior-volume     containers)
(quantity-type bottom-pressure     containers)
(quantity-type volume              contained-stuff)
(quantity-type pressure            contained-stuff)
(quantity-type level               contained-liquids)
(quantity-type pressure-difference fluid-paths)
```

The knowledge base also contains definitions and axioms for relations such as equivalence and order relations, expressed as slot specifications and forward- and backward-chaining rules.

14.5.2   Model Fragment Library: Liquid Flow

Much of the domain theory is expressed as a library of model fragments. The :participants and :conditions clauses specify the individual entities and structural conditions that must match objects and relations in the world for a model-fragment instance to be created.[10] The :quantities are defined for each model fragment instance. If the :operating-conditions are also satisfied, then the instance is active and the :consequences are asserted.

Contained Liquid   This domain theory reflects Hayes's (1985a) ontology for liquids. We distinguish between a container, a liquid substance, and the individual object that is the piece of liquid in the container.

```
(defModelFragment* CONTAINED-LIQUID
   :participants ((liq  :type contained-liquids)
                  (con  :type containers))
   :conditions ((container liq con))
   :consequences
```

---

[10]Instantiation of model fragments is a bit more flexible than suggested by the syntax of the examples presented here. Some of the participants in a model-fragment instance may be created on demand (section 14.5.3) in response to queries of conditions associated with participants already identified.

```
((q+0 (pressure liq) (level liq))
 (q+0 (level liq)    (volume liq))
 (q+0 (volume liq)   (mass liq))
 (>= (fluid-level con)    zero)
 (>= (bottom-pressure con) zero)
 (= (pressure liq) (bottom-pressure con))
 (= (level liq)    (fluid-level con))
 (correspondence (volume liq) (interior-volume con)
                 (level liq)  (height con))))
```

Fluid Flow Fluid flow requires source and destination containers, each with a contained liquid, and a fluid path between them that is aligned (i.e., open to flow). The flow rate is qualitatively proportional to the pressure difference across the fluid path, and tends to increase the mass of one contained liquid and decrease the other.

```
(defModelFragment* FLUID-FLOW
  :participants ((src    :type containers)
                 (dst    :type containers)
                 (fpath  :type fluid-paths)
                 (s-liq  :type contained-liquids)
                 (d-liq  :type contained-liquids))
  :conditions ((contents src s-liq)
               (contents dst d-liq)
               (fluid-connection src fpath dst)
               (aligned fpath true))
  :quantities (flow-rate)
  :consequences
    ((q+0 (flow-rate fluid-flow) (pressure-difference fpath))
     (add (pressure-difference fpath) (bottom-pressure dst)
          (bottom-pressure src))
     (I+ (mass d-liq) (flow-rate fluid-flow))
     (I- (mass s-liq) (flow-rate fluid-flow))))
```

Fluid Source A fluid source is modeled as a flow into a specified container and its contained liquid. If no other influence applies to the flow rate, it will be assumed constant. The source of the flow is not modeled.

```
(defModelFragment* FLUID-SOURCE
  :participants ((src :type fluid-sources)
                 (con :type containers)
                 (liq :type contained-liquids))
  :conditions ((flows-into src con)
               (contents con liq))
```

```
:quantities (source-flow-rate)
:consequences ((> (source-flow-rate fluid-source) zero)
               (I+ (mass liq) (source-flow-rate fluid-source)))))
```

Drain   A drain is a flow out of a container and its contained liquid, with rate influenced by the pressure of the contained liquid, but with unmodeled destination.

```
(defModelFragment* DRAIN-MF
   :participants ((drn  :type drains)
                  (con  :type containers)
                  (liq  :type contained-liquids))
   :conditions ((drains-outof drn con)
                (contents con liq))
   :quantities (drain-flow-rate)
   :consequences ((>= (drain-flow-rate drain-mf) zero)
                  (I- (mass liq) (drain-flow-rate drain-mf))
                  (Q+0 (drain-flow-rate drain-mf)
                       (bottom-pressure con)))))
```

Overflow   Overflow is modeled as a new outflow whose rate increases (rapidly) with the level of water over the top of the tank. Thus, when the tank is overflowing, the level of the water is above the top of the tank, and the amount of water in the tank is greater than its capacity.

```
(defModelFragment* OVERFLOW
   :participants ((con  :type containers)
                  (liq  :type contained-liquids))
   :conditions ((consider overflow con)
                (contents con liq))
   :quantities (rate delta-height)
   :operating-conditions ((> (level liq) (height con)))
   :consequences
     ((I- (mass liq) (rate overflow))
      (add (height con) (delta-height overflow) (level liq))
      (q+0 (rate overflow) (delta-height overflow)))))
```

14.5.3   Create Entities Only As Needed

An explicit description of an entity such as the contained liquid within a container is created only when needed by a model fragment instance, and when its existence is implied by other known relations. The defEntity* form specifies when an explicit

entity description is created on demand. If a suitable entity already exists, a new
one is not created.

```
(defEntity* c-liquid
    :goal (contents con c-liquid)
    :participants ((src  :type fluid-sources
                         :conditions ((flows-into src con)))
                   (con  :type containers))
    :consequences ((contents con c-liquid)
                   (isa c-liquid contained-liquids))
    :initially ((= (mass  c-liquid) zero)
                (= (level c-liquid) zero)))

(defEntity* dst-liquid
    :goal (contents dst dst-liquid)
    :participants
      ((src  :type containers)
       (dst  :conditions ((fluid-connection src ?path dst)
                          (contents src src-liquid)))
       (src-liquid :type contained-liquids))
    :consequences ((contents dst dst-liquid)
                   (isa dst-liquid contained-liquids))
    :initially ((= (mass  dst-liquid) zero)
                (= (level dst-liquid) zero)))

(defEntity* src-liquid
    :goal (contents src src-liquid)
    :participants
      ((src  :type containers)
       (dst  :conditions ((fluid-connection src ?path dst)))
       (dst-liquid :type contained-liquids
                   :conditions ((contents dst dst-liquid))))
    :consequences ((contents src src-liquid)
                   (isa src-liquid contained-liquids))
    :initially ((= (mass  src-liquid) zero)
                (= (level src-liquid) zero)))
```

14.6   Example: The Water Tank

Let us consider the familiar one-tank system, starting empty, with a constant rate
of inflow and an open drain (figure 14.1). We assert the existence of a container,
its contents, the source, the drain, and their relationships. We also assert that we
are considering the possibility of overflow from the tank.

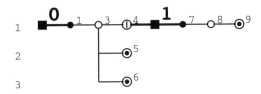

Figure 14.2
QPC behavior tree.

Model M_0 and initial state S_1 predict three behaviors, one of which, $[S_1, S_3, S_4]$, terminates with a region transition when the tank overflows. This leads to a new model M_1 and initial state S_7, which predict a single qualitative behavior terminating in an equilibrium state S_9.

```
(defscenario scene
    :comment "Tank with inflow and drain that may overflow."
    :entities ((a    :type containers)
               (drn  :type drains)
               (src  :type fluid-sources))
    :relations ((flows-into src a)
                (drains-outof drn a)
                (constant (height a))
                (> (height a) zero)
                (consider overflow a)))
```

We assume that the domain theory in section 14.5 has already been loaded. The behavior tree of models and qualitative states created by QPC in response to this scenario is shown in figure 14.2. We trace through the individual steps of the process in the following section.

14.6.1   Building the Initial Model

First, we create model-fragment instances for every model fragment whose structural conditions are satisfied. Those model-fragment instances whose operating conditions are also satisfied are considered *active* and are listed in the following trace.

```
Model SCENE.INITIAL-MODEL is the initial model.
Initializing model SCENE.INITIAL-MODEL.
Instantiated views for SCENE.INITIAL-MODEL:
    0. (%defentity-c-liquid-1 src a)
                                [%defentity-c-liquid-1.instantiation]
    1. (drain-mf drn a a.contents)        [drain-mf.instantiation]
    2. (fluid-source src a a.contents)   [fluid-source.instantiation]
    3. (contained-liquid a.contents a)
                                   [contained-liquid.instantiation]
    4. (container-mf a)              [container-mf.instantiation]
    5. (physob a.contents)               [physob.instantiation]
```

Once the complete set of active model fragments is known, we assert that the world is closed and transform the set of model fragments to a model in the form of a QSIM QDE.

```
Asserting that the world is closed.
Resolving influences.
Inferring that all uninfluenced vars are constant.
Resolving correspondences.
Resolving quantity spaces.
   The quantity spaces are totally ordered.
   Narrowing the qspaces.
   Asserting shared quantity spaces.
Collecting region transitions.

Defining a QDE.
   Cleaning up QDE for QSIM:
     every qspace must have a variable in a constraint,
     minf and inf are unreachable,
     unreachable values must be in a qspace,
     corresponding values must be in qspaces.
Constructing the QSIM QDE.
```

14.6.2 Creating an Initial State and Simulating

An initial state S_0 is created from the information available in the scenario description. State S_0 has two completions consistent with the constraints in the QDE, but S_2 violates the constraint on infinite values and infinite times. Starting from S_1, QSIM predicts the expected three behaviors for the water tank: overflow, equilibrium, and equilibrium at the top of the tank.

```
Building an initial state.
  Initial values:
          (dif-<a.fluid-level>-<a.height> ((minf 0) nil))
          (dif-<a.contents.level>-<a.height> ((minf 0) nil))
          (a.height ((0 nil) nil))
          (a.contents.level (0 nil))
          (a.contents.mass (0 nil))
          (fluid-source.instantiation.source-flow-rate ((0 nil) nil))
          (a.fluid-level (0 nil))

Run time: 0.050 seconds to initialize (S-1 S-2).
  Built initial state S-0, which has at most 2 consistent completions.

Simulating from initial state S-0.
Run time: 0.110 seconds to simulate 4 states.
  Generated 3 behaviors.
```

14.6.3   Building a Model after Overflow

The final state of the first behavior crosses a boundary of the current region, so the QPC model builder is invoked again to build a new model to predict the behavior of the overflowing tank. The magnitudes, but not the derivatives, of variables are inherited from the final state S_4 before the transition to the initial scenario after it.

```
Model M-1 follows SCENE.INITIAL-MODEL because of a transition.
Initializing model M-1.
  Model M-1 is a transition from SCENE.INITIAL-MODEL via S-4.
  Inheriting model assumptions:
      "[none]"
  Inheriting initial conditions assumptions:
      (region-active (:slot q>) (:quote a.contents.level)
                                (:quote a.height))
  Assert the qspace orderings from S-4.
  Assert the correspondences from S-4.
  Inheriting values from state S-4:
          (a.height (qsim::a-0 nil))
          (a.contents.level (qsim::a-17 nil))
          (drain-mf.instantiation.drain-flow-rate (qsim::d-2 nil))
          (a.contents.mass.scene.derivative (qsim::a-18 nil))
          (a.contents.mass (qsim::a-19 nil))
          (a.bottom-pressure (qsim::a-20 nil))
          (fluid-source.instantiation.source-flow-rate (qsim::f-0 nil))
          (a.fluid-level (qsim::a-21 nil))
```

```
(a.interior-volume (qsim::a-1 nil))
(a.contents.pressure (qsim::a-22 nil))
(a.contents.volume (qsim::a-23 nil))
```

Because the level of water is at the height of the container and increasing, the Overflow model fragment is instantiated and becomes active, albeit initially with flow rate zero.

```
Instantiating view OVERFLOW.
  A.CONTENTS -- ABSTRACT-LIQ3
  A -- ABSTRACT-CON4
Concluded zero Q= OVERFLOW.INSTANTIATION.DELTA-HEIGHT.
Instantiated views for M-1:
    0. (%defentity-c-liquid-1 src a)
                                 [%defentity-c-liquid-1.instantiation]
    1. (overflow a a.contents)              [overflow.instantiation]
    2. (drain-mf drn a a.contents)          [drain-mf.instantiation]
    3. (fluid-source src a a.contents)   [fluid-source.instantiation]
    4. (contained-liquid a.contents a)
                                  [contained-liquid.instantiation]
    5. (container-mf a)                     [container-mf.instantiation]
    6. (physob a.contents)                     [physob.instantiation]
```

Once the set of model fragments is complete, the world is closed and a QSIM QDE is constructed as before.

```
Asserting that the world is closed.
Resolving influences.
Inferring that all uninfluenced vars are constant.
Resolving correspondences.
Resolving quantity spaces.
  The quantity spaces are totally ordered.
  Narrowing the qspaces.
  Asserting shared quantity spaces.
Collecting region transitions.

Defining a QDE.
  Cleaning up QDE for QSIM:
    every qspace must have a variable in a constraint,
    minf and inf are unreachable,
    unreachable values must be in a qspace,
    corresponding values must be in qspaces.
Constructing the QSIM QDE.
```

14.6.4 Creating a New Initial State and Simulating

The initial state S_7 is constructed from the values inherited from S_4, plus the values obtained from the new `Overflow` model fragment. The information provided defines a unique initial state. QSIM then predicts a single qualitative behavior $[S_7, S_8, S_9]$, which terminates at an equilibrium state.

```
Building an initial state.
  Initial values:
        (dif-<a.fluid-level>-<a.height> (0 nil))
        (dif-<a.contents.level>-<a.height> (0 nil))
        (a.height (a-0 nil))
        (overflow.instantiation.delta-height (0 nil))
        (a.contents.mass.scene.derivative (a-18 nil))
        (a.contents.mass (a-19 nil))
        (a.contents.level (a-17 nil))
        (a.bottom-pressure (a-20 nil))
        (drain-mf.instantiation.drain-flow-rate (d-2 nil))
        (fluid-source.instantiation.source-flow-rate (f-0 nil))
        (a.contents.volume (a-23 nil))
        (a.contents.pressure (a-22 nil))
        (a.interior-volume (a-1 nil))
        (a.fluid-level (a-21 nil))

Run time: 0.030 seconds to initialize S-7.
  Built initial state S-7, which is complete.

Simulating from initial state S-7.
Run time: 0.130 seconds to simulate 6 states.
  Generated 1 behavior.
```

Since all behaviors terminate at equilibrium states, the simulation is now complete. Figure 14.2 shows the QPC behavior tree representing the models and behaviors. Figure 14.3 shows the first behavior, in which the tank overflows.

14.7 Large Knowledge Bases

A number of research groups, working in different domains, have constructed large knowledge bases with extensive domain theories for compositional modeling. Several of these are described in this section. Research efforts aimed at capturing the foundational knowledge underlying these technical domain theories are described by Lenat and Guha (1990) and Davis (1990).

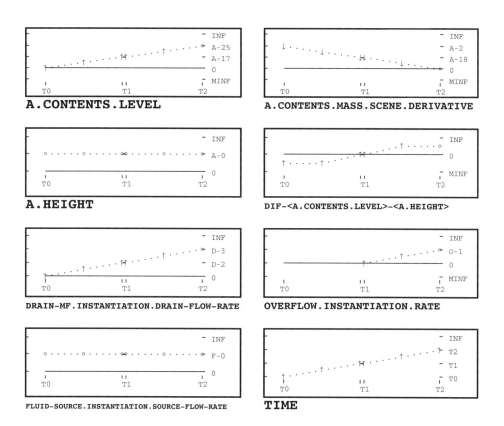

Figure 14.3
QPC behavior plot for overflow behavior.

14.7.1   Thermodynamics

Collins and Forbus (1989) have constructed a large-scale knowledge base of engineering knowledge about thermodynamics. The following description is extracted from their unpublished manuscript.

**Building Qualitative Models
of Thermodynamic Processes.**
J. W. Collins & K. D. Forbus

Engineering thermodynamics is concerned with the understanding of systems such as power plants, engines, refrigerators, and other energy conversion devices. Our goal is to provide the qualitative and ontological framework for the sorts of analyses found in a first year engineering thermodynamics course. Roughly, this means analyzing systems made of abstract fluid components, rather than detailed analyses of the properties of specific components. Thus we restrict ourselves to circumstances where we can ignore details of geometry. This restriction is implicit in many engineering thermodynamics textbooks. However, it does rule out some phenomena which engineers learn in their schooling. For instance, the FSThermo model is not concerned with how fluid properties change through nozzles or across blades in turbines. It does not capture the effects of scaling on heat transfer across surfaces. It also ignores the detailed dynamics of fluids. In particular, it ignores any inertial effects of fluid flow, the distinction between turbulent and laminar flow, and any effects of water hammer.

The FSThermo model captures a variety of physical processes, including fluid flows (liquid or gas, forced or free), heat flows, and phase transitions between the liquid and gaseous phases. Our model includes six basic kinds of concrete objects: physobs, containers, contained stuffs, paths, pumps, and compressors. This domain model can be used to build models of a variety of specific scenarios, including simplified versions of a refrigerator, a steam plant, and a thermal control system.

14.7.2   Botany

Porter, *et al.* (1988) have constructed a large, multi-function knowledge base about botany, organized around the many aspects of teaching scientific knowledge, especially explanation and tutoring. As discussed previously, Rickel and Porter (1992) have built a QPC knowledge base of model fragments describing the phenomena involved in water regulation in the plant at multiple time-scales. The following description was provided by Jeff Rickel.

Our group at the University of Texas is building a tutoring system for college-level botany. We are particularly interested in supporting "what if" questions, in which the student poses a hypothetical scenario (e.g., soil moisture decreasing) and asks for the effect on particular plant properties (e.g., growth rate). Our approach to such questions is to automatically construct a simplified model of the scenario appropriate for the question, use QPC to simulate this model under the scenario conditions, and use the model and simulation results to explain what happens and why.

Qualitative simulation is appropriate for this task for several reasons. First, the textbook knowledge encoded in our Botany Knowledge Base is largely qualitative. Botany textbooks present mostly qualitative relations among plant processes and properties because quantitative details vary greatly among different plants and because these quantitative details often are not known. Second, student questions are unlikely to provide the quantitative details needed to support a numeric simulation. Finally, college-level botany focuses primarily on the qualitative mechanisms of the plant, so quantitative details are unnecessary.

The domain theory pales in comparison to the scope of knowledge in our actual Botany Knowledge Base (BKB) (Porter *et al.*, 1988), but it is representative of the relevant knowledge in the BKB concerning these important plant mechanisms. The domain theory covers the uptake, transport, and loss of water in the plant; the plant's mechanisms for dealing with water stress (synthesis, consumption and transport of the ABA hormone, and movement of potassium ions and water into and out of guard cells that regulate water loss); and the production (via photosynthesis), consumption (via respiration), and transport (via the phloem) of carbohydrates in the plant. The descriptions of these processes are relatively simple, but they are fairly standard and reasonable high-level descriptions, and they are based both on textbook knowledge and consultations with domain experts. In addition to views containing influences, a number of the views provide reasonable range constraints on variables to prevent impossible or unlikely behaviors from being considered.

The simplest example is `gc-osmosis`, which addresses the question "Why do the stomates open when the level of potassium ions increases in the guard cells?" The relevant influences for this question are contained in `acc-gc-osmosis`. The aperture of the stomates is a function of the amount of water in the guard cells; a stomate is the opening between a pair of guard cells, and these cells become banana-shaped (thus enlarging the stomate) when they take up water. The water in the guard cells is influenced by the process of osmosis, which transfers water between the guard cells and adjacent accessory cells. The rate of this osmosis process is influenced by the amount of solutes in the guard cells, and potassium ions are the primary solute used by the plant to regulate osmosis. If osmosis is in equilibrium (i.e., no transport) and the level of potassium ions is increased to a new equilibrium value, water begins to osmotically enter the guard cells, and this increase in water there enlarges the stomates. When the increase in potassium levels off, the increasing pressure in the guard cells due to the increase in water eventually balances the influence of the increased potassium level, so osmosis stops and the system settles into a new equilibrium state.

14.7.3   Chemical Engineering

Catino (1993) constructed a large QPC domain theory within chemical engineering for the purpose of doing hazard and operability (HAZOP) studies of moderate-sized chemical process plants. The abstract of her doctoral dissertation, written under the supervision of Prof. Lyle Ungar, is quoted below.

**Automated Modeling of Chemical Plants
with Application to Hazard and Operability Studies**
Catherine A. Catino, Ph.D.
Department of Chemical Engineering
University of Pennsylvania

When quantitative knowledge is incomplete or unavailable (e.g. during design), qualitative models can be used to describe the behavior of chemical plants. Qualitative models were developed for several different process units with controllers and recycle, including a nitric acid plant reactor unit, and simulated using QSIM. In general, such systems produce an infinite number of qualitative states. Two new modeling assumptions were introduced, perfect controllers which respond ideally to a disturbance and ignore dynamics in controller variables, and pseudo steady state which ignores transients in all variables. Redundant constraints, reformulated equations, and quantitative information were also used to reduce ambiguity.

A library of general physical and chemical phenomena such as reaction and heat flow was developed in the Qualitative Process Compiler (QPC) representation and used to automatically build qualitative models of chemical plants. The phenomenon definitions in the library specify the conditions required for the phenomena to occur and the equations they contribute to the model. Given a physical description of the equipment and components present, their connectivity and operating conditions, the automatic model builder identifies the phenomena whose preconditions are satisfied and builds a mathematical model consisting of the equations contributed by these active phenomena. Focusing techniques were used to ignore irrelevant aspects of behavior. A dynamic condenser model was automatically generated illustrating QPC's ability to create a new model when a new phase exists.

Based on the ability to automatically build and simulate qualitative process models, a prototype hazard identification system, Qualitative Hazard Identifier (QHI), was developed which works by exhaustively positing possible faults, simulating them, and checking for hazards. A library of general faults such as leaks, broken filters, blocked pipes, and controller failures is matched against the physical description of the plant to determine all specific instances of faults that can occur in the plant. Faults may perturb variables in the original design model, or may require building a new model. Hazards including over-pressure, over-temperature, controller saturation, and explosion were identified in the reactor section of a nitric acid plant using QHI.

14.8   The Future

It seems clear that an enormously important area for research, development, and application of artificial intelligence methods is the creation and refinement of high-quality knowledge bases of model fragments for specific domains in science and engineering. Such knowledge bases will support model creation for computer-aided design, optimization of parameters, hazard and operability studies, system monitoring, fault detection and localization, automated explanation, and tutoring. The models that are created can be used for traditional numerical simulation, or in a deductive framework with explicit assumptions as in figure 13.1.

The value of such a knowledge base to society comes from reifying a body of knowledge as a shared asset, to be evaluated, refined, and extended as part of the collective knowledge of the culture.[11]

---

[11] For an important note of caution about the effect on individuals of reifying and externalizing a significant amount of society's technical knowledge, read Kurt Vonnegut's (1952) book *Player Piano*.

14.9   Problems

1. Translate the influence diagram in figure 14.1 into a set of direct and indirect influences. What knowledge did you apply? Assume that the resulting set of influences is closed, and translate it to a set of QSIM constraints. Add the simplest possible quantity spaces to define a QDE. Show that you can use QSIM to simulate this model to answer "what if" questions about given initial conditions.

2. Write a Lisp program to take a set of influences and return the corresponding set of constraints. Don't forget `constant` constraints for uninfluenced variables.

3. Use the fluid-flow domain theory in section 14.5 to create a model of the U-tube: two tanks connected at the bottom, permitting bidirectional flow. Generalize your solution to allow definition of general compartmental systems (cf. Jacquez, 1985, *Compartmental Analysis*).

4. Extend the domain theory in section 14.5 to include contained gases, evaporation, and condensation processes. These will depend (at least) on the shared surface area between the gas and the liquid in a container, and the vapor concentration of the gas. Then build the following models.

   • Evaporation to empty from a container open to the atmosphere.

   • Evaporation, perhaps to equilibrium, of an open container of water in a closed space.

   • Fill a tank with open drain to steady state liquid level, followed by evaporation to steady state humidity in a closed space.

5. Build a QPC domain theory for objects with mass, position, velocity, acceleration, and subject to forces such as gravity, springs, and air resistance. Demonstrate that you can build models of

   • an oscillating spring with and without friction;

   • a projectile under constant gravity, and under gravity decreasing with distance;

   • a falling object that may reach terminal velocity before reaching the ground.

6. (Research Problem.) Consider the classification of modeling assumption types in section 14.4.1. To what extent can the different types be considered independent dimensions? Examine a large number of different models and their assumptions, and

develop a theory of the constraints among choices within the different assumption types.

7. (Research Problem.) Augment the QPC domain theory in section 14.5 with order-of-magnitude information about bulk fluid flow, evaporation, and condensation. Implement a reasoner capable of identifying the dominant influences in a scenario. Demonstrate your reasoner's ability to construct appropriate models of

- evaporation as an *insignificant* influence on a bathtub being filled;
- evaporation as a *significant* influence on the level of a lake.

8. (Research Problem.) Extend the compositional modeling approach in the manner of SIMGEN (Forbus and Falkenhainer, 1990a; Forbus and Falkenhainer, 1990b; Amador *et al.*, 1993) to build numerical simulation models annotated with qualitative models to support explanation. Can partial numerical constraints be represented in individual model fragments, composable to complete numerical constraints when the model is built? Or should complete qualitative constraints be mapped to corresponding complete numerical constraints from a library after the model is built? Can we preserve the deductive structure of figure 13.1 by treating each transformation from a qualitative constraint to a numerical constraint as an explicit assumption?

A Glossary

attainable envisionment. The subset of states in the total envisionment reachable from a given initial state (or set of states).

behavior tree. The tree of qualitative states defined by the state completion, successor, and transition relations. Each path from root to leaf in this tree is a qualitative behavior.

comparative statics. The class of problems in which we attempt to find the relationship between an initial stable equilibrium state and the possible stable equilibrium state or states resulting from a small perturbation to the system.

corresponding value tuple. A tuple of qualitative values, one for each variable in a QSIM constraint, representing a consistent set of values for that constraint.

landmark. A qualitatively distinctive value in the range of a variable. A symbolic description of a particular number, whose numerical value may be unknown. The three predefined landmarks are `minf`, `0`, and `inf`.

limit analysis. The act of determining which among a set of changing variables will reach the landmarks they move toward.

operating region. The domain within which the current QDE is valid. Usually characterized by bounding landmark values in the quantity spaces of some variables in the QDE. A region transition is invoked if the value of a variable is equal to a bounding landmark and moving out of the current operating region.

parameter. Exogenously determined variable. Usually a constant in QSIM QDEs. (Formerly, and incorrectly, used to mean "variable.")

QDE. Qualitative differential equation. A qualitative abstraction of an ordinary differential equation (ODE).

qdir. Qualitative direction of change. The sign of the derivative of a variable at given qualitative state.

qmag. Qualitative magnitude. A description of the magnitude of a variable in terms of the landmarks in a quantity space. A value is described as either equal to a landmark value, or in an interval defined by two landmarks, usually the open interval defined by two adjacent landmarks.

qplot. The output format representing the qualitative behavior of a variable in a graph with the quantity space for the variable on the vertical axis, the quantity space for time on the horizontal axis, and representing the value of the variable at each qualitative state by a symbol for the qdir either at or between adjacent landmarks.

QSIM constraint. A qualitative abstraction of an algebraic, differential, or functional relation among reasonable functions. Determines which tuples of qualitative values for its variables are consistent.

Q2. The semi-quantitative reasoner that takes a behavior predicted by QSIM with interval bounds on landmark values, and derives tighter bounds on landmark values, or a contradiction refuting the behavior.

qualitative behavior. An alternating sequence of qualitative time-point and time-interval states describing the behavior of a reasonable function or set of reasonable functions. Often this set corresponds to a possible solution to a QDE model.

qualitative state. A description of the qualitative values of the variables in a QDE at a time-point or over a time-interval when that description remains constant. A *basic* qualitative state describes the values only with respect to the originally given landmark values.

qualitative value. A qualitative description of the value of a variable at a qualitative time-point or time-interval state. Consists of a qmag and a qdir.

quantity space. An ordered set of landmark values, defining the possible qualitative descriptions of the magnitude of a variable.

quasi-equilibrium assumption. The assumption that a system is always at, or very near, a point of stable equilibrium.

qval. Qualitative value.

reasonable function. A continuously differentiable function amenable to qualitative reasoning. It has only finitely many critical points over its domain, and its derivative approaches limits at the endpoints of the domain.

region transition. The point in a behavior when simulation stops because some variable has crossed the boundary of the operating region of the current QDE. The behavior either ends at that point or resumes after a discontinuous change, in the same or a different QDE.

sign-valued operators. Mappings from the extended real number line $\Re^* = [-\infty, +\infty]$ to the extended domain of signs $\mathcal{S}' = \{+, 0, -, ?\}$.

- $[x]_0 = sign(x) = \begin{cases} [+] & \text{if } x > 0 \\ [0] & \text{if } x = 0 \\ [-] & \text{if } x < 0. \end{cases}$

  $[x]$ as an abbreviation for $[x]_0$ is acceptable where no ambiguity is possible.

- $[x]_a = sign(x - a)$, where a serves as a reference value for the variable x.

- $[\dot{x}] = [dx/dt] = sign(dx/dt)$.

- $[x]_\infty = \begin{cases} [+] & \text{if } x = +\infty \\ [0] & \text{if } x \text{ is finite} \\ [-] & \text{if } x = -\infty. \end{cases}$

- $[x]_{(a,b)} = \begin{cases} + & \text{if } x \geq b \\ ? & \text{if } a < x < b \\ - & \text{if } x \leq a \end{cases}$

  when an interval (a, b) serves as the reference value.

total envisionment. The set of all possible states of a given QDE, and all possible transitions among them.

variable. A real-valued function of time.

B QSIM Functions

B.1 Qualitative Simulation

`define-QDE` *name &rest body*   [macro]

This macro creates a QDE with name *name* from user specifications provided as clauses in the *body* of the macro. The basic clauses are the following:

clause	documentation
quantity-spaces	Alist of variables and totally ordered lists of landmarks for that variable.
constraints	List of QSIM constraints and corresponding values.
transitions	List of transition rules.
independent	List of exogenous variables.

Additional clauses support extensions to QSIM or provide an alternative to `make-sim` for specifying style of simulation.

clause	documentation
unreachable-values	List of (*var val1 val2 ...*) lists, specifying prohibited qualitative transitions.
derive-M-constraint-for	List of dependent variables for which abstracted monotonic function constraints should be derived.
abstracted-from	List of entries (*constraint* <- *QDE*) specifying source of abstraction for a constraint.
text	Documentation string.
layout	List of lists of variables, specifying plot layout.

`make-new-state` *&key :from-qde :from-state :sim :assert-values :inherit :perturb :completions :assert-ranges :text*   [function]

This function creates a new state from user specifications for use as an initial or reference state for qualitative simulation. The state can be specified either in terms of a QDE, provided in the *from-qde* argument, or in terms of a reference state, provided in the *from-state* argument. It is an error to provide both. The QDE or reference state provides the initial quantity spaces and corresponding values for the new state. The *sim* argument allows the user to specify a sim, to control creation of this state and subsequent simulation from it. If *sim* is not provided, a new sim with default values is created and used.

The *assert-values* argument is an alist of variables and descriptions of qualitative values (qmags and qdirs). In case the new state is defined in terms of a reference state, *inherit* may provide a list of variables whose values are inherited, and *perturb* may provide an alist of variables and signs of small perturbations from the reference state that define initial values. The value of *completions* (default = T) determines whether an incomplete new state is completed or returned as is.

The *assert-ranges* argument specifies initial quantitative range values to be associated with certain landmark values. The value of *assert-ranges* is a list of list structures of the form ((*var lmark*) (*lb ub*)), where (*var lmark*) specifies a landmark, and (*lb ub*) specifies a range with endpoints in $\Re^*$. The value of *text* is a documentation string.

create-transition-state   *&key :from-state :to-qde :assert :inherit-qmag* *:inherit-qdir*   [function]

This function creates and links a new state in a new operating region specified by *to-qde*, following a region transition from the previous state *from-state*. Information about the new state is provided in *assert*, which specifies an alist of variables and qualitative value descriptions, and *inherit-qmags* and *inherit-qdirs*, which specify lists of variables for the indicated kind of inheritance. Both inheritance arguments can take the keyword value **:rest**, meaning all variables not otherwise specified.

make-sim   *&key* ... many ...   [function]

This function creates and returns a *sim*, which is the structure that encapsulates the control switches and parameters for qualitative simulation, as well as certain internal data structures such as agendas that allow a halted simulation to be resumed. Normally, a new sim with default values is created by **make-new-state**, and is accessed and used by **QSIM** when the qualitative simulator is called. The default values can be overridden by creating a sim explicitly with **make-sim** and passing it to **make-new-state** via its *sim* argument.

`make-sim` takes many different keyword arguments. Some of the most useful follow:

switch	purpose
:state-limit	Halt simulation after creating this number of states (default = 20).
:time-limit	Halt simulation after this time-point.
:ignore-qdirs	Ignore qdirs on variables in this list.
:no-new-landmarks	Create no landmarks for these variables.
:unreachable-values	alist of (var lm1 lm2 ...) specifying landmarks not allowed to be successor values.
:phase-planes	set of (v1 v2) pairs specifying phase planes for analysis by the non-intersection constraint
:cycle-detection	How to match states to check for cycles: :strong (the default), :weak, or nil.
:analytic-functions-only	Allow only analytic behaviors.
:HOD-constraints	Derive and apply second-order derivative constraints.
:SD3-constraints	Derive and apply third-order derivative constraints.
:Q2-constraints	Apply the Q2 semi-quantitative reasoning algorithm.
:KET-constraint	Derive and apply energy constraints.
:NIC-constraint	Apply non-intersection analysis to specified phase planes.
:cross-edge-envisionment	Envision by matching states across behaviors.
:nsim-constraints	Derive and apply numerical dynamic envelopes to bound behaviors.

QSIM   *state*   [function]

This function runs the QSIM qualitative simulator from *state* as initial state, with respect to the QDE in (state-qde *state*), controlled by the switch and parameter values in (state-sim *state*). The result is a behavior tree linked by *completion*, *successor*, and *transition* relations among states, rooted in *state*, which is the value returned.

QSIM-display   *state &key :reference-states*   [function]

This function displays the QSIM behavior tree rooted at *state* on a graphics terminal, providing the user with commands for navigating through the tree and selecting among modes of display. The value of *reference-states* is an alist of lists (*symbol refstate*), which causes each variable plot to include the value of that variable in *refstate*, labeled with *symbol*, plotted to the left of the dynamic behavior prediction.

B.2   Comparative Statics

QSEA   *&key :from-qde :initial-values :from-state :perturb :text*   [function]

This function returns a list of two states, (R S), representing the initial and final states of a comparative statics problem. Both R and S must be stable quiescent states, and S must be a small perturbation from R. If the problem has multiple solutions, the state S will be incomplete and its completions are the solutions.

A comparative statics problem is defined by a reference state and a perturbation. The reference state R is either provided explicitly as the value of the *from-state* argument, or is created from the *from-qde* and *initial-values* arguments. It is an error to call QSEA with both sets of arguments. The argument *perturb* is an alist of (*variable sign*) pairs. All other exogenous variables in S inherit their values from R.

QSEA-table   *state &key :reference*   [function]

This function displays a table of signs, representing the solution to a comparative statics problem. The reference state is the value of the *reference* argument, and the solution is the value of *state*. The table has one row for each variable x in *state* and one column for *state* or each of its completions. Each entry gives the sign $[x]_*$ of the qualitative value of x in *state* (or one of its completions) with respect to the reference value in *reference*.

B.2.1   Time-Scale Abstraction

tsa2   *&key :fast :slow :normal :perturb*   [function]

This function simulates the response of a two-level time-scale hierarchy to a perturbation, following the sequence described in figure 12.1. The arguments *fast* and *slow* specify QDEs for the two time-scales. *Normal* is an alist of variables and qualitative values specifying an equilibrium state shared by both QDEs. *Perturb* is an alist of (*variable sign*) pairs, and is used to specify the initial state for simulation. `tsa2` calls `qsim` to do the simulation, and `qsim-display` after each step. No useful value is returned.

B.3   Component-Connection Modeling

`define-component`   *name domain documentation clause**   [macro]

This macro defines a component for CC. The meaning of the clauses is described in section 13.3.1. The clause syntax is the following.

components A list of clauses specifying the embedded subcomponents of this component. Each clause has the following form:

(*component component-type*)

connections Each clause specifies any number of terminals of embedded subcomponents, with an optional name for the connection.

([*connection-name*] [(*component terminal*)]*)

terminal-variables A list of clauses of the following form:

(*terminal* [(*variable variable-type* [*quantity-space*])]*)

The only useful variable-types in a terminal are instances of the generic types `effort` and `flow`. The quantity space specification is optional.

component-variables A list of clauses of the following form:

([(*variable variable-type* [*quantity-space*])]*)

mode-variables A list of clauses of the following form:

(*variable* [*value*]*)

constraints A list of QSIM constraints, including corresponding values.

equivalence A list of clauses specifying an equivalence between a terminal of the component being defined and a terminal of one of the embedded subcomponents. Each clause has the following form:

(= *terminal* (*component terminal*))

build-QDE   *component*   [function]

Takes the name of a single component, which must have no terminals, and builds a QSIM QDE for the mechanism described.

CC-name   *qde &key :name :list :alist*   [function]

The CC-name format is a list of names for nested components, followed by a variable name defined in the innermost component. This can be translated to the corresponding QSIM name referring to a variable defined in the QDE produced by **build-QDE**. **CC-name** takes the QDE and a value for exactly one keyword argument, specifying the format for a data structure including one or more CC-names. It returns the same data structure with the corresponding QSIM variable names.

make-CC-state   *...same as* **make-new-state** *...*   [function]

Translates CC-names to QSIM variables and calls **make-new-state** with the same arguments.

CC-display   *...same as* **qsim-display** *...*   [function]

Translates CC-names to QSIM variables and calls **qsim-display** with the same arguments.

C Creating and Debugging a QSIM Model

C.1 Creating the Model

The creation of useful QSIM models is still something of an art. The best way to create a good model in the first place is to start with one of the examples in this book (or one supplied with the QSIM program) that resembles your problem, then copy and edit to get your desired model.

C.2 Checking the Model

C.2.1 Every Variable Must Be Constrained

If the value or direction of change of some variable is unconstrained, QSIM will guarantee that it is modeled as a *continuous* function, but the behavior tree will branch on all possible changes of direction at all possible places. This kind of intractable branching is called "chatter."

Most frequently, chatter arises because a `constant` constraint has been omitted from the `define-QDE`. Chatter can also arise if the direction of change of a variable X is constrained only by the constraint X = Y - Z, and both Y and Z are increasing. The ambiguity of qualitative addition means that X will branch on all possible directions of change. Two solutions to this problem are presented in chapter 10, one based on higher-order derivatives, the other on changing the level of description.

C.2.2 Constraints Must Be Meaningful

Each constraint must represent a meaningful relationship between its variables. This may seem obvious, but when one is debugging a model there is a strong temptation to insert an M^+ constraint just to make a problem disappear. Unless the constraint represents a genuine relationship between its variables, it will cause more problems later by preventing real behaviors from being predicted, a difficult bug to detect and fix.

C.2.3 Summarizing Constraints

A model can be summarized by collapsing adjacent constraints to eliminate variables and constraints, until the model reaches its simplest form, using algebraic rules such as these:

$$z = M^+(y), y = M^-(x) \quad \Rightarrow \quad z = M^-(x)$$

$$z = x + y, constant(y) \quad \Rightarrow \quad z = M^+(x)$$
$$z = y - w, y = M^-(x), w = M^+(x) \quad \Rightarrow \quad z = M^-(x)$$

A more complete set is given in Kuipers, 1984, Appendix D.

A model intended to be a one-tank equilibrium system should summarize to a model with two variables *level* and *rate* and the constraints

$$d(level)/dt \quad = \quad rate$$
$$rate \quad = \quad M^-(level).$$

See, for example, the water balance model (figure 6.11) and the sodium balance model (figure 6.14).

It is good practice to build and debug the simplest (i.e., fewest constraints; most abstract) model first, then incrementally refine it by expanding constraints to make explicit intermediate variables, parameters, and constraints.

C.3   Debugging the Initial State

The QSIM function `make-new-state` constructs one or more new states consistent with (a) the quantity spaces, constraints, and corresponding values obtained from a QDE or from a previously created state, and (b) variable values that are either asserted explicitly, or inherited or perturbed from a previous state.

The usual intent is for `make-new-state` to return a single complete qualitative state description. However, when the initial-state information is incomplete, QSIM will branch on all possible complete initial states consistent with the given information.

A trace option is available[1] to display the stages of this process: initial assertions, the result of local propagation, and all solutions to the constraint satisfaction algorithm. The meaning of these stages is explained in chapter 4.

C.3.1   No Initial State

The original set of values is inconsistent. The state completion trace will identify which constraint filtered out all possible values.

---

[1] Set `*show-completion-steps*` to `t` for a tabular presentation of state completion.

C.3.2   Too Many Initial States

Many states are consistent with the initial information. Analyze the state completion trace to determine whether all completions are valid, or whether important constraints, such as corresponding values, have been omitted.

C.4   Debugging the Behavior Tree

C.4.1   No Behaviors

It is possible for an apparently consistent sequence of states to be created before a constraint is violated and the behavior is determined to be inconsistent. Such a behavior is normally pruned by deleting its states from the behavior tree. If *all* behaviors turn out to be inconsistent, the tree is pruned back to the root, which is labeled inconsistent.

To debug such a situation, retain the inconsistent states in the behavior tree[2] so they can be examined explicitly to determine why they were filtered out. The final state of an inconsistent behavior is labeled with an explanation of how it was found to be inconsistent.

C.4.2   Too Many Behaviors

The most common manifestation of a modeling problem is an intractably branching tree of predicted behaviors, because QSIM cannot exclude enough behaviors at any given branch point.

The first step in debugging this problem is to understand the distinctions among the branches of the tree, to focus on the behaviors that should have been filtered out by QSIM. Some of the variables in the model will show essentially the same behavior on every branch; others show the differences in behavior that required the branch to be created. The QSIM interface provides an option for viewing all behaviors of a single variable. The nature of the undesired branch suggests what modification to the model is likely to eliminate it.

C.4.3   Chatter: All Possible Behaviors of a Variable

If one or more variables branch on all possible behaviors, while all others have little or no qualitative change in value, then those variables are likely to be essentially unconstrained, except by continuity.

---

[2]Set `*show-inconsistent-successors*` to `t` to make inconsistent states and behaviors visible.

The most common explanation is that some constraint (frequently `constant`) was omitted from the model. If the model is second-order or higher, it may be that the higher-order derivative methods of chapter 10 will be required.

C.4.4   A Variable Moves Outside Its Meaningful Range

A given model is only meaningful within certain limits, called the *operating region* of the model. For example, the amount of water in a tank cannot be negative, or greater than the capacity of the tank. These limits are expressed in two ways.

First, the endpoints of a quantity space are implicit operating region limits. Values outside those endpoints are not only *unreachable*, they are *inexpressible* within the model. Thus, if the quantity space for the variable `amount` is (`0 full inf`), then a qualitative value such as $amount(t_n) = \langle 0, dec \rangle$ has no successor and the behavior simply terminates. There are always implicit limits at $\pm\infty$. However, in most cases where a behavior terminates because some variable reaches an infinite value, a finite region transition was omitted from the model (e.g., the rope breaks).

Second, a qualitative value may be specified as representing a boundary of the current operating region. We can specify a boundary without a transition to a new operating region by including a form like

```
((level (top inc)) -> t)
```

in the `transitions` clause of the `define-QDE`, which terminates simulation in the current region when $level(t_n) = \langle top, inc \rangle$. Specifying a transition function, such as

```
((level (top inc)) -> tub-overflows)
```

in figure 6.3, terminates simulation in the current region and calls a function named `tub-overflows` to make the transition to a new region. Region transitions are discussed in detail in chapter 8.

C.4.5   A Variable Reaches an Unreachable Landmark

A variable might reach a landmark that should not actually be reached. For example, simulation of a model of blood pressure might yield behaviors where $BP(t) = 0$ or $BP(t) = \infty$. There are several approaches to this problem.

• The quantity space for BP may be augmented to include landmarks representing the actual limits of the operating region, perhaps with transitions to other models predicting the effects of disastrously high or low blood pressure.

- Additional constraints may be added to the model that have the effect of preventing the limits from being reached. For example, the constraint $heat = temp * mass$ will prevent $heat$ from reaching ∞ if $temp$ is constant and $mass$ is bounded.

- It is also possible to assert that a landmark in the quantity space is unreachable, by adding an `unreachable-values` clause to the `define-QDE`:

```
(unreachable-values (BP 0 inf) ...  )
```

Unreachable-value assertions must be used with caution. If the only behaviors of a model reach the specified landmark, even in the limit at $t = \infty$, the behavior tree will be mysteriously pruned back to its root. They should be regarded as a user-specified focus of attention that excludes certain possible behaviors. (See also figures 6.9, 6.12, and 6.15.)

C.4.6   Reaching Limits in Multiple Orders

Multiple behaviors may be distinguished by the order in which variables reach landmarks they are approaching. The validity of the alternate branches must be determined by carefully examining the combinations of values to see if they are reasonable. A problem may be correctable by a single new corresponding value tuple, by a chain of corresponding values through a sequence of adjacent constraints, or even by adding new constraints to hold the required corresponding values. (But recall the importance of constraints being *meaningful*.)

During simulation of the bathtub model (figure 6.3) we might consider two events, one being the point at which $amount(t)$ reaches $full$, and the other being the point at which $level(t)$ reaches top. The corresponding value pair (`full top`) associated with the constraint (`M+ amount level`) requires these two events to occur at the same time-point. Without the corresponding values, we would get another three-way branch according to the ordering of those events.

In a complex model, the ordering on genuinely unrelated events can cause substantial amounts of unnecessary branching, called *occurrence branching*. This issue has been addressed by Williams (1986); Fouché (1992); Clancy and Kuipers (1992); and Clancy and Kuipers (1993).

References

Abelson, H.; Eisenberg, M.; Halfant, M.; Katzenelson, J.; Sacks, E.; Sussman, G. J.; Wisdom, J.;, and Yip, K. 1989. Intelligence in scientific computing. *Communications of the ACM* 32:546–562.

Abelson, H., and Sussman, G. J. 1985. *Structure and Interpretation of Computer Programs*. MIT Press/McGraw-Hill, Cambridge, MA.

Addanki, S.; Cremonini, R.;, and Penberthy, J. S. 1989. Reasoning about assumptions in graphs of models. In *Proc. 11th Int. Joint Conf. on Artificial Intelligence*, San Mateo, CA. Morgan Kaufmann. 1432–1438.

Addanki, S.; Cremonini, R.;, and Penberthy, J. S. 1991. Graphs of models. *Artificial Intelligence* 51:145–177.

Alefeld, G., and Herzberger, J. 1983. *Introduction to Interval Computation*. Academic Press, NY.

Allen, J. F. 1984. Towards a general theory of action and time. *Artificial Intelligence* 23:123–154.

Amador, F., and Weld, D. 1990. Multi-level reasoning about populations. In *Proc. 4th Int. Workshop on Qualitative Physics*, Lugano, Switzerland.

Amador, P.; Finkelstein, A.;, and Weld, D. 1993. Real-time self-explanatory simulation. In *Proceedings of the Eleventh National Conference on Artificial Intelligence*, Cambridge, MA. AAAI/MIT Press.

Amsterdam, J. 1993. Estimating order from causal ordering. In *Proc. 7th Int. Workshop on Qualitative Reasoning About Physical Systems*, Orcas Island, WA.

Arnold, V. I. 1973. *Ordinary Differential Equations*. MIT Press, Cambridge, MA.

Bailey, A. D. Jr.; Kiang, M. Y.; Kuipers, B.;, and Whinston, A. B. 1991. Analytical procedures: Qualitative and causal reasoning in auditing. In Blocher, E., editor 1991, *Applications in Management Science, Volume 6, Accounting Applications in Management Science*. JAI Press, Greenwich, CT. 7–57.

Baker, A. B. 1991. Nonmonotonic reasoning in the framework of situation calculus. *Artificial Intelligence* 49:5–23.

Berleant, D. 1990. Probabilities of qualitative behaviors from probability distributions on inputs. Technical Report TR AI90-136, Artificial Intelligence Laboratory, Department of Computer Sciences, University of Texas at Austin.

Berleant, D., and Kuipers, B. 1991. Bridging the gap from qualitative to numerical simulation. Technical Report AI91-158, Artificial Intelligence Laboratory, Department of Computer Sciences, University of Texas at Austin.

Berleant, D., and Kuipers, B. 1992. Combined qualitative and numerical simulation with Q3. In Faltings, B., and Struss, P., editors 1992, *Recent Advances in Qualitative Physics*. MIT Press, Cambridge, MA.

Bhaskar, R., and Nigam, A. 1990. Qualitative physics using dimensional analysis. *Artificial Intelligence* 45:73–111.

Biswas, G., and Yu, X. 1993. A formal modeling scheme for continuous systems: focus on diagnosis. In *Proc. 13th Int. Joint Conf. on Artificial Intelligence*, San Mateo, CA. Morgan Kaufmann. 1474–1479.

Biswas, G.; Manganaris, S.;, and Yu, X. 1993. Extending component connection modeling for analyzing complex physical systems. *IEEE Expert* 8(1):48–57.

Bledsoe, W. W.; Kunen, K.;, and Shostak, R. 1985. Completeness results for inequality provers. *Artificial Intelligence* 27:255–288.

Bobrow, D. G. 1985. *Qualitative Reasoning about Physical Systems*. Bradford Books/MIT Press, Cambridge, MA.

Borchardt, G. 1992. Understanding causal descriptions of physical systems. In *Proceedings of the Tenth National Conference on Artificial Intelligence*, Cambridge, MA. AAAI/MIT Press.

Bousson, K., and Travé-Massuyès, L. 1993. Fuzzy causal simulation in process engineering. In *Proceedings of the Thirteenth International Joint Conference on Artificial Intelligence*, San Mateo, CA. Morgan Kaufmann.

Boyce, W. E., and DiPrima, R. C. 1969. *Elementary Differential Equations*. John Wiley, New York, second edition.

Brooks, R. A. 1981. Symbolic reasoning among 3-d models and 2-d images. *Artificial Intelligence* 17:285–348.

Brown, J. S.; Burton, R.;, and de Kleer, J. 1982. Pedagogical, natural language, and knowledge engineering issues in SOPHIE I, II, and III. In Sleeman, D., and Brown, J. S., editors 1982, *Intelligent Tutoring Systems*. Academic Press, New York. 227–282.

Buchanan, B. G., and Shortliffe, E. H. 1984. *Rule-Based Expert Systems: The MYCIN Experiments*. Addison-Wesley, Reading, MA.

Bylander, T. 1991. The qualitative difference resolution rule. In *Proceedings of the Ninth National Conference on Artificial Intelligence*, Cambridge, MA. AAAI/MIT Press. 824–829.

Catino, C. A. 1993. *Automated Modeling of Chemical Plants with Application to Hazard and Operability Studies*. Ph.D. Dissertation, Department of Chemical Engineering, University of Pennsylvania, Philadelphia, PA.

Cheung, J. T.-Y., and Stephanopoulos, G. 1990. Representation of process trends – part I. a formal representation framework. *Computers and Chemical Engineering* 14(4/5):495–510.

Chin, R. C. Y.; Hedstrom, G. W.;, and Howes, F. A. 1985. Considerations on solving problems with multiple scales. In Brackbill, J. U., and Cohen, B. I., editors 1985, *Multiple Time Scales*. Academic Press, New York.

Clancy, D. J., and Kuipers, B. J. 1992. Aggregating behaviors and tractable simulation. In *AAAI Design from Physical Principles Fall Symposium Working Notes*, Cambridge, MA. 38–43.

Clancy, D. J., and Kuipers, B. 1993. Behavioral abstraction for tractable simulation. In *Proc. 7th Int. Workshop on Qualitative Reasoning About Physical Systems*, Orcas Island, WA. 57–64.

Clement, J. 1983. A conceptual model discussed by Galileo and used intuitively by physics students. In Gentner, D., and Stevens, A., editors 1983, *Mental Models*. Erlbaum, Hillsdale, NJ. 325–340.

Coiera, E. W. 1992. Qualitative superposition. *Artificial Intelligence* 56(2–3):171–196.

Collins, J. 1989. Building qualitative models of thermodynamic processes. In *Proc. 3rd Int. Workshop on Qualitative Physics*, Stanford, CA.

Collins, J., and Forbus, K. D. 1987. Reasoning about fluids via molecular collections. In *Proc. 6th National Conf. on Artificial Intelligence*, San Mateo, CA. Morgan Kaufmann.

Collins, J. W., and Forbus, K. D. 1989. Building qualitative models of thermodynamic processes. Unpublished manuscript, Qualitative Reasoning Group, Beckman Institute, University of Illinois, Urbana, IL.

Crawford, J. M., and Etherington, D. 1992. Formalizing reasoning about change: A qualitative reasoning approach (preliminary report). In *Proc. 10th National Conf. on Artificial Intelligence*, Cambridge, MA. AAAI/MIT Press.

Crawford, J.; Farquhar, A.;, and Kuipers, B. 1990. QPC: A compiler from physical models into qualitative differential equations. In *Proc. 8th National Conf. on Artificial Intelligence*, San Mateo, CA. Morgan Kaufmann.

Crawford, J. M., and Kuipers, B. J. 1989. Toward a theory of access-limited logic for knowledge representation. In *Proc. 1st Int. Conf. on Principles of Knowledge Representation and Reasoning*, San Mateo, CA. Morgan Kaufmann.

Crawford, J. M., and Kuipers, B. J. 1991a. Algernon – a tractable system for knowledge representation. *SIGART Bulletin* 2(3):35–44.

Crawford, J. M., and Kuipers, B. J. 1991b. Negation and proof by contradiction in access-limited logic. In *Proc. 9th National Conf. on Artificial Intelligence*, Cambridge, MA. AAAI/MIT Press.

Dague, P. 1993a. Numeric reasoning with relative orders of magnitude. In *Proceedings of the Eleventh National Conference on Artificial Intelligence*, Cambridge, MA. AAAI/MIT Press.

Dague, P. 1993b. Symbolic reasoning with relative orders of magnitude. In *Proceedings of the Thirteenth International Joint Conference on Artificial Intelligence*, San Mateo, CA. Morgan Kaufmann.

Dague, P.; Deves, P.;, and Raiman, O. 1987. Troubleshooting: When modeling is the trouble. In *Proc. 6th National Conf. on Artificial Intelligence*, San Mateo, CA. Morgan Kaufmann. 600–605.

Dalle Molle, D. T. 1989. *Qualitative Simulations of Dynamic Chemical Processes*. Ph.D. Dissertation, Department of Chemical Engineering, University of Texas at Austin, Austin, TX. Available as UT AI Laboratory Technical Report AI89-107.

Dalle Molle, D. T., and Edgar, T. F. 1989. Qualitative modeling of chemical reaction systems. In Mavrovouniotis, M., editor 1989, *Artificial Intelligence Applications in Process Engineering*. Academic Press.

Dalle Molle, D. T.; Kuipers, B. J.;, and Edgar, T. F. 1988. Qualitative modeling and simulation of dynamic systems. *Computers and Chemical Engineering* 12:835–866.

D'Ambrosio, B. 1987. Extending the mathematics in qualitative process theory. In *Proc. 6th National Conf. on Artificial Intelligence*, San Mateo, CA. Morgan Kaufmann. 595–599.

D'Ambrosio, B. 1989. Extending the mathematics in qualitative process theory. In Widman, L. E.; Loparo, K. A.;, and Nielsen, N. R., editors 1989, *Artificial Intelligence, Simulation, and Modeling*. Wiley-Interscience, New York. 133–158.

Davis, R. 1984. Diagnostic reasoning based on structure and behavior. *Artificial Intelligence* 24:347–410.

Davis, E. 1987. Constraint propagation with interval labels. *Artificial Intelligence* 24:347–410.

Davis, E. 1990. *Representations of commonsense knowledge*. Morgan Kaufmann.

Davis, E. 1991. Axiomatizing qualitative process theory. Technical Report 590, NYU. Long version of the KR-92 paper.

Davis, E. 1992. Axiomatizing qualitative process theory. In *Proc. 3rd Int. Conf. on Principles of Knowledge Representation and Reasoning*, San Mateo, CA. Morgan Kaufmann. 177–188.

de Kleer, J. 1977. Multiple representations of knowledge in a mechanics problem-solver. In *Proc. 5th Int. Joint Conf. on Artificial Intelligence*, San Mateo, CA. Morgan Kaufmann. 299–304.

de Kleer, J., and Bobrow, D. G. 1984. Qualitative reasoning with higher-order derivatives. In *Proc. 4th National Conf. on Artificial Intelligence*, San Mateo, CA. Morgan Kaufmann.

de Kleer, J., and Brown, J. S. 1981. Mental models of physical mechanisms and their acquisition. In Anderson, J. R., editor 1981, *Cognitive Skills and Their Acquisition*. Erlbaum, Hillsdale, NJ.

de Kleer, J., and Brown, J. S. 1984. A qualitative physics based on confluences. *Artificial Intelligence* 24:7–83. Also in *Readings in Knowledge Representation*, Brachman and Levesque, editors, Morgan Kaufmann, 1985, pages 88-126.

de Kleer, J., and Brown, J. S. 1986. Theories of causal ordering. *Artificial Intelligence* 29:33–61.

de Kleer, J., and Williams, B. C. 1987. Diagnosing multiple faults. *Artificial Intelligence* 32:97–130.

Dean, T. L., and McDermott, D. V. 1987. Temporal data base management. *Artificial Intelligence* 32:1–55.

Dechter, R. 1992. Constraint networks. In Shapiro, S. C., editor 1992, *Encyclopedia of Artificial Intelligence*. John Wiley, New York, second edition.

DeCoste, D., and Collins, J. 1991. IQE: An incremental qualitative envisioner. In *Proc. 5th Int. Workshop on Qualitative Reasoning about Physical Systems*, Austin, TX.

DeCoste, D. 1991. Dynamic across-time measurement interpretation. *Artificial Intelligence* 51:273–341.

Dordan, O. 1992. Mathematical problems arising in qualitative simulation of a differential equation. *Artificial Intelligence* 55:61–86.

Dormoy, J., and Raiman, O. 1988. Assembling a device. In *Proc. 7th National Conf. on Artificial Intelligence*, San Mateo, CA. Morgan Kaufmann.

Doyle, J., and Sacks, E. 1991. Markov analysis of qualitative dynamics. *Computational Intelligence* 7:1–10.

Druzdzel, M., and Henrion, M. 1993. Efficient reasoning in qualitative probabilistic networks. In *Proceedings of the Eleventh National Conference on Artificial Intelligence*, Cambridge, MA. AAAI/MIT Press.

Dubois, D., and Prade, H. 1980. *Fuzzy Sets and Systems: Theory and Applications*. Academic Press, NY.

Dubois, D., and Prade, H. 1988. An introduction to possibilistic and fuzzy logics. In Smets, e. a., editor 1988, *Non-Standard Logics for Automated Reasoning*. Academic Press. Reprinted in *Readings in Uncertain Reasoning*.

Dvorak, D. 1992. *Monitoring and Diagnosis of Continuous Dynamic Systems Using Semiquantitative Simulation*. Ph.D. Dissertation, Department of Computer Sciences, University of Texas at Austin, Austin, Texas. Available as Technical Report AI92-170.

Dvorak, D., and Kuipers, B. J. 1989. Model-based monitoring of dynamic systems. In *Proc. 11th Int. Joint Conf. on Artificial Intelligence*, San Mateo, CA. Morgan Kaufmann. 1238–1243.

Dvorak, D., and Kuipers, B. 1991. Process monitoring and diagnosis: a model-based approach. *IEEE Expert* 6(3):67–74.

Falkenhainer, B. 1992a. A look at idealization. In *AAAI-92 Workshop on Approximation and Abstraction of Computational Theories*.

Falkenhainer, B. 1992b. Modeling without amnesia: making experience-sanctioned approximations. In *Proc. 6th Int. Workshop on Qualitative Reasoning about Physical Systems*, Edinburgh, Scotland.

Falkenhainer, B., and Forbus, K. D. 1988. Setting up large-scale qualitative models. In *Proc. 7th National Conf. on Artificial Intelligence*, San Mateo, CA. Morgan Kaufmann. 301–306.

Falkenhainer, B., and Forbus, K. D. 1991. Compositional modeling: Finding the right model for the job. *Artificial Intelligence* 51:95–143.

Farquhar, A. 1993. *Automated Modeling of Physical Systems in the Presence of Incomplete Knowledge*. Ph.D. Dissertation, Department of Computer Sciences, The University of Texas at Austin. Available as Technical Report AI93-207.

Forbus, K. D. 1983. Measurement interpretation in qualitative process theory. In *Proc. 8th Int. Joint Conf. on Artificial Intelligence*, San Mateo, CA. Morgan Kaufmann.

Forbus, K. D. 1984. Qualitative process theory. *Artificial Intelligence* 24:85–168.

Forbus, K. D. 1986. Interpreting measurements of physical systems. In *Proc. 5th National Conf. on Artificial Intelligence*, San Mateo, CA. Morgan Kaufmann. 113–117.

Forbus, K. D. 1989. Introducing actions into qualitative simulation. In *Proc. 11th Int. Joint Conf. on Artificial Intelligence*, San Mateo, CA. Morgan Kaufmann.

Forbus, K. D. 1990. The qualitative process engine. In Weld, D., and de Kleer, J., editors 1990, *Readings in Qualitative Reasoning about Physical Systems*. Morgan Kaufmann, San Mateo, CA.

Forbus, K. D. 1992. Pushing the edge of the (QP) envelope. In Faltings, B., and Struss, P., editors 1992, *Recent Advances in Qualitative Physics*. MIT Press, Cambridge, MA.

Forbus, K. D., and Falkenhainer, B. 1990a. Self-explanatory simulations: An integration of qualitative and quantitative knowledge. In *Proc. 8th National Conf. on Artificial Intelligence*, Cambridge, MA. AAAI/MIT Press. 380–387.

Forbus, K. D., and Falkenhainer, B. 1990b. Self-explanatory simulations: Scaling up to large models. In *Proc. 10th National Conf. on Artificial Intelligence*, Cambridge, MA. AAAI/MIT Press. 380–387.

Forbus, K. D., and Gentner, D. 1983. Causal reasoning about quantities. In *Proceedings of the Fifth Annual Conference of the Cognitive Science Society*. Lawrence Erlbaum and Associates. 196–206.

Forbus, K. D.; Nielsen, P.;, and Faltings, B. 1991. Qualitative spatial reasoning: The CLOCK project. *Artificial Intelligence* 51:417–471.

Forrester, J. 1961. *Industrial Dynamics*. MIT Press, Cambridge, MA.

Forrester, J. 1969. *Urban Dynamics*. MIT Press, Cambridge, MA.

Fouché, P. 1992. *Towards a Unified Framework for Qualitative Simulation.* Ph.D. Dissertation, Département Génie Informatique, Centre de Recherches de Royallieu Université de Technologie de Compiègne, France.

Fouché, P., and Kuipers, B. 1992. Reasoning about energy in qualitative simulation. *IEEE Transactions on Systems, Man, and Cybernetics* 22(1):47–63.

Franke, D. 1989. Representing and acquiring teleological descriptions. In *IJCAI-89 Model-Based Reasoning Workshop*, Detroit, Michigan.

Franke, D. 1991. Deriving and using descriptions of purpose. *IEEE Expert* 6(2):48–57.

Franke, D. 1992. *A Theory of Teleology.* Ph.D. Dissertation, Department of Computer Sciences, University of Texas at Austin, Austin, Texas. Available as Technical Report AI93-201.

Franke, D., and Dvorak, D. 1990. CC: Component-connection models for qualitative simulation – a user's guide. Technical Report AI90-126, Artificial Intelligence Laboratory, Department of Computer Sciences, University of Texas at Austin.

Freuder, E. C. 1978. Synthesizing constraint expressions. *Communications of the ACM* 21:958–966.

Gelfond, M.; Lifschitz, V.;, and Rabinov, A. 1991. What are the limitations of the situation calculus? In Boyer, R., editor 1991, *Automated Reasoning: Essays in Honor of Woody Bledsoe.* Kluwer Academic Press, Dordrecht. 167–179.

Genesereth, M. R. 1984. The use of design descriptions in automated diagnosis. *Artificial Intelligence* 24:411–436.

Goldmeier, E. 1972. Similarity in visually perceived forms. *Psychological Issues* 8(1). monograph 29.

Grossman, W., and Werthner, H. 1993. A stochastic approach to qualitative simulation using Markov processes. In *Proceedings of the Thirteenth International Joint Conference on Artificial Intelligence*, San Mateo, CA. Morgan Kaufmann.

Guyton, A. C. 1991. Blood pressure control – special role of the kidneys and body fluids. *Science* 252:1813–1816.

Hamscher, W. C. 1989. Temporally coarse representations of behavior for model-based troubleshooting of digital circuits. In *Proc. 11th Int. Joint Conf. on Artificial Intelligence*, San Mateo, CA. Morgan Kaufmann.

Hamscher, W. C. 1991. Modeling digital circuits for troubleshooting. *Artificial Intelligence* 51:223–271.

Hart, P. E.; Barzilay, A.;, and Duda, O. 1986. Qualitative reasoning for financial assessments. *AI Magazine* 7(1):62–68.

Hayes, P. J. 1979. The naive physics manifesto. In Michie, D., editor 1979, *Expert Systems in the Micro Electronic Age.* Edinburgh University Press, Edinburgh.

Hayes, P. J. 1985a. Naive physics 1: Ontology for liquids. In *Formal Theories of the Commonsense World.* Ablex Publishing Corporation, Norwood, NJ.

Hayes, P. J. 1985b. The second naive physics manifesto. In Hobbs, J. R., and Moore, R. C., editors 1985b, *Formal Theories of the Commonsense World.* Ablex Publishing Corporation, Norwood, NJ. 1–36.

Hellerstein, J. 1990. Obtaining quantitative predictions from monotone relationships. In *Proc. 8th National Conf. on Artificial Intelligence*, Cambridge, MA. AAAI/MIT Press. 388–394.

Hirsch, M., and Smale, S. 1974. *Differential Equations, Dynamical Systems, and Linear Algebra*. Academic Press, New York.

Hobbs, J. 1985. Granularity. In *Proc. 9th Int. Joint Conf. on Artificial Intelligence*, San Mateo, CA. Morgan Kaufmann.

Hollan, J.; Hutchins, E.;, and Weitzman, L. 1984. STEAMER: An interactive inspectable simulation-based training system. *AI Magazine* 5(2):15–27.

Hoppensteadt, F. 1966. Singular perturbations on the infinite interval. *Transactions of the American Mathematical Society* 123:521–535.

Horn, W. 1990. *Causal AI Models: Steps Toward Applications*. Hemisphere Publishing Company, New York.

IFIP Workshop on the Role of Knowledge Representation in Qualitative Reasoning, Islamorada, FL, February, 1992.

Ishida, Y. 1989. Using global properties for qualitative reasoning: a qualitative system theory. In *Proc. 11th Int. Joint Conf. on Artificial Intelligence*, San Mateo, CA. Morgan Kaufmann. 1174–79.

Iwasaki, Y. 1988. Causal ordering in a mixed structure. In *Proc. 7th National Conf. on Artificial Intelligence*, San Mateo, CA. Morgan Kaufmann. 313–318.

Iwasaki, Y., and Bhandari, I. 1988. Formal basis for commonsense abstraction of dynamic systems. In *Proc. 7th National Conf. on Artificial Intelligence*, San Mateo, CA. Morgan Kaufmann. 307–312.

Iwasaki, Y.; Fikes, R.; Vescovi, M.;, and Chandrasekaran, B. 1993. How things are supposed to work: Capturing functional knowledge in device design. In *Proceedings of the Thirteenth International Joint Conference on Artificial Intelligence*, San Mateo, CA. Morgan Kaufmann. 1516–1522.

Iwasaki, Y., and Levy, A. 1993. Automated model selection for simulation. In *Proc. 7th Int. Workshop on Qualitative Reasoning about Physical Systems*, Orcas Island, WA.

Iwasaki, Y., and Simon, H. A. 1986a. Causality in device behavior. *Artificial Intelligence* 29:3–32.

Iwasaki, Y., and Simon, H. A. 1986b. Theories of causal ordering: Reply to de Kleer and Brown. *Artificial Intelligence* 29:63–72.

Jacquez, J. A. 1985. *Compartmental Analysis in Biology and Medicine*. University of Michigan Press, Ann Arbor, second edition.

Kalagnanam, J.; Simon, H. A.;, and Iwasaki, Y. 1991. The mathematical bases for qualitative reasoning. *IEEE Expert* 11–19.

Karnopp, D.; Margolis, D.;, and Rosenberg, R. 1990. *System Dynamics: A Unified Approach*. John Wiley and Sons, New York, second edition.

Karp, P. D., and Friedland, P. 1989. Coordinating the use of qualitative and quantitative knowledge in declarative device modeling. In Widman, L. E.; Loparo, K. A.;, and Nielson, N. R., editors 1989, *Artificial Intelligence, Simulation and Modeling*. John Wiley and Sons.

Kay, H., and Kuipers, B. J. 1993. Numerical behavior envelopes for qualitative models. In *Proc. 11th National Conf. on Artificial Intelligence*, Cambridge, MA. AAAI/MIT Press. 606–613.

Kay, H., and Ungar, L. H. 1993. Deriving monotonic function envelopes from observations. In *Proc. 7th Int. Workshop on Qualitative Reasoning about Physical Systems*, Orcas Island, Washington. 117–123.

Kiriyama, T., and Tomiyama, T. 1993. Reasoning about models across multiple ontologies. In *Proc. 7th Int. Workshop on Qualitative Reasoning about Physical Systems*, Orcas Island, WA.

Kokar, M. 1987. Critical hypersurfaces and the quantity space. In *Proc. 6th National Conf. on Artificial Intelligence*, San Mateo, CA. Morgan Kaufmann.

Kokotovic, P.; Jr., O'Malley, R. Jr., and Sannuti, P. 1976. Singular perturbations and order reduction in control theory — an overview. *Automatica* 12:123–132.

Kreiss, H.-O. 1985. Problems with different time scales. In Brackbill, J. U., and Cohen, B. I., editors 1985, *Multiple Time Scales*. Academic Press, New York.

Kuipers, B. J. 1984. Commonsense reasoning about causality: Deriving behavior from structure. *Artificial Intelligence* 24:169–204.

Kuipers, B. J. 1986. Qualitative simulation. *Artificial Intelligence* 29:289–338.

Kuipers, B. J. 1987. Abstraction by time scale in qualitative simulation. In *Proc. 6th National Conf. on Artificial Intelligence*, San Mateo, CA. Morgan Kaufmann. 621–625.

Kuipers, B. J. 1988a. The qualitative calculus is sound but incomplete: A reply to Peter Struss. *Int. J. Artificial Intelligence in Engineering* 3(3):170–173.

Kuipers, B. J. 1988b. Qualitative simulation using time-scale abstraction. *Int. J. Artificial Intelligence in Engineering* 3(4):185–191.

Kuipers, B. J. 1989. Qualitative reasoning: Modeling and simulation with incomplete knowledge. *Automatica* 25(4):571–585.

Kuipers, B. J. 1993a. Qualitative simulation: then and now. *Artificial Intelligence* 59:133–140.

Kuipers, B. J. 1993b. Reasoning with qualitative models. *Artificial Intelligence* 59:125–132.

Kuipers, B. J., and Åström, K. 1991. The composition of heterogeneous control laws. In *Proceedings of the American Control Conference*. 630–636.

Kuipers, B. J., and Åström, K. 1994. The composition and validation of heterogeneous control laws. *Automatica* 30(2):233–249.

Kuipers, B. J., and Berleant, D. 1988. Using incomplete quantitative knowledge in qualitative reasoning. *Proc. 7th National Conf. on Artificial Intelligence*.

Kuipers, B. J., and Berleant, D. 1990. A smooth integration of incomplete quantitative knowledge into qualitative simulation. Technical Report AI90–122, Artificial Intelligence Laboratory, Department of Computer Sciences, University of Texas at Austin.

Kuipers, B. J., and Chiu, C. 1987. Taming intractable branching in qualitative simulation. In *Proc. 10th Int. Joint Conf. on Artificial Intelligence*, San Mateo, CA. Morgan Kaufmann.

Kuipers, B. J.; Chiu, C.; Dalle Molle, D. T.; and Throop, D. R. 1991. Higher-order derivative constraints in qualitative simulation. *Artificial Intelligence* 51:343–379.

Kuipers, B. J., and Kassirer, J. P. 1984. Causal reasoning in medicine: analysis of a protocol. *Cognitive Science* 8:363–385.

Kuipers, B. J., and Kassirer, J. P. 1985. Qualitative simulation in medical physiology: A progress report. Technical Report TM-280, MIT Laboratory for Computer Science, Cambridge, MA.

LeClair, S. R., and Abrams, F. L. 1988. Qualitative process automation. In *Proceedings of the 27th IEEE Conference on Decision and Control*, Austin, Texas. 558–563.

Lee, W. W. 1993. *A Qualitative Simulation Based Method to Construct Phase Portraits*. Ph.D. Dissertation, Department of Computer Sciences, University of Texas at Austin, Austin, Texas. Available as Technical Report AI93-194.

Lee, W. W., and Kuipers, B. J. 1988. Non-intersection of trajectories in qualitative phase space: A global constraint for qualitative simulation. In *Proc. 7th National Conf. on Artificial Intelligence*, San Mateo, CA. Morgan Kaufmann.

Lee, W. W., and Kuipers, B. J. 1993. A qualitative method to construct phase portraits. In *Proc. 11th National Conf. on Artificial Intelligence*, Cambridge, MA. AAAI/MIT Press.

Leitch, R., and Shen, Q. 1993. Prioritising behaviors in qualitative simulation. In *Proceedings of the Thirteenth International Joint Conference on Artificial Intelligence*, San Mateo, CA. Morgan Kaufmann.

Lenat, D., and Guha, R. 1990. *Building Large Knowledge-Based Systems*. Addison-Wesley, Reading, MA.

Levy, A. Y.; Iwasaki, Y.;, and Motoda, H. 1992. Relevance reasoning to guide compositional modeling. In *Proc. 6th Int. Workshop on Qualitative Reasoning about Physical Systems*, Edinburgh, Scotland.

Lifschitz, V. 1987. Formal theories of action (preliminary report). In *Proc. 10th Int. Joint Conf. on Artificial Intelligence*, San Mateo, CA. Morgan Kaufmann. 966–972.

Liu, Z., and Farley, A. 1990. Shifting ontological perspectives in reasoning about physical systems. In *Proc. 8th National Conf. on Artificial Intelligence*, Cambridge, MA. AAAI/MIT Press.

Lunze, J. 1992. Qualitative modeling of continuous-variable systems by means of nondeterministic automata. *Proc. 6th Int. Workshop on Qualitative Reasoning about Physical Systems*.

Lynch, R. 1986. The Oh! of pleasure. In Lynch, R., editor 1986, *Deep Breakfast*. Ray Lynch Productions, Music West Records, MWCD-102.

Mackworth, A. K. 1977. Consistency in networks of relations. *Artificial Intelligence* 8(1).

Mackworth, A. K. 1992. Constraint satisfaction. In Shapiro, S. C., editor 1992, *Encyclopedia of Artificial Intelligence*. John Wiley, New York, second edition.

Macsyma reference manual. MIT Laboratory for Computer Science. 1988.

Marino, R., and Kokotovic, P. 1988. A geometric approach to non-linear singularly perturbed control systems. *Automatica* 24:31–41.

Mavrovouniotis, M. L., and Stephanopoulos, G. 1987. Reasoning with orders of magnitude and approximate relations. In *Proc. 6th National Conf. on Artificial Intelligence*, San Mateo, CA. Morgan Kaufmann. 626–630.

Mavrovouniotis, M. L., and Stephanopoulos, G. 1988. Formal order-of-magnitude reasoning in process engineering. *Computers and Chemical Engineering* 12(9/10):867–881.

McCarthy, J., and Hayes, P. J. 1969. Some philosophical problems from the standpoint of artificial intelligence. In Meltzer and Michie, editors 1969, *Machine Intelligence 4*. Edinburgh University Press, Edinburgh. 463–502.

McCloskey, M. 1983. Naive theories of motion. In Gentner, D., and Stevens, A., editors 1983, *Mental Models*. Erlbaum, Hillsdale, NJ. 299–324.

McCloskey, M.; Caramazza, A.;, and Green, B. 1980. Curvilinear motion in absence of external forces: naive beliefs about the motion of objects. *Science* 210:1139–1141.

McCulloch, W. 1965. *Embodiments of Mind*. MIT Press, Cambridge, MA.

McDermott, D. 1982. A temporal logic for reasoning about processes and plans. *Cognitive Science* 6:101–155.

McDermott, D. V. 1983. Data dependencies on inequalities. In *Proc. 3rd National Conf. on Artificial Intelligence*, San Mateo, CA. Morgan Kaufmann.

McDermott, D. V., and Davis, E. 1984. Planning routes through uncertain territory. *Artificial Intelligence* 22:107–156.

Mead, C., and Conway, L. 1980. *Introduction to VLSI Systems*. Addison-Wesley, Reading, MA.

Moore, R. E. 1966. *Interval Analysis*. Prentice-Hall, Inc., Englewood Cliffs, NJ.

Moore, R. E. 1979. *Methods and Applications of Interval Arithmetic*. Studies in Applied Mathematics. SIAM, Philadelphia.

Murthy, S. S. 1988. Qualitative reasoning at multiple resolutions. In *Proc. 7th National Conf. on Artificial Intelligence*, San Mateo, CA. Morgan Kaufmann. 296–300.

Nayak, P. P. 1992a. *Automated Modeling of Physical Systems*. Ph.D. Dissertation, Department of Computer Science, Stanford University.

Nayak, P. P. 1992b. Causal approximations. In *Proc. 10th National Conf. on Artificial Intelligence*, Cambridge, MA. AAAI/MIT Press. 703–709.

Nayak, P. P. 1993. Order of magnitude reasoning using logarithms. In *Proc. 7th Int. Workshop on Qualitative Reasoning About Physical Systems*, Orcas Island, WA.

Nayak, P. P.; Joskowicz, L.;, and Addanki, S. 1992. Automated model selection using context-dependent behaviors. In *Proc. 10th National Conf. on Artificial Intelligence*, Cambridge, MA. AAAI/MIT Press. 710–716.

Newman, J. R. 1956. *The World of Mathematics*. Simon and Schuster, New York.

Ng, H.-T. 1991. Model-based, multiple-fault diagnosis of dynamic, continuous physical devices. *IEEE Expert* 6(6):38–43.

Nishida, T. 1993. Generating quasi-symbolic representation of three-dimensional flow. In *Proc. 11th National Conf. on Artificial Intelligence*, Cambridge, MA. AAAI/MIT Press. 554–559.

Nishida, T., and Doshita, S. 1987. Reasoning about discontinuous change. In *Proc. 6th National Conf. on Artificial Intelligence*, San Mateo, CA. Morgan Kaufmann.

Nishida, T., and Doshita, S. 1991. A geometric approach to total envisioning. In *Proc. 12th Int. Joint Conf. on Artificial Intelligence*, San Mateo, CA. Morgan Kaufmann.

Nishida, T.; Mizutani, K.; Kubota, A.;, and Doshita, S. 1991. Automated phase portrait analysis by integrating qualitative and quantitative analysis. In *Proc. 9th National Conf. on Artificial Intelligence*, Cambridge, MA. AAAI/MIT Press.

Patil, R. S.; Szolovits, P.;, and Schwartz, W. B. 1981. Causal understanding of patient illness in medical diagnosis. In *Proc. 7th Int. Joint Conf. on Artificial Intelligence*, San Mateo, CA. Morgan Kaufmann.

Porter, B.; Lester, J.; Murray, K.; Pittman, K.; Souther, A.; Acker, L.;, and Jones, T. 1988. AI research in the context of a multifunctional knowledge base: The botany knowledge base project. Technical Report TR AI-88-88, Artificial Intelligence Laboratory, Department of Computer Sciences, University of Texas at Austin.

Puccia, C. J., and Levins, R. 1985. *Qualitative Modeling of Complex Systems.* Harvard University Press, Cambridge, MA.

Raiman, O. 1986. Order of magnitude reasoning. In *Proc. 5th National Conf. on Artificial Intelligence*, San Mateo, CA. Morgan Kaufmann. 100–104.

Raiman, O. 1991. Order of magnitude reasoning. *Artificial Intelligence* 51:11–38.

Raiman, O., and Williams, B. 1992. Caricatures: Generating models of dominant behavior. In *Proc. 6th Int. Workshop on Qualitative Reasoning about Physical Systems*, Edinburgh, Scotland.

Rajamoney, S. A., and Koo, S. H. 1990. Qualitative reasoning with microscopic theories. In *Proceedings of the Eighth National Conference on Artificial Intelligence*, Cambridge, MA. AAAI/MIT Press.

Rajamoney, S. A., and Koo, S. H. 1991. Behavioral aggregation within complex situations: a case study involving dynamic equilibria. In *Proceedings of the Ninth National Conference on Artificial Intelligence*, Cambridge, MA. AAAI/MIT Press. 862–873.

Rayner, M. 1991. On the applicability of nonmonotonic logic to formal reasoning in continuous time. *Artificial Intelligence* 49:345–360.

Reiter, R. 1987. A theory of diagnosis from first principles. *Artificial Intelligence* 32:57–95.

Rickel, J., and Porter, B. 1992. Automated modeling for answering prediction questions: Exploiting interaction paths. In *Proc. 6th Int. Workshop on Qualitative Reasoning about Physical Systems*, Edinburgh, Scotland.

Rieger, C., and Grinberg, M. 1977. The declarative representation and procedural simulation of causality in physical mechanisms. In *Proc. 5th Int. Joint Conf. on Artificial Intelligence*, San Mateo, CA. Morgan Kaufmann.

Rose, P., and Kramer, M. A. 1991. Qualitative analysis of causal feedback. In *Proc. 9th National Conf. on Artificial Intelligence*, Cambridge, MA. AAAI/MIT Press.

Sacks, E. 1987a. Hierarchical reasoning about inequalities. In *Proc. 6th National Conf. on Artificial Intelligence*, San Mateo, CA. Morgan Kaufmann. 649–654.

Sacks, E. 1987b. Piecewise linear reasoning. In *Proc. 6th National Conf. on Artificial Intelligence*, San Mateo, CA. Morgan Kaufmann.

Sacks, E. 1990. Automatic qualitative analysis of dynamic systems using piecewise linear approximations. *Artificial Intelligence* 41:313–364.

Sacks, E. 1991. Automatic analysis of one-parameter planar ordinary differential equations by intelligent numerical simulation. *Artificial Intelligence* 48:27–56.

Saksena, V.; O'Reilly, J.;, and Kokotovic, P. 1984. Singular perturbations and time-scale methods in control theory: Survey 1976-1983. *Automatica* 20:273–293.

Samuelson, P. A. 1983. *Foundations of Economic Analysis*. Harvard University Press, Cambridge MA, enlarged edition. Original edition published 1947.

Sandewall, E. 1989. Combining logic and differential equations for describing real-world systems. In *Proc. 1st Int. Conf. on Principles of Knowledge Representation and Reasoning*, San Mateo, CA. Morgan Kaufmann. 412–420.

Schaefer, P. 1991. Analytic solution of qualitative differential equations. In *Proceedings of the Ninth National Conference on Artificial Intelligence*, Cambridge, MA. AAAI/MIT Press.

Schank, R. C. 1973. Identification of conceptualizations underlying natural language. In Schank, R. C., and Colby, K. M., editors 1973, *Computer Models of Thought and Language*. W. H. Freeman, San Francisco.

Shen, Q., and Leitch, R. 1992. Combining qualitative simulation and fuzzy sets. In Faltings, B., and Struss, P., editors 1992, *Recent Advances in Qualitative Physics*. MIT Press, Cambridge, MA.

Shen, Q., and Leitch, R. R. 1993. Fuzzy qualitative simulation. *IEEE Trans. on Systems, Man and Cybernetics* 23(4):1038–1061.

Shirley, M., and Falkenhainer, B. 1990. Explicit reasoning about accuracy for approximation physical systems.

Shoham, Y. 1988. *Reasoning About Change: Time and Causation from the Standpoint of Artificial Intelligence*. MIT Press, Cambridge, MA.

Shoham, Y., and McDermott, D. 1988. Problems in formal temporal reasoning. *Artificial Intelligence* 36(1):49–61.

Simmons, R. 1986. "Commonsense" arithmetic reasoning. In *Proc. 5th National Conf. on Artificial Intelligence*, San Mateo, CA. Morgan Kaufmann. 118–124.

Simmons, R., and Davis, R. 1987. Generate, test, and debug: Combining associational rules and causal models. In *Proc. 10th Int. Joint Conf. on Artificial Intelligence*, San Mateo, CA. Morgan Kaufmann.

Simon, H. A. 1952. On the definition of the causal relation. *The Journal of Philosophy* 49:517–528. Reprinted in H. A. Simon, *Models of Discovery*, Boston: D. Reidel, 1977.

Simon, H. A., and Ando, A. 1961. Aggregation of variables in dynamic systems. *Econometrica* 29:111–138.

Skorstad, G. 1992. Towards a qualitative Lagrangian theory of fluid flow. In *Proceedings of the Tenth National Conference on Artificial Intelligence*, Cambridge, MA. AAAI/MIT Press.

Söderman, U., and Strömberg, J.-E. 1991. Combining qualitative and quantitative knowledge to generate models of physical systems. In *Proc. 12th Int. Joint Conf. on Artificial Intelligence*, San Mateo, CA. Morgan Kaufmann.

Spanier, E. 1966. *Algebraic Topology*. McGraw-Hill, New York.

Spivak, M. 1967. *Calculus*. W. A. Benjamin, Inc., New York. [In my opinion, this is the finest book on the differential and integral calculus ever written.]

Stevens, S. S. 1946. On the theory of scales of measurement. *Science* 103:677–680.

Struss, P. 1988a. Global filters for qualitative behaviors. In *Proc. 7th National Conf. on Artificial Intelligence*, San Mateo, CA. Morgan Kaufmann.

Struss, P. 1988b. Mathematical aspects of qualitative reasoning. *Int. J. Artificial Intelligence in Engineering* 3(3):156–169.

Struss, P. 1990. Problems of interval-based qualitative reasoning. In Weld, D., and de Kleer, J., editors 1990, *Qualitative Reasoning about Physical Systems*. Morgan Kaufmann. 288–305.

Struss, P., and Dressler, O. 1989. Physical negation — integrating fault models into the general diagnostic engine. In *Proc. 11th Int. Joint Conf. on Artificial Intelligence*, San Mateo, CA. Morgan Kaufmann. 1318–1323.

Subramanian, D., and Genesereth, M. 1987. The relevance of irrelevance. In *Proc. 10th Int. Joint Conf. on Artificial Intelligence*, Los Altos, CA. Morgan Kaufmann.

Sussman, G. J., and Stallman, R. M. 1975. Heuristic techniques in computer-aided circuit analysis. *IEEE Trans. on Circuits and Systems* CAS-22(11).

Sussman, G. J., and Steele, G. L. 1980. CONSTRAINTS: a language for expressing almost-hierarchical descriptions. *Artificial Intelligence* 14:1–39.

Throop, D. 1991. *Model-Based Diagnosis of Complex, Continuous Mechanisms*. Ph.D. Dissertation, Department of Computer Sciences, University of Texas at Austin, Austin, Texas. Available as Technical Report AI91-162.

Top, J., and Akkermans, J. 1990. Bond-graph based reasoning about physical systems. In *Working Notes of the 2nd Model-based Reasoning Workshop*, Boston, MA.

Top, J., and Akkermans, J. 1991. Computational and physical causality. In *Proc. 12th Int. Joint Conf. on Artificial Intelligence*, San Mateo, CA. Morgan Kaufmann. 1158–1163.

Vescovi, M.; Iwasaki, Y.; Fikes, R.; and Chandrasekaran, B. 1993. CFRL: A language for specifying the causal functionality of engineered devices. In *Proceedings of the Eleventh National Conference on Artificial Intelligence*, Cambridge, MA. AAAI/MIT Press.

Vescovi, M., and Robles, J. 1992. Fuzzy diagnosis of continuous processes. In *Proc. 10th European Conf. on Artificial Intelligence*, Chichester, England. John Wiley and Sons.

Vinson, J., and Ungar, L. 1993. Qmimic: Model-based monitoring and diagnosis. In *Proc. American Control Conference (ACC-93)*, Piscataway, NJ. IEEE Service Center. 1880–1884.

Vonnegut, K. 1952. *Player Piano*. Dell Publishing Co., New York.

Waltz, D. L. 1972. Generating semantic descriptions from drawings of scenes with shadows. Technical Report AI-TR-271, MIT Artificial Intelligence Laboratory, Cambridge, MA.

Ward, A. C.; Lozano-Perez, T.; and Seering, W. P. 1989. Extending the constraint propagation of intervals. In *Proc. 11th Int. Joint Conf. on Artificial Intelligence*, San Mateo, CA. Morgan Kaufmann.

Weiss, S. M.; Kulikowski, C. A.; Amarel, S.; and Safir, A. 1978. A model-based method for computer-aided medical decision-making. *Artificial Intelligence* 11:145–172.

Weld, D. S. 1986. The use of aggregation in causal simulation. *Artificial Intelligence* 30:1–34.

Weld, D. S. 1990. Approximation reformulations. In *Proc. 8th National Conf. on Artificial Intelligence*, Cambridge, MA. AAAI/MIT Press. 407–412.

Weld, D. S. 1992. Reasoning about model accuracy. *Artificial Intelligence* 56:255–300.

Weld, D. S., and de Kleer, J. 1990. *Readings in Qualitative Reasoning About Physical Systems.* Morgan Kaufmann, San Mateo, CA.

Wellman, M. P. 1990. Fundamental concepts of qualitative probabilistic networks. *Artificial Intelligence* 44:257–303.

Wellman, M. P. 1991. Qualitative simulation with multivariate constraints. In Allen, J.; Fikes, R.; and Sandewall, E., editors 1991, *Proc. 2nd Int. Conf. on Principles of Knowledge Representation and Reasoning*, San Mateo, CA. Morgan Kaufmann.

Williams, B. C. 1984a. Qualitative analysis of MOS circuits. *Artificial Intelligence* 24:281–346.

Williams, B. C. 1984b. The use of continuity in a qualitative physics. In *Proc. 4th National Conf. on Artificial Intelligence*, San Mateo, CA. Morgan Kaufmann. 350–354.

Williams, B. C. 1986. Doing time: Putting qualitative reasoning on firmer ground. In *Proc. 5th National Conf. on Artificial Intelligence*, San Mateo, CA. Morgan Kaufmann. 105–112.

Williams, B. C. 1988. MINIMA: A symbolic approach to qualitative algebraic reasoning. In *Proc. 7th National Conf. on Artificial Intelligence*, San Mateo, CA. Morgan Kaufmann. 264–269.

Williams, B. C. 1991. A theory of interactions: Unifying qualitative and quantitative algebraic reasoning. *Artificial Intelligence* 51:39–94.

Wolfram, S. 1988. *Mathematica: A System for Doing Mathematics by Computer.* Addison-Wesley, Reading, MA.

Woods, E. 1991. The hybrid phenomena theory. In *Proceedings of the Twelfth International Joint conference on Artificial intelligence*, San Mateo, CA. Morgan Kaufmann.

Yager, R. R.; Ovchinnikov, S.; Tong, R. M.; and Nguyen, H. T. 1987. *Fuzzy Sets and Applications: Selected Papers by L. A. Zadeh.* John Wiley and Sons, NY.

Yeh, A. 1990. Finding the average rates of change in repetitive behavior. In *Proceedings of the Eighth National Conference on Artificial Intelligence*, Cambridge, MA. AAAI/MIT Press.

Yip, K. M. 1988. Generating global behaviors using deep knowledge of local dynamics. In *Proc. 7th National Conf. on Artificial Intelligence*, San Mateo, CA. Morgan Kaufmann. 649–654.

Yip, K. M. 1991a. Understanding complex dynamic systems by visual and symbolic reasoning. *Artificial Intelligence* 51:179–222.

Yip, K. M. 1991b. *KAM: A System for Intelligently Guiding Numerical Experimentation by Computer.* MIT Press, Cambridge, MA.

Yip, K. M. 1993. Model simplification by asymptotic order of magnitude reasoning. In *Proceedings of the Eleventh National Conference on Artificial Intelligence*, Cambridge, MA. AAAI/MIT Press. 634–640.

Zadeh, L. 1965. Fuzzy sets. *Information and Control* 8:338–353.

Zhao, F. 1991. Extracting and representing qualitative behaviors of complex systems in phase spaces. In *Proc. 12th Int. Joint Conf. on Artificial Intelligence*, San Mateo, CA. Morgan Kaufmann.

Index

Artificial Intelligence (selected titles)
Patrick Henry Winston, founding editor
J. Michael Brady, Daniel G. Bobrow, and Randall Davis, current editors

Artificial Intelligence: An MIT Perspective, Volumes I and II, edited by Patrick Henry Winston and Richard Henry Brown, 1979

NETL: A System for Representing and Using Real-World Knowledge, Scott Fahlman, 1979

The Interpretation of Visual Motion, Shimon Ullman, 1979

Turtle Geometry: The Computer as a Medium for Exploring Mathematics, Harold Abelson and Andrea di Sessa, 1981

Robot Manipulators: Mathematics, Programming, and Control, Richard P. Paul, 1981

Computational Models of Discourse, edited by Michael Brady and Robert C. Berwick, 1982

Robot Motion: Planning and Control, edited by Michael Brady, John M. Hollerbach, Timothy Johnson, Tomas Lozano-Perez, and Matthew T. Mason, 1982

Robot Hands and the Mechanics of Manipulation, Matthew T. Mason and J. Kenneth Salisbury, Jr., 1985

The Acquisition of Syntactic Knowledge, Robert C. Berwick, 1985

The Connection Machine, W. Daniel Hillis, 1985

Legged Robots that Balance, Marc H. Raibert, 1986

ACTORS: A Model of Concurrent Computation in Distributed Systems, Gul A. Agha, 1986

Knowledge-Based Tutoring: The GUIDON Program, William Clancey, 1987 AI in the 1980s and Beyond: An MIT Survey, edited by W. Eric L. Grimson and Ramesh S. Patil, 1987

Visual Reconstruction, Andrew Blake and Andrew Zisserman, 1987

Reasoning about Change: Time and Causation from the Standpoint of Artificial Intelligence, Yoav Shoham, 1988

Model-Based Control of a Robot Manipulator, Chae H. An, Christopher G. Atkeson, and John M. Hollerbach, 1988

A Robot Ping-Pong Player: Experiment in Real-Time Intelligent Control, Russell L. Andersson, 1988

The Paralation Model: Architecture-Independent Parallel Programming, Gary Sabot, 1988

Automated Deduction in Nonclassical Logics: Efficient Matrix Proof Methods for Modal and Intuitionistic Logics, Lincoln Wallen, 1989

Shape from Shading, edited by Berthold K.P. Horn and Michael J. Brooks, 1989

Ontic: A Knowledge Representation System for Mathematics, David A. McAllester, 1989

Solid Shape, Jan J. Koenderink, 1990

Theories of Comparative Analysis, Daniel S. Weld, 1990

Artificial Intelligence at MIT: Expanding Frontiers, edited by Patrick Henry Winston and Sarah Alexandra Shellard, 1990

Vector Models for Data-Parallel Computing, Guy E. Blelloch, 1990

Experiments in the Machine Interpretation of Visual Motion, David W. Murray and Bernard F. Buxton, 1990

Object Recognition by Computer: The Role of Geometric Constraints, W. Eric L. Grimson, 1990

Representing and Reasoning with Probabilistic Knowledge: A Logical Approach to Probabilities, Fahiem Bacchus, 1990

3D Model Recognition from Stereoscopic Cues, edited by John E.W. Mayhew and John P. Frisby, 1991

Artificial Vision for Mobile Robots: Stereo Vision and Multisensory Perception, Nicholas Ayache, 1991

Truth and Modality for Knowledge Representation, Raymond Turner, 1991

Made-Up Minds: A Constructivist Approach to Artificial Intelligence, Gary L. Drescher, 1991

Vision, Instruction, and Action, David Chapman, 1991

Do the Right Thing: Studies in Limited Rationality, Stuart Russell and Eric Wefald, 1991

KAM: A System for Intelligently Guiding Numerical Experimentation by Computer, Kenneth Man-Kam Yip, 1991

Solving Geometric Constraint Systems: A Case Study in Kinematics, Glenn A. Kramer, 1992

Geometric Invariants in Computer Vision, edited by Joseph Mundy and Andrew Zisserman, 1992

HANDEY: A Robot Task Planner, Tomas Lozano-Perez, Joseph L. Jones, Emmanuel Mazer, and Patrick A. O'Donnell, 1992

Active Vision, edited by Andrew Blake and Alan Yuille, 1992

Recent Advances in Qualitative Physics, edited by Boi Faltings and Peter Struss, 1992

Machine Translation: A View from the Lexicon, Bonnie Jean Dorr, 1993

The Language Complexity Game, Eric Sven Ristad, 1993

The Soar Papers: Research on Integrated Intelligence, edited by Paul S. Rosenbloom, John E. Laird, and Allen Newell, 1993

Three-Dimensional Computer Vision: A Geometric Viewpoint, Olivier Faugeras, 1993

Contemplating Minds: A Forum for Artificial Intelligence, edited by William J. Clancey, Stephen W. Smoliar, and Mark J. Stefik, 1994

Thinking between the Lines: Computers and the Comprehension of Causal Descriptions, Gary C. Borchardt, 1994

Rules of Encounter: Designing Conventions for Automated Negotiation among Computers, Jeffrey S. Rosenschein and Gilad Zlotkin, 1994

Qualitative Reasoning: Modeling and Simulation with Incomplete Knowledge, Benjamin Kuipers, 1994